I0024656

Beyond Man

Black Outdoors *Innovations in the Poetics of Study*
A series edited by J. Kameron Carter & Sarah Jane Cervenak

Beyond Man

Edited by
An Yountae &
Eleanor Craig

Race, Coloniality, and Philosophy of Religion

Duke University Press *Durham and London* 2021

© 2021 Duke University Press
All rights reserved
Cover designed by Matthew Tauch
Text designed by Aimee C. Harrison
Typeset in Portrait Text Regular and ITC Franklin Gothic
by Westchester Publishing Services

Library of Congress Cataloging-in-Publication Data

Names: An Yountae, editor. | Craig, Eleanor, [date] editor.
Title: Beyond man : race, coloniality, and philosophy of religion /
    edited by An Yountae and Eleanor Craig.
Other titles: Black outdoors.
Description: Durham : Duke University Press, 2021. | Series: Black outdoors |
    Includes bibliographical references and index.
Identifiers: LCCN 2020040898 (print) | LCCN 2020040899 (ebook) |
    ISBN 9781478011880 (hardcover) | ISBN 9781478014027 (paperback) |
    ISBN 9781478021339 (ebook)
Subjects: LCSH: Religion—Philosophy.|Racism— Religiousaspects— Christianity.|

    Imperialism. | Decolonization. | Eurocentrism—History. | Civilization,
    Western—Christian influences. | Civilization, Modern—Philosophy.
Classification: LCC JV51 .B49 2021 (print) | LCC JV51 (ebook) | DDC 210—dc23
LC record available at https://lccn.loc.gov/2020040898
LC ebook record available at https://lccn.loc.gov/2020040899

Cover art: Dell Hamilton, untitled. 22 in. × 30 in. Monotype, collage, colored pencil,
    ink, black gesso, charcoal, acrylic, and oil pastel on paper. Courtesy of the artist.

CONTENTS

ACKNOWLEDGMENTS

WE THANK THE CONTRIBUTORS TO THIS VOLUME—those who from day one believed in the project and helped it gather momentum and those who added their energies later in ways that kept our collective thinking fresh and flexible. We owe extra thanks to Mayra Rivera for introducing us and suggesting that we collaborate and for hosting space to deepen authors' engagements with one another at Harvard in 2018. We are grateful to J. Kameron Carter and Sarah Jane Cervenak for joining our efforts to the wider conversations about settler colonialism and Black studies taking place in the Black Outdoors series.

Sandra Korn at Duke University Press has guided this project with thoughtfulness, enthusiasm, and patience. Our anonymous reviewers provided invaluable advice, particularly on the introduction, and we are indebted to their wisdom.

Participants and audience members in the American Academy of Religion exploratory session Race, Coloniality, and Philosophy of Religion in November 2017 launched this work into a dynamic conversation. Attendees at the Colloquium on Coloniality, Race, and Philosophy of Religion at Harvard Divinity School in November 2018 provided valuable feedback on several chapters in progress. We especially wish to thank David Kim, Elaine Padilla, and Santiago Slabodsky for their contributions to this process.

Over the years of this project, Eleanor experienced the kind of deep care that instills hope for an otherwise world through the support and friendship of Leena Akhtar, Ariel Berman, Karlene Griffiths, Janhavi Madabushi, Kris Trujillo, and too many others who are neglected here. Toby Oldham, Dante and Rafaél Craig, and Noe Montez bring sustaining joy to every day. Yountae is grateful for the support of the College of Humanities and the Department of Religious Studies at California State University, Northridge.

Eleanor Craig and An Yountae

Introduction

Challenging Modernity/Coloniality
in Philosophy of Religion

DOES *PHILOSOPHY OF RELIGION* name a genre of thought or a delimited tradition? Can it be more broadly conceived to encompass modes of critical theorizing that have not heretofore been considered part of the field? This volume is an intervention, but it is also an experiment. It represents our belief, for lack of a better word, that it is possible and valuable to apply the categorical designation *philosophy of religion* to decolonial and anticolonial projects that rearrange the epistemological assumptions of much of the work carried out under that heading. The project at hand requires accounting for the dual forms of violence that define Euro-descended Christianity by its others while paradoxically claiming to represent and speak to humanity in its totality. This claim, today as in centuries past, is coherent only if the non-European and non-Christian are understood as less than human. The highest and lowest levels of evaluation are thus directly connected: those said to do philosophy are those who (really) count as human.

Introductory textbooks on philosophy of religion usually introduce the field as a series of inquiries into the nature and existence of God. It is common to see chapters devoted to categories of argument—cosmological, teleological, ontological—including debates over their articulation and validity. Defined as an inquiry into the rationality of theism, philosophy of religion deploys a familiar lineup of thinkers: Anselm, Thomas Aquinas, and Immanuel Kant are constants; occasionally William James is included to discuss religious experience, or William Paley for argument from design.[1] Logical grapplings with morality and evil, especially (but by no means limited to) their exploration through theodicy, are rehearsed in fairly consistent ways across such texts. One might begin with Spinoza or with Job and put varied emphasis on the work of Irenaeus or Augustine, but the outlines of the problem are the same: one must reckon, rationally if not necessarily confessionally, with God's goodness and power in the face of evil.

Philosophy of religion is thus presented to beginning students as an analytic project with known and agreed-upon starting points, even as the answers offered to foundational questions vary to some extent. Students receive a chronology and classification of argument that sets down implicit and explicit ideas about what philosophy of religion *is*. Their participation in the discourse is invited with the (again, explicit or implicit) understanding that they too will start at the beginning, undertaking these old (timeless) questions of widespread (universal) significance.

We can neither ignore nor fully respond to the discourses and histories contained in the tradition of thought just described. Despite the limitations of its methodological patterns and recurringly foregrounded questions, this tradition must be acknowledged to contain curiosity, variation, creativity, and valuable modes of questioning. While the present collection is not determined to assert itself as *analytic* philosophy of religion, we remain interested in how some of the philosophy's thinkers and their various entanglements might be repurposed to understand the development of race and coloniality, as well as the ongoing reformulation of philosophy and religion themselves.

Despite these dynamic processes, the repetition and reproduction of the same thinkers and ideas across volumes reinstates with each publication the putative foundations of the field. These introductory texts performatively solidify which issues, thinkers, and methods are valid and important for philosophy of religion. They regard and present themselves as merely restating what is already known, while in fact continuously reconstituting boundaries and exclusions. We are interested in how this consensus was formulated and why it persists—what elisions, even violence, must be enacted to legitimate canonical decisions and declare them settled.

The present volume, however, is as eager to pursue neglected trajectories of thought as to reveal their absence or suppression. Critical theorizing about humanity and morality has never been the exclusive domain of European thinkers, just as European thought has never truly addressed the condition of all humanity. That so much philosophy of religion proceeds as if this were not the case is, on the one hand, our starting observation and, on the other, a critical lens that we hope those invested in the field as it stands would try on through engagement with the writings collected here. Put differently, we aim to reconfigure what philosophy of religion is understood to mean such that European Man is put in proper perspective as, in Sylvia Wynter's words, a "local culture's" definition of the human.[2]

Our work, too, takes place in a context that must be accounted for. Precisely because we see ourselves working with and sometimes within the field as it stands, we are calling for a reexamination of assumptions about its origins and boundaries and for a critique of the historical processes through which these assumptions came to be. More important, we find it imperative to probe the ways in which such normative philosophical inquiry into religion has reinforced the inscription of coloniality into the global epistemic framework. Questions of method, universality, and historical context thus arise from multiple directions at once.

The religious turn in French philosophy, concepts of pluralism and secularity, and comparative studies that displace the universality of Christian thought have garnered significant attention in philosophy of religion over the past two decades. Its relevance for addressing issues of ecology, social inequality, democratic theory, and religion's place in politics is argued as both a defense of and challenge to the field's accumulated ways of producing knowledge.[3] These important initiatives rework the sedimented habits of thought and argument that would tightly guard the label philosophy of religion. Yet the basic canon of thinkers and texts is left relatively untouched as scholars work to determine how it might be applied or revised in present contexts. These various calls for revision may be spurred by many of the same forces as the present collection, yet they continue to affirm a core or lineage that we would emphasize is only one possible center among others.

Race, Coloniality, Modernity

THE TERM *coloniality* as used in recent scholarship indicates the epistemic dominance of western and Eurocentric modernity, including its suppression of methodological critiques and alternate modes of thought. Coloniality is the universalization and normalization of matrices of power

that historically enacted colonization itself and the presumption of superiority that these forces collectively grant to discourses articulated from
colonizing and western perspectives. The notion of modernity/coloni-
ality advanced by Aníbal Quijano, Enrique Dussel, María Lugones, and
Walter Mignolo gave rise to a critical scholarship that, under the banner
of "decolonial thinking" or the "decolonial turn," situates the inception of
modernity (and therefore the beginning of post/decolonial thought and
movements) in the Spanish colonial encounter of 1492. *Coloniality* names
the regime of power that outlasts formal colonial governance, sustained in
neocolonial power relations that reaffirm and reproduce Eurocentrism, as
well as the construction of ideas of Europe and whiteness over and against
colonized, racialized others.

Decolonial thought indexes colonial relations as a complex web of
power that weaves together political-material relations and epistemic production. That is, the rise of the modern western episteme is intimately
linked to the material conditions that colonial encounter facilitates. Con-
versely, the encounter with, or rather the invention of, the colonial other
feeds the modern western episteme and constructions of its own subjecthood. Wynter refers to this ideal subjecthood—or, better, mode of
being—with its common self-designation, *Man*. She designates with *Man*
the hegemonic installation of a particular understanding of the human
based in the norms of western modernity: secular, rational, bourgeois,
and of course white.

The overrepresentation of Man as the universal or universalizable category of the human depends for its claims to attainment and coherence
on the (invention of the) racial/colonial other. It figures indigeneity, then
Blackness, as the materialization of ontological lack, the antithesis of Man
that defines it by contrast.[4] Wynter's analysis parallels the observations
of other decolonial thinkers who also view modernity and coloniality as
inseparable. Numerous voices articulating anticolonial visions and alternative modes of thought in the Americas have existed since the beginning
of colonization, though their presence in the western academy is more
recent. The discourses on which this collection builds are rooted not first
or only in what is commonly labeled philosophy of religion but in long
genealogies of radical and revolutionary Indigenous, antiracist, Black, and
mestizo/creole philosophies.

Naming a few key thinkers can, then, establish helpful points of reference without declaring these to be necessary or exclusive starting points.
Dussel's philosophy of liberation intervenes with questions of power,

violence, and geopolitics in philosophical discussions usually guided and dominated by Eurocentric views. Influenced by Emmanuel Levinas's critique of metaphysics, Dussel views European modernity as a totalitarian myth. Deconstructing the myth of modernity's universality involves situating it within the global matrix of power that invented the original inhabitants of the Americas as the other. In the spirit of Karl Marx, the necessary task of philosophy for Dussel is to transform both the material and epistemic conditions that classify, subjugate, and violate the colonial other of Eurocentric modernity. Both dominant and suppressed forms of thought in the post-1492 worldview are entangled in the global matrix of power that reinforces its attendant universals at the expense of the other. What does it mean to do philosophy and philosophy of religion when, as Wynter and Dussel demonstrate, the act of thinking about the cogito and the world is already conditioned by such power relations? We argue that the central materials for this work cannot be reduced to theological concepts or segregated from the problems of power that shape political life. The contributors to *Beyond Man* demonstrate that radical thinkers' quests to interrogate and dismantle the apparatus of systemic violence offer challenges, vocabularies, and epistemic alternatives for doing philosophy of religion.

Questions of philosophy, race, and power are poignantly articulated in the work of the Martinican revolutionary Frantz Fanon, whose influence on this volume is evident. Like Wynter, Fanon analyzes how racial-colonial ideology shapes the symbolic register grounding philosophical signification. He thus challenges the prevalent apolitical readings of dominant philosophical concepts and frameworks. The modern western subject—and the definition of the human it presupposes—is projected as an ideal that necessarily contrasts with what its colonized, racialized others (supposedly) embody. The universal subject signifies the ontological norm, while its other embodies the antithesis of being.

Fanon's take on Maurice Merleau-Ponty's corporeal schema, for instance, demonstrates the ways in which critical studies of race and colonialism can reconfigure philosophical conversations. For Merleau-Ponty, the body schema refers to the knowledge of one's body and orientation as the expression of one's "manner of being in the world."[5] For Fanon, what informs the orientation of racialized/colonized beings is not a body schema but a racial epidermal schema.[6] With this, Fanon develops his notion of sociogeny, a concept that Wynter takes up in turn, which challenges the dominant ontogenetic definition of the human. Our corporeal, embodied existence is not only given and determined biologically. Rather, sociogeny suggests that our existence is also created socially. Fanon thus locates inescapable racialization at the beginning of human life while denouncing the stark dualisms of whiteness and Blackness, colonizer and colonized, that constitute the world of signification into which social beings are born. The phenomenological perception of our own selves and of the world cannot transcend social relations. In ways that foreshadow later theories of racial formation, Fanon claims that racialized existence is an ongoing invention.[7]

While Fanon has made invaluable contributions to conversations about philosophy, race, and coloniality, the implications of his thought for thinking about religion have yet to be thoroughly explored. In his influential work "Necropolitics," Achille Mbembe engages Fanon through the terms of political theology as sharpened by Giorgio Agamben's discussion of sovereignty, exclusion, and violence.[8] The situation of colonial occupation and governance described by Fanon in *The Wretched of the Earth* represents, for Mbembe, the mechanism through which the coloniality of necropower operates. The theologico-political problem at hand revolves around the sovereign, who represents "the capacity to define who matters and who does not, *who* is disposable and who is not."[9]

In another compelling theological vein, Lewis Gordon has suggested reading Fanon through the lens of theodicy. Fanon denounces colonial metaphysics for being Manichaean (dualistic), its bipartite view dividing the world into species of absolute good and absolute evil. According to Gordon, Fanon denounces this worldview as a secularized form of theodicy, a theological rationalization of a dualistic division of humanity into insiders and outsiders.[10] While Gordon leaves the religious implications of this reading unexplored, he opens one door to possible dialogue between Fanon and the study of religion—a line of thought both An Yountae and Joseph R. Winters explore in this volume.

Religion's role in coloniality, underexplored in the work of Fanon, is a major (though still underappreciated) focus for Wynter, another guiding figure in this collection. Wynter understands religion to be constitutive of the modern colonial world order and traces the role of religion—and its refraction through the secular—in the reproduction of the colonial order of knowing/being. Against the secularist narrative of the triumph of reason over religion, Wynter probes ways in which the old theological logic operates within and erects the modern western scientific worldview. The transition from religious cosmovision to secular worldview took place alongside the sacralization of secular rationality as the absolute parameter of truth—a process that required relegating religion to the sphere of non-reason, associated with the enchanted worldview of the colonial other. The relationship between the theological and the political, and the corresponding problem of the secular, thus cannot be understood as an isolated European construct. Wynter demonstrates that the modern western secular subject is informed and haunted by a theology that takes shape in and through the colony and slavery.[11] Religion in its more explicit forms retained more influence than Wynter directly accounts for, but she demonstrates that the secular and its racializing outcomes have an inescapable theological shape.

The gendered status of Man, noted but not extensively pursued in Wynter's work, cannot be overlooked. What Lugones calls the coloniality of gender, through which "the modern hierarchical dichotomous distinction between men and women became known as characteristically human and a mark of civilization," also plays a key role in these developments.[12] Non-European and non-Christian arrangements of gender were taken as marks of unredeemed bestiality and primitiveness, and the need to instill European frameworks of gender and kinship was used as a key justification for colonial domination and brutality.[13] These dynamics are evident in Eleanor Craig's analysis of the Laws of Burgos, which attempt to manipulate and alter Taíno understandings of gender. They also come to the fore in Vincent Lloyd's depiction of the ways C. L. R. James internalized certain colonialist class and gender norms. As readers of Fanon are also aware, via Fanon's complicated understanding of gender and masculinity, the coloniality of gender is both crucial to colonizing strategy and insidiously extant in much anticolonial and decolonial thinking.

Religion, Eurocentrism, and Racial Order

Thanks be to nature, therefore, for the incompatibility, for the spiteful competitive vanity, for the insatiable desire to possess or even to dominate! For without them, the excellent natural predispositions in humanity would eternally slumber undeveloped.—Immanuel Kant, "Idea for a Universal History with a Cosmopolitan Aim"

PURUSHOTTAMA BILIMORIA AND ANDREW IRVINE'S edited volume *Postcolonial Philosophy of Religion* poses the decolonization of philosophy of religion as a necessarily comparative project. Several crucial insights

emerge in this work, including a critical awareness that both colonialist and postcolonial theory tend to be written by cultural elites and the
recognition of the need to engage seriously and relationally with non-
Christian traditions in any reassessment of philosophy of religion's meaning and potential. *Beyond Man* seeks to reckon in a sustained way with
Christian coloniality and to simultaneously problematize the notion that
starkly and essentially distinct traditions simply exist to be compared.[14]
One of its key limitations is the centrifugal force still arguably granted to
Christian thought and history. Yet as Mayra Rivera points out (chapter 2),
Christianity itself is a tricky and perhaps limited label when applied to the
traditions of the colonized and formerly colonized. Vincent Lloyd notes
that Christian theology can exert force on thinkers who have explicitly
renounced it, suggesting that it might be better to name these influences
than to take their denial at face value (chapter 4). In short, it is no simple
thing to say what Christianity is, what it does, to whom it belongs, or
whose actions it shapes.

This, of course, has something to do with the constitution of religion as
a modern concept and of Christianity as one (albeit exalted) subheading.
That there are mutually constitutive histories of race and religion—as concepts and categories—is broadly recognized, even when this fact's significance for philosophy of religion is not fully elaborated. J. Kameron Carter
persuasively argues that western Christian attempts to disown Christianity's Jewish roots made possible modern racial imaginaries. In *Race: A
Theological Account*, he traces the connections between Kant's anthropology and his eschatological political vision. Carter observes that Kant
places "the Jews as the sole negative racial other" and that this negation
inflects his other racial classifications.[15] Race and religion are imbricated
not only with each other but with the modern, and crucially Christian,
nation-state that they justify and enable.[16] Tomoko Masuzawa elaborates
how nineteenth-century classificatory categories that dealt with religion
consolidated a narrative in which "those nations of Aryans—whether
Greece, Persia, or India—had shown in various epochs of their history the
capacity to transcend their national particularities, hence their propensity
for universality." She claims that Christian universalism is thus secondary
to and derivative from Aryan universality.[17] In Theodore Vial's account,
"because [race and religion] share a mutual genealogy, the category of religion is always a racialized category, even when race is not explicitly under
discussion." This remains true in contemporary studies of comparative religion that unwittingly reproduce "the same hierarchies of Kant, Herder,

Schleiermacher, and Müller."[18] Vial aims to draw the gaze fixed on the Enlightenment forward in time, arguing that modern race and religion are still taking shape in post-Enlightenment German thought.

Our historicizing approach follows the decolonial strategy of beginning with the so-called long sixteenth century, or what Wynter refers to as the 1492 worldview. We insist that while significant shifts of course did occur in the eighteenth and nineteenth centuries, race and religion are more accurately understood when viewed as the trajectories of European colonial projects that began in the age of discovery. This is not to fixate on a debate about origins, or whether or not early modern ideas are equivalent to later ones. It is as much an orientation as a truth claim, a methodology that asks how the stories of race and religion might be told differently if the starting point is 1492 rather than Kant. It is also a method for interrogating the ways in which, as Carter states in this volume, western conceptions of sovereignty—from subjectivity to the state—are "never not colonial."

Nelson Maldonado-Torres observes that the invention of the universalizing category of religion "opened up a universe of signification" that naturalized a racial ontological hierarchy.[19] The "discovery" of nonreligious subjects, meaning the decidedly Christian assessment that Indigenous people had nothing that qualified as religion, initiated the possibility of anthropological thinking that classified some beings as "ontologically limited" and inhuman. It was this division of humanity into those who did and did not qualify as human beings that Maldonado-Torres sees as "opening the doors of modernity."[20] This is not to say that hierarchies were somehow determined and settled in that moment: Indigenous people were nonetheless, in paradoxical ways, conceived of as possible subjects of the Catholic church. Colonial thinking denied this status to enslaved African people, seen as property (nonbeing) but also associated with "Moors," who were "in defiance of the Christian order."[21]

Joint hierarchies of race and religion thus have a long lineage that transforms but endures with the emergence of secularism. While for nineteenth-century European scholars, "having religion no longer provides the ultimate or definitive concession of full humanity," the anthropological assumptions put in place under that logic remain. Colonized people's religion was recognizable for European scholars and publics through demonstrations of its proximity or similarity to Christianity, and religion itself was deemed less qualifying than "the capacity to think beyond religion and to organize their society rationally."[22] Masuzawa connects this pattern to the narrative of secularization that holds the liberation of political, economic, and civil life from church authority as a sign of societal maturation. The colonized or "primitive" were seen as "thoroughly in the grip of religion," atavistically subscribing to "prelogical" modes of thought and belief.[23] Religion thus went from qualifying peoples as human to being a potential liability that could, through excess or irrationality, evince cultural inferiority and backwardness.

Philosophy of religion's relationship to race and coloniality is also tightly connected to European understandings of the term *philosophy* from the eighteenth century on. The dominant understanding and definition of philosophy has a particular genealogy that was born out of the modern imaginary of the west. It is an endless reproduction of self-referentiality in which "the narrative returns the west to itself despite its various transformations."[24] Philosophy becomes a homogenizing discourse, a reiteration of sameness, as its particular trajectory is transformed into a universality. That trajectory cites as its initial articulation a reified and exclusively European origin.

The claim of philosophy's Greek roots intentionally portrays Europe as the first and greatest agent of critical and rational thinking while relegating non-western traditions of philosophical thinking to culture and religion. Greek thought is then taken as the forebear of universal norms and ideals of science, medicine, aesthetics, ethics, and politics (democracy), all of which reflect the universal progress of history, while non-western traditions are identified as lacking rational rigor, critical perspective, and universal relevance.

This narrative of lineage relies on a number of distortions, oversimplifications, and erasures. In his recent book, *Isonomia and the Origins of Philosophy*, Kojin Karatani displaces western metaphysics' and political philosophy's age-old claims of Greek origin by identifying their source in Ionia, an ancient Greek colony in Anatolia. The reduction of philosophy's root to a single European origin also underestimates the long and persisting influence that Arabic-Islamic thought had on western philosophy during the Middle Ages. The thirteenth-century Arabic-Latin translation movement had a significant impact on the formation of European disciplines of science and humanities, particularly in natural philosophy, metaphysics, logic, and ethics. Indeed, it was Ibn Rushd's (Averroes) original reading of Aristotle that reintroduced Aristotle to Europe. Ibn Rushd's influence persists widely through the western philosophical tradition, most notably in the work of Spinoza—however, this history is always underplayed within the intellectual genealogy.

Before the eighteenth century, philosophers often attributed philosophy's origin to places outside of Europe, such as India, Egypt, China, and Persia.[25] According to Robert Bernasconi, the eighteenth-century reinvention of philosophy as a western tradition was due to a specific question that needed to be addressed: the existence of what seemed like philosophy in China.[26] Around this time, historians of ideas began to deny the existence of philosophy in Africa and Asia. While religion had previously been a marker of civilization, it became a category used to distinguish non-European spiritual cosmologies from the rational operations of philosophy.[27]

This period coincides with both Enlightenment philosophies of rational humanity and the surge in scientific theories of race. Europe's self-referential identification of philosophy's origin cannot be examined outside of the history of colonial encounters and the development of scientific racism. It is against this backdrop that Kant's well-known racist anthropology and Georg Wilhelm Friedrich Hegel's exclusion of Africa from world history must be understood. Kant's preoccupation with anthropology and geography (he offered more courses on those subjects than on logic or metaphysics) is indicative of their critical place in his philosophical thinking. If what constitutes the human in its fully realized capacity is the ability to think and will, it is the white European who materializes, or can materialize, this ideal. Unlike Jean-Jacques Rousseau, who postulates the ideal human nature as a hypothetical concept, the Kantian cosmopolitan vision of moral reason does not shy away from indicating the specific racial group that embodies—or is destined to eventually embody—the ideal of critical reason.[28] Kant's racist anthropology is inseparable from his moral philosophy.

Kant's "Idea for a Universal History with a Cosmopolitan Aim" is thus significant not only for what it represents about his own ideas but also—perhaps even more so—for the many strands of philosophical and theological thought consolidated therein. From a contemporary standpoint, "it is as if this essay were a crucible in which Kant sought to synthesize the purified and transformed views of his predecessors, condensing them into a comprehensive political and cultural history with a philosophical moral. It is itself an instance of the integration of history and philosophical reflection that it heralds."[29] This historical and philosophical integration is possible because of Kant's undergirding teleology, which is evident in the fact that universal history is an idea that emerges for Kant in spite of what one can observe of human action. A philosopher observing fellow human beings would be unable to "presuppose any rational *aim of theirs*."[30] And if one took a more collective view, it would appear that "everything in the large is woven together out of folly, childish vanity, often also out of childish malice and the rage to destruction."[31] For Kant, however, it is also necessary and observable that everything in nature is constructed to fully realize its development. One must take this species-level view of "rational beings who all die" to detect nature's purposiveness with respect to immortal humanity. Within Kant's teleological narrative, (western) European states have traveled only a short way toward their ultimate destiny. Yet they are ahead of other places and peoples and "will probably someday give laws to all the others."[32]

Hegel's view of world history is structured by a similarly teleological progression in which "the History of the world travels from East to West."[33] Asia represents the childlike stage of the Spirit, whereas Christian Europe is the consummation. The first Man of reason arose, remarks Hegel, among the ancient Greeks, who understood freedom to be the essence of human being but who nonetheless engaged in slavery. Christian German nations "were the first to attain the consciousness, that man, is free: that it is the freedom of Spirit which constitutes its essence."[34] He excludes Africa from the global cartography of reason in which the Spirit's movements are registered. Africa is associated with backwardness and immaturity: "the land of childhood, which lying beyond the day of history, is enveloped in the dark mantle of Night."[35] He claims that Africa is "no historical part of the world; it has no movement or development to exhibit."[36]

The entanglement of Hegel's philosophy and colonial history nonetheless takes place in unexpected sites. Susan Buck-Morss's important work *Hegel, Haiti, and Universal History* argues that Hegel's master-slave (lordship-bondage) dialectic was inspired by the Haitian slave revolt, rather than the French Revolution as is commonly claimed by intellectual historians. Buck-Morss's work shows how the historical event that likely inspired Hegel's lordship-bondage dialectic is muted in his own work as well as in historical and theoretical interpretations of his ideas. Intellectual histories and Hegelian historiography continually affirm the assumption of Europe as self-generating; the evident connection between Europe and its colony is viewed as material and external, at most. The constitution of Europe's self-knowledge occurs internally, thus maintaining the Hegelian thesis of universal history that in its temporal progression moves from the archaic periphery to its consummation, namely, Europe.

Revising these genealogies is a matter not simply of exposing the racist moments tainting an intellectual history but of understanding the extent to which philosophical claims are inseparable from questions of narrative, context, and power. The discipline of philosophy's reluctance to critically engage race, gender, class, and sexuality continues to produce (with some exceptions) universalizing philosophical knowledge that neglects history, context, and power. Despite its unparalleled influence on a wide range of critical theories, the field of philosophy as commonly recognized remains relatively immune to the various challenges emerging from global geographies of power and knowledge. A similar tendency prevails in radical philosophical (neo-Marxist and postmodern) critiques of modernity and capitalist globalization when Europe remains the sole agent and referent of knowledge production.

Some have, in search of an alternative to rationalism, turned to Spinoza's monism or to existential-phenomenological sources such as Søren Kierkegaard, Martin Heidegger, Emmanuel Levinas, and Jacques Derrida. These thinkers are often presented as correctives to the limits of western thought, as offering an autocritical lens. They point to matters of contingency and contradiction that attend western metaphysics characterized by the problems of ontotheology, Platonic dualism, Aristotelian substance metaphysics, and the suppression of difference. The twentieth-century tradition of phenomenology signals a turn to the structure of experience and the way the subject's consciousness is constituted by the other and the surrounding world. By suspending presence (the presence of truth), phenomenology seeks to displace the sovereign subject: the self-possessed subject of modern metaphysics yields to alterity. Inspired by the phenomenological tradition inflected by Levinas, Derrida's later writings on ethics and religion signal for many a defining critique of the impasse of western metaphysics.

Deconstruction and phenomenology's contributions to analyzing the limitations and potential of western philosophy cannot be underestimated. What calls our attention, however, is that they are often viewed as solutions to the problems of and epistemic violence done by western metaphysics (especially when the reception of these works is devoid of analytics of power). The phenomenological constitution of the self and the world does not take place in a power vacuum, nor is the self who is "in the world" (à la Heidegger) interrogating the meaning of Being unaffected by the social relations of power that condition them. Fanon's phenomenological analysis of racialized subjectivity shows how the approach to the question of meaning and existence always unfolds in the matrix of power relations conditioning the individual's existence. The questions of the self's existence/formation in relation to the other and the world cannot be reduced to the philosophical categories of abstract universals. Rather, Fanon shows how the self is always already given to the world, a world constituted by myriad others whose participation in the constitution of the subject's consciousness as well as its body schema is conditioned by power.

A related elision takes place when European feminist philosophy is treated as decisively addressing gender—in subjectivity or for philosophical writing. In the existential-phenomenological tradition, Simone de Beauvoir demonstrated women's assigned place of otherness in relation to men.[37] Common to Beauvoir's and Fanon's analyses is the centrality of otherness (negation) in the constitution of the subject. A close examination of the rational-universal western subject reveals what it hides: those whose exclusion makes the being-there of the subject (the Euro-Christian Man) possible. Yet it is an entirely more complex task to weave together an understanding of how race *and* gender operate in these constructions of being and in the aspirations they engender in those thereby excluded.

An emerging body of literature brings race and coloniality to the forefront of philosophical discourse. Linda Alcoff, Robert Bernasconi, Lewis Gordon, María Lugones, Achille Mbembe, Eduardo Mendieta, Charles Mills, Lucius Outlaw, Shannon Sullivan, and George Yancy have been offering in recent years (and in many works already cited here) theoretical frameworks and directions for the philosophical study of race and coloniality. Nelson Maldonado-Torres, in particular, has elaborated the ways in which these issues intersect with studies and definitions of religion.

Discourse on political theology has undertaken a parallel and related critical turn. Inspired to varying degrees by the question of the theologico-political (and still, for some, the Schmittian notion of the sovereign), some strands of the debate retain an emphasis on continental philosophers invested in questions of law, sovereignty, and violence (such as Derrida, Agamben, and Slavoj Žižek). These conversations examine the dominant political system's sanction of violence under the name of the sovereign, as well as the justification and delivery of violence through more intricate modes of biopolitics. A more recently emerging group of voices also contests political theology's Eurocentric orientation, its historical embeddedness in Euro-Christian analytics, and its neglect of nonwhite and non-western interlocutors. The works of Shawn Copeland, Gil Anidjar, J. Kameron Carter, Hussein Ali Agrama, Santiago Slabodsky, Vincent Lloyd, Houria Bouteldja, An Yountae, and Devin Singh—several of whom appear in this volume—are among those who analyze the problems of political theology in conversation with non-western, nonwhite, and non-Christian interlocutors. These thinkers would not univocally classify their work as political theology. Yet they are cumulatively reworking the ways that relationships among politics, theology, and other social processes are imagined.

Beyond Man assumes, but also strives to demonstrate, the inseparability of colonialism and anti-Blackness in philosophy and theology. We hope that it also contributes to discourses that are bringing multiple strands of liberatory thought into collaborative conversation. Willie James Jennings's work provides repeated reminders that the influence of coloniality on Christian theology has been both chosen and contingent. Jennings exercises a materialist, historicizing orientation that the authors in this collection mirror. For Jennings, economic and social arrangements are fundamentally relational—between humans but also between humans and the land.[38] These arrangements come about over time, through processes of transformation and (conscious and unconscious) decision-making. We share this preoccupation with examining how religious thinking *takes shape*, a method that emphasizes that both punctual moments of crisis and embedded, seemingly intractable situations of exploitation are continually created. This approach calls attention to the historical situatedness of any form of philosophy.[39] Our authors engage Black radical traditions and others in the typically conceived decolonial circle (U.S. Latinx philosophy, Latin American/Caribbean philosophy, and Indigenous philosophies) without supposing that there are clear, necessary boundaries between these categories. Our contributors are in conversation with both "traditional" modes of philosophical scholarship and the many crucial endeavors that have already initiated the work of thinking critically and constructively about race, coloniality, and philosophy of religion.

Decolonizing Philosophical Trajectories

If you do not embody Kant's and Foucault's local history, memory, language, and "embodied" experience, what shall you do? Buy a pair of Kant and Foucault's shoes; or, look around you and think about what has to be done in the same way that Kant and Foucault looked around themselves and thought about what had to be done?—Walter Mignolo, *The Darker Side of Western Modernity*

The most profound ethical relation in the zone of nonbeing is not that of the master with another master, but that of a slave with another slave. At the end, it is not only the master who can start a relation.—Nelson Maldonado-Torres, "Race, Religion, and Ethics in the Modern/Colonial World"

QUESTIONING THE NORMATIVE STATUS of the term *philosophy* as well as attempting to reclaim and decolonize the term itself certainly involve deconstructing the racist history haunting the archive of philosophical canons. Underlying this problem, however, is the epistemic edifice that sanctions exclusion and hierarchy, which is inseparable from the colonial ideology driven by Europe's imperialist desires and racializing (racist) worldviews. Exposing the complex entanglement of knowledge and power underneath philosophy and philosophy of religion's disciplinary designations clarifies the stakes and politics of categorization and canonization. Just as the notion of religion cannot be detached from the long history of European imperialism in which it played an instrumental role in denying the humanity of non-Europeans, the normative category of philosophy was crucial for reason's imperial design. In its imaginary of the modern world, Europe is the sole possessor and producer of philosophical knowledge, while non-Europe is the receptacle of ancient wisdom and art. Similarly, Christianity is constructed as a religion compatible with the secular-liberal values of rationality and democracy, while nonwestern religions are constructed as overly mystical and outdated.

This is why rethinking the term *philosophy* is important. Philosophy has placed itself at the center of knowledge (as the queen of science). Its rigid normative parameters delineate which methods, texts, sites, and modalities of thinking are properly part of its domain, the voices of these judgments uttered "by an authority who adjudicates what we will and will not count as legitimate knowledge. These are voiced by one who seems to know, who acts with the full assurance of knowledge."[40] Reflecting on her academic journey within and outside of the disciplinary boundary of philosophy, U.S. philosopher Judith Butler remarks that "philosophy has become another to itself."[41] As a feminist philosopher teaching in the Department of Rhetoric, she finds herself being labeled as a "theorist." She notes that many important philosophers who are working with gender and race are housed outside of philosophy departments.[42] It is no coincidence that important philosophical thinkers from outside the traditional

European canon are often labeled as theorists, critics, artists, writers, or poets—or vaguely, thinkers. Philosophy as a concept and field maintains self-segregation from analytics of power, key tools of analysis considered highly important and relevant in almost every discipline of humanities and social sciences.

We understand the endeavor of reclaiming philosophy of religion as working to push the normative boundaries that calcify the discipline rather than prescribing another normative orientation that would rectify the field. The genealogies of the thinkers in whose work our contributors locate alternative possibilities are, generally speaking, found in contexts of struggle (anticolonial, antiracist, antipatriarchal). Its members are often grounded in, or at least in close contact with, emancipatory political movements—inspiring them, challenging them, and strategizing their ways forward. Such work has sparsely and sporadically made its way into the field of religious studies, in ways this volume aims to deepen and expand.

Two concepts from Juliet Hooker's *Theorizing Race in the Americas* helpfully frame the collective work of this project. The first is a hemispheric approach that connects struggle in and theory about the United States or North America with Caribbean and Latin American histories and discourses. For Hooker, an "intellectual hemispheric genealogy" allows one to trace U.S. and Latin American thought about race in ways that are attuned to contextual specificity and useful for understanding the evolution of present-day racial ideology.[43] The present collection aims for hemispheric relationality, albeit always with an eye to transatlantic histories and relations. Its engagements with Black studies, alongside Caribbean and Latin American history and philosophy, suggest important overlaps and points of convergence for the study of (de)coloniality.

While hemispheric thinking is not Hooker's invention, we adopt that approach in a spirit framed by the second concept we borrow from her work: that of "juxtaposition as a methodological alternative to comparison."[44] As much as colonialism and coloniality are patterned modes of universalization and domination, they play out in disparate ways across time and space and target differently positioned others. The theories and tactics of those who contest these forces are likewise impossible to unify. Yet it would be disingenuous and undesirable to render these contexts distinct and comparable—because much of Caribbean thought is also Black studies, because many U.S. racial dynamics were incubated in Caribbean contexts, and because Latin American thinking on race is formatively connected to how other parts of the hemisphere are *imagined* to be. Rather than "assuming prior difference" in order to compare discrete contexts and approaches, we set these efforts side by side. We urge readers in turn to resist comparison, which can elide "the boundaries between traditions as contingent products of political power," and to notice "the resonances and/or discontinuities between traditions of thought" as they appear in this work.[45] The contributors to this volume share many notes of common purpose but are not univocal. Rather than smooth over controversies among us, we welcome notes of tension and discord as marking sites for the continuation of this work.

IN "DECOLONIAL OPTIONS FOR A FRAGILE SECULAR," Devin Singh probes the complex connection between modernity and secularity, which is often underexplored or muted in the mainstream conversation headed by figures such as Charles Taylor and José Casanova. If decolonial theorists complicate widespread accounts of modernity and secularity by exposing their coconstitutive role in colonial history, Singh troubles them further by tracing their connection with the evolution of a capitalist economic system and the ensuing material conditions. He looks at secularization's influence on the inception of capitalism, in which the evolving economic systems of production, accumulation, and exchange served the needs of colonial enterprises. Against the myth of the secular (secular modernity as the edifice of western civilization), Singh probes the undying power of religion in the secular public realm by demonstrating how changing conceptions of economy in western social life are always imbricated with religious ideas, whether in explicit theological language (premodern time) or secular terms (during and after modernity). Despite the collusive tie between secularity and modernity/coloniality, Singh does not want to reject the contributions of the secular altogether. Rather, he is interested in preserving important contributions and the potential of the secular space for protecting difference in a way that takes a decolonial vantage point and breaks with the account provided by European modernity.

While Singh argues the need to preserve a version of secularity, Mayra Rivera highlights the multiplicity of valences that religion can have for political resistance. In "Embodied Counterpoetics: Sylvia Wynter on Religion and Race," Rivera explores the various roles that religion plays in Wynter's work. Wynter elaborates both the ways that Christianity gave systematic shape and justification to coloniality and the ways that an anticolonial spirit was nurtured in Caribbean religious practice, Christian and otherwise. Religion in the latter vein can work as counterpoetics, incubating "states of feeling" that play a key role in the reinventions of the human to which Wynter aspires. The importance of African cultural inheritance in Wynter's treatment of ritual challenges both secular humanist condescension and European hegemony; it requires letting go of aspirations to align with or become that which was "never meant to foster our well-being." Religion itself is neither good nor bad. The question is what ways of life, religious and otherwise, will nurture "the states of feeling needed to counter dehumanization"—embodied counterpoetics that can resist both coloniality and capitalism.

In a chapter examining the Laws of Burgos (Leyes de Burgos) of 1512–13, Eleanor Craig argues that these "Royal Ordinances for the Good Government and Treatment of the Indians" constitute a moral philosophical document that consolidates emerging justifications for colonial intervention and expansion. Craig reads the laws as simultaneously continuing and diverging from preceding European thought on salvation, culture, and conquest. While the Laws were a document of governance, they were never executed to any extent that resembled their prescriptions. They also were composed in a context in which Spanish colonizers were having to engage directly (with likely intentional and unintentional forms of misunderstanding) with Indigenous moralities and epistemologies. Craig argues that at stake in the Laws are colonialist self-justifications that, while intended to lessen outright brutality, were primarily concerned with reconciling colonial violence with eternal salvation. This chapter asserts that the Laws' frequent invocation as an early human rights document deserves further attention, since it points to tendencies to elevate the morality of dominating groups that endure to this day. It also argues that the Laws ought to be included in genealogies of race that are often construed as having their roots in the Enlightenment.

In "The Puritan Atheism of C. L. R. James," Vincent Lloyd grapples with the complex legacy of James's work and person. James defines activity as fundamentally collective, referring to practices that resist systems of racial and capitalist domination; activity is what performs and creates the new society in the midst of the old. In James's thought, workers possess wisdom derived from everyday confrontations with domination and the creative resources needed to shape an alternative world order. The revolutionary intellectual or agitator inhabits a set of tense contradictions, elaborating a theory that fundamentally questions the need for their contributions. Middle-class intellectuals, by James's own account, are far less accountable to social collectivities than are members of the working class. Lloyd presents James's late confession to having committed sexual assault at the age of sixteen in order to raise questions about this founder of Black revolutionary theory's understanding of power and domination. He identifies a steady undercurrent of violence beneath middle-class respectability, depicting James in a puritan stance of alienation from his own desires and from the recognition of women as human. The bourgeois revolutionary more generally, Lloyd observes, is in a stance of constant complicity: "For the middle class broadly—for whites, for men, for those in the Global North, for those without disability—there is no redemption." Neither violence nor its confession comes as a surprise, even when they contradict one's stated commitments to follow others' (women's or the working class's) desires. This chapter raises crucial and unsettling questions about who can truly desire, or fully participate in, struggles for liberation.

Ellen Armour is concerned with another form of complicity. Her chapter on decolonizing engagements with photographic objects and media advocates contemplative attention—not just to what the photograph might represent but also to how its constitution, like the viewer's own, is immersed in biodisciplinary power. Against the conventional assumption that the photographic image represents the truth before one's eyes (seeing is believing), she suggests, following Errol Morris, that we see in photographs what we already believe to be true (believing is seeing). Armour invokes Ariella Azoulay's exploration of photography's potential to activate a resisting gaze, termed the *civil gaze*. While the civil gaze offers a compelling account of photography's role in cultivating a transformative political imagination, Armour finds it insufficient for decolonizing spectatorship as it tends to assume a sovereign subjectivity. Perhaps, Armour suggests, a careful inquiry into Christianity's entanglement in the condition of seeing and believing might shed light on decolonizing spectatorship, as the mediation between belief and visual image has occupied a central place in Christian history.

Sovereign subjectivity is, moreover, a fundamentally racial ideal that is part of what J. Kameron Carter portrays as the cannibalistic ritual of colonialism. Carter's reading of Aimé Césaire observes that the coconstruction of the political and the theological, or "racial capitalism and colonialism as theological discourse," undergirds both humanist Man and its attendant versions of sovereignty and transcendence. The metabolization of Indigenous and Black life and labor for capitalist profit is a consumption of flesh and blood, a eucharistic practice in which the racial capitalist liturgy organizes "matter into a violent and restricted economy of value." Césaire portrays the bodies and comments of legislators in the French National Assembly as they promote murderously violent responses to the 1946–47 anticolonial revolts in Madagascar. He observes how, in this ritual repetition of coloniality, the politicians' discourse transfigures the bodies of the colonized into both blood sacrifice and something to be eaten—consumed, then excreted. These are the movements that ceremonially produce the Christian community, the nation-state, and the idea of western civilization. They rehearse, moreover, a "violent metaphysics of matter" that has justified various forms of classed, raced, and gendered extraction and exploitation since the Middle Ages.

Blackness as "anticolonial antisacrament" refuses consumption and digestion and lodges itself in the colonial machinery as *remains*. It testifies to the failed totality of race and is itself a site of seemingly impossible possibility, a secreted "erotic reserve" that bears fugitive relation to western Christian capitalist discourse and governance. Négritude, Carter argues, rearranges sacrality and teleology through a poetics that operates in excess of this sacrificial political theology. In a mode that Carter terms *fecopoetics*, Césaire's *Cahier d'un retour au pays natal* interrupts the incorporative "self-corpsing" by which the colonized participate in their own consumption. Carter with Césaire pursues an alternate sacrality marked by desire and multiplicity, a recoding of language and fugitive reimagining of materiality and self.

An Yountae also challenges Christian notions of sacrifice that rely on and inscribe colonialist ideology. An reads Fanon's controversial notion of violence through the lens of theodicy by juxtaposing Fanon with Job. Fanon views the problem of colonialism as a metaphysical problem reified by a Manichaean division, a theodicean ontology that separates good (the white colonizer) from evil (the Black/Native colonized). An observes that colonial theodicy offers a simple answer to the question of divine justice: redemption through violence and sacrifice. Fanon's intervention, for An, is a critique of the redemptive violence that demands sacrifice. Fanon rearticulates violence by breaking from an instrumentalist understanding that sets up the binary of violence/nonviolence. Many of the critiques directed at Fanon's notion of violence, such as Hannah Arendt's, emanate from the instrumentalist framework, which views violence as pure means.

An argues that Arendt's position on violence—and the liberal discourse of nonviolence—denounces certain forms of violence while legitimizing others. To explicate Fanon's notion of violence, An juxtaposes Fanonian absolute violence with Walter Benjamin's notion of divine violence. Like Benjamin's divine violence, Fanon's absolute violence is irreducible to particular moments and actions. Rather, it is always in excess and elsewhere. It does not aim at replacing the social order but at terminating it entirely. Fanon's critique of colonial metaphysics is further refined by An as a critique of colonial theology and sovereignty via Delores Williams and Achille Mbembe. Against the colonial theodicy that demands sacrifice, Fanon urges the end of theodicy and the abolition of the world and the theology that give birth to such a theodicy.

Filipe Maia's "Alter-Carnations: Notes on Cannibalism and Coloniality in the Brazilian Context" recounts "the life and swallowing" of the first episcopal priest in Brazil, Bishop Pero Fernandes Sardinha (1495–1556), who was captured and devoured by a Caeté warrior. This chapter analyzes the anthropophagic ritual in the Tupi philosophical context as a mode of deterrence and vengeance that was also an honorable mode of death, one that recognized the bravery and strength of the rival so eaten. It reads Oswald de Andrade's "Cannibalist Manifesto" for the ways that the text playfully deconstructs Brazilian origins and "ontological nationalism," drawing attention to abjected and secreted dimensions of both Portuguese and Brazilian mythologies. For Maia, the eating of Bishop Sardinha is a eucharistic encounter that presents "a pathway to theorize cannibalism as a mode of relation that resists coloniality precisely by incorporating it." While a Freudian interpretation of originary incorporation would indicate the installment of patriarchal laws and civilizing logics, Andrade instead envisions it as an act of embracing the totem. Maia delivers a theological reflection on anthropophagy as sacrament—as a regenerative, digestive act in which coloniality might be disintegrated and transformed. This incorporative process, a kind of communion, has the potential to bring about "a new social-material-subjective reality" and thus new incarnations.

Joseph R. Winters reads the notion of the sacred, one of the key conceptual notions in the modern study of religion, as it inscribes an ontological distinction separating the pure from the impure, order from chaos, and being from nonbeing. By juxtaposing the sacred in the work of the historian of religion Mircea Eliade and in the works of Sylvia Wynter and Frantz Fanon, Winters unravels the particular understanding of the sacred undergirding the colonial imaginary. According to Eliade, the sacred provides the ontological ground for participating in being. But his vision of the sacred corroborates the racial/colonial imaginary of the west, as he refers to occupation of foreign land as participation in the sacred. Eliade's sacred, Winters observes, is posited *contra* opacity and darkness so that whiteness is associated with the sacred while Blackness represents profanity. The connection between the ontological distinction and racial/colonial demarcation is further clarified by Wynter, who views the emergence of European Man in opposition to its others as a transference of the Christian distinction between spirit and fallen flesh. Man, according to this framework, consecrates the world by expansion and by subjugation of darkness and nonbeing. Winters finds in Fanon's poetics potential for reconfiguring the sacred. Fanon's final prayer, directed to his body, suggests an alternative sense of the sacred, the sacred gone astray that remains faithful to the ungrounding and unsettling nature of the flesh.

Carter traces Césaire's "shamanic poet journeys" into their experimental remaking of political and narrative logics; these projects play with and disorient the "totemic or racial masks and scripts" that structure anti-Black theopolitics. Maia notes a totemic embrace in the alternative sacrament that cannibalizes and incorporates the colonizer. Amy Hollywood picks up on these multivalent, multidirectional circulations of the totem in her response to this volume. She affirms that passionate attachments to whiteness and westernness are inextricable from coloniality and capitalism. These passions belie philosophy's rational self-image, itself an object of affective investment. But they can also distract from the epistemic dimensions of contemporary social and ecological crises. Hollywood locates in Sigmund Freud's *Totem and Taboo* an ambivalence over colonization on the part of the colonizers and posits mourning and melancholia as key structural elements of colonialist, racial, and capitalist thinking. Just as the Laws of Burgos anxiously attempt to formalize colonizing ethics, the law of the father incorporated in the totem meal reproduces the violence to which it responds. "European savagery is displaced, continuously, onto those whose land and resources and bodies it exploits." It repeats and reconstitutes itself in every attempt to deny that it is driven by desire, belief, or other nonsecular forces. Disparate readings of cannibalism and colonial metabolism each rely, Hollywood notes, on the subjective positionings from which they depart; mourning and melancholia occur differently for colonizers and colonized. For writers in this volume who straddle categories of privilege and subjection (race, gender, sexuality, and class, to name but a few), philosophy necessarily takes forms of "analysis, critique, and self-exposure" that register loss differently in each instance.

ALL OF THE CONTRIBUTORS TO THIS VOLUME are situated in the United States two decades into the twenty-first century. When writing about thinkers in other times and places, we are nonetheless writing toward questions posed by our respective positions and (particular and collective) histories in relation to this location. Such questions include, What is to be done with liberal ideals that, though faulty and even disingenuous, sometimes provide recognizable language to protest some of the worst forms of inequality and injustice? Under what conditions, and for whom, does hope for large-scale social change hold out against a world that seems thoroughly subsumed by racial capitalist logics? What must be learned from histories of Black radicalism for decolonial thought and practice today—in particular, how does the realization of radical political potential necessitate steady and simultaneous reassessments of class, gender, sexuality, and more?

None of these issues is new, and we do not claim any originality in combining them. Yet it may be that something about the time and place in which we are all living—separately and together—has created our common urge to pursue these questions in relation to philosophy of religion. It is also important to acknowledge that we are all scholars trained, though critically, in traditions of western Christianity. While each of our chapters challenges religion's homogenizing association with European intellectual trajectories, they collectively emphasize Christianity's broad interactions with diverse forms of political thought. The emphasis on a western, and largely Christian, religious perspective is not meant to reinforce Christian hegemony, though that is of course its risk. It rather reflects our particular focus on the complex connection between the Americas and the modern European imaginary that was mediated by the overwhelming presence of Christianity in the Americas through (post-, neo-, and ongoing) colonial history. This positioning is not intended to erase the cartography of intellectual and political struggle emerging from non-Christian religious communities and texts or to undermine the guiding role that Indigenous epistemologies play in decolonial scholarship. Rather, it acknowledges our focus and limits while aiming to avoid a tokenizing or comparativist approach.

There is a danger that "the epistemic privilege of the first world," which has been central in our training (even when we find ourselves excluded by its norms), might cause us to lose sight of the dynamic just described. None of us can imagine that we are fully Man or fully untouched by the biases that have propelled Man's status as the consummate thinker and knower.[46] These writings exhibit that tension and wrestle with it openly in hope that more can be done and addressed when these dynamics are explicitly named. To the extent that philosophies of religion are thoroughly embedded in violent hierarchies, they may seem an unlikely site for launching decolonial and antiracist interventions. Yet, for these same reasons, scholars of religion, and particularly philosophy of religion, may be situated in an especially "useful site to disrupt broader trends of understanding and constructing humanity."[47]

In her groundbreaking essay "Mama's Baby, Papa's Maybe," Hortense J. Spillers observes that Black femininity is "a meeting ground of investments and privations in the national treasury of rhetorical wealth."[48] Knowledge created by those positioned socially as Black and woman reveals the fantasies, constrictions, and delusions of what passes for rationality in a white supremacist culture. Aisha Beliso-De Jesus observes, however, that to divide modes of thought by identity has proved "a neutralizing system used to manage difference."[49] Much of what has been counted as womanist, queer, and postcolonial theology would call into question basic features and structures of what is widely considered philosophy of religion if it were not categorically contained under these particularizing labels. As Beliso-De Jesus suggests, it is far from benign to add identities adjectivally in this way; to suggest that there may be Black, transnational, queer, or Asian philosophy of religion sets that work apart from philosophy of religion proper.[50] This categorization continues to set "real" thought in implicit contrast to other modes presumed to be "personal quests, marks of belonging, or anecdotes of inclusion." It denies "a relational understanding of power" that would not simply apply the brakes to Eurocentric overgeneralizations but would ask how racial and racially gendered dominance are intrinsic to nonadjectivized philosophy of religion's self-understanding.[51]

We are seeking a philosophy that actively decolonizes thought, always keeping in view the challenge of defining philosophical writing's relationship to action and practice. This problem is not peculiar to decolonial methods and is in fact taken up by thinkers for whom coloniality is not a matter of direct concern. The question of what compels right action is, after all, at the center of Kantian thinking on morality. It is also, in spite of repeated attempts at resolution, a difficulty that continues to haunt contemporary normative philosophical discourse that, "epistemically speaking, moral theory does not give us the knowledge it promises, and pragmatically speaking, it does not give us the goodness we need."[52] In this volume's discursive context, this means that certain questions must for the time being remain open: Is there constitutively decolonial thought, or is decoloniality always a matter of the act and effects of specific philosophical interventions? Is the transferability of decolonial operations best determined by analyses of comparison, relation, or something else entirely? Is there a precise or necessary relationship between one's social positioning and the methods or sites one selects for critique?[53]

Through this same understanding of the opportunities and dangers of interdisciplinary categorization, we would insist that the present collection is a work within and about philosophy of religion. To suggest that C. L. R. James, Frantz Fanon, and Sylvia Wynter might participate in philosophy of religion is a purposeful expansion of the term. It is not, however, a request (or even demand) for inclusion but rather a statement of fact. Hegel's notions of religion and Spirit and Kant's historical teleology do not exist without cultural and racial hierarchies. To question those hierarchies, their validity as well as their effects on centuries of scholarship and politics, necessarily intervenes in—*and performs, actually constitutes*—philosophy of religion. We do not aim to secure the comprehensiveness of philosophy of religion by adding to its competencies issues of race and coloniality. Rather, we argue their centrality for reading and interpreting the normative tradition. To read decolonially is to undo certain possibilities of approach, even as one offers others.

We do not take the European philosophical tradition as our necessary primary ground and starting point. In their introduction to *Postcolonial Philosophy of Religion*, Bilimoria and Irvine suggest that philosophy of religion as a form of knowledge must be reconfigured to account for, respond to, and address the experiences of colonized people.[54] However, the relationship between knowledge and experience is precisely what is at issue. Decolonizing philosophy of religion cannot be a straightforward matter of inserting the experiences of colonized and racialized persons to qualify or even determine the content and propositions of philosophical work. A more fundamental and epistemologically oriented examination is needed. We want to ask instead how philosophy of religion is itself a colonialist project and what other options develop among those who not only experience racism and colonization but actively work against their ways of seeing and shaping the world.

Notes

1 See Gale, "William James"; and Wynn, "William Paley."
2 That local culture, as Wynter also notes, is porous and internally contested; the steadiness of the definition itself signals multiple modes of violence and erasure. Wynter, "Pope," 30.
3 Farneth, *Hegel's Social Ethics*; Hackett and Wallulus, *Philosophy of Religion*; Roberts, *Encountering Religion*; and Schilbrack, *Philosophy and the Study of Religion*.
4 Wynter, "Beyond the Word of Man"; and Wynter, "Unsettling the Coloniality."
5 Merleau-Ponty, *Phenomenology of Perception*, xli.
6 Fanon, *Black Skin, White Masks*, 110.
7 The terminology of racial formation was popularized by Michael Omi and Howard Winant in *Racial Formation in the United States*, first published in 1986 and now in its third edition (2015).
8 Mbembe, "Necropolitics"; see also Agamben, *Homo Sacer*.
9 Mbembe, "Necropolitics," 27.
10 Gordon, *Introduction to Africana Philosophy*, 77.
11 Wynter, "Beyond the Word of Man," 641–42.
12 Lugones, "Methodological Notes," 72–73.
13 Lugones, "Colonialidad y género"; see also Silverblatt, *Modern Inquisitions*; and Tortorici, *Sins against Nature*.
14 This is more a difference in emphasis and framing than a disagreement; many of Bilimoria and Irvine's contributors provide key resources for the work we are doing here.
15 Carter, *Race*, 104.
16 Carter, *Race*, 39–40.
17 Masuzawa, *Invention of World Religions*, 205–6.
18 Vial, *Modern Religion, Modern Race*, 1, 10.
19 Maldonado-Torres, "Race, Religion, and Ethics," 703.
20 Maldonado-Torres, "AAR Centennial Roundtable," 651.
21 Maldonado-Torres, "AAR Centennial Roundtable," 657.
22 Maldonado-Torres, "Race, Religion, and Ethics," 708.
23 Masuzawa, *Invention of World Religions*, 16.
24 Mandair, *Religion and the Specter of the West*, 4.
25 Park, *Africa, Asia, and the History of Philosophy*, 1.
26 Bernasconi, "Philosophy's Paradoxical Parochialism."
27 Park, *Africa, Asia, and the History of Philosophy*, 1.
28 Eze, "Color of Reason," 106–18.
29 Rorty and Schmidt, "Introduction," 1.
30 Kant, "Idea for a Universal History," 11.

31 Kant, "Idea for a Universal History," 10–11.

32 Kant, "Idea for a Universal History," 21.

33 Hegel, *Philosophy of History*, 195.

34 Hegel, *Philosophy of History*, 207.

35 Hegel, *Philosophy of History*, 91.

36 Hegel, *Philosophy of History*, 99.

37 Beauvoir, *Second Sex*.

38 Jennings, "Disfigurations of Christian Identity," 69–70.

39 See also Isasi-Díaz and Mendieta, *Decolonizing Epistemologies*. This collection models the kinds of contextual reading and writing of philosophy to which our volume also aspires.

40 Butler, *Undoing Gender*, 233.

41 Butler, *Undoing Gender*, 233.

42 Butler, *Undoing Gender*, 243–44.

43 Hooker, *Theorizing Race*, 5. We are indebted to Christina Davidson for pointing out the applicability of Hooker's work and the concept of juxtapositional analysis (more on this later) to this project.

44 Hooker, *Theorizing Race*, 13.

45 Hooker, *Theorizing Race*, 13.

46 Wynter has coined the term *Man* as a reference to Europe's modern/colonial imaginary and its hegemonic installation of rational-secular subjecthood over against the colonial/racial other.

47 Beliso-De Jesus, "Confounded Identities," 313.

48 Spillers, "Mama's Baby, Papa's Maybe," 65.

49 Beliso-De Jesus, "Confounded Identities," 326.

50 Beliso-De Jesus attributes to Spillers the insight that "identity . . . is an obscuring regime that performs a metaphysical operation of separation as a form of governance." Beliso-De Jesus, "Confounded Identities," 331.

51 Beliso-De Jesus, "Confounded Identities," 328.

52 Westphal, "Empty Suitcase," 48.

53 The editors of this volume, for instance, come from two quite different experiences of being Asian American, yet none of the chapters, including our own, take those identities as their explicit focus. We would not downplay the role our personal lives play in shaping the perspectives from which we write. At the same time, we are invested in relational understandings of race and coloniality that require us to follow other historical and philosophical trajectories.

54 Bilimoria and Irvine, "Introduction," 4–5.

Bibliography

Agamben, Giorgio. *Homo Sacer: Sovereign Power and Bare Life.* Translated by Daniel Heller-Roazen. Stanford, CA: Stanford University Press, 1998.

Beauvoir, Simone de. *The Second Sex.* Translated and edited by H. M. Parshley. New York: Vintage, 1974.

Beliso-De Jesus, Aisha. "Confounded Identities: A Meditation on Race, Feminism, and Religious Studies in Times of White Supremacy." *Journal of the American Academy of Religion* 86, no. 2 (2018): 307–40.

Bernasconi, Robert. "Philosophy's Paradoxical Parochialism: The Reinvention of Philosophy as Greek." In *Cultural Readings of Imperialism: Edward Said and the Gravity of History*, edited by Keith Ansell-Pearson, Benita Parry, and Judith Squires, 212–26. London: Lawrence and Wishart, 1997.

Bilimoria, Purushottama, and Andrew Irvine. "Introduction: The State of Philosophy of Religion and Postcoloniality." In Bilimoria and Irvine, *Postcolonial Philosophy of Religion*, 1–5.

Bilimoria, Purushottama, and Andrew Irvine. *Postcolonial Philosophy of Religion.* New York: Springer, 2009.

Buck-Morss, Susan. *Hegel, Haiti, and Universal History.* Pittsburgh: University of Pittsburgh Press, 2009.

Butler, Judith. *Undoing Gender.* New York: Routledge, 2004.

Carter, J. Kameron. *Race: A Theological Account.* Oxford: Oxford University Press, 2008.

Eze, Emmanuel Chukwudi. "The Color of Reason: The Idea of 'Race' in Kant's Anthropology." In *Postcolonial African Philosophy: A Critical Reader*, edited by Emmanuel Chukwudi Eze. 103–40. Cambridge, MA: Blackwell, 1997.

Fanon, Frantz. *Black Skin, White Masks.* New York: Grove, 1967.

Fanon, Frantz. *The Wretched of the Earth.* New York: Grove, 1963.

Farneth, Molly. *Hegel's Social Ethics: Religion, Conflict, and Rituals of Reconciliation.* Princeton, NJ: Princeton University Press, 2017.

Freud, Sigmund. *Totem and Taboo.* In *On Murder, Mourning and Melancholia*, translated by Shaun Whiteside, 1–166. London: Penguin, 2005.

Gale, Richard M. "William James and Religious Experience." In *Philosophy of Religion: The Key Thinkers*, edited by Jeffrey J. Jordan, 100–17. London: Continuum, 2010.

Gordon, Lewis. *An Introduction to Africana Philosophy.* Cambridge: Cambridge University Press, 2008.

Hackett, Jeremiah, and Jerald Wallulus. *Philosophy of Religion for a New Century: Essays in Honor of Eugene Thomas Long.* Dordrecht: Kluwer Academic, 2004.

Hegel, Georg Wilhelm Friedrich. *The Philosophy of History.* Translated by J. Sibree. Mineola, NY: Dover, 2004.

Hooker, Juliet. *Theorizing Race in the Americas: Douglass, Sarmiento, Du Bois, and Vasconcelos*. New York: Oxford University Press, 2017.

Isasi-Díaz, María, and Eduardo Mendieta, eds. *Decolonizing Epistemologies: Latina/o Theology and Philosophy*. New York: Fordham University Press, 2012.

Jennings, Willie James. "Disfigurations of Christian Identity: Performing Identity as Theological Method." In *Lived Theology: New Perspectives on Method, Style, and Pedagogy*, edited by Charles Marsh, Peter Slade, and Sarah Azaransky, 67–88. Oxford: Oxford University Press, 2016.

Jordan, Jeffrey. *Philosophy of Religion: The Key Thinkers*. London: Continuum, 2011.

Kant, Immanuel. "Idea for a Universal History with a Cosmopolitan Aim." In *Kant's Idea for a Universal History with a Cosmopolitan Aim: A Critical Guide*, edited by Amélie Oksenberg Rorty and James Schmidt, 9–23. Cambridge: Cambridge University Press, 2009.

Karatani, Kojin. *Isonomia and the Origins of Philosophy*. Durham, NC: Duke University Press, 2017.

Lugones, María. "Colonialidad y género." *Tabula Rasa*, no. 9 (2008): 73–101.

Lugones, María. "Methodological Notes toward a Decolonial Feminism." In *Decolonizing Epistemologies*, edited by Ada María Isasi-Díaz and Eduardo Mendieta, 68–86. New York: Fordham University Press, 2011.

Maldonado-Torres, Nelson. "AAR Centennial Roundtable: Religion, Conquest, and Race in the Foundations of the Modern/Colonial World." *Journal of the American Academy of Religion* 82, no. 3 (2014): 636–65.

Maldonado-Torres, Nelson. "Race, Religion, and Ethics in the Modern/Colonial World." *Journal of Religious Ethics* 42, no. 4 (2014): 691–711.

Mandair, Arvind-Pal. *Religion and the Specter of the West: Sikhism, India, Postcoloniality, and the Politics of Translation*. New York: Columbia University Press, 2016.

Masuzawa, Tomoko. *The Invention of World Religions: Or, How European Universalism Was Preserved in the Language of Pluralism*. Chicago: University of Chicago Press, 2005.

Mbembe, Achille. "Necropolitics." *Public Culture* 15, no. 5 (2003): 11–40.

Merleau-Ponty, Maurice. *Phenomenology of Perception*. London: Routledge, 2012.

Mignolo, Walter. *The Darker Side of Western Modernity: Global Futures, Decolonial Options*. Durham, NC: Duke University Press, 2011.

Omi, Michael, and Howard Winant. *Racial Formation in the United States*. 3rd ed. New York: Routledge, 2015.

Park, Peter. *Africa, Asia, and the History of Philosophy: Racism in the Formation of the Philosophical Canon, 1780–1830*. Albany: State University of New York Press, 2014.

Roberts, Tyler. *Encountering Religion: Responsibility and Criticism after Secularism*. New York: Columbia University Press, 2013.

Rorty, Amélie Oksenberg, and James Schmidt. "Introduction: History as Philosophy." In *Kant's Idea for a Universal History with a Cosmopolitan Aim: A Critical Guide*, edited by Amélie Oksenberg Rorty and James Schmidt, 1–8. Cambridge: Cambridge University Press, 2009

Schilbrack, Kevin. *Philosophy and the Study of Religion: A Manifesto*. Hoboken, NJ: Wiley-Blackwell, 2014.

Silverblatt, Irene. *Modern Inquisitions: Peru and the Colonial Origins of the Civilized World*. Durham, NC: Duke University Press, 2004.

Spillers, Hortense J. "Mama's Baby, Papa's Maybe: An American Grammar Book." *Diacritics* 17, no. 2 (1987): 64–81.

Tortorici, Zeb. *Sins against Nature: Sex and Archives in Colonial New Spain*. Durham, NC: Duke University Press, 2018.

Vial, Theodore. *Modern Religion, Modern Race*. New York: Oxford University Press, 2016.

Westphal, Merold. "The Empty Suitcase as Rainbow." In *Saintly Influence: Edith Wyschogrod and the Possibilities of Philosophy of Religion*, edited by Eric Boynton and Martin Kavka, 48–62. New York: Fordham University Press, 2009.

Wynn, Mark. "William Paley and the Argument from Design." In *Philosophy of Religion: The Key Thinkers*, edited by Jeffrey J. Jordan, 54–75. London: Continuum, 2010.

Wynter, Sylvia. "Beyond the Word of Man: Glissant and the New Discourse of the Antilles." *World Literature Today* 63, no. 4 (1989): 637–48.

Wynter, Sylvia. "The Pope Must Have Been Drunk, the King of Castile a Madman: Culture as Actuality and the Caribbean Rethinking of Modernity." In *The Reordering of Culture: Latin America, the Caribbean, and Canada in the Hood*, edited by Alvina Ruprecht and Cecilia Taiana, 17–41. Ottawa: Carleton University Press, 1995.

Wynter, Sylvia. "Unsettling the Coloniality of Being/Power/Truth/Freedom: Towards the Human, after Man, Its Overrepresentation—An Argument." *CR: The New Centennial Review* 3, no. 3 (2003): 257–337.

Devin Singh

1 Decolonial Options for a Fragile Secular

IN HIS ESSAY "Two Theories of Modernity," Charles Taylor seeks to correct what he see as the more prevalent "acultural" reading of modernity
with a cultural reading. The former speaks of a presumed set of universal
human tendencies toward rationalization that manifest in diverse locales.
The latter acknowledges the context-specific practices in western culture
that contributed to the rise of the phenomenon called modernity and
with it certain characterizations of rationality and universality. Thus, the
former attends to culture and context as an afterthought, as the site where
the stable core of universal and inevitable tendencies manifests itself with
some modulation according to the spaces of its deployment. The latter
brings cultural and contextual concerns into a reading of modernity itself.
Taylor resists the ways the former approach often construes modernity,
whether positively or negatively, as a type of loss, and he asserts that its
novel content should be recognized.[1] He emphasizes the need to locate
the emergence of the modern in an assemblage of values, institutions, and
practices in late medieval Europe before speaking of its alternative manifestations elsewhere. In short, modernity must be culturally located and
evaluated.

In speaking of "alternative modernities," Taylor's assessment leaves out
attention to *submerged* cultural practices and identities that attend the

birth of the modern. Neglecting such perspectives, Taylor's essay seems to imply that the emergence of alternative modernities in colonial contexts unravels according to spontaneous local logic and practice, rather than partly as the result of the colonial encounter. Swinging perhaps too far to the pole of acknowledging local cultural diversity, he neglects crucial power dynamics and questions of domination and exploitation so central to modernity's development, particularly in relation to the colonies.

Contra Taylor, the opposition, I suggest, should be read less as one between acultural and cultural constructions of modernity than as one between dominant and subjugated stories of the modern. Rather than argue merely for a contextual corrective to abstract notions of modernity, it is necessary to highlight the fractures and disjunctures *within* modernity itself, even when socially and culturally grounded. While one fulcrum of change and development at the center of modernity was indeed late medieval Europe, retrieving this cultural context alone misses Europe's mutual imbrication and coconstitution with others construed as peripheral or external to this geospatial imaginary. Discourses of alternative modernities should highlight the varying stories told within this genealogy.[2] Critical in such a discussion are the awareness and mapping of the power locations and political economies of the various storytellers involved.

The presence of various modernities in colonial spaces betrays the reality that, as Enrique Dussel is careful to maintain, the logic of the dominated is always already constitutive of the European identity being exported.[3] We cannot think Europe without thinking the underside, those constructed as the counterpoint to the Eurocentric self being forged. The modernities emerging in the colonies form a complex part of European manifestations but are not merely extensions of it. Neither are they simply "alternatives" to it. A thoroughgoing, culturally situated analysis of modernity would need to include the colonial encounter, such that both European and colonial modernities are coordinated and related.

Such coimplicated, emerging modernities are centrally marked by the interlaced ideas of the secular, secularity, and secularization, notions that arise in early modernity with the colonial encounter and in tandem with the category of religion.[4] Both religion and the secular require each other as differential categories. As theorists of the secular highlight, the secular sphere was in part *theologically* constructed by and on behalf of religio-cultural others during European ascendency, as a means of ostensibly protecting religious freedom and religious minorities.[5] To be sure, the secular was also used to monitor and police difference, especially as the category of religion was marshaled to enumerate the other both in Europe and in colonized territories. Yet the secular was also championed as a space for the employment of concepts such as tolerance, value neutrality, and the provisional suspension of judgment in matters of diverging opinion, valuation, and analysis. Institutional structures and legal discourse interacted with theological and broader philosophical value claims to enforce, by means of the state's problematic monopoly on violence, a tenuous peace that allowed the other to exist.

Amid the contemporary celebration of our "postsecular" era with its supposed resurgence of religion, I argue that a pause is called for to consider the vital role played by the secular. I suggest that a decolonial vantage point, one that breaks with and speaks back to and otherwise than European modernity and its categories of knowledge, might offer resources for reconfiguring and preserving elements of this fragile sphere. In this chapter, I first dwell briefly on the notion of the secular that I have in mind. I then turn to decolonial thought as an aid in assessing the interpenetration of categories of religion, secularity, and modernity. I return to the question of the secular and consider it from decolonial vantage points, which help bring attention to secularization's links to the inception of capitalism, particularly around primitive accumulation, colonial resource extraction, and the creation of indebted subjects. Formations of the secular correlate to material networks linking Europe and the colonies and invoke processes such as the mobilization of race, the privatization of land, and the profanation of poverty. Given that the secular and the religious are tied to Europe's relation with the colonial world, decolonial reflection is linked with the futures and fates of religion and the secular. I gesture toward a notion of the secular as a theoretically legitimated space to allow for and protect difference and disagreement. Theologies and religious reflection interested in a nuanced defense of the secular might consider decolonial perspectives for alternatives to how secularity is predominantly displayed and deployed, linked as it has been to Eurocentric conceptions of modernity.

The Precarious Secular

THE HISTORY OF THE SECULAR is as vexed as stories of its origins, and my intervention seeks to avoid a simplistic celebration and retrieval of this concept. But present discourses on the postsecular and on religious resurgence reveal problematic tendencies. Fundamentalisms and neo-orthodoxies persist. Each set of discourses in its own way exploits the turn to difference and to particularity in late modernity in order to reassert a master narrative. Violence against the secular order is articulated through political decisions invoking religious messianism and manifest destiny. Militaristically, it appears in contemporary wars of religion, articulated along national and economic lines, whether in state-sanctioned military occupations or nonstate and so-called terrorist insurgencies. Rhetorically, it appears in decrying the secular as a heresy, either as the spawn of an error in ontology or as a realm given over to Satan, for instance.[6] Such approaches align with and often blur into discourses about the postsecular that celebrate the triumph, persistence, or return of religion and enthusiastically offer their postmortem assessments of the secular. Paradoxically, much current talk of religious resurgence simply fits the story European modernity told itself about itself. Taking modernity's claim of linear and progressive secularization at face value, such perspectives celebrate secularization's apparent failure without interrogating the functions of the narrative or its mythological status.

As José Casanova has claimed, however, one of secularization's main characteristics involves the institutional differentiation of spheres.[7] This need not go hand in hand with a decrease in or suppression of religion or religiosity. Indeed, history belies this purported agonism, and Casanova notes the persistence of religious communities, institutions, and practices alongside and often because of the secular differentiation of spheres. The question is thus not why religion persists or why secularization develops unevenly. The interesting question is the why of the story of the secular itself. Why did modernity need to tell itself this tale, simultaneously fashioning and repressing the religious other, yet always maintaining its specter on the horizon? Such religion (as a category and as its loosely mapped and mercurial phenomena) remains present, and the commotion around its resurgence may be more about the return of the repressed in modernity's consciousness than about any new empirical developments in global religiosity.

My interest is in preserving the important contribution of a secular space as one sociopolitically and discursively constituted to *protect difference*. Indeed, the institutional differentiation of spheres, which Casanova highlights, appears as the constructive and productive edge of the secular. One might trace the secular's emergence as a way for religious others in Europe to seek space to pursue their own patterns of life free from more openly violent modes of initially ecclesial and subsequently state intervention. Notions of the secular were furthermore marshaled in the academy to create a space that allowed a pragmatic and provisional peace for the sake of inquiry. Put bluntly, heresy could be explored without fear of the flame and stake. The hope in both cases is to bracket out reprisals from power owing to difference and disagreement. At one level, this marks the case for academic freedom, but at a broader, societal level, it signals a political value for the preservation of space to allow lives lived in a variety of nonconforming trajectories.

Admittedly, we find ourselves in delicate territory, for genealogies of the secular highlight that part of its own ideological success involves its being posited as a response to wars of religion. The secular is often touted as an advance, as a rational response to destabilizing religious irrationality. Such tales miss the violence of the imposition of the secular itself.[8] They also neglect the ways state structures employ notions of secularity to police difference. Indeed, the enforcement of the secular is directly bound up with the colonial project and the pacification of culturally and politically, and hence religiously, threatening others. Also suppressed are the ways colonial administrations touted secular values but imposed normative Christian visions on a subjugated populace. Yet we cannot escape this problematic tension, and to my mind this is no reason to reject the constructive contributions of the secular. Decolonial redeployments of the secular may thus aim to mobilize its ostensible *protection* of difference while acknowledging, reckoning with, and resisting its operations in *policing* such difference.

Given the genealogy of the secular as emerging in tandem with the concept of religion and being used in part to coordinate European identity vis-à-vis colonial otherness, discourses of decoloniality offer one resource for its reconceptualization. Decolonial difference acknowledges the problematic nature of a space constructed both to make room for cultural others and yet also to monitor and regulate them. Such a vantage point at once recognizes itself as the colonial underside to such a realm and yet seeks to move beyond the opposition. It appropriates what is productive and life affirming in such discourses, while contributing previously silenced voices to shore up and reconfigure such a space. We must face the troubled legacy of secular spaces and ideals while recognizing some of the goods that may be afforded by such spheres.

A Tenuous Typology of Decoloniality

DECOLONIAL THOUGHT is associated with the work of scholars such as Aníbal Quijano and Walter Mignolo, developed in conversation with the project of Enrique Dussel.[9] It locates itself simultaneously within and without the story of modernity. Rhetorically, it recognizes the colonial element present in developments in the modern and at the same time seeks to move beyond binaries to allow the telling of other stories. It is not simply an antagonistic response to modernity and colonialism, nor is it simply a problematization of the contradictions within Eurocentric thought. Rather, it brings a variety of local and Indigenous voices to the table to contribute to a rich and diverse picture of what we call the story (and, hence, stories) of modernity and with it, by implication, religion and the secular.

What follows is a tenuous typology marking out the variants in theoretical responses to colonialism, in order to help further situate decolonial thought. This typology is proffered with all the caveats and qualifications necessary for such an attempt. It is to be considered a loose classification with a host of exceptions and possible alternative configurations. The power moves typically latent in classification systems must also be acknowledged outright. This heuristic should not be reified. This typology is a provisional and general grouping of the ways discourses on coloniality have developed, distinguishing between anticolonial, postcolonial, and decolonial approaches. Furthermore, this historical development in terminology does not negate the fluidity exhibited by these terms and their capacious deployment in the present, often with overlapping meanings.

Anticolonial thought characterizes the early to mid-twentieth-century liberation movements associated with forging a national consciousness and independent state apparatus after colonialism. Anticolonial thought is often categorized as modernist, seeking to realize the promise of Enlightenment emancipation and self-determination, but this time among the repressed nations. Anticolonial thought takes up Enlightenment ideals, not uncritically but dialectically, in antagonism to the discourse of the oppressor. As such, it seeks to overcome illegitimate colonial violence with legitimate revolutionary violence.[10] Anticolonial thought is often associated with Marxian analysis and essentialist constructions of racial and national identity, motivating sociopolitical liberation movements as extensions of the march of history. The local, Indigenous vanguard becomes the bearer of the promise of emancipation, translating it into enculturated narratives in ethnic, religious, and national parlance. Frantz Fanon may be the figure most often associated with this approach.[11] One can add to this Gamal Abdel Nasser, Aimé Césaire, Ernesto "Che" Guevara, and a variety of theorists and political leaders associated with the strategic nonaligned countries, which came to be constituted as the third world.[12] Anticolonial thought privileges the *when*: the when of liberation, the when of self-determination, the when of social justice. It temporalizes and historicizes, as justice is sought and worked out progressively on a national scale.

Postcolonial thought is often seen as a contextualized extension of the poststructuralist and deconstructive turns in European philosophy and literary theory. Although it is unfairly characterized as merely mimetic of such European discourse, it does emerge in critical conversation with the likes of Michel Foucault and Jacques Derrida, for instance. Postcolonial thought questions anticolonialism's apparent commitment to a modern narrative of linear development and liberation according to Enlightenment standards. If anticolonialism is primarily concerned about the when, we might say that postcolonial thought privileges the *who*. It seeks to trouble notions of subjectivity, of static ontologies and enclosed selves, and hence incorporates discussion of hybridity and of fluid and dynamic notions of identity. A hybrid, interstitial space and identity is not a blending or mixing but a restless movement of liminality. Postcolonial thought takes anticolonialism's colonizer/colonized binary and disrupts it by positing a unitary yet always open colonial subject, a mutual indwelling of both poles. Thinkers such as Homi K. Bhabha and Gayatri Chakravorty Spivak are often located in this approach.[13] Both anticolonialism and postcolonialism inherit the ongoing debates between Marxian and poststructuralist theorists about the limits and liabilities of each side's approach, particularly when it comes to political practicability.[14]

If anticolonialism is marked by the *when* and postcolonialism by the *who*, decolonial thought asks about the *where*. It asks about the where in terms of a geopolitics of knowledge, both globally and in its construction within the academy.[15] Decolonial thought situates knowledge production in its various locales and seeks to let local voices, histories, and paradigms speak back to and transform the master narrative of modernity set forth with European ascendancy. Thus, while postcolonial thought has laid bare some of the fractures within the monolithic story of modernity, decolonial thought adds to this the multiple other stories of modernity seen from a variety of vantage points. For instance, Mignolo invites us to reconsider the globe around 1500 as a polycentric world of multiple regional empires and alliances. Europe had not yet sought to eclipse all others in writing its history as the one world history. It had not yet reclaimed Greco-Roman thought as its own, renarrating its origins as rooted in the classical world. While certainly engaged in crusades, it had not yet inserted itself problematically into every area of the globe. Mignolo invites us to shift perspectives and paradigms from universalism toward a pluriversalism.[16] What are the other histories and frameworks that might have developed independently from the eventual master tale, and how are they transformed and shaped in interaction with the colonial expansion of Europe's provincial narrative?

Decolonial thought not only asks about the where but also seeks to reconfigure the when and who of the aforementioned approaches. Like postcolonial thought, it questions the when of anticolonialism's reliance on a modernist narrative of linear, progressive emancipation. It accepts the disruption by poststructuralist discourse of such temporalities. Yet it challenges the move to derive this disruption from European poststructuralist debates. It seeks to speak new modes of the when based on alternative temporalities outside of Europe and capitalism's "homogenous, empty time."[17] Furthermore, while the anticolonialists sought to realize the self through emancipation and attainment of the European universal ideal, postcolonial thought addressed the hybridity, fracturing, and erasure of the self, the disruption of a fixed and stable subject, as discussed in deconstruction and poststructuralism. Alternatively, decolonial thought rethinks the who of postcolonial thought, looking to ideas of life and flourishing from local stories, traditions, and trajectories, outside what it sees as the Eurocentric purview of these former conversations. What local resources are available for the performative and discursive construction of the self and selves in distinction from imposed identities or even those bound up with the colonizer?

One example of this approach, drawn from Black studies, is the positing of Europe as periphery, as Cedric Robinson has done.[18] For much of world history and at the height of what even Europe considers the classical age, Europe was a backwater, a hinterland and insignificant outpost. African, Near Eastern, and Asian civilizations constituted "the real"; Europe was the negation. Europe was excluded by Greco-Roman thought as barbarian. Not until centuries later, hemmed in on the east by superior empires, did European nations invade the western hemisphere, initiate colonization, and begin to constitute themselves self-consciously as a continental unit, doing so in part by a revisionist retrieval of Greco-Roman thought, now construed as Europe's own heritage. Robinson's approach has a productively destabilizing effect, opening up refigurations of history and knowledge. What might it do to think Europe as negation, to think Eurocentrism in a minor key?

Decolonial thought also asks about the epistemic construction of knowledge in the academy, the ways such approaches largely depend on a fixed set of categories of western science. This approach seeks a reconfiguration of the very edifices of disciplinary distinctions and academic divisions of labor. It is not merely about expanding and diversifying existing structures but about allowing them to be transformed. Decolonial thought seeks to have its own conversations outside the hegemony of a Eurocentric academy and to appropriate such discourses and speak back on its own terms, if and when it wills. It is a thinking *otherwise* than coloniality, a response to, a rejection and dismissal of, but ultimately a deliberate alternative to—as opposed to a direct opposition to—Eurocentric modernity. Decolonial criticism is perhaps a later iteration of theoretical reflection on the condition of coloniality and its epistemic registers, appearing in academic conversations after anti- and postcolonial discussions. But Mignolo and others claim that this type of thinking has been going on throughout the project of the modern. While it is arguably a more recent way of framing the scholarly discussion, decolonial thought itself is not new.

Originary Occlusions:
Primitive Accumulation and Secularization

FRAMING QUESTIONS of the secular within concerns about coloniality helps to highlight secularization's relation to the primitive accumulation necessary at capitalism's inception, as well as the secular's implications for the expropriated and exploited labor needed for colonial extraction and capital production. As Karl Marx notes, since the generation of capital requires capital, the question arises of where the initial capital came from that fueled the rise of industry in early modern markets. The founding myth of primitive accumulation provided by classical political economists, Marx remarks, plays "about the same part as original sin in theology."[19] Initially, some were naturally predisposed to industry and commerce, and others were given to sloth and lack of ingenuity. The former instinctively added value to the world and also created opportunity and incentive for the latter. If the latter had no creativity, the tale goes, they could at least be motivated to work, offering the only commodity and value they had, their labor power.

Of course, Marx notes, history looks quite different and "is written in the annals of [hu]mankind in letters of blood and fire."[20] Actual primitive accumulation includes the pushing of peasants off common lands, the privatizing of public land through enclosure, the appropriation of church and public lands and goods by states and new corporate actors, and changes in access to land and the materials of production—now mediated through wage labor. As Marx summarizes: "The spoliation of the church's property, the fraudulent alienation of the State domains, the robbery of the common lands, the usurpation of feudal and clan property, and its transformation into modern private property under circumstances of reckless terrorism, were just so many idyllic methods of primitive accumulation."[21]

Marx's invocation of church property here signals primitive accumulation's links to secularization. Indeed, the term *secularization* itself was first employed in this era specifically to denote this transfer of church land and property into the hands of secular rulers and states and the aristocrats who supported them. The history of secularization, of the radical changes in the religious landscape and imaginary of Europe and its colonies, is linked to the founding and development of capitalism.

By theorizing the site and mechanisms of primitive accumulation in relation to secularization, we glimpse the complex interweaving of the religious/secular assemblage with significant material-economic transformations on the ground, as well as with developments in discourse around race, space, and economy. This reveals secularization's links to economic transformations during colonial modernity, ones that remain central to the project of global capitalism as a form of late-stage colonialism.

While secularization, at least in its early modern deployments in Europe, had as its focal point the institutional and material transfer of ecclesial property into state hands, Hans Blumenberg cautions that we should not let such early material designations overdetermine the metaphorical application of secularization.[22] Nevertheless, such a historical marker is important for linking discourse about the emerging secular differentiation of spheres to material appropriation and matters of economy, as well as antagonistic struggles between ecclesial and state power and between landowning and laboring classes. This anchor prevents discussions of secularization from simply being about apparent changes in theological key, told as mere intellectual history (whether as decline, progress, or shift), and calls attention to the links between such ideational developments and changes in economic and political-institutional relations.

The Reformation upheaval included new debates about and redefinitions of the nature of poverty, taking as one key site of critique the medieval distinction between sacred and involuntary poverty. In Frank Ruda's telling phrase, "Luther profanes poverty."[23] As he elaborates:

> The reformation ousts poverty from its holy throne and destroys in this way the privilege of a class that imagines itself to be the sole possessor of truth. Luther thereby shatters the medieval economy of salvation that had become dilapidated and that had previously been able to assign a seemingly fixed place to poverty. Before Luther, voluntary rejection of property and refusal of worldly possessions is integrated into an economy of salvation by the fact that the beggar is "promised spiritual support" in return.[24]

Clergy and mendicant orders relying on alms for support were thrust out into the newly profaned space of the public sphere. Soon work would come to be the sole determinant of access to money and render alms an at-best secondary, temporary, and remedial means of acquiring funds. Thus, in thinking secularization as the transfer of land and property from church to state, we must likewise think it as the transfer of vulnerable and precarious bodies from spiritual-ecclesial to public exchange economies. Even as serfs and peasants were excluded from land through enclosure acts and then permitted to work only as "free" wage laborers, orders of the religious poor were shifted to the ranks of the proletariat or to the rabble and precariat, those excluded even from the labor economy.

Part of the formation of dependent labor is thus bound up with narratives that undo ideals of sacred poverty, the place of almsgiving, and transcendent vocation. Whether or not one critiques the medieval sacralization of poverty—and there is good basis for such critique—it functioned as part and parcel of frameworks that enjoined the wider community to care for and support such poor as a mode of spiritual discipline. Such supports were stripped away in the secularizing processes initiated in part by the Reformation. These transformations must be held together with what are sometimes construed as related "goods" of this period: the dismantling of rigid and often theologically legitimated social hierarchies, including those fixing one's destiny as poor; new freedom for self-determination, despite higher exposure to risk; and state protections against local abuses, even if such laws typically favored the wealthy.

Yet the process of secularization must not be read as subtraction, as if religious legitimation was removed to allow bare state and economic regulatory mechanisms free rein. Religious discourse was reconfigured during this time, often lending support to emerging market patterns. This is significant in complicating attempts to link the secular with primitive accumulation, as if secularism goes hand in hand with the emergence of capitalism. While secularization is historically correlated with transformations associated with early capitalism, causation remains elusive. Furthermore, when it becomes clear that apologists for capitalism moved fluidly between secular and religious discourses to further their claims, easy binaries are quickly troubled.[25]

To this end, Jordy Rosenberg's illuminating study of discourses on enthusiasm in seventeenth- and eighteenth-century England examines how religiously inflected—and at times motivated—narratives of secularization functioned specifically to occlude the mechanisms of early capitalist accumulation.[26] Rosenberg explores the migration of sentiments about enthusiasm as it "was reconceived as a principle of social comportment, in some cases as key to the peaceful functioning of civil society."[27] What we find are critiques of religious fanaticism and enthusiasm coming from within religious traditions and marshaled to serve the emerging market system and its relations of production and exchange.

For instance, Rosenberg tracks the metaphor of bondage in and escape from Egypt as used in England in the service of land privatization, as the commons was gradually enclosed. Ideals extolling Protestant England as a space of free exchange, unencumbered by ecclesial control, allegorize escape from Egypt and the despoliation of the Egyptians to serve a narrative of secularizing progress. Secularization was a way to shore up the state and corporate class as saviors from religious tyranny (a form of institutional enthusiasm). Such liberation and salvation brought with it land enclosures, the erosion of Poor Laws, and the emergence of police forces to protect private estates. As Rosenberg claims:

> This secularization narrative posits a distinction between a dangerously religious past and a rational, ideal present. But the point to take from this is not so much that the early eighteenth century was invested in secularization in and of and for itself. Rather, because this narrative is organized around the figure of accumulation at the level of the state, what it does is simultaneously allegorize *and occlude* the contemporary accumulative conditions of British development as an attribute of a distant and violently religious past.[28]

Thus, the critique of religious enthusiasm served to allegorize and periodize history around the problem of primitive accumulation. Rather than being identified with the mechanisms of land conquest and the extraction of surplus labor value under capitalism, such accumulation was relegated to a mythic past whose determinants included religious tyranny. Such despotic rule, like the pharaohs of old, extracted wealth from an oppressed populace toiling under superstitious beliefs. Many of these discourses were marshaled by English Protestant thinkers—or those steeped in such Reformed contexts—to celebrate the move away from continental Catholicism. In contrast to a simplistic secular-versus-religious binary in which the former designates nonreligion or atheism, the debate over and use of secularization rhetoric often took place *within* religiously identified milieus.[29]

Rosenberg summarizes Marx's critique of such a narrative: "In the mythic past produced by the political economists, religious terror and theocratic tyranny—rather than the transformation of the countryside, the inauguration of the imperial nation-state, the creation of the plantation system, and the birth of commercial capitalism—produced the initial accumulations of profit."[30] The temporalization of modernity and, in particular, of modern economy made use of the fanatic and enthusiast tropes to construct a chaotic religious past against which staid, rational, enlightened capitalism asserted itself as a savior. The transfer of church property into the hands of princely estates in England also served to deliver ecclesial land tenants into the hands of new, private landlords. An entire class of indentured labor was made available, removed from direct access to its land, and now dependent on the landowning class. Citing Blumenberg with approval, Rosenberg claims that secularization in this sense had less to do with any decline or transmutation of theological into worldly values and more with the creation of free and alienated capitalist labor.[31] In other words, the process of secularization eroded traditional communal ideals and practices that had anchored medieval peasants in a complex web of mutual relations of care, dislocating them into a new, "free" world of isolated laborers toiling for a wage.

Secularization discourses were mobilized in capitalist global spatializations as well. Policing the religious fanatic can be seen not only internally, in Europe's own nation-state formation and land privatization, but externally as well. The spatial reasoning implicated in nation-state territorialization, tied as it was to secular logic as the spatial relegation of religion to a private sphere, manifested in the management of colonial space and differently coded bodies.[32] Here, confrontation with colonial and non-European others played into Europe's self-fashioning and the geopolitics of early capital, the plantation system, and resource extraction.[33] The figure of the fanatic—and the religious fanatic, in particular—aided in colonial projects of racial and ethnic demarcation and control. Cool-headed rationality, serving bureaucratic administrations, was the vaunted subjective posture against which the "exuberant natives" were contrasted. Europe's civilizing project—both internally and externally—invoked the figure of the undisciplined fanatic, the savage in the wilderness, as its counterpoint.[34]

Portraying colonial and cultural others as irrationally religious and bestial was thus bound up with what Nancy Fraser has highlighted as the expropriation of labor in the colonies. This dynamic must be read together with the exploited labor of the newly formed European proletariat.[35] Models of primitive accumulation must hold both sites together, for expropriated and enslaved labor was central to, and not merely an extension of, the emergence of capitalism as well as its maintenance. Even as secularization marks material transfers of wealth on the continent, together with land enclosures and the policing of property and persons, it signals the management of colonial others who needed regulation through forced labor and brutal disciplinary practices, often with the aid of theological justifications, counterintuitive as this alliance might seem.

As Jorge Cañizares-Esguerra's work has shown, the English colonizers imitated and incorporated earlier Spanish and Portuguese patterns of oversight and governance of natives and slaves, even while decrying and distancing themselves from the "superstition" and "tyranny" of their Catholic predecessors.[36] English colonial narratives portray the Spaniards "explicitly as papist enemies whose caravels and galleons constantly threaten the survival of the young" English colonies. Yet the Spanish "colonies also appear implicitly as the reference upon which to measure both failure and success."[37] Thus, the secular discourses of liberal English Protestants, observed by Rosenberg to describe European primitive accumulation as liberation from implicitly Catholic tyranny, manifest in transmuted narratives of the English as more humane and enlightened colonizers than the Spanish—tales that mask the reinscription of brutal management practices.

Attending to the neglected economies of secularization thus complicates understandings of the term. Here we see it deployed as an ideological narrative that employs notions of religion to obfuscate political and economic transformations taking place in Europe and its colonies at the time. Tales of religious decline, enlightenment, or the liberation of reason may coincide with new modes of labor extraction and the concentration of wealth and resources in the hands of an elite minority class. Secularization thus ties together the category of religion, exploited peasant labor and enclosures, and colonial enslavement and extraction. We need to think (at least) these three trends together in relation to stories of modernity. Thus, questions about the status of belief or models of God in light of secularization, for instance, pertain as well to the status of global relations around capital flows, labor, land, and racialized and gendered subjects.

Decoloniality and the Secular: Contributions and Interventions

IN LIGHT OF THE MUTUAL IMPLICATION of secularization and colonial appropriation, how might we relate the foregoing typology and discussion of decoloniality to refigurations of the secular? At the outset, I note Mignolo's caveat that it would be problematic to

> take secularization as *the* sacred truth and impose, by military force if necessary, the secular on societies who do *not necessarily have a problem* with giving a priority to the sacred or with weaving together the sacred and secular. . . . Once we bring geo- and body politics into the realm of knowledge and understanding, we realize that secular modernity has its own politics, which do not necessarily coincide with the needs, visions, and desires of everyone on the planet, and that new projects (ethical, political, epistemic) are emerging in which secular modernity is being transcended by multiple projects of epistemic decolonization.[38]

Thus, the relationship to the secular manifest in European society will be different in postcolonial settings. The decolonial *where* resituates talk of secularity in different locales. In retrieving and reconfiguring the anticolonial *when*, we must recall that secularism was not uniformly embraced in the post/colony as a mode of liberation as it was in Europe. As Vijay Prashad outlines in his people's history *The Darker Nations*, as liberation movements worked to forge national consciousness and independence, religion could well be invoked as one support among others for the purposes of identity demarcation, solidarity, and hope.

These recollections serve as a reminder that what should be sought is not a body of doctrine concerning the secular, particularly in its vulgar construal as the absence of religious belief and practice. The secular that I am grasping for here is a form with minimal content, an ethical framework or horizon toward which communities might strive. Emerging in connection with the wars of religion and state-church conflicts, it is not exhausted by them and thus need not remain bound by the oppositional fixation of the secular versus the religious. The secular here is a set of commitments to protect difference and frame the possibilities for discussion and interchange. Questions persist about whether this is merely a liberal pluralism superintended by soft power that remains unthreatened.[39] To mitigate this possibility, commitments to discursive neutrality and openness must be supplemented with material and institutional structures that ensure just resource distribution and access.

Furthermore, the possibility of securing an ostensibly neutral space free from retaliation without the enforcement of an overarching sovereign mechanism of control and oversight remains a live point of debate. Acknowledgment must also be made that any ethical framework, no matter how lean or minimalist, is culturally derived and situated. Thus, the assertion of an ethical commitment to the protection of difference and a space for free and neutral inquiry, debate, and dissent must articulate the power interests bound up with such desires. This allows for their examination, contestation, and potential alteration. As Ranu Samantrai concludes in her case for a secular Britain, "A secular political culture must not be the imposition of a majority culture on recalcitrant minorities but a meeting ground on which the two can meet, transform each other, and perhaps create new alignments. . . . While the best result of the former may be a separate but equal coexistence, the latter holds out the possibility of a transformation of the whole."[40] Yet concerns persist about how such a "meeting ground" might be institutionally, legally, and inclusively secured and about what centers of capital and other resources may sustain it while resisting the power interests and structural biases that appear always to creep in. These tensions remain at the conceptual growth edge of such hopes and visions.

In seeking to redress the modes of violence needed to preserve and police the secular, a violence whose necessity must be vigorously contested, one step may be to rekindle theological justifications for such a sphere. Religious paradigms might construe the secular as part of their own gift to global humanity. In other words, such traditions might marshal symbols, narratives, mythologies, and ethical norms that support a realm of peaceful coexistence and the toleration of difference as in the interests of those religious communities and of humanity at large. In light of the paucity of such efforts today, such rhetoric is often viewed as foreign or heterodox when it is espoused by various traditions. If defenses of the secular can be marshaled from within various religious imaginaries, immanent measures may thus emerge to protect such spaces. Arguably, the state's role as violent gatekeeper for the secular might then be mitigated. In other words, as religious and nonreligious humanistic traditions draw on their resources to formulate justifications for a secular sphere, support for the secular is not left to the state alone. The secular need not be constructed in opposition to religious self-understandings, and such rapprochement may liberate the fragile secular from the administrative governance of state structures.

A methodology informed by comparative secularisms may allow us to reorient, expand, and redefine our understandings of the relevant institutional practices related to this sphere. As Janet R. Jakobsen and Ann Pellegrini write:

> One of the major insights of the project of the comparative study of secularism(s) has been to challenge the holistic nature of the secularization narrative in which any secularism represents development along a single path. By differentiating the secularization narrative itself, historical sociologists have shown that secularism need not always be read as the telos of development. The comparative study of secularism has thus intervened not only in the linear narrative of secularization, but also in its accompanying narratives: development, modernization, evolutionary inevitability. By interrupting secularism's just-so story, the comparative study of secularism challenges the view that either nations had moved through the process of modernization or they had not, they were either developed or undeveloped, modern or antimodern.[41]

Similar cautions apply here as in the field of comparative religions. As scholars have troubled the supposed univocity of the concept of religion, we must disrupt a singular notion of the secular that serves as the implicit hermeneutical background for comparison. Are we importing a specifically western, Protestant notion of secularity? Do we assume it as a fixed, already constituted social object for analysis? Or is it constructed by our analysis? With these and other caveats in mind, however, the project may be useful.

In addition to synchronic analysis that undertakes side-by-side assessments of secular options, comparative historical approaches, those demonstrating alternate models across time, may provide fruitful alternatives to consider. One example is that of the so-called Islamic Golden Age from the ninth to the fourteenth century.[42] Under the Abbasid Caliphate, the Islamic empire experienced a period of relative stability and a cultural milieu supporting scientific discourse and inquiry, interfaith cooperation and interchange, protection of religious minorities, and economic advance.[43] The earliest forms of academic peer review occurred in this period, as did the earliest universities. Economics saw innovations such as double-entry book-keeping, which would propel the growth of banking in Italy and the inception of capitalism. It is also well known that the retrieval and preservation of Greek thought in this period provided Europe with resources for philosophy and theology. How might the practices and institutions of this form of cosmopolitanism have impacted emerging European concepts of secularity as the institutionalized support of neutral inquiry, that is, of inquiry that provisionally brackets certain normative values and permits the entertaining of alternative value systems, for the sake of breakthroughs in thought as well as new possibilities for life and praxis, without reprisals from institutional and political power? How might arguments, resources, and structures from this period be retrieved and incorporated to rehabilitate modes of secular space today?

Another decolonial approach would be to rethink various conceptual foundations of the secular as it has been deployed from a Eurocentric perspective. Temporality is one starting point, considering the etymological roots of the secular as a temporal suspension, a moment of "worldly" time, the *saeculum*. Eurocentric secularization imports with it a notion of linear history progressing toward a specific horizon, undergirded as it may be with a repressed or evacuated Christian redemption narrative.[44] The secular as conceived and championed in European modernity stems in part from a confident and triumphalist grounding in an ultimate realization through *eschaton* and Parousia, however reconfigured.

What might the alternative temporal ontologies of certain African philosophical systems, such as those of the Akan, do to alter the concept? Here, authentic being and the real are in the past, as founding moments, and successive iterations diminish in significance as they increase in distance from that past.[45] The future is nonexistent, literally nonbeing, but comes into partial being in the continuous present through our actions. What foundations for a space bracketing out power reprisals and conceptual violence might be marshaled from such a perspective? How might forms of African Christian thought incorporate such notions of alternative African temporalities and offer a different reading of the need for and nature of the secular?[46] While such a temporal scheme risks positing the present and future as decline and hence potentially and problematically reinforces narratives of lament over secularization as a loss of tradition, it need not necessarily lead to such positions. Such a temporal ontology may disrupt assumptions of future-oriented eschatological progress modeled on Christ's return and fruitfully reconfigure the logic supporting the secular, presenting the future of the secular as an open flow dependent on participatory coconstruction rather than as a closed horizon of certain destiny.

Examples and possibilities are as diverse and plentiful as non-European cultural schemas. A decolonial vantage point of breaking with and speaking back to modes of European modernity and its narrowly defined secular sphere provides one model for constructive engagement. My hope is that religious and nonreligious actors will continue to see the viability and importance of something like the secular sphere and will work to preserve it. I am advocating a self-conscious construction of the secular for the sake of peace and meaningful engagement, a construction on sociopolitical grounds and shored up with theological and other cultural-ideological discourses of meaning making and legitimation. Such support claims may be based on ideas of the good discernible within the religious or humanistic value systems from which one theorizes. Indeed, one key point of interfaith dialogue and cooperation may emerge around preserving a secular sphere, a contingent and value-neutral space, recognizing that it may exist for value-laden, often radically nonneutral, and possibly theological reasons. Such reasons may draw on sacred scriptures, theological systems, or rituals and have as ends certain goods like peaceful coexistence, the flourishing of life, and unfettered inquiry in the service of life.

Such inquiry would ideally be set free to be regulated by the logic internal to the structures and aims of that inquiry itself rather than by external dictates or powers. Here, condemnations and reprisals from power are bracketed out, fostering a pragmatic embrace of immanence and contingency. In contrast to a stripping away of the religious to reveal some mythical secular core, diverse religious and nonreligious perspectives contribute to a third space, between religiously construed particularism and statist, secular universalism. Thus, the postsecularity currently being lauded need not entail a jettisoning or dismissal of the secular. Rather, a critical part of its postsecular mandate might include a more rigorously theorized and theologized—and hence legitimated—secular sphere.

Notes

1 Taylor, "Two Theories of Modernity," 176. For Taylor here, *culture* indicates loosely "a constellation of understandings of person, nature, society, and the good" (179).

2 E.g., Dipesh Chakrabarty sets forth the material basis of two histories of capital, one that attends to the mechanisms of labor, value, and production in capitalist processes and one that limns the detritus, the excluded yet vital elements of living labor and noncapitalist exchange that are deemed external to the system yet function as necessary supplements. Indeed, for Enrique Dussel, this category of living labor forms the epistemic counterpoint to the totalizing narrative of capital and, with it, modernity. See Chakrabarty, *Provincializing Europe*; and Dussel, *Towards an Unknown Marx*.

3 Dussel, *Invention of the Americas*.

4 See, e.g., Masuzawa, *Invention of World Religions*.

5 See, e.g., Asad, *Formations of the Secular*; and Casanova, *Public Religions*.

6 Radical Orthodoxy, of course, regards the secular as a form of heresy, a perverse ontology, and the prime source of conceptual and social malaise in modernity. See, e.g., Milbank, *Theology and Social Theory*. For satanic imagery, I have in mind the "Great Satan" metaphor used by Ayatollahs Khomeini and Khamenei, among others, to depict the United States and "western values" more broadly. While these accusations are not leveled at secularism alone, secularity is part of the assemblage often condemned. American evangelicals also invoke such satanic imagery when condemning aspects of secular culture at home or abroad, placing them on the spectrum with the ayatollahs. Decolonial vantage points reveal the long workings of the Satan trope in the policing of othered bodies in the interests of material accumulation. See, e.g., Federici, *Caliban and the Witch*; and Taussig, *Devil and Commodity Fetishism*.

7 Casanova, "Rethinking Secularization."

8 See, e.g., Cavanaugh, *Myth of Religious Violence*.

9 See, for instance, Quijano, "Coloniality of Power"; Mignolo, "Geopolitics of Knowledge"; Mignolo, "Delinking"; and Dussel, *Posmodernidad y transmodernidad*.

10 The Haitian Revolution is often cited as paradigmatic of this tendency. See, e.g., James, *Black Jacobins*.

11 Fanon, *Wretched of the Earth*. Of course, the retrieval of Fanon for more recent decolonial projects challenges the relegation of Fanon merely to anticolonial discourse.

12 This history is explored in Prashad, *Darker Nations*.

13 Bhabha, *Location of Culture*; and Spivak, *Critique of Postcolonial Reason*.

14 Dirlik, "Postcolonial Aura."

15 As Nelson Maldonado-Torres notes, while modern social theory has undergone a spatial turn, as it did an earlier sociolinguistic one, such spatiality has largely remained confined to Europe. See Maldonado-Torres, "Topology of Being."

16 Mignolo, "Delinking." See also Mignolo, *Darker Side*.

17 On "homogenous, empty time," see "Theses on the Philosophy of History," in Benjamin, *Illuminations*, 261. For decolonial subversions of such temporality, see, for instance, the importance of the "where" of time in the introduction, "Time on the Move," in Mbembé, *On the Postcolony*.

18 Robinson, *Anthropology of Marxism*, 33; and Robinson, *Black Marxism*. See also Gordon, *Introduction to Africana Philosophy*.

19 Marx, *Capital*, 873.

20 Marx, *Capital*, 875.

21 Marx, *Capital*, 895.

22 Blumenberg, *Legitimacy of the Modern Age*.

23 Ruda, *Hegel's Rabble*, 6.

24 Ruda, *Hegel's Rabble*, 6, quoting Geremek, *Poverty*, 47.

25 Furthermore, to the well-established association between religion and the rise of capitalism, new studies demonstrate not only that no clear correlation exists between capitalism and disenchantment but that strident religious cases were made for capitalist enchantment. See Coleman, *Spirit of French Capitalism*; and McCarraher, *Enchantments of Mammon*.

26 Rosenberg, *Critical Enthusiasm*. See also Rosenberg, "'Accumulate! Accumulate!'" On the political uses of the fanatic trope, see Toscano, *Fanaticism*.

27 Rosenberg, *Critical Enthusiasm*, 10.

28 Rosenberg, *Critical Enthusiasm*, 58.

29 As Richard Amesbury trenchantly observes, while secular discourse can represent religion as its other—in the case of Islam and Catholicism, for instance—it also represents it as "its fraternal twin, having developed in tandem with it"—in the case of "an idealized form of liberal Protestant Christianity." Amesbury, "Secularity," 11.

30 Rosenberg, *Critical Enthusiasm*, 61.

31 Rosenberg, *Critical Enthusiasm*, 104–5.

32 On modern nation-state territoriality, see Schmitt, *Nomos of the Earth*. On its temporality, see Koselleck, *Futures Past*. On the secular as spatializing religion, see Amesbury, "Secularity."

33 Mignolo argues that Marx failed to account for the centrality of coloniality in primitive accumulation, playing into the mythology of a linear development to European capitalism that extended to the colonies, rather than recognizing the colonial encounter as originally constitutive of the capitalist moment. See Mignolo, "Enduring Enchantment," 274–76.

34 Achille Mbembé captures the connotation of the Native as the passionate and fanatic other requiring rational control: "The native was also recognizable by his/her exuberance, ability to enjoy the present to the full, grace of movement, insatiable pride, intrigue, and playfulness. . . . Not knowing how to write, she/he registered nothing. . . . The native was a great child crushed by long atavism, was incapable of autonomous thought and could make no distinction between vice and virtue." Mbembé, *On the Postcolony*, 33. On calm rationality in market engagement, see Singh, "Irrational Exuberance."

35 Fraser, "Expropriation and Exploitation."

36 See, e.g., Cañizares-Esguerra, *Puritan Conquistadors*.

37 Cañizares-Esguerra, introduction to *Entangled Empires*, 2.

38 Mignolo, "Delinking," 488.

39 See the trenchant institutional diagnosis of this phenomenon in Hulsether, "Grammar of Racism."

40 Samantrai, "Continuity or Rupture?," 117.

41 Jakobsen and Pellegrini, "Introduction," 13.

42 The "golden age" nomenclature remains contested.

43 Critics may point out that such stability corresponded to a strong sovereign, that such secular inquiry was superintended by the heavy, if at times benevolent, hand of central authority and oversight. This must be acknowledged and must lead not to simplistic dismissal but to dialogue with European celebrations of free inquiry that also rely on and presume the strong arm of sovereignty, such as Immanuel Kant's model of enlightened public dialogue under the watchful eye and firm command of Frederick the Great of Prussia. See Kant, "Answer."

44 Paradigmatic of this view of secular history as flattened Christian eschatology is Löwith, *Meaning in History*. One early vision of such Christian temporal structure is explored in Markus, *Saeculum*. On the coconstruction of historical temporality and sovereignty in the medieval period, see Davis, *Periodization and Sovereignty*.

45 See, e.g., Mudimbe, *Invention of Africa*. I pose this challenge of alternate temporalities to Milbank in light of his own postsecular triumphalism in Singh, "Provincializing Christendom."

46 See, e.g., Oduyoye, *Introducing African Women's Theology*; and Mbiti, *Bible and Theology*.

Bibliography

Amesbury, Richard. "Secularity, Religion, and the Spatialization of Time." *Journal of the American Academy of Religion* 86, no. 3 (2018): 1–25.

Asad, Talal. *Formations of the Secular: Christianity, Islam, Modernity*. Stanford, CA: Stanford University Press, 2003.

Benjamin, Walter. *Illuminations*. Translated by Harry Zohn. New York: Harcourt, 1968.

Bhabha, Homi K. *The Location of Culture*. London: Routledge, 1994.

Blumenberg, Hans. *The Legitimacy of the Modern Age*. Translated by Robert M. Wallace. Cambridge, MA: MIT Press, 1983.

Cañizares-Esguerra, Jorge. Introduction to *Entangled Empires: The Anglo-Iberian Atlantic 1500–1830*, edited by Jorge Cañizares-Esguerra, 1–15. Philadelphia: University of Pennsylvania Press, 2018.

Cañizares-Esguerra, Jorge. *Puritan Conquistadors: Iberianizing the Atlantic, 1550–1700*. Stanford, CA: Stanford University Press, 2006.

Casanova, José. *Public Religions in the Modern World*. Chicago: University of Chicago Press, 1994.

Casanova, José. "Rethinking Secularization: A Global Comparative Perspective." *Hedgehog Review* 8, no. 1–2 (2006): 7–22.

Cavanaugh, William T. *The Myth of Religious Violence: Secular Ideology and the Roots of Modern Conflict*. New York: Oxford University Press, 2009.

Chakrabarty, Dipesh. *Provincializing Europe: Postcolonial Thought and Historical Difference*. Princeton, NJ: Princeton University Press, 2000.

Coleman, Charly. *The Spirit of French Capitalism: Economic Theology in the Age of Enlightenment*. Stanford, CA: Stanford University Press, 2021.

Davis, Kathleen. *Periodization and Sovereignty: How Ideas of Feudalism and Secularization Govern the Politics of Time*. Philadelphia: University of Pennsylvania Press, 2008.

Dirlik, Arif. "The Postcolonial Aura: Third World Criticism in the Age of Global Capitalism." In *Contemporary Postcolonial Theory: A Reader*, edited by Padmini Mongia, 294–320. London: Arnold, 1996.

Dussel, Enrique. *The Invention of the Americas: Eclipse of "the Other" and the Myth of Modernity*. Translated by Michael Barber. New York: Continuum, 1995.

Dussel, Enrique. *Posmodernidad y transmodernidad: Diálogos con la filosofia de Gianni Vattimo*. Mexico City: Universidad Iberamericana Plantel Golfo Centro, 1999.

Dussel, Enrique. *Towards an Unknown Marx: A Commentary on the Manuscripts of 1861–63*. Translated by Yolanda Angulo. London: Routledge, 2001.

Fanon, Frantz. *The Wretched of the Earth*. New York: Grove, 1965.

Federici, Silvia. *Caliban and the Witch: Women, the Body, and Primitive Accumulation*. Brooklyn, NY: Autonomedia, 2008.

Fraser, Nancy. "Expropriation and Exploitation in Racialized Capitalism: A Reply to Michael Dawson." *Critical Historical Studies* 3, no. 1 (2016): 163–78.

Geremek, Bronislaw. *Poverty: A History*. Cambridge, MA: Blackwell, 1991.

Gordon, Lewis. *Introduction to Africana Philosophy*. Cambridge: Cambridge University Press, 2008.

Hulsether, Lucia. "The Grammar of Racism: Pluralism and the Birth of the Interdisciplines." *Journal of the American Academy of Religion* 86, no. 1 (2018): 1–41.

Jakobsen, Janet R., and Ann Pellegrini. "Introduction: World Secularisms at the Millennium." *Social Text 64* 18, no. 3 (2000): 1–27.

James, C. L. R. *The Black Jacobins: Toussaint L'Ouverture and the San Domingo Revolution.* 2nd ed. New York: Vintage Books, 1963.

Kant, Immanuel. "An Answer to the Question: What Is Enlightenment? (1784)." Translated by Mary Gregor. In *Practical Philosophy*, edited by Mary Gregor, 11–22. Cambridge: Cambridge University Press, 1996.

Koselleck, Reinhart. *Futures Past: On the Semantics of Historical Time.* New York: Columbia University Press, 2004.

Löwith, Karl. *Meaning in History.* Chicago: University of Chicago Press, 1957.

Maldonado-Torres, Nelson. "The Topology of Being and the Geopolitics of Knowledge: Modernity, Empire, Coloniality." *City* 8, no. 1 (2004): 29–56.

Markus, R. A. *Saeculum: History and Society in the Theology of St. Augustine.* Rev. ed. Cambridge: Cambridge University Press, 1988.

Marx, Karl. *Capital: A Critique of Political Economy.* Translated by Ben Fowkes. Vol. 1. London: Penguin Books, 1976.

Masuzawa, Tomoko. *The Invention of World Religions, or, How European Universalism Was Preserved in the Language of Pluralism.* Chicago: University of Chicago Press, 2005.

Mbembé, Achille. *On the Postcolony.* Berkeley: University of California Press, 2001.

Mbiti, John S. *Bible and Theology in African Christianity.* Nairobi: Oxford University Press, 1986.

McCarraher, Eugene. *The Enchantments of Mammon: How Capitalism Became the Religion of Modernity.* Cambridge, MA: Harvard University Press, 2019.

Mignolo, Walter. *The Darker Side of the Renaissance: Literacy, Territoriality, and Colonization.* Ann Arbor: University of Michigan Press, 1995.

Mignolo, Walter. "Delinking." *Cultural Studies* 21, no. 2 (2007): 449–514.

Mignolo, Walter. "Enduring Enchantment: Secularism and the Epistemic Privileges of Modernity." In *Postcolonial Philosophy of Religion*, edited by Purushottama Bilimoria and Andrew Irvine, 273–91. New York: Springer, 2009.

Mignolo, Walter. "The Geopolitics of Knowledge and the Colonial Difference." *South Atlantic Quarterly* 101, no. 1 (2002): 56–97.

Milbank, John. *Theology and Social Theory: Beyond Secular Reason.* 2nd ed. Oxford: Blackwell, 2006.

Mudimbe, V. Y. *The Invention of Africa: Gnosis, Philosophy, and the Order of Knowledge.* Bloomington: Indiana University Press, 1988.

Oduyoye, Mercy Amba. *Introducing African Women's Theology*. Sheffield, UK: Sheffield Academic Press, 2001.

Prashad, Vijay. *The Darker Nations: A People's History of the Third World*. New York: New Press, 2007.

Quijano, Aníbal. "Coloniality of Power, Eurocentrism, and Latin America." *Nepantla: Views from South* 1 (2000): 533–80.

Robinson, Cedric. *An Anthropology of Marxism*. London: Ashgate, 2001.

Robinson, Cedric. *Black Marxism: The Making of the Black Radical Tradition*. Chapel Hill: University of North Carolina Press, 2000.

Rosenberg, Jordy [Jordana]. "'Accumulate! Accumulate! That Is Moses and the Prophets!': Secularism, Historicism, and the Critique of Enthusiasm." *Eighteenth Century* 51, no. 4 (2010): 471–90.

Rosenberg, Jordy [Jordana]. *Critical Enthusiasm: Capital Accumulation and the Transformation of Religious Passion*. New York: Oxford University Press, 2011.

Ruda, Frank. *Hegel's Rabble: An Investigation into Hegel's Philosophy of Right*. London: Continuum, 2011.

Samantrai, Ranu. "Continuity or Rupture? An Argument for Secular Britain." *Social Text 64* 18, no. 3 (2000): 105–22.

Schmitt, Carl. *The Nomos of the Earth in the International Law of the Jus Publicum Europaeum*. Translated by G. L. Ulmen. New York: Telos, 2003.

Singh, Devin. "Irrational Exuberance: Hope, Expectation, and Cool Market Logic." *Political Theology* 17, no. 2 (2016): 120–36.

Singh, Devin. "Provincializing Christendom: Reviewing John Milbank's *Beyond Secular Order*." *Syndicate: A New Forum for Theology* 2, no. 6 (2015): 177–83.

Spivak, Gayatri Chakravorty. *A Critique of Postcolonial Reason: Toward a History of the Vanishing Present*. Cambridge, MA: Harvard University Press, 1999.

Taussig, Michael T. *The Devil and Commodity Fetishism in South America*. 30th anniv. ed. Chapel Hill: University of North Carolina Press, 2010.

Taylor, Charles. "Two Theories of Modernity." In *Alternative Modernities*, edited by Dilip Parameshwar Gaonkar, 172–96. Durham, NC: Duke University Press, 2001.

Toscano, Alberto. *Fanaticism: On the Uses of an Idea*. London: Verso, 2010.

Mayra Rivera

2 Embodied Counterpoetics

Sylvia Wynter on Religion and Race

SYLVIA WYNTER CLOSES HER ESSAY "The Pope Must Have Been Drunk, the King of Castile a Madman" with a poetic affirmation: "Human beings are magical. Bios and Logos. Words made flesh, muscle and bone animated by hope and desire, belief materialized in deeds."[1] The statement encapsulates a recurrent idea in Wynter's heterogeneous explorations, that is, that being human is a matter of culture as much as biology. But the adoption of Christian language here is surprising, coming from a theorist known for her discussions of how Christian ideas shaped problematic conceptions of the human. Indeed, in much of her later work, Wynter emphasizes the destructive effects of a Christian Word that made way for western colonialism and race. The hope, desire, and belief animating countercolonial deeds are mentioned often but only briefly and indirectly.

I have been intrigued by Wynter's references to the transformation of beliefs into flesh as well as by her calls to invent new *genres* of being human. I wanted to understand her view of the possibilities for and mechanisms by which such transformation could take place. Was Wynter gesturing toward a theory of corporeality shaped by Caribbean decolonial poetics? This search led me to her early work, where she theorized cultural transformation as "metamorphosis" and developed this concept partly through studies of "unofficial" religious practices. These early analyses of religion inform her later theorizations of the human.

In this essay, I focus on Wynter's theorization of religion as inextricable from coloniality. Focusing on religion, I examine the relationship between the encompassing and persisting power of colonialism/racism and the possibilities of embodied contestation and transformation. Bringing together these two aspects of Wynter's work is difficult, however, because her approaches to each are vastly different. Her writings on coloniality offer a view from a distance, analyses of epistemological and ontological shifts over long periods of time across vast regions. They are detached descriptions of underlying orders of knowledge. In contrast, she looks at the dynamics of transformation from the ground level, observing or imaginatively reconstructing the movements of practitioners in dance and mourning, in labor and revolt.[2] Thus, the sections of my own discussion seem to pull in opposite directions—the first toward an (imaginary) global viewpoint, the second and third toward the earth. But the contrast between the two vectors is revealing. The style fits the topic. Coloniality and racism are global, all-encompassing forces, but they ultimately impinge on us at the level of bodies. Reading Wynter's later work in light of the earlier has helped me appreciate not only the multivalent role of religion in her thinking but also her interest in how collective action can counter the overwhelming power of coloniality and racism—and even at times create something new.

Wynter's descriptions of the human being as praxis have received deserved attention among Caribbean scholars, who recognize her as a decolonial theorist in the tradition of Aimé Césaire, Frantz Fanon, C. L. R. James, and George Lamming, among others. She is also of particular interest to scholars of religion because Wynter is one of very few critics of coloniality that take seriously its religious dimensions, not only as a tool of colonial ideology, but also as a resource for its subversion.[3] Like Latin American decolonial theorists, Wynter begins her story of the invention of race with the Spanish Empire and the conquest of America, rather than with the European Enlightenment. This historical scope makes visible the links between the discourses of the Reconquista in Spain and the conquest of America as well as the connections between the theological arguments about the nature of the Amerindians and later conceptions of humanity and its others. Throughout her discussions of coloniality, Wynter does not simply mention this or that element of Christian thought but considers the implications of specific theological ideas—monotheism, original sin, and heaven, among others. Her analyses of the complex relationship between Christianity and race take unexpected turns. She tracks the resonances between medieval Christian ontology and biological race. But she also describes "degodding" or secularism as a condition of possibility for modern conquest and its racial hierarchies of being. Secular understandings of the human can be even more totalizing than those based on creeds, she suggests. Her arguments are multilayered and do not yield a simple theory of secularism or of the relationship between religion and race. But they offer rich provocations and crucial questions that traverse studies of coloniality, race, and religion.

The Emergence of Man

WYNTER'S ACCOUNT of the emergence of our current understanding of race is based on an examination of changes between medieval and modern worldviews. This aspect of her work is influenced by Michel Foucault's *The Order of Things*—especially by his "archaeological" method and his studies of the development of the human sciences and the concomitant invention of Man. Like Foucault's, Wynter's work is not history but rather a comparative study that draws from disparate disciplines to uncover their shared episteme. Her explorations cover vast distances in time and space, but they are not comprehensive. She relies on examples that illuminate the shifts between historical epochs or the repetitions of particular patterns across different areas of knowledge. She places disparate discourses next to each other to make visible the convergences between colonial, racial, and religious imaginaries that would otherwise be occluded.[4]

The Order of Things identifies significant "discontinuities in the episteme of the Western culture," both between the Renaissance and the classical period (beginning in the mid-seventeenth century) and between the classical and the modern (from the beginning of the nineteenth century). Each episteme sustains a particular order of knowledge. What seems logical and stable and precise is also, in a different time or a different place, absurd or altogether unthinkable. For example, the emergence of biology is not the effect of a better understanding of life but a manifestation of broader cultural changes, from which life emerged as a thing existing independently from religious ideas, something to be studied *scientifically*. "Up until the eighteenth century . . . life does not exist: only living beings," Foucault states.[5] Life is part of the present order of knowledge and its ways of being. The shift to a biological understanding of life is thus not progress toward objective truth, as the historical narratives often represent it, but a result of changes that make possible and legitimate particular forms of knowledge. Epistemes shape not only what can be *thought* but also what subjects can *be*. The emergence of the human sciences implies a way of understanding the knower—as both the subject and the object of that knowledge. Foucault calls him simply *man*. "Before the end of the eighteenth century," Foucault writes, "*man* did not exist—any more than the potency of life. . . . He is quite a recent creature."[6]

Wynter deploys a similar analytic strategy to address the particularities of the modern concept of the human ("Man"), even as she moves it to regions beyond Foucault's analyses—conceptually and geographically. Like Foucault, Wynter points to significant changes in epistemes, culminating in the emergence of biology as our main discourse of the human. These changes transform what it means to be human—in theory and in practice—with devastating consequences for colonized peoples. Although she refers, loosely, to Foucault's periodization, her own story begins earlier than *The Order of Things* does. Wynter examines the shift from medieval Christianity to humanism, emphasizing the role of theology as a dimension of western culture. Analyzing the shifts in western cultural epistemes entails, for her, tracking the changes in the Christian order of being. She sees that emphasis as a point of difference from Foucault. "Although Foucault, in his analysis of the processes by means of which the classical episteme was replaced by our own, had proposed that these epistemes be seen as being discontinuous with each other, what he oversaw was that such a discontinuity, like the earlier discontinuity that had been effected by the classical episteme itself, was taking place in the terms of a continuous cultural field, one instituted by the matrix Judeo-Christian formulation of a general order of existence."[7] I would counter that Wynter's statement applies only to *The Order of Things*, for he focuses on Christian ideas elsewhere, pointing to the emergence of scientific and cultural concepts out of Christian theological categories, notably the concepts of sin and the flesh. But Wynter's attention to religion and colonialism does result in a distinct understanding of the role of Christianity in the colonial order of being.

The medieval Christian order was structured according to the assumed ontological difference between the perfection of the heavens and the fallenness of the world. This division in turn organized the hierarchies between clergy and laypeople, theological knowledge and human knowledge, livable regions and unlivable ones. The dogma of original sin encapsulates that order.[8] In the Christian story, with the Fall, "all humans are . . . made the recipient of this Adamic negative inheritance and were therefore bearers of this universal mode of the abject."[9] That is, *all* humans lack in true being. "Redemption from this legacy, for the layman, could only be obtained through . . . baptism," the path into Christian identity.[10] Access to full being was premised on the rejection of the prebaptismal self—a death performed in the *ritual* that constitutes the means of admission into the redeemed community. This is what Wynter calls the "Word of the Christian"—or the Sacred Logos. This "Word" includes the ontological division between being and nonbeing as well as the prescribed practices of self-negation.

Geography mapped out the Christian ontological division between being and nonbeing spatially, as a demarcation between livable and in-habitable regions. On one side of the divide were the "temperate regions centered on Jerusalem—regions that because held up above the element of water by God's Providential Grace, were habitable—and, on the other, those realms that, because outside this Grace, had to be uninhabitable."[11] Venturing beyond the boundaries of the grace-filled regions would be unthinkable.

The voyages of conquest presuppose a shift in episteme, one that would make such exploration conceivable, Wynter argues. It would entail questioning the subordination of lay knowledge to theological truths as well as the "nonhomogeneity" between geographic regions. Often celebrated as the triumph of reason over belief, the shift was really the emergence of a new way of being human tied to conquest and slavery.[12]

The transition began in Christianity itself, where human rationality began to be described as a divine quality that allowed humans to choose to rise above the fallen world and stand closer to God. Bringing about changes in orders of knowledge requires taking an outside position, standing on alternative ground, Wynter often suggests.[13] The humanists sought in classical Greco-Roman texts alternative models for a vision of a world that was not subordinated to the church. By rejecting theology as the only source of knowledge and denying the authority of the clergy, humanism was asserting the value of human knowledge. It claimed, for instance, the validity of knowledge derived from observing the movements of the stars or from studying history, even as grounds for questioning theological teaching. Theological knowledge would no longer be the arbiter of lay knowledge. This shift is not simply the development of new ideas. Inasmuch as humanism makes possible and authorizes new ways of knowing and experiencing the world, it makes possible and authorizes new ways of being human. In place of the birth by baptism into a Christian being, Wynter argues, the Re*naissance* is the *birth* of Man defined by Reason.

Wynter describes the humanist order as "hybridly secular and religious," because while it redefines Man as a rational creature, it still depends on God to guarantee the rational nature of the human. Furthermore, humanism does not abandon the fundamental logic of original sin; it just displaces the realms of being and nonbeing from heaven and earth to the human.

The debates of Valladolid between Juan Ginés de Sepúlveda and Bartolomé de las Casas (1550–51) exemplify the tensions between competing views within Christianity as they confront the "New World." The issue at stake was the right of the king of Castile to subject the Amerindians. But the significance of the debate is that the arguments revolved around the status of Indians as human beings, which was treated as an inquiry into their rationality. Sepúlveda, a humanist and translator of Aristotle, based his defense of the conquest on Aristotle's theory of "natural slavery" as well as on Augustine's argument that slavery is a punishment for sin.[14] His position was that the Indians were slaves by nature, displaying "an innate weakness of mind and inhuman and barbarous customs."[15] They are as different to the Spaniards as "monkeys are to men," he claimed.[16] Las Casas's defense of the Indians entailed challenging the applicability of the category of natural slave to the peoples of the Americas. He explained it by appealing to cultural evolution. Turning to classical writers like Aristotle and Cicero, in addition to Thomas Aquinas, Las Casas argued, "All the races of the world are men, and the definition of all men and of each of them, is only one and that is reason."[17] If their behavior was starkly different, even seemingly abhorrent, it was not because of an inherent flaw in their capacity for rationality. Although he did not dispute the existence of "natural slaves," Las Casas argued that to describe such a large population (all Amerindians) as natural slaves would imply attributing significant error to the order of Creation. The differences in the Amerindians' behavior, he argued, were the effect of their primitive culture and religion. Culture was necessary to transform barbarians into civilized men. The Indians were as the Spaniards had been at previous stages in their development, when their culture had not yet achieved the level of civility it now possessed. Thus, the Spaniards had the *duty* to teach the Amerindians as children until they achieved the level of civility of European Christians, not the *right* to subject them as slaves.

The opposing theological arguments of Sepúlveda and Las Casas were articulated on the basis of a congruent definition of the human—to be human is to be a Man of reason, which is demonstrated in government and religion. Perhaps Sepúlveda's dichotomy between man and the barely human, rather than the scale of cultural attainment offered by Las Casas, most clearly corresponds to the view that Wynter presents as the displacement of the Christian order into a coloniality of being. The "Adamic enslavement to Original Sin was transferred to that of potential human enslavement to sensory nature."[18] Yet regardless of whether the perceived inferiority is described as natural (Sepúlveda) or as cultural/religious (Las Casas), a system that equates humanity with reason would place Indigenous peoples outside. The Indigenous peoples were "discursively constructed as . . . irrational Human Others to . . . Man."[19]

That ontological position of otherness was eventually transferred to the enslaved Africans. There are conflicting accounts of the justifications offered for the enslavement of Africans rather than Amerindians. Wynter offers a theological one. Even before the conquest of America, the enslavement of non-Christians, including Africans, had been accepted on theological grounds, on the basis of their being "enemies of Christ." They had learned about and still rejected Christ. But that argument could not be made of Amerindians. The Requerimiento had been an unconvincing attempt to fit Amerindians into the category of enemies of Christ. The document (in Castilian, of course) rushed through the history of the church, beginning with St. Peter and ending with the requirement: "We ask and require you that you consider what we have said to you, and that you take the time that shall be necessary to understand and deliberate upon it, and that you acknowledge the Church as the Ruler and Superior of the whole world." Those who refused would rightfully be enslaved. An argument for enslaving Africans was based on a similar logic, that it was better to enslave Africans than Amerindians: unlike the Amerindians, Africans were enemies of Christ and thus *should* be enslaved to protect Amerindians. This argument is all the more significant because it was presented by none other than Las Casas.[20]

Religious and racial justifications cannot be so easily set apart, however.[21] Portuguese literatures had justified the wars in Africa as both a search for slaves and the extension of the Reconquista against the "Moors."[22] As Wynter observes, Portuguese colonialism had produced symbolic representations of Africans as lacking and animal-like, which were described as manifestations of their depravity, resulting from sin.

These symbolic representations were easily absorbed into a new order in which such characterizations appeared as proof of lack of rationality rather than of sin. This allowed Africans and peoples of African descent to be "assimilated to this Irrational Other category, as its extreme form."[23]

The shift from religious identity to rationality as the foundation of the ontological order is often inconspicuous, but it has lasting implications. Wynter describes it as the "fatal error of the West's degodding": "While, as Christians, Westerners could see other peoples as also having gods," even if considering their religions as resulting from error, as Las Casas did, the humanists' Man was "overrepresented as the supra-creedal human itself."[24] Degodding leaves us with only one version of Man. The realms of being/nonbeing shift from divine/human to rational/irrational—Man and his others.

This is what Wynter calls the "Word of Man."

The third episteme in Wynter's account, our current order of knowledge, is marked by the emergence of biology. Wynter still considers this part of the Word of Man, but it marks a shift from definitions of the human as a rational being to the human as a natural organism. A definition of the human in purely biological terms bolsters the assumed universality of Man. If a scientist in Europe can extrapolate the traits he identifies in one organism to all organisms of the same species, then he can imagine using a similar approach for humans.[25] He extrapolates the ideal traits of Man as he finds them in his own context to humanity as a species. This makes it possible to represent a "'local culture' conception of the human as if this conception were isomorphic with the human species itself."[26] The "local culture" assumes its own universality, conflating Man and human. This conflation "enables the well-being of this specific category of the human to be represented as if its well-being, too, were isomorphic with the well-being of the human species as a whole."[27] To uncover the particularity of Man is also to question its role as the foundation for social transformation.

The biological order of knowledge produces yet another displacement in the structure of being and nonbeing, this time based on a logic derived from evolutionary science. Differences that had previously been attributed to divine will are now ascribed to "natural selection," Wynter argues, in a simplistic, though pervasive, interpretation of natural selection. In Darwinian theory, evolution is contingent, guided by a multiplicity of factors—including environmental forces and accidents—that make the results unpredictable. Evolutionary theory does not predict progressive development toward perfection—a fact that troubled Darwin himself. But in its popular reception, natural selection was misinterpreted as selection of the best and strongest—which led to its transmutation into eugenics. Wynter's comments apply to the view of evolution as progress. Nature is represented as the power that selects particular species for survival and further complexity, based on their inherent superiority. Supernatural causation is replaced by natural causation but still imagined as supracultural.

Only at this point do we arrive at a purely secular conception of the human, Wynter argues. Race emerges in tandem with this secular understanding of the human, imagined as its hidden law—one that accounts for the uneven distribution of being. Thus, race "took the place both of Original Sin" and of the doctrine of enslavement to the bodily senses as the principle of human depravity and degeneracy.[28]

Those who are marked as lacking in true being experience the effects of this secular conception of the human externally—as social, political, and economic forces. But we also experience it internally—as self-abjection. The Word of Man is a powerful script that shapes us affectively. Wynter notes the similarities between this self-abjection and original sin. "Like the lay man of medieval-Christian Europe who could realize optimal being as a baptized, redeemed feudal Christian subject only through his or her autophobic aversion to prebaptismal being as the embodiment of 'fallen natural humanity' enslaved to Original Sin," Wynter observes, "the Antillean subject had to become reflexively autophobic to its own specific physiognomic being as the condition" of becoming Man.[29]

Frantz Fanon had suggested this link between racial self-abjection and the Christian idea of original sin. He wrote, "I read white books and little by little I take into myself the prejudices, the myths, the folklore that have come to me from Europe. . . . Without thinking, the black man selects himself as an object capable of carrying the burden of original sin. The white man chooses the black man for this function."[30] Because of the implicit negation of true being in colonized subjects, Fanon famously stated, "every ontology is made unattainable in a colonized and civilized society."[31] Wynter explicates and develops Fanon's insight by tracking the transformations through which the Christian logic of sin is carried into modern visions of the human, now operating through the notion of race.

No one escapes the force of these cultural conceptions of the human. These ideas shape our desires, our behavior, our being. But we can relate to them differently. Those defined as other in relation to Man may be enchanted by Man, as if our well-being depended on it, and accept carrying the burden of original sin. Or we may become disenchanted with Man.

Metamorphoses

Their recreation of a culture and a religion in which their gods could sustain and affirm their humanity was a central moment of their struggle to rehumanize themselves.—Sylvia Wynter, "Black Metamorphosis"

CARIBBEAN WRITERS HAVE SOUGHT to break their enchantment with the Word of Man, Wynter often observes. They have exposed Man as a local cultural construct masking itself as supracultural by foregrounding other stories—of African ways of life, of Caribbean rebellions against slavery, of the invention of Caribbean ways of being human. Steeped in that intellectual tradition, Wynter too sought to retrieve such stories, to give an account of stubborn refusals and creative self-transformations. This mode of research is different from the broad analytics I have described so far, for which Wynter is well known. But in these stories I find concrete models for what Wynter means by inventing new genres of being human, what she envisions as this ongoing praxis.

In her unpublished manuscript "Black Metamorphosis," written in the early 1970s, Wynter sets out to demonstrate that the retention and reinvention of African cultures and religions allowed the peoples of the Caribbean to survive in the new land and to resist their dehumanization. The plantation system—which Wynter insists is the origin of capitalism— required turning culturally diverse African peoples into a homogenized commodity. The violence of the plantation is clear evidence of dehumanization. And so are the attempts to deprive the enslaved of their ancestral traditions, of spiritual, geographic, and communal ties. Surviving it required nothing short of the reinvention of the self. They reinvented themselves as "natives" of the Caribbean. Drawing from historical and theoretical sources, inspired by the anthropological approach of Melville Herskovits, and armed with Marxist theory, Wynter analyzes such reinventions. She examines the religious practices of particular African groups in relation to practices in the Caribbean—mainly in Jamaica—to describe the processes as well as the aims and significance of such transmutations. She finds fragments of African religious practices in later reinvented rites, theologies, dances, and music in the Caribbean and beyond.

The discursive dehumanization of Amerindians and Africans entailed the claim that they had no culture or religion. Wynter calls this the "myth of cultural void" or the "Sepúlveda syndrome," to point to its origins in the debates of Valladolid I discussed in the previous section. Twentieth-century postcolonial intellectuals had to contend with the legacy of such myths.[32] Negritude as well as Amerindian and African *indigenismo* movements should be read, Wynter argues, as countering the Sepúlveda syndrome by revaluing African traditions. Both movements "implied a return to a lost autochthonous Golden Age, both mythic and real, a rehabilitation of the ancient gods, sprung from their homeland, a renaissance of the complex culture that had defined their being."[33] That rehabilitation was a kind of "spiritual return"—a transformation of the veneration of the ancestors into a rich intellectual pursuit. Contrary to the common representation of negritude as a nostalgic and impossible return, Wynter argues that the revaluation of African culture and religion was necessary for claiming Caribbean modes of being human against and beyond colonial discursive violence. Africa constituted the alternative ground from which to counter the universalization of Man. Haitian Jean Price-Mars and Senegalese Léopold Sédar Senghor are key examples of this in negritude and African indigenismo, respectively.[34] And they provide Wynter the metaphors and conceptual language for her own reading and theorization of Jamaican culture.

Price-Mars describes Haitians as the descendants of the people who had "the most moving history in the world," for they had suffered and survived "the transplantation of a human race into a stranger soil, in the worst possible biological conditions."[35] This history must be reclaimed, because the fact that the "the transplantation had taken root and grown 'under the worst possible biological conditions' was strong testimony to the viability of the original African culture and to the creativity of the culture-bearers, the slaves."[36] Whereas this remarkable process of self-creation might have faded from the public discourses and from the Haitian sense of identity, it is inscribed in folklore. Folklore is at once "the agent and the product of that cultural metamorphosis."[37] Turning to folklore, Wynter seeks to read those inscriptions and, most important, to understand *how* such metamorphoses took place.

Wynter makes Price-Mars's metaphor of transplantation her own, referring often to African cultural and religious elements as "seeds" and to the Caribbean as the "strange soil" in which the "transplantations and transformations" take place, giving the Caribbean its current form.

(*Transplantation* may appear more frequently than *metamorphosis* in the manuscript as it stands.) These agricultural metaphors serve her well, because much of her research focuses on practices of relating to the land. Drawing from Senghor, she describes culture as "the expression of the relationship between man [*sic*] and his natural environment. . . . Man adapts himself to Nature, at the same time as he adapts Nature to his own exigencies."[38] Capitalism undermines this mutual relationship, redefining "Nature as land, conceivable only in terms of property, *laid bare of myth, custom, tradition*"—a clear departure from the African and Indigenous traditions of those enslaved by it.[39] The interweaving of culture and nature had shaped Native people's attitude toward the earth and was thus crucial for their well-being. But from the time of the conquest, "an economic and instrumental civilization could make us believe that one part of the process, the transformation of Nature by Man is the very essence of culture."[40] I would add that cultures that did not adopt that instrumental relationship with nature are more likely to be described as "folklore" than "culture." Wynter associates the countercapitalist relation between human and nature—in which nature and human shape each other—specifically with the retention of African *religions*. This is not, however, because she assumes a modern belittling of both reverence for nature and religion as forms of faulty or primitive reason but rather because she rejects the hierarchical distinction between culture (as valuable) and religion (as naive). This distinction is, after all, indebted to local modes of European thought that she seeks to counter.[41]

Wynter looks for evidence of the transplantation of African beliefs in the practices around the plots of land given to plantation slaves for self-sustenance. Having access to land afforded them the opportunity to organize as a community outside the plantation, even if not independent from it—and to transplant their beliefs by practicing rituals that embodied their relationship to the earth in ways that contradicted the logic of the plantation. They "transplanted an old theology into a new soil."[42] Furthermore, as Price-Mars argued, they "humanized the landscape by peopling it with gods and spirits, with demons and puppies, with all the rich panoply of man's imagination."[43] Their orientation toward the earth shaped their burial rites as much as their fertility dances and was to become "the central grid" for the transformation of old beliefs into a new reality—into new ways of being human.[44]

The settlements of Maroons—slaves who ran away and settled in the mountains, from where they staged revolts, often with Indigenous peoples—offer a fuller example of transplantation. "From the description of early clashes with the Maroons, we see that they were organized in settlements which were almost exact replicas of their former patterns of life in Africa. The land was tilled, crops cultivated, religious feasts celebrated with song and dance. Above all, in these early stages their former African religions, *gradually metamorphosed*, were openly carried on."[45] The majority of Maroons in Jamaica were Ashanti-Fanti, and their religion centered on the earth; "the earth was not only goddess, Asase Afua," she explains, "and the source of all sustenance, it was also the place where their ancestors were interred."[46] The rites expressed these beliefs and, most important, materialized their orientation. Feasts and festivals ensured them good crops. Proper burial rituals assured the passage of the dead to the realm of the ancestors and thus "acknowledged and strengthened the tie between the life of man and of the earth."[47] The Maroons transplanted these beliefs into the new soil, where the relation to the earth mediated the creation of new communal bonds with the living and the dead. Burial rituals reconnected them with ancestors and eventually transformed Africa into the metaphor for the other world, the realm of the ancestors.

Slave revolts expressed the new culture of the Maroon, which had transformed patterns of warfare.[48] Wynter is particularly interested in the oaths and dances because they express the connections between religious and collective action. "The oath sworn by kissing the earth," she observes, "bound each man not only to the other men of the group, but to the whole world of ancestors," showing the transformation of the religions of the earth to support the formation of a new collective identity and the revolt against dehumanization.[49] Pointing to Herskovits approvingly, Wynter asserts, "The centrality of the *religious focus*" was "the centrality of the *rebellious impulse* by which the slave, refusing to accept his status as merchandise, never ceased to reinvent himself as human and to recognize himself as such through the reinvention of the gods."[50] Recovering the history of such revolts is necessary to counter colonial narratives of the passivity and objectification of the enslaved. But revolt was not the only expression of their resistance, Wynter argues; "the reinvention of a culture was an even more significant part of the black revolt than the occasional physical revolts. For the latter sprang from the seedbed, the ideology, *the emotional states of feeling* of the former. Negated as men, the blacks rebelled in periodic uprisings and in the ongoing creation of a culture, in order to be."[51] Reinventing culture would support alternative ways of being, possibly through generations.

Wynter's descriptions of these transplantations and transformations establish the parameters of her investigation of later religious and cultural practices. Practices and rituals were the mechanisms for the metamorphosis of religion and, Wynter's later works suggest, of being.[52] The relation to the earth as a communal bond would give rise to Caribbean culture, she argues. Wynter's most developed research on this topic focuses on dance, both the religious dances of myalism and those of Jonkonnu, generally considered secular. Through analyses of their history, function, and form, Wynter tracks the African elements in those dances and, most important, the history of their transformation in Jamaica, especially as means of communal formation. Pointing to the religious dimensions—even forgotten ones—is for Wynter a way to connect the dances to the counterpoetics of the Maroon and their emotional states of feeling. This explains why myalism was forbidden on the plantation, for it was suspected that its dances incited revolt. "Both [myalism and Jonkonnu] passed on elements of their rituals, beliefs, and dances to the surviving dances and versions of folk religion that exist today."[53] The dances sheltered rebellious impulses, even as they were significantly transformed into other cultural forms.

Christianity would threaten these dances—wanting to send African gods into exile, as Wynter puts it. But instead they took root in Christianity itself. Precisely through its connections with transformed African traditions, Christianity became "indigenous" to the Caribbean. Native Christianity was rejected by the official church, but Native Christians adopted the Bible, interpreting it freely, making it speak to their situation. They embodied Christianity differently from European preachers, praying and healing through dance. "The unofficial religion of the slaves or natives drew Christianity into its Indigenous cultural dynamic and transformed it," connecting with the hidden or forgotten liberating elements in Christianity, "freeing its original revolutionary impulse."[54] The cultural dynamic of transplantation and transformation, by which the African gods became the roots of Caribbean being, also altered Christianity.[55]

The metamorphosis of Christianity in the Caribbean is exemplified by the well-known Morant Bay rebellion (1865), led by Baptist elder Paul Bogle. "What is important to note with the 1865 rebellion," Wynter writes, "was that the rebellion was a rebellion expressed in religious metaphors, in religious terms." His Christianity was a Native one, "part of that Afro-Christian fusion," which served to protect rebellious impulses through changing conditions. "*The phraseology of the revolt was religious* as it had been under slavery but this time it was Afro-Christian. . . . Much of the ritual and the metaphors of freedom came from the Bible, but the spirit that infused it, that matrix that expressed the dynamic of revolt was part of the same continuum that had created Jonkonnu/Myalism."[56] The letter was Christian; the spirit was African. But it is the creativity of the rebels that transforms these elements into a vital force. Later movements would claim the Morant Bay rebellion as their tradition and Bogle as their ancestor. Indeed, Wynter herself claims later unofficial Christian prophetic movements in the Caribbean as precursors to the anticolonial movements and thus implicitly to her own praxis.[57] I will return to this.

A vital force once expressed in slave revolt erupts in a Christian movement. Wynter is interested in what makes it possible for a community—Maroon, myalist, Baptist, or political—to rebel against the seemingly inescapable force of empire and racialization. Creativity fuels these transformations, through ongoing processes of selecting fragments from old beliefs, bringing them into new frameworks to establish relations between peoples, experiences, and geographies and weave a new sense of collective identity through material practices. Old beliefs are expressed and transformed through the material practices of relation to the land and embodied through bodily practices in song and dance. Although this remains implicit in "Black Metamorphosis," I think it explains Wynter's swift shift from her discussion of religion to art. "All art is born from religion," she states.[58]

Tracking the transmission of religious sensibility through art entails expanding the archive. The analyses in "Black Metamorphosis" grow unwieldy, packing in example over example through more than nine hundred pages. She describes patterns of transplantation and transformation continuing to be embodied in disparate cultural practices—from the structure of political parties to the rhythms of popular songs. Bedwardism and Garveyism, Rastafarianism and reggae, work songs and jazz, all carry in them the seeds of a religious/cultural sensibility that, when cultivated, can spark rebellion. They constitute the counterpoetics of the Americas that may negate the negation of Black humanity.

In Wynter's depictions of African survivals, gods, like seeds, undergo metamorphosis. Fragments of African rituals seem, at times, to have their own power to kindle and sustain human metamorphosis. This power is not absolute, however, but relative to their effectiveness in human lives. Gods and rituals lose their power—become petrified. Indeed, the weight of Wynter's argument lies in the reinvention of religion more than merely in the retention and continuation of beliefs and practices. Her subject is metamorphosis. However, as the manuscript moves into more recent cultural forms, I detect an unresolved tension between her desire to revalue African traditions as sources for Caribbean culture and the insistence on the ongoing transformation of culture and thus of being. At certain points, "Black Metamorphosis" is so intent on identifying survivals of African cultures that it seems to undermine the depth of transformations. Why is it so important to return over and over to African cultures if her purpose is to illuminate their reinvention? Identifying African cultural roots allows Wynter to relativize European culture; it reminds us that we do not need to accept European definitions of our being and that we should not try to transform ourselves into the likeness of images that were never meant to foster our well-being. We have other resources from which to draw. And, in fact, we have been doing so since the beginning and should embrace that legacy, as Price-Mars and other negritude writers did. But appeals to origins easily turn into genealogical causality—as if we could derive behavior from origins. Identifying retentions enables examination of their alteration—particularly those aimed at challenging the imposition of racist ways of being. Ultimately, the goal is to assert the possibility and the need to continue reinventing ways of being human.

The processes of reinvention, as we have seen, are embodied. Wynter mentions in passing that in oral cultures, memory is "maintained, reconstructed, represented, and in essence, reinvented in the very flesh of each generation."[59] And thus she emphasizes such practices as the vehicle for the transplantation and transformation of religion. She calls the process "metamorphosis," evoking the work of Fanon, who described the effect of racism using images of bodily transmutation.[60] The scope and method of Wynter's work are significantly different from those of *Black Skin, White Masks*, yet "Black Metamorphosis" is similarly attentive to the corporeal dimensions of racialization—to the constitution of bodies in relation to both Bios and Logos. Her view of metamorphosis includes not just the involuntary effect of exposure to a racist culture but also the transformation brought about through intentional and creative practice.

Carving Being

PERHAPS WYNTER'S MOST detailed depiction of how religious imaginaries can be intentionally and creatively embodied is her novel *The Hills of Hebron*—one of her earliest works, published in 1962.[61] Like "Black Metamorphosis," the novel explores the praxis of transformation through religion. It focuses on a Jamaican Afro-Christian community that sets itself apart from Pocomanians and Baptists, as well as from Marxists and Garveyites.

The fictional "New Believers" embody the rebellious impulse of the Maroons—as Wynter describes it in "Black Metamorphosis"—and incorporate it into their Native Christianity. They escape from the city to create their own community in the (fictional) hills of Hebron, where they reestablish a vital connection to the land and reimagine a god to affirm their humanity. The narrator makes explicit the ancestral roots of the community's resolve. "The instinct for survival was as strong in them as in their slave ancestors. Some weight of memory in their blood carried the ghosts of dark millions who had perished, coffined in the holds of ships, so that some could live to breed more."[62] Like their ancestors, the New Believers longed for all they had "lost in their trespass across the seas, across the centuries": "gods and devils that were their own" but also the material elements that constituted their daily lives, "familiar trees and hills and huts and spears and cooking pots . . . their own land in which to see some image of themselves."[63] Their longings and their inventiveness were expressed in theological language and embodied in ritual.

Wynter found her inspiration for the main characters of the novel in the legendary prophets Bedward (1859–1930) of Jamaica and Jordan (d. 1928) of Guyana, whose religious movements exemplify Indigenous and rebellious forms of Christianity. Bedward identified with Bogle, the leader of the Morant Bay rebellion I mentioned before. Bedward's message emphasized "the need for land and justice, the injustices associated with White rule, and the necessity of setting up social welfare schemes that addressed the needs of the aged, infants, sick, and illiterate."[64] Jordan, an "extraordinary prophet-storyteller," "never hesitated to bring biblical characters into his pagan mytho-poetic folk legends," spinning "tales of redemption and escape."[65] Wynter combines Bedward's and Jordan's personalities and stories in the main character of the novel, Moses, the first leader of the New Believers.

Creating a fictional account of these movements, spinning her own tales of rebellion and transformation, allows Wynter to flesh out her view of metamorphosis by offering detailed observations of her characters and their inner lives in relation to their material environment. In contrast to the focus on collective identity that characterizes "Black Metamorphosis," *The Hills of Hebron* describes how individual personality and gifts inform the interpretation and embodiment of religious ideas in ways that affirm and reshape practitioners' humanity. Moses uses his gifts as a storyteller to bring biblical stories to life and lead his followers into the hills to build a community on their own land and seek a way of life that sustains their well-being. They leave behind the God of the Baptist church for a God in their own image who is partial to them. Moses's preaching physically transforms his followers, transfiguring their bodies with hope. They enliven Hebron with their myths and their God, with their worship and their labor. Their beliefs and their land sustain their attempt to create a way of life that affirms their humanity.

But the community struggles with external pressures and internal betrayals. Moses is a charismatic patriarchal leader, but his need for recognition leads to his demise. While at the Cockpit Centre market, he runs into a group of people gathered around a speaker, whom he assumes is a prophet. "'Friends and comrades, this is a new time, a new century, a new day. All over the world a new race of men arise to greet the morning. One race, black, brown or white, the race of those who work!' Moses hears him say.[66] The speaker, who has just returned from the United States, where he got an education, is captivating the audience with his analysis of their plight. "Because here in this island, it is we who plant the seeds of wealth, but it is others, thousands of miles away, who reap the harvest. The big white gods who rule us from their palaces up in Kingston call themselves empire-builders, but they didn't build the Empire, we did, we built the Empire with our sweat, with the blood of our ancestors whom they bought and sold like cattle. Today we carry this Empire on our backs."[67] Moses too is enthralled by the speaker until he realizes that the very people who once ridiculed his preaching are there listening to a message that makes no appeal to the Bible or a Black God. Envy takes hold of him. "All that the man said that they would do, he, Moses, had already accomplished. . . . Up in Hebron they were already free, neither workers nor capitalists, only New Believers owning everything in common, safe from the flood of want on Mount Ararat. And refuged in the arms of God."[68] But he had failed to convert those whom this man is convincing. The audience keeps shouting in response, establishing a rhythmic exchange between speaker and audience, until they break out in song. But the man reprimands them—"no hymns," this is not a church.[69] They are to believe only in the "religion of Man." Moses is desperate. He tells them that he has seen God, a Black God, who has come to liberate them. But the group mocks his claim to be the son of a Black God by daring him to crucify himself.

Back in Hebron, Moses can no longer find his God. In despair, he begins to plan his crucifixion. The prophet had imagined this act of self-immolation as the best proof of his divinity. When the New Believers realize Moses's plan, they believe, "beyond all doubt, that the Son of God would die to save them." Yet they see the true desire behind Moses's sacrifice. "The blackness which was their secret shame would be atoned for, would become their pride, their joy"—a salvation not from sin but from race.[70] It is a ritual of self-abjection, a fatal defeat revealed in Moses's last cry: "God is white after all. . . . God is white!"' There is no liberation, just death. The leader who had shown remarkable creativity in turning biblical stories into visions of hope, who had cunningly stolen land from the masters to establish a self-sustaining community where all had shelter, food, and dignified clothing, succumbed to the desire to prove himself to the followers of the Word of Man.

Moses's perverse ritual brings destruction to the New Believers. As if "entombed" with Moses, the community loses its vitality.[71] Their ritual dances become "ossified," for they have forgotten the dances' intention. Their "rituals of existence" become a mere repetition of gestures and actions they have done before, but these practices can no longer enliven them. A drought leaves their land lifeless, and lassitude takes hold of their bodies.

The next leader of the New Believers, Obadiah, has to experience a deeper conversion than Moses. Wynter imagines his transformation as a process of carving. Before he moved to Hebron, Obadiah's trade had been carving. And he is described as a carving himself. Creative practice and self-transformation are linked. Toward the end of the novel, Obadiah learns that his particular technique may have roots in the methods used by his African ancestors. Carving is thus presented as an African survival but also as the product of the creative agency of the artist who transforms received knowledge and is himself transformed through it. What Obadiah receives from Africa—as both trade and art—is a way of relating to the social and material world, but the product will be his own expression of that tradition materialized in the particular elements he finds in the thickly wooded hills of Hebron the New Believers have claimed as their own. He carves out of the depth of his anguish, of "the story of Hebron, of their search for God . . . out of this, the dream and the reality."[72] Obadiah "created consciously," an intentionality that is consistent with Wynter's portrayal of the invention of Caribbean identities. He is "trying to embody in his carving his new awareness of himself and of Hebron."[73] Furthermore, his carving becomes part of his own body and by extension of the community of Hebron.[74]

While the novel foregrounds the humanizing impulse that leads Moses's followers to Hebron and to their Black God, in the end it points to a shift away from those beliefs. Why are they "shut amidst these arid, thorny, almost inaccessible hills, straining for the embrace of God"? Obadiah wonders.[75] The wood carvings that reconnect Obadiah with the traditions of his ancestors allow him to envision a different way of relating to the world beyond the hills of Hebron, connecting them with communities past and future. Obadiah's vision includes some aspects of the message of the speaker at the marketplace—they would embrace commerce and seek education. But Obadiah would transplant his vision to the soil of Hebron. "To explain it to them he would need the words and the rhythms, not of a sermon, but a song."[76] Obadiah realizes this has to be a slow process, for his vision will only be meaningful if it becomes theirs too. Ultimately, "what he was asking of them now was for a new response to a new ritual, a new morality, a new right and wrong, a new God."[77]

"Beliefs materialized in deeds"—in the everyday rituals of existence as much as in worship and art. In the novel, as in "Black Metamorphosis," rituals connect dreams, material elements, and bodies, as Obadiah's carving had done. But rituals are not meant to be immutable. They cease to be effective when they can no longer mediate relationships to the sociomaterial environment in ways that sustain and transform life. Wynter returns to the nexus of beliefs/cultures and bodies in her later theorizations of "sociogenesis," elaborating on Fanon's statement that culture "is what a human being creates *and what creates a human being*."[78] Through *sociogenesis*, she seeks to describe the mechanisms by which culture not only defines what it means to be human but also materially shapes human bodies, this time in dialogue with evolutionary biology and cognitive science. But in those writings the attention to the role of individual, embodied creativity that infused her literary works is submerged. The specific trees and hills and cooking pots, the heat or relentless rain, the distinct movements of bodies in spiritual procession or rhythmic dance, are rare in her later works. Gods and demons are mostly gone.

Religion as Counterpoetics

At the very time when it most often mouths the word, the West has never been further from being able to live a true humanism—a humanism made to the measure of the world.—Aimé Césaire, *Discourse on Colonialism*

RELIGION IN WYNTER'S CORPUS is an inherent part of the colonial order of being, but it has also been a reservoir of sensibilities to refuse its prescriptions. Her analyses are informed by Karl Marx's theory of religion and thus indirectly by Ludwig Feuerbach's. She makes this explicit in "Black Metamorphosis," where she cites Marx's statement "Religion is simply the recognition of man in a roundabout way."[79] And she repeatedly asserts that particular gods affirm and sustain specific forms of humanity. However, her early engagements with religion do not read like theoretical elaborations on Marxism or any theory of religion but rather as attempts to capture a feature of life that can only be perceived obliquely through religion. Furthermore, her goal is not to uncover religion as misguided delusion or to promote, in Marx's words, "the abolition of religion as the illusory happiness of the people."[80] Instead, she challenges what she considers a misreading of Marx's much-quoted description of religion as "the opium of the masses."[81] Wynter counters that there is a significant distinction between the religion of the plantation/capitalist system and the religion of those dehumanized by that system. "While the official religion is the opium of the people, the unofficial religion serves two functions: to sustain a sense of identity in the face of increasing pressures, and to *structure those states of feeling* that wait their moment to erupt."[82] Such eruptions may seem like "spontaneous resistance," but they are oriented by affects that have been shaped and transmitted through embodied practices like ritual, song, and ceremony.[83]

Wynter describes the possibilities of refusing the imposition of the Word of Man as the mobilization of affective energies and bodily performance in specific sociomaterial contexts. Unofficial religion can be a reservoir of humanizing feelings and sensibilities. Religious stories, images, and beliefs are the "structures" that those feelings take. Ritual is the means by which such feelings are embodied, transmitted, and transformed.

Far from denouncing religious beliefs as illusory just because they are not factual, Wynter treats them as productive forces in human existence that should be engaged consciously and ethically. Wynter is, after all, a writer and literary critic, attuned to the constitutive power of the imagination. Her theory of religion should be understood as part of her broader argument that human beings are shaped by their cultural creations as much as by evolutionary forces—by Logos as much as by Bios. Religious ideas can be at the same time a human creation and a vital potency that nourishes or destroys possibilities for being. Thus, the reinvention of religion cannot be disentangled from the reinvention of ways of being human.

Secular cultures have no higher claim to truth than do religious communities. We may ask of both: What kind of ills can they cure? What redemptions do they offer, and for whom? What are the socioeconomic conditions under which they work or fail? The modern technoscientific mode of perceiving, understanding, and being in the world should be subjected to the same types of contestations that we deploy against, for instance, Haitian Voodoo—one of Wynter's contemporary examples; the effectiveness of the former is as bound to its material context and its local cultural understanding of the world as that of the latter.[84] Our shared understanding of the very word *secular* is the effect of being disciplined in a specific cultural system, Wynter adds, one that construes religion as private or unreal—a system based on a belief in its own supracultural nature.[85]

This way of understanding religious beliefs implies their continuity with the dogmas of secular culture. As I discussed in the first section, Wynter interprets humanism as a displacement rather than an obliteration of the Christian division between being and nonbeing, which authorized lay humanists while confining those deemed as lacking rationality to nonbeing. This ontological construct shaped affects—not least by inducing autophobic feelings. The Word of Man has its own rituals, its own ways to instruct us of what it means to be a Man and what practices—social, economic, sexual, and aesthetic—will help us embody the image of Man. But we seldom question the truths of Man or challenge its prescriptions. We occlude their origin. In statements that evoke Feuerbach's description of religion, Wynter argues that societies create genres of being human and then repress the knowledge that they are a human invention. Thus, Wynter calls for her readers to become disenchanted, not with religion, but with Man.

Today we need to become disenchanted with secular understandings of the human in order to free ourselves to invent new ones. This may entail adopting the perspective of the outsider to our own current order of being. Wynter invites us to imagine the shock of the Cenú Indians, for instance, when informed that the pope had given the Spanish crown their lands. Their response? "The pope must have been drunk, the king of Castile a madman."[86] This is probably why she considers the unofficial prophetic movements of the Caribbean the precursors of anticolonial struggles. Religion offered them affective and imaginative resources to take the outsider's perspective to counter the inscriptions of Man.

I stated before that Wynter does not seek to dispel religion. But she is willing to concede its disappearance. In *The Hills of Hebron*, she describes the characters' Native Christian practices empathically, highlighting the longings for rehumanization at the core of their beliefs. But she also portrays how their rituals lost their power, leaving them as petrified beings in a lifeless land. In her discussion of the U.S. intervention in Haiti, Wynter describes indigenismo's attempts to revitalize Voodoo as a positive revaluation of Haitian culture. But in her view, the crucial concern was the devastation of the world for which Voodoo had been a vital way of life. In that case, she argues, liberation entailed disenchantment from both creolized Christian theology and secular Marxist ideology. When the context changes, the affective energies once transmitted by religious rituals may activate other cultural practices.

Where the gods no longer sustain the affirmation of identities beyond the Word of Man, where rituals no longer ground the invention of new ways of being, literature would have to play that role. "One might say [literature] would have to take their place."[87] This is why she invites scholars to learn from the first humanists, those who sought to challenge the medieval Christian order of being. We need to be *heretics* against our own order of knowledge—imbedded in the structure of academic disciplines. Most significantly, we may return to the humanists to remind ourselves of the power of the imagination. "For the humanists had glimpsed here that . . . man was indeed double; that he invented for himself a second self and then acted to verify this self, acting 'from role sustaining motives in a dramatic reality.'"[88] Perhaps because this statement is meant to inspire changes within the academy, it shifts the site of the invention of new ways of being human from the unofficial religious practices of the Antilles to the scholarly practices of the humanists. I find this shift difficult, lacking the vital and embodied dimensions of her discussions of religious practices like cultivating the land and staging rebellions, dancing and burying the dead. But it clarifies how she envisions the role of scholars in bringing about new ways of being.

Wynter suggests a kind of transplantation of some of the religious functions to the secular humanities. "The great rupture that transformed the *mythos* and *theologos* into a secular order of things" leads humanists to insist "on the uniqueness of those narratives defined as 'literature' precisely because of the new role that these ordering narratives of secular man . . . would play."[89] Since our modes of figuration shape our modes of self-understanding, "in secular society, literature, as well as the arts in general, would come to play a ritual . . . function."[90] Literary critics are the new theologians—for good or ill.[91] But her invocations of the secular remain provisional and cautious; after all, the rupture that gave birth to humanism is also the origin of race. Thus, Wynter argues that the much-needed reinvention of the humanities entails the "un/writing of our present normative defining of the secular mode of the Subject."[92] This new humanism is a heresy in relation to Man—not necessarily against religious modes of being. A humanism "to the measure of the world" refuses the totalizing impulse of the first. This is why she warns against the "stigmatization of so-called 'primitive cultures,'" in which religious practices are privileged sites of counterpoetics.[93] Challenging the prevalent order of knowing and being requires stepping outside of it—literally or imaginatively—which would mean imagining ourselves outside of the limits imposed by modern forms of secularism.

Taking the perspective of the outsiders may prove impossible, however, without the affective resources to do so. "The mutations at the level of the aesthetic-affective" are the hardest.[94] "The Ceremony Must Be Found," Wynter argues, quoting a poem by John Peale Bishop.[95] Writers and artists are well equipped for the task of self-invention. No wonder she considers their practice rooted in religion. But what rituals or ceremonies will sustain the states of feeling needed to counter dehumanization and guide us to embody new genres of the human?

I titled this essay "Embodied Counterpoetics" to point to the importance of being as poiesis in Wynter's understanding of religion and to foreground what is less explicit in the appeals to literature: the role of embodied and grounded practices by means of which we may cultivate affective orientations and intentionally re-create ourselves. Indeed, it is through her descriptions of rituals that Wynter offers her most compelling theorization of corporeality—where the body is both the vehicle and the product of self-transformation. And this sensibility undergirds her understanding of the role of the arts—particularly dance. Are the humanities equipped to guide us toward this sense of embodied counterpoetics as both imaginative discourse and transformative practice—to counter the colonial and capitalist forces that shape our being? Do we need to invent new rituals, a counteraesthetic and a counterethics?

Notes

1 Wynter, "Pope," 35.
2 She explicates the connection between beliefs and bodies in discussions of behavioral and evolutionary science, focusing on how beliefs shape desires, which in turn shape practice. But there she adopts a different language, the language of science rather than religion. Wynter, "Towards the Sociogenic

Principle." She has also explored this topic in close readings of Caribbean literatures. But these are subjects for another essay.

3 This work has been receiving attention among scholars of religion interested in the connections among Christianity, coloniality, and race—like An Youn-tae and J. Kameron Carter, who contribute to this volume.

4 In her early work, Wynter has problematized conventional understandings of history, arguing, in a Marxist tone, that "history in the Caribbean is fiction: 'a fiction written, dominated, controlled by forces external to itself.'" Edwards, "'Talking about a Little Culture,'" 29, quoting Wynter's "Novel and History." In her works on coloniality of being, however, Foucault's archaeology of thought is a more defining source than her Marxist sensibility.

5 Foucault, *Order of Things*, 160.

6 Foucault, *Order of Things*, 308.

7 Wynter, "Unsettling the Coloniality," 318. Wynter uses the problematic designation *Judeo-Christian*. When I am not quoting her directly, I use the term *Christian*, which more accurately describes the theological concepts she is analyzing.

8 For her analyses of original sin, Wynter draws on the works of Julia Kristeva, Jacques Le Goff, and Anthony Pagden, among others.

9 Wynter, "Beyond the Word of Man," 641.

10 Wynter, "Beyond the Word of Man," 641.

11 Wynter, "Unsettling the Coloniality," 278–79.

12 Wynter, "Unsettling the Coloniality," 279.

13 Foucault is clear that he bracketed the question of causality from *The Order of Things*. Wynter just treats it indirectly in the context of humanism but is more explicit when calling for intentional transformation.

14 Pagden, *Fall of the Natural Man*, 112–13.

15 Sepúlveda cited in Pagden, *Fall of the Natural Man*, 115.

16 Pagden, *Fall of the Natural Man*, 117.

17 Pagden, *Fall of the Natural Man*, 140.

18 Wynter, "Beyond the Word of Man," 641.

19 Wynter, "Towards the Sociogenic Principle," 43.

20 Las Casas later repented of having taken this position.

21 The Spanish notion of "purity of blood" similarly blurs the boundary between religious and inherited differences.

22 See also Blackmore, *Moorings*.

23 Wynter, "Towards the Sociogenic Principle," 43.

24 Wynter, "Unsettling the Coloniality," 299.

25 Wynter identifies Isaac Newton as an example.

26 Wynter, "Pope," 29.

27 Wynter, "Pope," 29.

28 Wynter, "Beyond the Word of Man," 642.

29 Wynter, "Beyond the Word of Man," 643.

30 Fanon, *Black Skin, White Masks*, 191–92.

31 Fanon, *Black Skin, White Masks*, 109.

32 Vincent Brown offers a clear example of this legacy in the words of a University of Chicago professor in 1919: "The Negro, when he landed in the United States, left behind almost everything but his dark complexion and his tropical temperament." Brown, "Social Death and Political Life," 1234.

33 Sylvia Wynter, "Black Metamorphosis: New Natives in a New World," n.d., 14, Institute of the Black World Records, MG 502, Box 1, Schomburg Center for Research in Black Culture, New York Public Library, New York.

34 In other works, Wynter explains how other Caribbean thinkers contributed to this project—notably, Nicolás Guillén and Aimé Césaire. See, for instance, Wynter, "Beyond the Word of Man"; and Wynter, "Pope."

35 Price-Mars quoted in Wynter, "Black Metamorphosis," 16. Wynter uses Price-Mars's statement as the epigraph for her essay about Jonkonnu. Wynter, "Jonkonnu in Jamaica."

36 Wynter, "Black Metamorphosis," 16.

37 Wynter, "Black Metamorphosis," 18.

38 Wynter, "Black Metamorphosis," 18.

39 Wynter, "Black Metamorphosis," 19 (emphasis mine).

40 Wynter, "Black Metamorphosis," 1.

41 Seeking, imagining, and conjuring practices of relating to the earth had an added significance in the early twentieth century, when colonialism meant that claims of belonging to the land of one's birth could not be taken for granted.

42 Wynter, "Black Metamorphosis," 72.

43 Wynter, "Jonkonnu in Jamaica," 35. Wynter adopts this framework, stating that "the Maroons humanized their mountainous interior with adaptation." "Black Metamorphosis," 72.

44 Wynter, "Black Metamorphosis," 49.

45 Wynter, "Black Metamorphosis," 72 (emphasis mine).

46 Wynter, "Black Metamorphosis," 76. I wonder, though, if it is necessary to claim this origin to assert the transplantation of rituals and communal practices.

47 Wynter, "Black Metamorphosis," 76–77.

48 Wynter, "Black Metamorphosis," 80.

49 Wynter, "Black Metamorphosis," 77.

50 Wynter, "Black Metamorphosis," 77 (emphasis mine).

51 Wynter, "Black Metamorphosis," 83 (emphasis mine).

52 When I use the term *mechanism*, I am *not* imagining an industrial process but rather a slow chemical reaction in which new bonds are created that produce significant transformations.

53 Wynter, "Jonkonnu in Jamaica," 41. I can't help playing in my mind the lyrics of the Puerto Rican group Truco y Saperoco: "Me tienen miedo / me tienen temor / cuando yo toco esta plena / mezclada con guaguancó" (They are afraid of me / they are fearful of me / when I play this *plena* / mixed with *guaguancó*).

54 Wynter, "Black Metamorphosis," 180.

55 Wynter, "Jonkonnu in Jamaica," 44.

56 Wynter, "Black Metamorphosis," 178 (emphasis mine).

57 Scott, "Re-enchantment of Humanism," 137.

58 Wynter, "Jonkonnu in Jamaica," 36.

59 Wynter, "Black Metamorphosis," 140.

60 See Rivera, *Poetics of the Flesh*, 125–26.

61 For a full discussion of the novel's relation to Wynter's theoretical works, see Rivera, "Where Life Itself Lives."

62 Wynter, *Hills of Hebron*, 52.

63 Wynter, *Hills of Hebron*, 52.

64 Price, "'Cleave to the Black,'" 46.

65 Carew, "Fusion of African and Amerindian Folk Tales," 7.

66 Wynter, *Hills of Hebron*, 215.

67 Wynter, *Hills of Hebron*, 216.

68 Wynter, *Hills of Hebron*, 223.

69 Wynter, *Hills of Hebron*, 223.

70 In "Poetics and the Politics," Wynter similarly states, "The cross of Christ was made of wood. The Cross of the Freetown Christian was an arrangement of genes: black skin, lips, eyes that existed to negate, perversely, the white skin of Christ. They took up the cross and walked. They endured their passion . . . and proceeded to sweat in thick English flannels, to answer in Latin, endure the incongruity of their passions, and to re-enact the Crucifixion not as tragedy but as farce" (87).

71 Wynter, *Hills of Hebron*, 244.

72 Wynter, *Hills of Hebron*, 300.

73 Wynter, *Hills of Hebron*, 283.

74 Wynter, *Hills of Hebron*, 299.

75 Wynter, *Hills of Hebron*, 22.

76 Wynter, *Hills of Hebron*, 305.

77 Wynter, *Hills of Hebron*, 310.

78 Wynter, "Towards the Sociogenic Principle," 33 (emphasis mine).

79 Quoted in Wynter, "Black Metamorphosis," 74.

80 Marx, "Critique of Hegel's Philosophy," 171.

81 Refuting Richard Wright's reading of Marx, she writes, "Wright, like all positivist Marxists, took the line extracted from a larger or more complex statement by Marx that 'religion is the opium of the people' [at] its face value,

without distinguishing those moments when religion serves as 'opium' from those other moments when it has served as a humanizing and revolutionary ideology for great movements of the people" ("Black Metamorphosis," 57).

82 Wynter, "Black Metamorphosis," 180.
83 Wynter, "Black Metamorphosis," 180.
84 Wynter, "Pope."
85 Wynter, "Pope," 29.
86 Wynter, "Pope."
87 Wynter, "Ceremony," 50.
88 Wynter, "Ceremony," 23.
89 Wynter, "Ceremony," 50.
90 Wynter, "Ceremony," 51.
91 Wynter, "Ceremony," 51.
92 Wynter, "Ceremony," 22.
93 Wynter, "Ceremony," 49.
94 Wynter, "Ceremony," 52.
95 Wynter, "Ceremony."

Bibliography

Blackmore, Josiah. *Moorings: Portuguese Expansion and the Writing of Africa*. Minneapolis: University of Minnesota Press, 2009.

Brown, Vincent. "Social Death and Political Life in the Study of Slavery." *American Historical Review* 115, no. 5 (2009): 1231–49.

Carew, Jan. "The Fusion of African and Amerindian Folk Tales." *Caribbean Quarterly* 23, no. 1 (1977): 7–21.

Césaire, Aimé, *Discourse on Colonialism*. New York: Monthly Review Press, 1972.

Edwards, Norval. "'Talking about a Little Culture': Sylvia Wynter's Early Essays." *Journal of West Indian Literature* 10, no. 1/2 (2001): 12–38.

Fanon, Frantz. *Black Skin, White Masks*. New York: Grove, 1967.

Foucault, Michel. *The Order of Things: An Archeology of the Human Sciences*. New York: Random House, 1970.

Marx, Karl. "Critique of Hegel's Philosophy of Rights." In *Marx on Religion*, edited by John Raines, 167–86. Philadelphia: Temple University Press, 2011.

Pagden, Anthony. *The Fall of the Natural Man: The American Indian and the Origins of Comparative Ethnology*. Cambridge: Cambridge University Press, 1982.

Price, Charles Reavies. "'Cleave to the Black': Expressions of Ethiopianism in Jamaica." *New West Indian Guide* 77, no. 1/2 (2003): 31–64.

Rivera, Mayra. *Poetics of the Flesh*. Durham, NC: Duke University Press, 2015.

Rivera, Mayra. "Where Life Itself Lives." In *Beyond the Doctrine of Man: Decolonial Visions of the Human*, edited by Joseph Drexler-Dreis and Kristien Justaert, 19–35. New York: Fordham University Press, 2019.

Scott, David. "The Re-enchantment of Humanism: An Interview with Sylvia Wynter." *Small Axe*, no. 8 (2000): 119–207.

Wynter, Sylvia. "Beyond the Word of Man: Glissant and the New Discourse of the Antilles." *World Literature Today* 63, no. 4 (1989): 637–48.

Wynter, Sylvia. "The Ceremony Must Be Found: After Humanism." *boundary 2* 12/13 (1984): 19–70.

Wynter, Sylvia. *The Hills of Hebron*. 1962. Kingston: Randle, 2010.

Wynter, Sylvia. "Jonkonnu in Jamaica: Towards the Interpretation of Folk Dance as a Cultural Process." *Jamaica Journal* 4, no. 2 (1970): 34–48.

Wynter, Sylvia. "Novel and History, Plot and Plantation." *Savacou*, no. 2 (1971): 95–102.

Wynter, Sylvia. "The Pope Must Have Been Drunk, the King of Castile a Madman: Culture as Actuality, and the Caribbean Rethinking of Modernity." In *The Reordering of Culture: Latin America, the Caribbean and Canada in the Hood*, edited by Alvina Ruprecht and Cecilia Taiana, 17–41. Ottawa: Carleton University Press, 1995.

Wynter, Sylvia. "The Poetics and the Politics of a High Life for Caliban." In Lemuel Johnson, *Highlife for Caliban*, 85–110. Trenton, NJ: Africa World Press, 1995.

Wynter, Sylvia. "Towards the Sociogenic Principle: Fanon, Identity, the Puzzle of Conscious Experience, and What It Is Like to Be 'Black.'" In *National Identities and the Sociopolitical Changes in Latin America*, edited by Mercedes F. Durán-Cogan and Antonio Gómez-Moriana, 30–66. New York: Routledge, 2001.

Wynter, Sylvia. "Unsettling the Coloniality of Being/Power/Truth/Freedom: Towards the Human, after Man, Its Overrepresentation—an Argument." *CR: The New Centennial Review* 3, no. 3 (2003): 257–337.

Eleanor Craig

3 We Have Never Been Human/e

The Laws of Burgos and the Philosophy
of Coloniality in the Americas

THIS CHAPTER INTERPRETS the Laws of Burgos (Leyes de Burgos) as a philosophical document that posits an ideal relationship between colonizers and Indigenous persons from a colonialist perspective. More fully titled the Laws of Burgos: Royal Ordinances for the Good Government and Treatment of the Indians (Las Leyes de Burgos: Ordenanzas para el buen regimiento y tratamiento de los indios), these 1512 pronouncements are explicitly concerned with the spiritual salvation of Indigenous persons on the island the Spanish named Hispaniola (La Española, present-day Dominican Republic and Haiti).

Castilian law was, from the Spanish perspective, the default law for new colonies in the Caribbean. The Laws of Burgos, issued on December 27, 1512, with an official supplement ratified July 28, 1513, are frequently cited as an early human rights document and the first of their kind in the Americas. A typical lay interpretation of the Laws goes as follows: "The Laws of Burgos issued on Dec. 27, 1512, by Ferdinand II, the Catholic, regulated relations between Spaniards and the conquered Indians, particularly to ensure the spiritual and material welfare of the latter, who were often severely treated."[1] This narrative suggests two decisive shifts—one causing the Indians to become royal subjects and another implementing "spiritual and material" improvements to remedy the injustices created by colonization.

I argue, against this popular interpretation, that the Laws of Burgos did not advocate justice for Indigenous persons. Invoking overlapping Christian and humanist universalisms, the Laws at best attempt to set limits on violence performed under specific conditions (e.g., on those not considered slaves). Yet their larger philosophical work is not to prevent violence at all but to integrate its justifications into religious philosophies of salvation and the soul. Even on a theoretical level, the Laws do not forbid violence but describe ideal conditions for "the persistence of violence made functional and coherent."[2] This resonates with long-standing questions about the extent to which concepts of rights develop to manage and rationalize, rather than eradicate, injustice. My argument also intersects at this juncture with critiques of Enlightenment-derived political liberalism from critical race and anticolonial perspectives. A discourse of rights that fails may not be a matter of unfortunate mistakes or omissions but part of the logic of dominance. I acknowledge that claims to human rights can be essential elements of political strategy for subjugated persons and groups. Yet I also participate in philosophical and political critiques of human rights discourse that argue its historical entanglement with colonial and imperial projects.[3]

Written by a committee of theologians and jurists, the Laws express awareness that Indigenous persons suffer brutal, often lethal, conditions at the hands of Spanish colonists. A quasi-humanist rhetoric combines exhortations for Spanish colonizers to treat Indigenous people with gentleness and justice with instructions to ensure Indians' religious conversion and indoctrination. The Laws give a wide range of commands, covering issues from food and clothing provisions to enforcement of monogamous marriage to forced relocation. They insist that the Indians bound to Europeans for labor ought to be clothed, fed, and protected from overwork. They set guidelines for the proper way to keep Indian laborers in *encomienda* (a state of indenture), with little suggestion that this state conflicts with commands to observe kindness and fairness.

I am reading the Laws as a document of *moral* religious philosophy, since the Spanish moral self-image is prominently at stake in their declarations. The Laws foreshadow, in this way, forms of thought usually attributed to Enlightenment texts that posit civilized European Man as teacher and guardian of his various others. In the latter part of this chapter, I fleetingly point to resonances with Kantian logic. This is not to assert a causal relationship or even direct influence. Whether a matter of context or political positioning, anxieties about the degradation Europeans might experience through their colonial adventures are not evident in Immanuel Kant's political writings. Yet Kant is cited as an originator of both human rights and racist societal hierarchies in ways that make his work a worthwhile juxtaposition. I do not claim that the same phenomena are occurring in the Laws as in Kant's texts, whatever that would mean. It may nonetheless warrant further study that combining racism and what is now called human rights was a philosophical move that was methodologically established long before Kant arrived on the scene and well rehearsed by the time he wrote of peace between nations or universal history.

This chapter revises narratives of both continuity and break as they are frequently applied to Spanish colonialist thought and praxis. That is, there are breaks in spite of similarities with and extensions of previous theorizations, continuities in spite of definite shifts. What this means will be better contextualized, but, generally speaking, it refers to the following pair of claims about genealogies of European thought: On the one hand, 1492 ushered in a new world order, one that posed direct and perhaps unprecedented challenges to the colonizing society's epistemologies. On the other, the Spanish colonial mindset was not born all at once, fully formed; its various elements were historically enabled, though not thereby predetermined. Nor did this phase of coloniality determine the shape and content of other forms that followed (such as British entry into South Asia and North America)—forms that expanded, contested, and diverged from it in important ways. In reading the Laws of Burgos philosophically, I thus see them as an important moment that both participates and intervenes in a tradition of theopolitical philosophy.

My main argument, however, concerns the Laws themselves. In classifying them as a document that performs and consolidates a philosophy of religion, I trace the way that submission to empire is required for legible spiritual salvation. At the same time, imperial authorities demonstrate in these laws an anxiety about their own moral status. This is what I initially found most curious: the extensive rhetorical effort in the Laws of Burgos to foreground the state of Indians' souls, which functioned as a corrective and protective measure to benefit the souls of European colonizers. I read the Laws as an exemplary instance of broader trends in philosophies of rights in the Americas, though this chapter does not attempt the historical argument necessary to thoroughly support that claim.

Reception and Philosophical Context

THAT THE LAWS OF BURGOS had little effect on Spanish-Indigenous relations in Hispaniola is uncontroversial. Those who point out that the Laws did little to ameliorate conditions or prevent the maltreatment of Indigenous persons agree that "although many of the various aspects of the Laws of Burgos had good intentions, the laws were largely unenforceable. Regardless of their enforceability, however, the laws represent Spain's first attempts to limit the abuse of the indigenous peoples of the New World by the Spanish."[4] This interpretation holds that there was an unfortunate gap between intent and delivery, theory and practice. While the qualifying "various aspects of" suggests that perhaps not all motivations were benevolent, the Laws are seen as a step in the direction of greater morality and humanity. They marked an initial effort to recognize Indigenous rights, and the tragedies with which the Laws are associated result from their failure to govern.

An even stronger way of reading the Laws proclaims their positive valence as a paradigm shift, as sites of ennoblement that foretell decolonial thought. Enrique Dussel writes that liberation theology in Latin America began with Dominican friar Antonio de Montesinos's 1511 Advent sermon decrying the treatment of Indigenous people on Hispaniola.[5] Ivan Petrella, with Dussel, sets in this same lineage Bartolomé de las Casas, "who heard Montesino's [sic] sermons first hand and subsequently converted from being a slaveholder to being the primary advocate for Indian rights."[6] Thus, the Laws of Burgos are entered into a tradition of social justice thought seen as critiquing the basic structure of colonial society. "In both Montesinos and Las Casas, therefore, we see the two parts that have since characterized Liberation Theology: on the one hand, the denunciation and revision of theological ideas; and on the other, the attempt to rethink and revise the institutions (thus the Laws of Burgos and the New Laws of 1542) that undergird structural oppression."[7] This narration would suggest that the Laws were fundamentally intended to intervene in the structure of colonial relations and to deliver justice (however conceived) for Indigenous persons and communities.[8]

Others argue that the Laws, even in theory, commanded little that would substantially improve conditions for Indigenous people. Many of these critics acknowledge that the Laws did not prescribe justice in practical or theoretical terms but rather situate them in a progressive narrative. This argument from historical distance was articulated nearly a century ago: "To an observer of the twentieth century they seem, in their practicable measures, a cold-blooded sanctioning of existing conditions. In many respects, however, they were a long step in advance over the preceding unregulated and irresponsible exploitation of the Indians."[9] While the laws did not lay the groundwork for liberation, such a reading argues, they ought not to be read by present-day social and political standards. They were an incremental improvement and deserve credit for setting limits to colonial brutality and instrumentalization of human life.

In a less sanguine vein, Rick Dyson points out that the Laws were written because "Spanish conquistadors had no qualms with torturing, killing, and raping natives in their quest for treasure."[10] Yet here again, the Laws' failure is posed as a gap between theory and practice: "Ideally, the natives were allowed to retain ownership of their lands, raise crops and livestock to feed themselves, and work only a small portion of time on the projects of their *encomenderos*. In practice however, the natives were overworked and exploited by the very Spaniards assigned to protect them."[11] Distracted by greed, the Spanish colonizers forgot their responsibility for converting their charges to Christianity.

Across the range of interpretations offered thus far, the Laws are seen as mitigating colonial conditions. I would argue instead that they were written to affirm and entrench coloniality and colonial legitimacy. In categorizing permitted forms of violence and their limits, the Laws envision a more sustainable, well-managed violent order.

Epistemological Breaks and Continuities

COLONIZATION RAISED new philosophical questions for imperial actors. There are thus certain stark discontinuities in European, and especially Iberian, thought from 1492 forward. While the political and economic ramifications are most obvious, María M. Portuondo has written of ways in which early New World encounters challenged established Spanish hermeneutics. Knowledge itself had to be reworked in areas of "vastly different magnitudes" and kinds. These challenges were more and less easily resolved, from Ptolemaic reasoning about which geographic regions were inhabitable to the overall "validity of the ancient philosophical canons to explain the world."[12] Portuondo notes that thinkers trained in Aristotelian natural philosophy sought to accommodate objects (or "products") from New Spain, for reasons ranging from curiosity to direct service for the purposes of empire.[13]

Yet important legal, theological, and philosophical precedents existed before colonization, and their accumulated modes of reasoning shaped justifications for Spanish colonization.[14] The multiple phases of crusades within Europe and targeting North Africa joined military strategies to religious philosophies of colonial expansion. To cite just a couple of instances: German emperors invaded Slavic territories, backed by "hierocratic canonical discourse" that justified the slaughter of pagan "infidels" if they posed any (perceived) threat to Christians. As these projects of conquest and conversion were being carried out, Emperor Frederick II (1194–1250) overturned historical reliance on Roman papal permission when he "proclaimed the power to destroy, convert, and subjugate all barbarian nations" in his role as Holy Roman emperor.[15]

Papal authority continued to be a nexus of controversy in the fourteenth century in debates about Lithuanian Christianization and the implications for sovereignty.[16] Pope Innocent IV in *Quod super his* declared "that infidels possessed the same natural-law rights as Christians."[17] Based on these arguments, jurist Paulus Vladimiri advocated in the early fifteenth century that the Knights Templar had no valid claim to Lithuania and that Poland should be given dominion over its governance and Christianization. Since the Lithuanians had committed no clear violations of natural law, he argued, they could not be subject to papal interference.[18]

The 1417 special commission that decided the matter set a standard that invasion, seizure of property, and conquest were not warranted in the Lithuanian case.[19] The decision, however, left significant room to justify those very acts. Official affirmation of the natural-law rights of infidels provided a framework and vocabulary for deciding when such rights were relinquished. Self-defense, for instance, was a lawful justification for war that was cited in the Reconquista. Colonial ventures into the Canary Islands were rationalized by "the 'nearly wild' Canarians [being] in obvious and continued violation of natural law."[20] While the balance of monarchical and papal power remained unsettled, legal norms emerged in these contexts that paved the way for philosophically justifying New World colonial projects.

Admitting the multiple ways in which one could narrate continuity and change, even in these sketchy allusions to wider contexts, raises an important caution against oversimplifying—historically or theoretically—the ways in which Spain was exceptional or precedent setting in its modes of conquest or colonial justifications. Such views, sometimes captured in so-called Black Legend and White Legend mythologies, not only involve

factual distortions but emphasize calculations of relative blame and inno-
cence that distract from direct interrogations of colonial ideologies.

The point is thus not to locate coloniality's origin in something specific
about Spanish thought and culture in order to assign ultimate responsibility for centuries of violence and oppression to a single source (the Black
Legend approach). I do wish to draw out underappreciated commonalities
between sixteenth-century Spanish religio-juridical reasoning and certain
ideas associated with Enlightenment philosophy, but this does not make
the former the sole, necessary cause of the latter. This effort also challenges
attempts to set Spanish coloniality and racial thinking apart from other,
particularly western European, forms presented as more collaborative or
somehow beneficial (as White Legend mythology would do). I especially
do not suppose that Spanish conquest was less exploitative, violent, or degrading than any other; colonial ideology presents many striking continuities across contexts. The precise content of the generalizations that can
be made, and the ways in which they ought to be nuanced or qualified in
particular instances, is necessarily an ongoing site of study.

Colonial Entanglements

SPANISH EPISTEMOLOGIES, even in early sixteenth-century Hispaniola,
were not uncontested in the colonial context. They were recorded and ar-
chived in ways that Indigenous Taíno thought was not, but both were active and operated with various degrees of conflict or synchronicity at different moments. José R. Oliver demonstrates that a network of political,
spiritual, and familial ties were woven by caciques (leaders) on Hispaniola
and Puerto Rico in the early 1500s. Thus, the web of cultural understanding into which Spanish colonizers stepped was simultaneously more diverse and more connected than they realized. This was true for spiritual
and metaphysical understandings as well. According to Oliver, Spanish
chroniclers "failed to realize (or did not care) that the caciques' conduct-
ing war and deciding on other important political actions required the
full engagement of . . . other partible and dividual nonhuman beings: the
cemí idols."[21] Oliver focuses on cemí-human relationships and the ways
they guided Taíno actors in their relations with Spaniards.

Whatever Spanish actors made of Taíno beliefs, they found it practi-
cally and strategically worthwhile to participate in Taíno rituals for select
purposes. The condition of indentured labor that had been established by
the time of the Laws of Burgos was a lopsided settlement that followed the

extremely brutal 1503–4 conquering of Higüey in Hispaniola. The framing of the conflict as a just war (because it erupted when cacique Cotubanamá led an attack on eight Spanish sailors, which was itself retribution for the murder of another cacique) was deployed as a rationale for enslaving Indigenous people as the private property of Spanish colonists.[22] The terror of battle and its losses led the caciques, including Cotubanamá, to agree to terms of surrender that stated that their people would serve and work for the Spaniards. This pact "was ceremonially sanctioned by a guaitiao ritual between Esquivel and Cotubanamá, a custom that was by now familiar to the Spanish."[23] This sort of participation would become another element of violation when colonizers failed to uphold agreements thus observed.[24]

While it is well known that Spanish intellectuals engaged early in colonial life with debates about the humanity of Indigenous persons and the implications for slavery, Oliver stresses Indigenous speculation about the inhuman strength and immortality of the Spanish.[25] This topic was taken up during the "secret war council meeting of the caciques . . . held in the winter of 1510, probably in the settlement of Agüeybana II."[26] In one experiment, an appointed delegation drowned a Spanish traveler in the Guaorabo River and observed the body's decomposition over the following days.[27]

In 1511, just one year before the Laws of Burgos, a cacique of Boriquén (Puerto Rico) named Agüeybana II ordered the execution of Spanish nobleman Cristobál de Sotomayor. Sotomayor had been granted Indians in encomienda but was discontented with his allotment and had directly broken "the pact cemented by name exchange and sister/wife-giving." These conflicts are generally cited as the reason for his killing, though Oliver claims it was also an extension of the investigation into Spanish mortality.[28] What is known with more certainty is that Sotomayor's ambush and execution were followed by an island-wide Indigenous uprising.[29] The political and strategic actions taken by Taínos show them grappling in multiple ways with the apparent imperviousness of Spanish persons to what they considered moral and physical human limitations.

This section is a small glimpse into the ways that Taíno thought posed moral and metaphysical challenges to Spanish Christian frameworks. (Taíno thought was and is much broader and more diverse than represented here; the term *Taíno* itself is debated because it risks overgeneralization.) And, just as important, Spanish actions violated the moral, physical, and metaphysical assumptions of Indigenous thinkers and actors. What I mean to convey in this section, echoing a point more thoroughly made by many Indigenous scholars, is that colonialist worldviews did not simply or (ever) fully replace the worldviews of those they colonized.[30] To the contrary, colonizers interacted and contended with Indigenous methods, practices, and ideas even as they steadily proclaimed the right to subsume others. The distinctive forms of thought that developed in this period of Spanish history, or history from Spanish perspectives, arose in such contexts of contentious engagement.[31]

This means that while I amplify resonances with philosophical sites spread across the eighteenth through twenty-first centuries, the Laws of Burgos have much more proximate past, present, and future relationships that must be considered in my own reading. This is an act of close reading with an eye to context. Its aims are genealogical in the Nietzschean-Foucauldian sense, in that it pursues a history of the present but retains significant uncertainty—an agnosticism, perhaps—about what, precisely, is thereby explained.

A glance at the intervening time period may be helpful. María Elena Martínez asserts that among colonial projects with their own respective economic, political, and religious agendas, the Spanish colonial world is characterized by having forged societal organization by "religion, lineage, and blood."[32] Her work explicates in depth how racial and biological logics were jointly configured in seventeenth-century Spanish imperial thought. These matrices of race and biology were also infused with religious reasoning about virtue, civilized religious practice, and potential for salvation. The Laws of Burgos are an important precursor to Martínez's study, as they laid groundwork for aligning evangelism with racialized labor structures in ways that posited shared but unequal humanity. A century after the Laws of Burgos, then, the issues of concern to the Laws' authors and addressees continued to hold a prominent place in moral, legal, and religious discourses. I take it as an open line of inquiry how and to what extent these frames of thought directly shape present-day versions of Euro- or Anglocentrism and white supremacy. At the same time, this period of colonial history would be essential in any attempt to construct a genealogy of settler nativist thought in the Americas.

Methodology and Animating Questions

A WORD ABOUT METHOD IS IN ORDER, since I am proposing to read a legal document as a philosophical and theological text. I would assert that a deconstructive, rhetorically oriented reading of this text is necessary to understand the conflicts it is trying to resolve and the structures of argument it seeks to legitimate. Yet it still might seem odd to examine a product of theological and juridical debate for its articulation of a worldview. Indeed, that the Laws of Burgos do not represent a consensus is key, because this demonstrates that they were decided in a field that contained other live options. Because the Laws are widely agreed to have lacked practical efficacy, their primary significance was the work they performed as a theoretical text. The Laws are not a record of what *was* but of what was justified. They record an instant in an intellectual process that constructed Christian morality and a spiritualized hierarchy to support, even demand, colonialist action. These hierarchies are sustained by a soteriological frame that equates Indigenous submission with salvation. They are, I would submit, a work of ideal theory imagined from one side of the relationship between colonized and colonizer.

The Laws' explicit aim of protection is bound up with rationalizations for exploitation, and the "rights" the Laws afford must be understood as fundamentally conditioned by this unequal and coercive arrangement. Insofar as the Laws are frequently cited as the basis for contemporary notions of human rights and international law, this analysis raises questions about the assumed power relationships embedded in that genealogy. That the Laws share structures of racial reasoning with eighteenth- and nineteenth-century sources raises additional challenges to common assumptions about the timeline along which racial ideas associated with either the Reformation or Enlightenment humanism might have developed. This chapter's discussion takes place amid lively and necessary debates about precisely when and how race developed in anything resembling its current form. At the same time, it urges recognition that ideas about race are constantly forming and re-forming. The history of racial thought provides pieces that are picked up, reworked, reiterated, and reanimated across time and space.

Racial categories were formulated differently in Renaissance and early modern Spain than in the contemporary United States and transnational contexts. What I suggest in this chapter is that something about the ways racial concepts form and spread today might echo or build on the former. This, again, is not about assigning ultimate blame for the past or present but opening up new avenues for accountability that recognize coloniality traveling through modes of discourse that we might be inclined to give the benefit of the doubt. This would point to political questions such as, When Indigenous rights are at stake, what baseline demands are made redemptive conditions for their recognition? What dimensions of justice are elided by the terms of negotiation? How do the presumed good intentions of actors driven by a colonialist mindset *still* operate in the service of racial, economic, and labor exploitation?

Behind such practical concerns is a set of philosophical inquiries about theological inheritance. What difference does it make that violence is carried out in the name of salvation (rather than for bare material motives)? Why are those who exploit so frequently preoccupied with establishing their *moral* rightness in doing so? How are these questions both symptomatic of tensions within philosophy of religion and philosophical problems to be analyzed?

More specifically for the context at hand, what is the philosophical import of insisting that the Indians are not slaves? What is the extant philosophical valence of the desire to recover the Laws as a document of rights rather than blunt exploitation? How are these forms of philosophy also philosophies *of* religion? I hope to collect and magnify points of both clarity and contradiction within the Laws themselves—not in order to fully answer these questions but to sharpen the lenses through which they can be repeatedly, continually asked.

Exegesis

Whereas, the King, my Lord and Father, and the Queen, my Mistress and Mother (may she rest in glory!), have desired that the chiefs and Indians of the Island of Española be brought to a knowledge of our Holy Catholic Faith, and,

. . .

Whereas, it has become evident through long experience that nothing has sufficed to bring the said chiefs and Indians to a Knowledge of our Faith (necessary for their salvation), since by nature they are inclined to idleness and vice [*porque de su natural son ynclinados a oçosidad e malos visyos*], and have no manner of virtue or doctrine (by which Our Lord is disserved), and that the principal obstacle in the way of correcting their vices and having them profit by and impressing them with the doctrine is that their dwellings are remote from the settlements of the Spaniards.—Laws of Burgos

THE PROCLAIMED PURPOSE of the Laws of Burgos is to instruct the "chiefs [cacyques, or caciques] and Indians" in Catholic doctrine and practice.[33] Its logical premise is that the Indians' physical distance from the Spaniards poses an insurmountable obstacle to their religious instruction. These difficulties are claimed to be fundamentally rooted in Indigenous persons' "nature," which is declared predisposed to immorality and laziness. Indeed, this preamble to the Laws claims that their only reason for returning to their own villages after working is "to do with themselves what they will, without any regard for virtue" (*para hazer de sy lo que les biene a la boluntad syn aver rrespeto a ninguna cosa de birtud*).[34] Nature directs behavior without mediation, and not only do Taínos allow it to govern, but they actively and consciously will for it to do so.

That coerced laborers would wish to be left alone when not working is interpreted as a lack of virtue and a rejection of Christian faith. While their nature is cited as the root source of difference from Europeans, some aspect of the given situation is deemed mutable because the proposed solution is an immanent one. What is needed is uninterrupted education that directly imparts doctrine and constant contact with living examples of virtue. The main resolution of the Laws, as articulated by the preamble, is to relocate Indigenous persons to live near Spanish settlements. "Therefore, for these reasons and for many others that could be adduced, it was agreed that for the improvement and remedy of all the aforesaid, the said chiefs and Indians should forthwith be brought to dwell near the villages and communities of the Spaniards who inhabit the Island, so that they may be treated and taught and looked after as is right and as we have always desired."[35] Proximity to colonizers is presented as a remedy for the "evils and hardships" presently faced by the Indians, and the relationship of exploitation is framed as one of patronage and tutelage.[36] Any mention of Spanish interests apart from the physical and spiritual salvation of others is notably absent.

If it seems glaringly obvious that the desire to move Indigenous persons into a closer orbit of Spanish control was not philanthropic, it is still worth asking why the authors of the Laws went to such rhetorical trouble. Why, in short, is there a (perceived) need to frame the exploitative promotion of Spanish economic and ideological interests as benevolence? This is not only a matter of sincerity, of the extent of deceit or delusion on the part of the Laws' authors. It is also a question about the requirements of the theological reasoning to which they feel themselves bound.

The expression of exasperation with which the Laws begin, that "nothing has sufficed" to lead the Indians to adopt the Christian faith and virtue, points to the ways in which spiritual care as conceived by the council at Burgos resembles and requires cultural assimilation. Several provisions require direct religious instruction in doctrine, including instruction and (forced) practice in "the Ten Commandments and the Seven Deadly Sins and the Articles of the Faith, that is, to those he thinks have the capacity and ability to learn them." The Laws declare that progress in acquiring this knowledge should be closely tracked and regularly examined, "but all this shall be done with great love and gentleness."[37] This is, I would argue, a key intervention of the Laws of Burgos. Insofar as they were conceived in response to the moral crisis passionately outlined by Antonio de Montesinos in his 1511 Christmas Eve sermon (referenced above and in the following), the Laws strive to reconcile domination with Christian love.

Conversion in the Laws of Burgos's context was both moral and cultural. Spiritual care was joined tightly to assimilatory demands for Indigenous persons to acquire certain practices and abandon others. The Laws order the construction of churches and the overseeing of Indians' daily attendance at prayers. Not only must they be made to attend, but "the person who has them in encomienda shall be obliged" to see that they "cross themselves and bless themselves, and together recite the *Ave Maria*, the *Pater Noster*, the *Credo*, and the *Salve Regina*." The overseeing party should observe how well the prayers are recited and "correct the one who is wrong."[38] Mass and feast days as well as confession are instructed to be observed with priests when at all possible. And these special days ought to be marked by providing better food than on other days of the week.[39] The proposal is one of tight control over bodily expression and experience, and the Laws charge Spanish estate holders to ensure that Indians become participatory agents in Christian observance as they receive knowledge and instruction.

In some instances, the Laws' authors cite the importance of adhering to aspects of Indian culture and an Indigenous worldview. Hierarchies internal to Indian societal arrangements are to be reflected in giving those of higher rank lighter work tasks. Caciques and their wives ought to be better dressed than others, and their sons "shall be given to the friars of the Order of St. Francis who may reside on the said Island" to receive education in reading, writing, and "our Holy Catholic Faith." The assumption is that the sons, after four years of instruction, will be qualified to teach others, "for the Indians will accept it more readily from them."[40] These accommodations of Indigenous social structures are considered instrumental to the larger project of training Indigenous subjects into new roles and beliefs. A more ambiguous concession is that "since we have been informed that if the Indians are not allowed to perform their customary dances [*areytos*] they will receive great harm," performances are allowed on Sundays, feast days, and any time they can be observed without compromising their assigned labor.[41]

Spanish perceptions of Indigenous gender, such as the role of sons or the treatment of caciques' wives, raises questions about how legible or shared understandings of gender and family were between Spanish and Taíno actors. Among those who have given sustained attention to Taíno formulations of gender, the scholarly consensus is that while there were some typical divisions of roles and labor according to both class and gender, "gender roles among the Taíno were generally nonexclusive in most activities, ranging from political leadership and fighting as warriors to food and craft production."[42] The more rigid gender structures to which the colonizers subscribed both altered Indigenous practices and read their "prior" state through culturally particular lenses.

The Laws carefully prescribe what Indians' religious, cultural, and familial activities ought to look like, citing concern that their obligated work not interfere with their bodily well-being or spiritual salvation. The Laws are concerned with guaranteeing appropriate rest, limiting the time that Indians held in encomienda could be made to work in gold mines (five months a year, followed by forty days of rest during which they would still plant food for their own subsistence and receive religious instruction).[43] They declare that Indians who are seriously ill must receive confession and last rites from priests, who "shall go with a Cross to the Indians who die and shall bury them."[44] Infants must be baptized "within a week of birth or before, if it is necessary," thus assuring their eternal fate.[45]

These protective guidelines are bound up with non-spiritual measures that reflect European customs and aesthetics. Any Spanish settler given Indians in encomienda is "obliged to give to each of them a hammock in which to sleep continually; and they shall not allow them to sleep on the ground, as hitherto they have been doing."[46] There is also a mandatory clothing allowance that is to be given to each Indian once a year (one gold peso).[47] The practical and spiritual furthermore intertwine in ways that conflate cultural norms with morality. The Laws, for instance, prescribe monogamous and permanent matrimony as the only appropriate kind, specifying "that they may not take wives related to them"; they name this a matter of salvation.[48] The Laws are thus concerned not only with bodily survival and Christian conversion but with inculcating ways of living—forms of kinship, modes of dress, and manner of sleep—that would mirror Spanish examples.

Some of the passages overtly concerned with care or rights might reflect pragmatic concerns about maintaining a labor force. For instance, pregnant women and mothers of young children are to be kept out of the mines and away from planting, activities considered dangerous for the infants. It bears noting, first, that women would still be expected to work during these times ("kept on the estates and utilized in household tasks") and, second, that Indigenous reproduction would have been a source of future laborers.[49] Finally, all of the Laws' protections are valid "unless they are slaves, for these may be treated by their owner as he pleases."[50] The Laws are meant to limit certain types of abuses toward a certain class of forced workers. They do not, however, entail a recognition of universal humanity or inalienable human rights.

What is ultimately most striking about the rhetoric of the Laws is their casual juxtaposition of declared concern for Indians' well-being with calculated ways to control as much of Indigenous life as possible. While the explicit rationale is care for their good treatment and salvation, these are considered compatible with—and even require—layered forms of violence. The same Indians who are to be attended to when sick and fed adequately are also to be forced from their homes (which will be destroyed), made to study and practice Christianity, and monitored in nearly every aspect of life.[51] It can be debated whether the Laws' real motives were solely economic, cynically covered over with spiritual care, but that is not my aim. Whether or not Spanish authorities truly believed their mission to be the furtherance of Catholic salvation (and this no doubt varied among the relevant actors), the Laws of Burgos accept and seek to extend the legitimacy of captive labor.

Situating the Laws in Philosophies of Religion

ON DECEMBER 24, 1511, Fray Antonio de Montesinos preached the famous sermon in which he excoriated his colonial Hispaniola audience for mortal sins of cruelty and neglect toward Indigenous people. Bartolomé de las Casas was in attendance and records the Dominican monk Montesinos as having said, "And why don't you look after their spiritual health, so that they should come to know God, and they should be baptized, and that they should hear Mass and keep the holy days? Aren't they human beings? Have they no rational soul? Aren't you obliged to love them as you love yourselves?"[52] This sermon is widely thought to have galvanized the anxieties and energies that led to the Laws of Burgos.[53] Its declarations that "these innocent people" are human, rational, and entitled to love assert certain forms of universalism and equality. The sermon railed against the Indians' enslavement, oppression, and neglect in illness, bemoaning that the Spanish colonists would "work them to death to satisfy [their] greed."[54] Humanity and rationality are cited as *shared* by colonizers and colonized and as mandating against oppression (though, crucially, not efforts at conversion). This prefigures Enlightenment suppositions of the universal capacity to reason, as well as the proposition that rational humanity ought to be the basis for self-governance and freedom.

At the same time, these criteria could be seen as providing the terms by which self-governance and freedom could be contested or revoked. If a people were found not to be innocent or rational, their humanity might be questioned or scaled accordingly. Kant called, on the one hand, for recognition of a united purpose and destiny for the "human species."[55] Yet he explicitly conceived of a condition in which those with higher attainment of reason, civilization, and morality would rightfully govern others.[56] A universal capacity for reason, developed unequally among individuals and races, was the classical nineteenth-century justification for indefinite, in Uday Singh Mehta's words "infinitely patient," imperial domination.[57]

The Laws of Burgos are written for a context in which Spanish conquest subjected Indigenous communities to mass death from massacres, disease, and forced labor. The Laws signal awareness of these facts and a measure of concern but work to maintain and justify the existing structures of power and labor. Not only was the issue of Indigenous humanity not resolved with the passage of the Laws (as discussed in Mayra Rivera's contribution to this volume), but the recognition and "good treatment" they prescribe calls for new forms of violence: uprooting Indigenous people from their homes and destroying their villages, coercively imposing Christian indoctrination, and forcing assimilation to European standards of dress, diet, and family structure—even sleep. The humanity afforded to Indians by the Laws of Burgos is partial and conditional, as concerned with the self-degradation of Spanish oppressors as with the harm to those oppressed.

Even as they evidently serve Spanish self-interest, the Laws strive to create a colonizing self-image that can hold the colonizers as the Indians' rightful instructors and governors. The overlaps between economic, political, ideological, and religious motivations caution against an assessment that the Laws were unconcerned with Spanish morality. Yet the Laws did not make Indigenous persons human, nor colonizers humane—

even by colonizing standards. Their shortcomings in granting human rights and humane treatment were not a gap between theory and practice but a structural component of their internal logic.

This argument strongly resembles anticolonial critiques of modern liberalism, which usually examine European thought from the seventeenth century forward. Martínez points out that Spanish colonialism forged a type of universalism that preceded and foreshadowed aspects of "the politics of nationhood, liberalism, and Enlightenment."[58] In her work with British colonial archives, Lisa Lowe has expressed the trouble with liberalism as a contradictory universalism because, "in the very claim to define humanity, as a species or as a condition, its gestures of definition divide the human and the nonhuman, to classify the normative and pathologize deviance."[59] In continuity with the demands the Laws of Burgos laid on Indigenous people's bodily conduct, labor, and appearance, Lowe observes that, "while violence characterizes exclusion from the universality of the human, it also accompanies inclusion or assimilation into it."[60] This chapter has endeavored to make clear the violence behind inclusion in a preliberal context, challenging, albeit indirectly, attempts to draw stark distinctions between the multiple ideologies that animated *and continue to animate* coloniality.

By loosening these temporal divisions, the philosophical dimensions of coloniality rise to the surface. Yet this is also an argument about temporality itself and the ways that the violence of racialization and coloniality repeats and continues. "The operations that pronounce colonial divisions of humanity—settler seizure and Native removal, slavery and racial dispossession, and racialized expropriations of many kinds—are imbricated processes, not sequential events; they are ongoing and continuous in our contemporary moment, not temporally distinct nor as yet concluded."[61] This emphasis on imbrication rather than progression, relation rather than comparison, is where I would locate both the importance of the Laws of Burgos and the larger effort to which this chapter contributes.

Colonial and racial baggage trails the language of human rights. There are certainly contexts today in which calls for human rights are part of crucial advocacy strategies to mobilize justice on behalf of persons without other forms of legal standing (such as citizenship or nonincarceration). Language with a problematic history can still serve an important role in making harm recognizable and even in making substantive claims about what would constitute justice. However, humanization still frequently requires legible evidence of rationality and morality.[62] And the structure of thought in which natural endowments generate hierarchies of humanity does not make a clean jump from Aristotle to Kant. The Laws are one site along the way at which racial and civilizational ideals are molded anew.

Notes

1 *Encyclopædia Britannica Online*, Academic ed., s.v. "Indies, Laws of the," accessed October 30, 2018, https://www.britannica.com/event/Laws-of-the-Indies.
2 Valle, "José de Acosta," 22.
3 See, for instance, Schippers, *Critical Perspectives on Human Rights*.
4 Chuchiak, "Laws of Burgos," 1:184.
5 Dussel, *Teología de la liberación*, 11, cited in Petrella, "Intellectual Roots of Liberation Theology," 359.
6 Petrella, "Intellectual Roots of Liberation Theology," 360.
7 Petrella, "Intellectual Roots of Liberation Theology," 360.
8 A similar discourse attaches to the writings and preaching of Francisco de Vitoria (and, beyond Spanish contexts, the work of Hugo Grotius), also commonly cited as originating international law. Vitoria's *De Indes Noviter Inventis* (1532), like the Laws of Burgos, asserted certain Indigenous rights while ultimately affirming conquest itself. Kinsella, *Image before the Weapon*, 61–63. Anghie, "Francisco De Vitoria." Thanks to J. Kameron Carter for our discussion on this point.
9 Simpson, *Encomienda in New Spain*, 50.
10 Dyson, "Law of Burgos," 212.
11 Dyson, "Law of Burgos," 213.
12 Portuondo, "America and the Hermeneutics of Nature," 78.
13 Portuondo, "America and the Hermeneutics of Nature," 80–82.
14 At the same time, there was never a univocal Spanish consensus about the colonial project's justifications. Mayra Rivera's chapter picks up on some of the ways that questions about Spanish sovereignty, Indigenous humanity, and Indigenous rights continued to be debated in the decades following the period I focus on here.
15 Williams, *American Indian*, 61.
16 Williams, *American Indian*, 62–63.
17 Williams, *American Indian*, 64–65.
18 Williams, *American Indian*, 66–67.
19 Williams, *American Indian*, 66–67.
20 Williams, *American Indian*, 67, 70.
21 Oliver, *Caciques and Cemí Idols*, 193.
22 Oliver, *Caciques and Cemí Idols*, 195.
23 Oliver, *Caciques and Cemí Idols*, 196.

24 Oliver, *Caciques and Cemí Idols*, 197.

25 As early as 1495, "experts" were trying to determine Indigenous people's ontological and legal status ("el estatuto ontológico y jurídico de los indios"). Sagarra Gamazo, "El indigenismo castellano," 58.

26 Oliver, *Caciques and Cemí Idols*, 207.

27 Oliver, *Caciques and Cemí Idols*, 208.

28 Name exchanges and "women giving" were modes by which caciques solidified agreements with one another and were also used in relations with Spanish officials. Oliver, *Caciques and Cemí Idols*, 191. That Indigenous women would have thus entered into Spanish family structures is significant, especially since one of the concerns of religious and political authorities in the Laws of Burgos is to enforce European rules about marriage and kinship, as described in the following analysis.

29 Oliver, *Caciques and Cemí Idols*, 209–10.

30 This argument is made pointedly and poignantly in Palmer, "Devil in the Details."

31 See also Anderson-Córdova, *Surviving Spanish Conquest*.

32 Martínez, *Genealogical Fictions*, 16.

33 This section uses a Spanish version of the text with its original spellings as well as an English translation: Altamira, "Texto de las Leyes de Burgos"; and *Laws of Burgos*.

34 *Laws of Burgos*, 12; Altamira, "Texto de las Leyes de Burgos," 24.

35 *Laws of Burgos*, 14.

36 *Laws of Burgos*, 14.

37 *Laws of Burgos*, 18.

38 *Laws of Burgos*, 17.

39 *Laws of Burgos*, 19, 20.

40 *Laws of Burgos*, 26–27, 29.

41 *Laws of Burgos*, 25.

42 Deagan, "Reconsidering Taíno Social Dynamics," 602.

43 *Laws of Burgos*, 24.

44 *Laws of Burgos*, 22.

45 *Laws of Burgos*, 23.

46 *Laws of Burgos*, 28.

47 *Laws of Burgos*, 29.

48 *Laws of Burgos*, 26.

49 *Laws of Burgos*, 27.

50 *Laws of Burgos*, 34.

51 "I command you, our said Admiral officers and judges and officers, to have the lodges of the said villages burned, since the Indians will have no further use for them: this so they will have no reason to return from whence they have been brought." *Laws of Burgos*, 16.

52 Quoted in Aspinall, introduction to *Montesinos' Legacy*, 2.

53 Shortly after word of the sermon reached him, the king assembled a junta of theologians and jurists who produced the Laws of Burgos. It is also the case, however, that a junta was called to Burgos significantly earlier, in 1508, to discuss bureaucratic reorganization in New Spain. Sagarra Gamazo, "El indigenismo castellano," 64. The Laws, indeed, seem to be the product of a series of inquiries and debates that proceeded for a decade before their issuance.

54 Aspinall, introduction to *Montesinos' Legacy*, 2.

55 Kant, "Idea for a Universal History," 21.

56 "For if one starts from *Greek* history . . . then one will discover a regular course of improvement of state constitutions in our part of the world (which will probably someday give laws to all the others)." Kant, "Idea for a Universal History," 21. Aristotelian resonances, particularly with regard to natural qualifications for governance and servitude, pervade the Laws more broadly. My thanks to An Yountae for noting that they are heightened at this particular point. Lesley Byrd Simpson notes that this Aristotelianism was heavily inflected by feudal hierarchical conventions, the "principle of *commendatio*" allowing encomenderos to imagine their governance as imitating or mirroring royal forms. Simpson, in *Laws of Burgos*, 2, 10.

57 Mehta, *Liberalism and Empire*, 30.

58 Martínez, *Genealogical Fictions*, 15.

59 Lowe, *Intimacies of Four Continents*, 6.

60 Lowe, *Intimacies of Four Continents*, 6.

61 Lowe, *Intimacies of Four Continents*, 7.

62 This is evident today in the arguments made by advocates for immigrant rights who urge that Central Americans migrating northward into Mexico and the United States are making an eminently reasonable choice—often in desperation and with the moral weight of protecting one's family or forgoing criminality.

Bibliography

Altamira, Rafael. "El texto de las Leyes de Burgos de 1512." *Revista Historia de América* 4 (1938): 5–79.

Anderson-Córdova, Karen Frances. *Surviving Spanish Conquest: Indian Fight, Flight, and Cultural Transformation in Hispaniola and Puerto Rico*. Tuscaloosa: University of Alabama Press, 2017.

Anghie, Antony. "Francisco De Vitoria and the Colonial Origins of International Law." *Social and Legal Studies* 5, no. 3 (September 1996): 321–36.

Aspinall, Diana E. Introduction to *Montesinos' Legacy: Defining and Defending Human Rights for 500 Years*, edited by Diana E. Aspinall, Edward C. Lorenz, and J. Michael Raley, 1–16. Lanham, MD: Lexington Books, 2014.

Chuchiak, John F., IV. "Laws of Burgos." In *Encyclopedia of Latin America: Amerindians through the Age of Globalization*, edited by J. Michael Francis, 1:183–84. New York: Facts on File, 2010.

Deagan, Kathleen. "Reconsidering Taíno Social Dynamics after Spanish Conquest: Gender and Class in Culture Contact Studies." *American Antiquity* 69, no. 4 (2004): 597–626.

Dussel, Enrique. *Teología de la liberación: Un panorama de su desarrollo*. Mexico City: Potrerillos, 1995.

Dyson, Rick. "Law of Burgos." In *Conflict in the Early Americas: An Encyclopedia of the Spanish Empire's Aztec, Incan, and Mayan Conquests*, edited by Rebecca M. Seaman, 212–14. Santa Barbara, CA: ABC-CLIO, 2013.

Kant, Immanuel. "Idea for a Universal History with a Cosmopolitan Aim." In *Kant's Idea for a Universal History with a Cosmopolitan Aim: A Critical Guide*, translated by Allen Wood, edited by Amélie Oksenberg Rorty and James Schmidt, 9–23. Cambridge: Cambridge University Press, 2009.

Kinsella, Helen M. *The Image before the Weapon*. Ithaca, NY: Cornell University Press, 2011.

Laws of Burgos 1512–1513: Royal Ordinances for the Government and Good Treatment of the Indians. Translated by Lesley Byrd Simpson. San Francisco: J. Howell, 1990.

Lowe, Lisa. *The Intimacies of Four Continents*. Durham, NC: Duke University Press, 2015.

Martínez, María Elena. *Genealogical Fictions: Limpieza de Sangre, Religion, and Gender in Colonial Mexico*. Stanford, CA: Stanford University Press, 2008.

Mehta, Uday Singh. *Liberalism and Empire: A Study in Nineteenth-Century British Liberal Thought*. Chicago: University of Chicago Press, 1999.

Oliver, José R. *Caciques and Cemí Idols: The Web Spun by Taino Rulers between Hispaniola and Puerto Rico*. Tuscaloosa: University of Alabama Press, 2009.

Palmer, Vera B. "The Devil in the Details: Controverting an American Indian Conversion Narrative." In *Theorizing Native Studies*, edited by Audra Simpson and Andrea Smith, 266–96. Durham, NC: Duke University Press, 2014.

Petrella, Ivan. "The Intellectual Roots of Liberation Theology." In *The Cambridge History of Religions in Latin America*, edited by Virginia Garrard-Burnett, Paul Freston, and Stephen C. Dove, 359–71. Cambridge: Cambridge University Press, 2016.

Portuondo, María M. "America and the Hermeneutics of Nature in Renaissance Europe." In *Global Goods and the Spanish Empire, 1492–1824*, edited by

Bethany Eram and Bartolomé Yun-Casalilla, 78–99. Basingstoke, UK: Palgrave Macmillan, 2014.

Sagarra Gamazo, Adelaida. "El indigenismo castellano (1492–1524)." In *Leyes de Burgos de 1512: V Centenario*, edited by Rafael Sánchez Domingo and Fernando Suárez Bilbao, 51–88. Madrid: Dykinson, 2012.

Schippers, Birgit, ed. *Critical Perspectives on Human Rights*. London: Rowman and Littlefield, 2018.

Simpson, Lesley Byrd. *The Encomienda in New Spain: Forced Native Labor in the Spanish Colonies, 1492–1550*. Berkeley: University of California Press, 1929.

Valle, Ivonne del. "José de Acosta: Colonial Regimes for a Global Christian World." In *Coloniality, Religion, and the Law in the Early Iberian World*, edited by Raúl Marrero-Fente and Santa Arias, 3–26. Nashville, TN: Vanderbilt University Press, 2013.

Williams, Robert A. *The American Indian in Western Legal Thought: The Discourses of Conquest*. New York: Oxford University Press, 1990.

Vincent Lloyd

4 The Puritan Atheism of C. L. R. James

C. L. R. JAMES was the preeminent Black revolutionary theorist of the twentieth century. He was also an atheist and a rapist. As an octogenarian, he dictated to his helper, a white woman in her twenties, twin confessions, one of his deconversion from Christianity and one of his youthful violence against women. How are these three badges—revolutionary, atheist, and rapist—connected? The easy answer would be to talk about the hubris and machismo that necessarily accompany political and religious leadership. To imagine you know the path to revolution, to overthrowing the ways of the world altogether, necessarily places you in a godlike position, disposing you to place yourself over others, be they comrades, gods, or, all too often, women.[1] Yet the case of James cannot be explained so easily. The novelty and power of his account of revolution lies in its rejection of the agency of the professional revolutionary, ceding the role of revolutionary protagonist to the subaltern and trenchantly attacking those revolutionaries who would understand themselves as inseminators of the revolution. James is serious about his atheism, not just as a rejection of God but as a thoroughgoing critique of all substitute gods, including himself—at least in theory. What, then, can we make of his rape confession? I suggest that we read this as part of James's sense of tragedy. I do not mean a tragic outlook in general but the specific tragic condition faced by the middle classes understood broadly: those individuals formed by systems of domination but neither the prime beneficiaries nor the prime victims of domination. This is the situation of James himself: a middle-class colonial subject formed in the Christian virtues and educated in the European classics. For James, the middle-class subject must become a revolutionary but cannot become a revolutionary: the best efforts at this transformation will go deeply wrong, as evidenced by James's confessed violence against women.

There was never a better atheist than James. At least this, *atheism*, is one way of characterizing his life's work in philosophy. If we say that Ludwig Feuerbach inverted Georg Wilhelm Friedrich Hegel, placing the absolute in Man rather than above him, with the divine merely a projection of Man's ideals, and that Karl Marx attacked the absolute within Man, leaving the human to flourish in the world without any abstractions whatsoever, James goes one step further. If Feuerbach's inversion pushed Hegel toward atheism, and Marx pushed Feuerbach toward a more complete atheism, James explicates Marx in a way that completes the purge of theism's remnants. He and his colleagues spent a great deal of time reflecting on this move of Marx's; indeed, it was they who first translated and disseminated Marx's crucial early writings in English. Who was this human that remained after Feuerbach's deified Man, stripped of ideals, embracing species being? Marx offers rather apophatic reflections, making suggestions as to what the human in socialism is not, plus descriptions that are really more words of praise for this status than precise characterizations.

In an era of humanism, when the problem of Man was on the lips of many (even if this mainly consisted of reiterating that there was some such problem), it was tempting to read Marx's early writings as part of a humanist canon. But this would be to refuse what distinguishes Marx from Feuerbach and to reduce the seriousness of Marx's atheism. James set out to add content to the human in a way that cuts off the possibility of humanism. Atheism at its finest: he sought to dethrone the last of the gods, the last of the sovereigns, our belief in ourselves as gods, as sovereigns. This idolatry arises when the human who remains after the defeat of Man—after all the supposedly universal but actually culturally and psychologically specific traits associated with Man are stripped away—is static, just there. Marx's reluctance to fill out socialist humanity can be read as an apophatic instinct, and apophaticism encourages such stasis: the object (the human) about which we speak, which our words negate and praise, just stands on a pedestal, as it were, venerated.

The human, however, is not static but active, and activity is at the heart of what makes the human human. Abstraction obscures this, giving the human a list of qualities and ascribing these to Man (or God). But *activity* itself is a rather mysterious term; what can it mean? The slogan about *doing* rather than *being* is more evocative than illuminating and so would not seem much of an advance beyond apophasis. James makes three points by way of clarification. First, activity means *social* practice, doing together rather than just doing. Second, activity means struggle. This is because of the way the world is. The Christian might say fallen. Others might say tragic. Here, James remembers his Hegel. Human activity does not mean struggling against the world; rather, activity is defined by the friction produced by activity itself. Every time one sets out to accomplish this or that, unexpected results follow, prompting more activity, prompting more unexpected results—and this is activity's essence. Otherwise, activity would be wheels spinning without touching the ground, which is to say, again, abstraction, taking *this* step based on *these* reasons to achieve *that* desired outcome, which (supposedly) is necessarily achieved.

Third, activity takes place against the background of domination. The forces of capitalism and their representatives can never properly be described as participating in human activity. They are striving to live in a world of abstraction, a world where instrumental reason has the last word. Such a capitalist logic, such ideology, attempts to color the whole world, for everyone. Activity names resistance. Whatever activity may look like at the *eschaton*—spending all day painting, singing songs, and eating ambrosia—is of no interest in this world; if anything, it distracts. For the world is doubly fallen: not only is it riven with contradictions, but there are interconnected systems of domination that seek to make those contradictions invisible. Activity means struggling together against all those forces that would suppress contradiction, that is, against the forces of capitalism, which make capitalism appear as an earthly god and which attempt to cloud the distinction between domination and resistance. (While James places particular emphasis on capitalism as *the* fundamental system of domination, one of his innovations in Marxist theory was elevating the role of racial domination to something like coequal status, and he shows an openness to treating other systems of domination, such as patriarchy, similarly.)

It would be improper to say these insights were new to James, for in the Marxist tradition all are interpreters of Marx, explicating what Marx already said so rightly, unpacking it for readers of the day—as the Christian theologian only interprets the scripture and tradition that have come before, unpacking rather than innovating. James and his colleagues claimed no more. Their task was to uncover the core of Marx's method and to apply it to the present day. The gods that Marx fought would inevitably reappear in new guises, and his atheism must again be embraced so that these avatars could be smashed as idols. For James, this meant telling a story of the present day in which human activity, what he would sometimes call the "self-activity of workers," contested the forces of capitalism, what he would sometimes call "official society." (Again, *capitalism* should be read as more or less interchangeable with all interlocking systems of domination, including racism.) This is the grand struggle of world history: the human is not revealed at the end of history, after the defeat of capitalism, but already exists in history, as capitalism is contested. The new society exists within the old. "Our task then is to recognize the new society, align ourselves with it, and record the facts of its existence."[2] The first-person pronoun here refers to the revolutionary, the committed Marxist, and here is the seismic shift in Marxism that James champions. He agrees that the proletariat is the agent of history (the proletariat is where the self-activity of workers is most powerfully found), but he takes this proposition even more seriously than his contemporaries. To posit that a party or a set of revolutionaries is an agent of history is to commit a new idolatry, he charges. Revolutionaries must fully subordinate themselves to the new society, proto-socialism, that already exists in the world today wherever workers are struggling together against capitalism, for example, on the factory floor. If we read James broadly, *capitalism* stands for interlocking systems of domination, so struggle means struggle against any of these systems: not only against capitalism and its representatives in the factory but also against racism, sexism, colonialism, ableism, and much else.

James was developing these ideas in the United States from the late 1930s to the early 1950s, when he was at his intellectual prime.[3] He wrote his two great literary works before (*The Black Jacobins*, on the Haitian Revolution) and after (*Beyond a Boundary*, on cricket) this time, but his political-philosophical thought reached its culmination in between. James was born in Trinidad in 1901 to a middle-class family invested in learning; his father was a schoolteacher. James left Trinidad for England in 1932 having read widely, taught, and begun literary writing of his own, and he had developed the typical colonial ambivalence toward the metropole. He had political intuitions—against British colonial rule, on the side of the working classes, like the subject of his first nonfiction book, the Trinidadian labor leader Arthur Cipriani—but not a political-philosophical project.[4] This he received, in excess, from the British left, first Communists, then Trotskyites. They had a ready-made political-philosophical system into which James could place his intuitions, and they had a set of periodicals and institutions in which James's political formation could continue and his intellectual life could flourish. The great product of this period was his book *The Black Jacobins*, and in this work his own distinctive political voice, running beyond the Trotskyite line, was clearly evident. James narrated a finely textured story of poor Black Haitians as agents of history, struggling against the domination of the colonial government, all of the wealthy and much of the middle classes, and the racially privileged. No revolutionary party was needed to motivate or guide the poor Black Haitians: the forces of domination were enough motivation, and the skills of resistance naturally acquired in contexts of domination were enough guidance. In other words, good organizing does not need outside guidance, just fidelity to the experience of those enduring domination.

In 1938, James came to the United States to lecture; visited Leon Trotsky in Mexico, where they debated the role of Blacks in the Marxist movement; and decided to remain in the United States. He organized farmers in Missouri and participated in some other on-the-ground political activity, but for the most part he immersed himself in a world of ideas and surrounded himself with an eclectic group of like-minded intellectuals, most notably Raya Dunayevskaya, a Russian Jew who had been Trotsky's assistant, and Grace Lee (later Boggs), a Chinese American organizer who had recently obtained a doctorate in philosophy. By collaborating intensely and tapping new theoretical resources, with Lee translating Hegel and Marx from the German and Dunayevskaya translating Vladimir Lenin from the Russian, these three became the leading lights in what became known as the Johnson-Forest tendency of the Trotskyite movement. They produced hundreds of pages of political-philosophical reflections, printed pamphlets and books, and built an organization aimed at putting their ideas into practice. During these years, through this collaborative process, the most innovative and rigorous ideas associated with James came together. These ideas are most clearly expressed in the book *Facing Reality*, written with clarity and urgency because it was motivated by the Hungarian Revolution.[5]

Eventually, this fruitful period of collaboration would end. Dunayevskaya and Lee would take their organizing work to Detroit, and eventually each would go their own way, taking handfuls of followers with them.

James was a victim of the Red Scare: he was deported in 1953 but not before writing a study of Herman Melville during his immigration detention and having it sent to each U.S. congressperson.[6] James would try his hand at West Indian politics, assisting his former student and the first prime minister of Trinidad, Eric Williams, and would lecture widely, but he ended his life largely alone in a small London apartment. After leaving the United States and his comrades, James's thought lost its verve; he would write cultural criticism that drew on fragments of the magisterial intellectual project he had developed in the United States, but his time as a contributor to political philosophy had ended.

What was happening during those decisive years for James's thought? The Trotskyites were struggling to articulate what was going wrong with the Soviet Union, and just how wrong. Since Trotsky's expulsion and Joseph Stalin's alignment with Winston Churchill and Franklin Delano Roosevelt in the war, it was clear something must be gravely amiss with the Soviet project. James and his colleagues had been pushing Trotskyites to recognize the centrality of the self-activity of the working class when history seemingly proved them right. In 1956, Polish and then Hungarian workers attempted to seize control of the means of production without the help of a guiding party, indeed against that party, locating power at the local level, in workers' councils, rather than in the state. With the exuberance of theorists proved right, James and his colleagues wrote *Facing Reality*, their pointed meditation on the significance and implications of centering political philosophy on the self-activity of workers.

"The whole world today lives in the shadow of state power," they begin. "It transforms the human personality into a mass of economic needs to be satisfied by decimal points of economic progress" (1). For them, state power was just as much a problem if the state was the United States or the Soviet Union, "One-Party State or Welfare State." Despite the rhetoric of these states, in them the people no longer govern, and the state is set up as a god.[7] It is the state that governs the people, bureaucracy that rules. Yet the state does not have the last word. "Against this monster, people all over the world, and particularly ordinary working people in factories, mines, fields, and offices, are rebelling every day in ways of their own invention" (5). There, in the self-activity of working people directed against the domination of bureaucracy in both its democratic and Communist forms, we find the new society: socialism.

There is no need for intellectuals with special knowledge to catalyze the masses. Indeed, with the advance of capitalism, intellectuals are more and more becoming technicians, effectively bureaucrats aligned with state interests. To gather intellectuals, even organic intellectuals, in anything like a traditional revolutionary party would only sever "workers with an instinct for leadership from the masses" (10). The revolutionary party promises to teach workers how to fight capitalism, but workers already possess this knowledge. It promises to instill discipline so that struggle can proceed collectively and strategically. But the working class is already disciplined by the process of work itself in a way that can be mobilized for collective action. There is no need to impose extra discipline; if such discipline is necessary, it is the bourgeoisie and the high-minded intellectuals who need it, not workers. The occasional worker who acts stubbornly is quickly and relatively painlessly brought in line by his fellows. Further, when workers are allowed to organize their own work, they naturally find ways to incorporate as effectively as possible those with different capacities, older workers, women workers, and workers with disabilities. Because of the friction produced by the labor process, by systemic domination as well as local pressures to produce, "the overwhelming preponderance of all the classic human virtues is on the side of the shop stewards" (71). Only the semblance of virtues is to be found among the aristocracy of earlier days or the managerial classes of today. Actual virtue is forged in struggle, and that is what the working class faces on a daily basis—and these virtues look strikingly similar to the ancient virtues. Moreover, while the term *struggle* suggests an unwelcome burden, in fact workers "glory in the struggle," and despair is foreign to them (73). After all, only there, in struggle, is humanity realized. Official society, in contrast, is a site of decay and demoralization, requiring incentives to motivate continued activity.

In today's world, the forces of domination are intensifying; correspondingly, the new society is emerging all the more vibrant. With the increasing power of systems of domination, the space for ambivalence fades; the middle class is now "dominated by rationalist ideas" (82), and even ostensibly political writers more often than not "attach themselves to one of the great bureaucratic social and political machines" (83).[8] Not only writers: "professional agitators," who once may have had a role catalyzing working-class mobilization, are now employed by both the Communist state and the democratic state to harness the political energy of the working class, fully integrated into official society.

What is the role of the revolutionary with middle-class origins, then? What is the role of people like James and his colleagues? If they are to form revolutionary organizations, they must let these groups be guided by workers' activity. Workers are the agents of history, and if liberation is to be achieved for all, including for those in the middle class, it will be through the actions of workers. What the middle class can do, then, is equip workers with the resources to recognize their own activity, their own participation in struggle, and with information about the struggles of other workers at a geographic or historical distance. Official society tries to suppress such information. The revolutionary organization also has an important role in informing workers about the machinations of official society. Finally, the revolutionary organization develops Marxist theory and applies it to situations that arise in the present. All of these tasks are not done *by* middle-class supporters, *for* working-class men and women. Rather, the revolutionary organization itself properly consists of a mix of intellectuals of middle-class origins and members of the working class, and the decisions of the organization are the result of working through the friction created by this mix.

The revolutionary organization does not just declare the truth, taking the point of view of God. It struggles with itself to strip away confusion and move toward right action. Workers "reject slogans and instructions of what to do" because "they know what to do"—they confront domination in the workplace every day, and they respond creatively, inaugurating the new society (136). But workers do not have access to a record of those struggles, nor to the struggles of others, nor to the second-order reflection on those struggles that constitutes Marxist theory—so the right political intuitions acted upon in local, factory-floor struggles are not developed into the ideas that could lead to a revolutionary transformation that would end systems of domination altogether. In turn, those equipped to write history and to theorize have their views contaminated by their formation in the middle class. Hence, it is only by embracing the friction created when members of the two groups work together that genuine insights can be obtained.

In sum, James and his colleagues rediscover and fully embrace the Hegelian legacy in the Marxist tradition.[9] Hegel's project represents the continual, inevitable challenge to all idolatry. "Contradiction, even antagonism, is the source of all life and movement. It is from the confrontation of fundamental ideas with the reactions of workers that new ideas emerge and new energy is created" (159). The job of the revolutionary organization is to create the arena in which these contradictions can be worked; paradigmatically, this means a newspaper, not with party doctrine but with the voices of workers at its core, curated in a way that stages encounters between workers' intuitions, broader stories of struggle, and Marxist theory. There is no need for Marxist intellectuals to condescend to workers by "popularizing" theoretical ideas. If that feels necessary, then the intellectual is not sufficiently fluent in the language and culture of the workers. James and his colleagues put these ideas into practice in Detroit, running newspapers that centered the voices of workers.[10] Yet another idolatrous temptation presents itself: to take the task of amplifying subaltern voices to be the primary goal of organizing. In *Facing Reality*, two temporalities are operative and essential. There is the time of struggle, when workers' voices are centered but always in creative (dialectical) tension with history and theory. Then there is the time of revolution, inevitable but unpredictable. Struggle in the present offers a foretaste of a world without domination, of the new society. But it should not be confused with the new society itself, fully realized, for that will be seen only after the revolution, when all systems of domination have been eliminated once and for all.[11]

IN THE LAST DECADE OF JAMES'S LIFE, he lived alone in a tiny flat in the London neighborhood of Brixton. While his intellectual work was achieving increasing visibility among leftist students, scholars, and activists, he himself remained largely isolated. He was surrounded by books, and he read regularly and watched television. Then his eyesight failed. He came in contact with a recent Cambridge graduate, Anna Grimshaw, who befriended him. She would spend hours at his apartment every day, talking with him and helping him in various ways, including by taking down notes for an autobiography he intended to write.[12] Grimshaw's relationship with James grew so intense that she moved to an apartment across the street from his so that she could spend even more time with the aging intellectual. At least in its broad contours—intense intellectual discussion between James and a white woman in her twenties—this relationship looked quite similar to James's relationships with Constance Webb (who would become his second wife) and Selma Deitch (who would become his third). James and Grimshaw toiled for years on his autobiography, but it never came together; finally, they decided that the best way to introduce new readers to James's work would be through a chronologically organized collection of his writings, the *C. L. R. James Reader*.

James's autobiography did not see the light of day for good reason. It is, for the most part, a tedious text.[13] Much ink is expended recalling the internecine struggles of Trotskyite organizations and various episodes in James's life—quite lifelessly. James wrote in different genres over the course of his life: at times as party propagandist and theorist, at times as cultural critic, and at times literarily, often imitating the style of his first literary love, William Thackeray. James's cricket writing, and particularly *Beyond a Boundary*, is so outstanding because it affords him the opportunity to mix these three genres, bringing out the best in each. In contrast, his purely political writings, his purely literary writings, and his cultural criticism are each to some degree unsatisfying, exhibiting competence but not excellence. James tried to integrate genres again in his autobiography, but for whatever reason—perhaps simply age—he did not succeed. There are fragments of brilliant cultural criticism, captivating anecdotes, and expositions of political positions, but they do not work together, and the text as a whole is dominated by a frustrating imperative to convey the facts exhaustively. James has clearly rehearsed these facts so frequently that they come off as overwrought and often self-defensive. Plus, James was notoriously long-winded. As his publisher Frederic Warburg once put it, "Excess, perhaps, was James' crime, an excess of words whose relevance to the contemporary tragedy was less than he supposed."[14]

In addition to the many fragments of autobiographical writing over which James and Grimshaw labored, there are a series of outlines for the text as a whole. One version is strictly chronological, with the first chapter covering the first nine years of James's life (because "much of the work that I have done can now be traced to my West Indian origin"); the second chapter covering the next twenty-one years, until James left for England (showing "an exceptional grasp of life in the West Indies and a tendency towards a political solution"); and so on. Some drafts of the autobiography are interrupted by two thematically arranged fragments, one on religion and one on "women and sex." These two fragments strike a discordant note. They introduce a confessional genre, different from the genres in which James usually operates. There is no dry recitation of political facts, no cultural analysis, and only stilted anecdotes. In short, the smoothness of James's self-presentation breaks when he encounters these two topics, religion and "women and sex"; it is as if, strangely, the author, so polished throughout his life, has suddenly decided to offer backstage access, perhaps because that is what he imagines an autobiography is supposed to do, perhaps because this is what he enjoys dictating to Grimshaw.[15]

As James tells it, his parents were members of Trinidad's Black lower middle class, but both embraced the life of the mind, his mother through her own reading and his father through teaching. In his view, his early days were crucially formative: "I believe that much of my attitude in writing and speech to this day are a continuation and maturity of some ideas which remained in my mind before I was a 9 year old." His mother possessed an emotional, but serious, piety. She felt her faith, and she performed it, with the requisite involvement in church life. "She guided her life completely by the Protestant religion and the social discipline and manners which the English version of Protestantism imposed on middle class people everywhere." His father's faith was more of a mystery. They lived across the street from their Anglican church, and his father taught the choir and played the organ, but he did not show evidence of faith felt in his heart, as it were. Despite this, James's father did show a supererogatory commitment to assist the church, to the extent that when the (white) minister went to England for six months for medical treatment, James's father became the substitute minister. Yet even this, in James's telling, had a quality of duty, and a taxing duty at that. When the priest returned, James's father stopped attending church for six months, the same amount of time he had officiated at the church.

James describes himself, in childhood, as hearing much about religion at church and Sunday school and from his own reading of John Foxe's *Book of Martyrs*. Yet, in retrospect, James concludes, "I did not believe nor did I disbelieve anything." Rather, "it was a routine that I went through." He was confirmed. He took communion. But he neither fully felt nor fully thought through Christianity. What he did feel and appreciate, particularly as he grew older, was the sense that his sins could be cleansed through communion. (It is tempting to read James's recitations of his imperfections with respect to "women and sex" as participating in this sort of cleansing— stating his sins not to God or a priest but to a white woman.) James became frustrated. Before taking communion he would promise not to sin again—and then he would sin. His doubts expanded as he read more. He came across an English free-thought magazine, the *Rationalist Annual*, which he read "over and over," absorbing its attacks on the credibility of the Bible. As his doubts grew, he went to see a Catholic priest and then an Anglican minister. Both offered unsatisfying answers: they told him to read more and decide whether or not he wanted to believe. James queried an acquaintance who was studying theology and was told, essentially, that Christianity is about mystery. He began drifting away from his faith.

Then, one day, James experienced a sudden deconversion.[16] He was working as a teacher at Queens Royal College in Port of Spain, modeled on the English public school experience. It was a stormy afternoon. The boys were working at their desks. In a flash, James reached a definitive conclusion regarding religion: "I was finished with it and would not be in any way concerned with it in the future. That belief I have held to for the past half century." This was an intellectual conclusion, based on reasons, but it resulted in a sort of atheist faith. At first, the young James was a zealot: "I flaunted my newfound beliefs." He would take every opportunity to challenge his mother's beliefs. He devoured Voltaire and other Enlightenment thinkers on religion. This lasted only a few months. Then James was able to encounter the Christianity of others without taking offense or provoking an argument; he would even show sympathy. "I had recovered my notoriously calm and disciplined approach to everything."

James reflects that Christianity still had a hold on him as a young adult, despite his intellectual rejection of it, because he did not immediately find a replacement. Reading European philosophy and the classics of world religions left him cold. Finally, he found the replacement he was looking for in the African American slave spirituals, as sung by Paul Robeson. In those ancient songs, composed by Black women and men enduring unimaginable suffering, James found an embrace of "the response of a human being to the beauty and harmony of nature" but also a sense that these pleasures were not ultimate. They fortified the soul for engagement with the social world, for struggle. The spirituals recognize that there is evil in the world, real deep, but evil does not have the last word. Beyond the beauty and suffering of the moment was a grand drama of struggle against all forms of domination, a struggle that would ultimately end in victory. This was a sort of religiosity that James could embrace, that he would write about in his first published short story, "La Divina Pastora," and it was the sort of religiosity he would find in the African American communities in Missouri where he worked as a labor organizer in the 1930s.

The middle-class Christian-colonial mores that James would take from his mother did not fall away when he embraced atheism nor when he learned of the spirituality of the enslaved. He repeatedly characterizes himself as a "Puritan" in the mold of his parents. He never saw his parents drunk, and he reports that he himself has never been drunk. He does not swear because his parents did not swear. James lost belief in religion, but in a sense he retained the practice of religion. Indeed, James's great book, *Beyond a Boundary*, where James describes his "puritanical view of the world," may be read as an encomium to the virtues, describing how they contribute to the play of cricket and how cricket leads to their development.[17]

This puritanism presumably accounts for James's vexed relationship with "women and sex." The essence of religious practice, in the Trinidad of James's youth, was a code of sexual conduct. Eventually he decides to devote a full chapter of his autobiography to this topic, "women and sex," and this is the one extract from the text that he decides to publish—though it was ultimately not included in the collection of writings about James for which he offered it.[18] As such, James (with Grimshaw) worked and reworked this text into something like a polished form, though without diminishing the text's oddity. It is, essentially, a confession. In the world of middle-class Trinidadians, sex was to be between married men and women. Sexual mores were a key differentiator between the middle class and the supposedly promiscuous lower class. James identified with the middle class, and eighty years of pent-up thoughts about his sexual history are released onto the page seemingly without restraint. He begins with his first awareness of his body's sexuality: between the ages of eleven and twelve or thirteen, he lived with his aunts and slept on a sofa in their living room. He began to masturbate, though without fantasy: "It was a purely physical act." Then his classmates began talking about the sexual acts they aspired to perform with girls in their circle, and they shared dirty pictures. James reports that he took offense at the latter, thinking them "degrading and without any value whatsoever." Then, James recalls, he was so absorbed in reading and in cricket that he forgot about girls.

After graduating from high school, James and his circle of male friends would encounter women at dances and parties. They treated these encounters essentially as games. From their perspective, in personal conduct men were not subject to moral restraints, but women were. The man's goal was seduction; the woman's goal was to resist being seduced. "She would or she would not and you could persuade her or you could not." This was the context, James writes, for his encounter with a certain virgin when he was twenty-two or twenty-three years old. She allowed her clothes to be removed and let James do anything he liked to her, except for penetrative sex. James clinically reports, "She allowed me to enter her vagina to the extent of about an inch or less. That she would allow, but further than that I was not to go, and I obeyed." The young woman was pleased that James obeyed, and she returned to his apartment two or three more times. But then James began to be "rather tired of it—not angry, because I understood her point of view." He consulted an older man who informed him that such women really wanted to have sex; they just did not want to admit it. They did not want the responsibility of allowing sex, and they wanted to be able to charge rape if their promiscuity was discovered. James's consultant told him he ought to go ahead and take the woman; otherwise, she would find a different man with whom to consort. James describes his own ambivalence: he had an intuition that women were exploited, but he was inexperienced and trusted the older man's judgment. If this had occurred twenty years later, he reflects, he would have dismissed the man's advice outright, but at the time James recollects facing a dilemma. He decided to break off the relationship. "I was a very moral person, that is to say I lived by moral ideas, and I made up my mind then that I was finished with seduction, partial sexual relations, intimacy without penetration, and the whole bag of tricks by which our young men in Trinidad lived." He decided that whenever he was interested in a woman, he would simply ask her whether she would be willing to sleep with him. He would do this when he was sure that the woman was calm and not intoxicated. "From that day to the present, I have never seduced anybody."

This James declares definitively—and then, at the conclusion of the chapter, he vividly describes his favorite seduction. It was 1936, James was in London, and he would exchange glances with a neighbor woman. "Whether she was tall or short, plump or thin, beautiful or plain, race or nationality, I do not propose to go into. She was what she was." They happened to attend the same party one evening. James asks a mutual friend to introduce them. He proposes meeting. She says she is available any time. He says he will visit her at nine Monday morning. He readies himself and arrives at her house; they shake hands, and he reports that their hands did not let go until they were done making love. They sit on her sofa, and James (a "very moral person") says to her, "Now we have to tell your husband about this." She decides to break off the relationship, but their affair continues. "We were too close, physically and spiritually, to live so near to one another" without making love. Eventually, she and her husband moved away, and the affair definitively ended. James reflects that he still hopes to meet her again one day. "She would have put on a little weight, and she would be a little gray. But she would be as she was on that Monday morning, a human being made to order for another human being." This may not exactly be seduction, but neither is it exactly love or romance. The woman is, after all, "made to order." It is her self, beyond any particular characteristics, that matters, or at least that is what James says, raw attraction of souls, but really? This woman may not have affected the puritan mores of the middle-class Trinidadian women James would try to seduce, but is this not seduction nonetheless?

The anecdotes and reflections that James offers follow what he reports to have been his first sexual experience, one that can only be described as rape. He was sixteen. The girl was his age. "It was a curious episode," James recalls. What was strange about it? "She said, 'No and no and no and no,' and actually fought me for a while. And then [she] gave in completely." James raped the girl. According to his recollection, after he had completed the act, the girl told him that "if there was anything else that [he] wished that she would give it to [him]," which he seems to interpret as voicing desire for him: "She obviously wanted me to come back again." However, James declares that he lost interest—until he changed his mind: "That happened once or twice more with her. And then, events happened and we went our different ways." In contrast to all of James's professed ambivalence about seduction—which is essentially about how the practice does not allow him to get what he wants—the primal sexual encounter for James is rape followed by submission, and about this episode he voices no ambivalence.

Indeed, later in life James will reflect (to Grimshaw) on his inability to do more with women than have his way with them. "I am a well-behaved person," he reflects, yet "my virtues as a husband were entirely negative." He left his first wife (about whom he says nothing of substance, not even her name) in Trinidad when he went to England; she later declined to join him. This may not be surprising, given that she once told him, "The only time you have any pleasure with me is when you are on top of me." James's second wife, the white American actress and activist Constance Webb, would say to him, "Tell me what you want from me, what you want me to do. . . . Tell me something." To his first wife, James reflects, "I did not know what to say." With respect to Webb, "I could tell her nothing because I had only the vaguest idea of what she was speaking about."[19] On further reflection, James realizes he has a prejudice against women that has prevented him from fully engaging with them. He neglected to "pay any attention to them as human beings," "as personalities."[20]

James liked women to say what they wanted, to say that they wanted to sleep with him, and then he would give it to them. In *Facing Reality*, James and his colleagues write that workers "say precisely what they want and when" (165). The task for the intellectual, and for the revolutionary organization, is simply to listen carefully and to work collectively toward giving workers precisely what they want. James himself is incapable of saying what he wants. He can ask questions, of women and workers, and he can attempt to satisfy the desire of others, but he is left stammering when pressed to articulate his own desire. This problem, effectively existential, is the political problem James and his colleagues are trying to work through in *Facing Reality*. God has been rejected. All gods. What does it mean to desire properly without God? Does it mean that James embraces a variety of forms of human flourishing, desiring disparate goods, through politics, culture, and sport, as Alasdair MacIntyre contends?[21]

No. When James embraces the spirituality of the songs sung by Robeson, he is embracing flourishing under the shadow of domination together with faith in the struggle against all forms of domination, in what the enslaved call Zion. Only the epistemic injustice effected by the forces of domination makes it seem as if worldly goods are the proper objects of desire. This confusion is the product of the middle-class culture in which James was formed—in particular, the middle-class colonial culture, where colonial subjects insecure in their status invest all the more affective energy in maintaining the bourgeois virtues. Just below the surface is violence, rape. The middle-class world is made possible by colonialism, racism, capitalism, and patriarchy, even as it presents as genteel. As such, the middle-class world is riven by contradictions. (James's own autobiographical narrative, despite its confident recitation of facts, itself contains numerous factual contradictions.) James realizes those contradictions and realizes the solution: alignment with the proletariat. But it is impossible, for he was formed in the middle class, with commitments to modes of domination baked into his being no matter how hard he tries to identify with the proletariat.

Put another way, James is a puritan atheist through and through. His mode of resisting a puritan formation in the middle class is to embrace atheism, religious and political. But because of his unshakeable formation, that atheism can never be as thoroughgoing as his political philosophy calls for: it remains a puritan atheism. His political philosophy extols an atheism that comes naturally to the proletariat: at the level of ideas, suspicion of all bosses and masters; at the level of practice, building power through local organizing to challenge those false gods. But for James, an intellectual formed in the middle class, atheism operates only at the level of ideas, not at the level of activity, even as those ideas laud activity. In contrast, the working class, never formed by bourgeois religion, never invested in the bourgeois virtues, can embrace atheism fully, becoming the proper revolutionary subject.[22]

Middle-class life is tragic because it either is self-deceptive, ignoring the contradictions and violence that constitute it, or is a failure, attempting to resolve its contradictions by embracing the proletariat but never succeeding.[23] Only the shadow of flourishing is possible, and that only by the security offered by willful blindness, puritanism, or a continuous attack on oneself, one's own formation—by atheism, a puritan atheism. Either way, sins will be committed, people will be hurt, and relationships will be broken. For James, even confessing this guilt, a confession displaced from priest-confessor to woman-confessor, commits further wrongs, does more violence. For the middle class broadly—for whites, for men, for those in the Global North, for those without disability—there is no redemption. There is only suffering: suffering in vain or suffering aligned with struggle, suffering that might, even with the violence it inflicts, support the redemption of the subaltern and so the redemption of the world.

Notes

1 While James's case is more complex, some of this conventional manliness certainly is at work. He reports that immediately after he published his book on world revolution, "all doubt as to the effectiveness of my sexual activities disappeared. I had always previously been careful to see that I did not ejaculate too early [but] in time with the woman whom I was with. But that concern disappeared entirely." Undated document, C. L. R. James Papers, box 2, folder 13, Rare Book and Manuscript Library, Columbia University Library, New York. For a reading of James along these lines, see Johnson, "Sex and the Subversive Alien."

2 Lee, Chaulieu, and Johnson, *Facing Reality*, 125. Hereafter cited parenthetically in the text.

3 James's authorized biography, recounting many of these events, was written by Paul Buhle: *C. L. R. James: The Artist as Revolutionary*.

4 James, *Life of Captain Cipriani*.

5 Cornelius Castoriadis was also involved in the writing of this book and is credited, along with James and Boggs, as a coauthor, although he likely had limited involvement in the final writing and editing.

6 James, *Mariners, Renegades, and Castaways*.

7 James and his colleagues develop this point further, with force, in *State Capitalism and World Revolution*. All texts from this period were collaborative and published under pseudonyms. In later editions, James is credited as author and others as "collaborators."

8 But James and his colleagues also assert that the middle classes "have shown themselves all over the world increasingly ready to follow the example of the

workers" (114). I read this apparent contradiction as a symptom of James's fundamental ambivalence about the status of the middle class.

9   They undertook an intensive study of Hegel and the Marxist appropriation of Hegel's legacy, published as *Notes on Dialectics*.

10 See Boggs, *Living for Change*.

11 "The violent seizure of power is not the main preoccupation of workers and peoples. . . . But they know that when the moment comes they can overthrow any power, government or otherwise, which seeks to enslave them" (164).

12 See "C. L. R. James in the 1980s: A Conversation with Anna Grimshaw," 1991, James Papers, box 28, folder 3.

13 For the undated manuscript material, see James Papers, boxes 4, 5.

14 Warburg, *Occupation for Gentlemen*, 215.

15 Compare the sometimes confessional nature of James's letters collected in James, *Special Delivery*.

16 While James presents his deconversion as sui generis, he later notes that the father of his friend and fellow Trinidadian revolutionary George Padmore converted from Anglicanism to Islam, inspired by Edward Blyden's critique of Christianity's racism.

17 James, *Beyond a Boundary*, 18.

18 Buhle, *C. L. R. James: His Life and Work*. The document can be found in the James Papers, box 2, folder 3; a copy exists in Paul Buhle Papers, box 7, Tamiment Library and Robert F. Wagner Labor Archive, Elmer Holmes Bobst Library, New York University, New York.

19 George Lamming fictionalizes the relationship between James and his third wife in his novel *Natives of My Person*. Lamming has the Selma character reflect on the James character and his comrades involved in political work, "To hear them predict the future that could come if circumstances allowed their plans to operate, it was like waiting for heaven. . . . In spite of the indignities done to me, I couldn't help seeing them with some favor. . . . His interest had been given to a larger love" (330–31).

20 James never did come to see that his most philosophically fruitful period was made possible by collaboration, in thought and writing, with two women with whom he had substantial and prolonged intellectual exchanges.

21 MacIntyre, *Ethics*, ch. 5.4. Contrast this with the reading of James's "queer" attachments in Ellis, *Territories of the Soul*, ch. 1.

22 Sylvia Wynter reads *Beyond a Boundary* as especially concerned with extolling the working class, whereas I read James's work as especially concerned with the ambivalence of the middle class. See Wynter, "In Quest of Matthew Bondsman."

23 In *Conscripts of Modernity*, David Scott argues that tragedy is the organizing principle of James's mature work.

Bibliography

Boggs, Grace Lee. *Living for Change: An Autobiography.* Minneapolis: University of Minnesota Press, 1998.

Buhle, Paul. *C. L. R. James: The Artist as Revolutionary.* London: Verso, 1988.

Buhle, Paul, ed. *C. L. R. James: His Life and Work.* London: Allison and Busby, 1986.

Ellis, Nadia. *Territories of the Soul: Queered Belonging in the Black Diaspora.* Durham, NC: Duke University Press, 2015.

James, C. L. R. *Beyond a Boundary.* Durham, NC: Duke University Press, 2013.

James, C. L. R. *The Black Jacobins: Toussaint L'Ouverture and the San Domingo Revolution.* New York: Vintage, 1989.

James, C. L. R. *The C. L. R. James Reader.* Edited by Anna Grimshaw. Oxford: Blackwell, 1992.

James, C. L. R. "La Divina Pastora." In *C. L. R. James Reader,* 25–28.

James, C. L. R. *The Life of Captain Cipriani: An Account of British Government in the West Indies.* Nelson, UK: Coulton, 1932.

James, C. L. R. *Mariners, Renegades, and Castaways: The Story of Herman Melville and the World We Live In.* New York: privately printed, 1953.

James, C. L. R. *Notes on Dialectics.* Detroit: Facing Reality, 1948.

James, C. L. R. *Special Delivery: The Letters of C. L. R. James to Constance Webb, 1939–1948.* Edited by Anna Grimshaw. Oxford: Blackwell, 1996.

James, C. L. R. *State Capitalism and World Revolution.* Detroit: Facing Reality, 1950.

Johnson, W. Chris. "Sex and the Subversive Alien: The Moral Life of C. L. R. James." *International Journal of Francophone Studies* 14, no. 1/2 (2011): 185–203.

Lamming, George. *Natives of My Person.* Ann Arbor: University of Michigan Press, 1992.

Lee, Grace, Pierre Chaulieu, and J. R. Johnson [C. L. R. James]. *Facing Reality.* Detroit: Correspondence, 1958.

MacIntyre, Alasdair. *Ethics in the Conflicts of Modernity: An Essay on Desire, Practical Reasoning, and Narrative.* New York: Cambridge University Press, 2016.

Scott, David. *Conscripts of Modernity: The Tragedy of Colonial Enlightenment.* Durham: Duke University Press, 2005.

Warburg, Frederic. *An Occupation for Gentlemen.* Boston: Houghton Mifflin, 1960.

Wynter, Sylvia. "In Quest of Matthew Bondsman: Some Cultural Notes on the Jamesian Journey." In Buhle, *C. L. R. James: His Life and Work,* 54–68.

Ellen Armour

5 Decolonizing Spectatorship

Photography, Theology, and New Media

Human beings live in a world that is simultaneously real and virtual, material and symbolic, sensate and mediated.—Robert Hariman and John Louis Lucaites, *The Public Image: Photography and Civic Spectatorship*

Photographs . . . trade simultaneously on the prestige of art and the magic of the real. They are clouds of fantasy and pellets of information.—Susan Sontag, *On Photography*

THE PUBLICATION AND CIRCULATION in the fall of 2015—first on social media and then via legacy media—of photographs of the drowned body of Alan Kurdi, a three-year-old Syrian boy, washed up on a Turkish beach and then in the arms of a soldier who picked him up, proved a dramatic moment in the global response to the ongoing Syrian refugee crisis.[1] Though hardly the first (or the last) photographs of Syrian refugees to appear in either news or social media, the photos of Kurdi encapsulated the plight of the refugees with particular pathos and power, moving many to take some kind of action on their behalf. A story in the *Guardian*, for example, documented a dramatic increase in donations to a refugee-aid start-up in Britain, Help Refugees.[2] The *New York Times* reported that the photograph helped catapult Justin Trudeau, a liberal, to power in Canada and prompted many Canadians to get involved in refugee resettlement programs.[3] But the

Guardian also reported that ISIS used the same photographs to condemn those fleeing their would-be caliphate for the west for exposing their children to apostasy, fornication, sodomy, and liberalism.[4]

That same fall, a seemingly successful protest led by Native Americans against the Keystone XL pipeline (designed to carried oil across the border between the United States and Canada, which raised serious environmental concerns) was ending, and another beginning, this one at the Standing Rock Sioux Reservation against the proposed Dakota Access Pipeline. As photographs of (and stories about) the protest circulated on social media, the protests caught the attention of legacy media as the protestors grew not only in number but in kind. Organizers ended up drawing to their aid not just the usual suspects (environmental activists, for example) but a remarkably wide range of allies, including religious leaders from various faith traditions and U.S. military veterans. Indeed, among the most powerful photographs from the months-long protest was one of a group of veterans kneeling in formation before tribal leaders to ask forgiveness for the military's role in colonizing Native Americans and stripping them of their land, a striking contrast to photos of law enforcement's threats to the camps and the protestors.[5] The protest continued well into 2017, ending as construction began on the pipeline that June. (In January 2021, in one of his first acts after assuming the U.S. presidency, Joe Biden revoked the permit for the Keystone XL pipeline.)

THIS CHAPTER IS A BRIDGE BETWEEN MY MOST RECENT BOOK, *Signs and Wonders: Theology after Modernity*, and my current book project, "Seeing Is Believing: Theology, Visual Culture, and the New Media." Both projects center on photography's role in crucial challenges—national and global, theological and philosophical, social and political—that we face as we live into modernity's anticipated end, challenges that reflect the legacy of colonialism (among other isms) and implicate photography. These challenges are the effects, I argue in *Signs and Wonders*, of the outworking of two forms of power that the philosopher Michel Foucault identifies as distinctively modern: biopower and disciplinary power (biodisciplinary power, for short).[6] Coursing through modern institutions like prisons, clinics, and asylums (as well as the modern school, workplace, and family), disciplinary power is a system of carrots and sticks that seeks to mold human beings into docile subjects: self-avowed delinquents, compliant patients, obedient workers, good boys and girls. Biopower harnesses disciplinary power to serve its goal of nurturing human life by eliminating (social and biological) abnormality. Per LaDelle McWhorter, I argue that biodisciplinary power is both productively and destructively racist.[7] While attributions of abnormality are to be found throughout the human race, it has an uncanny knack for finding a stubbornly resistant host in certain populations (colonized or enslaved peoples and their descendants, for example). Thus, these populations feel biodisciplinary power's most virulent and violent effects in concentrated form. Thanks in no small part to its role in colonization, Christianity is deeply imbricated in colonial biodiscipline. To colonize was to civilize, and to civilize was to Christianize. To Christianize was to reorganize Indigenous "family values," if you will—including sexual mores—to conform to a more Victorian model. That meant remaking colonized subjects into proper men and women (to the degree that this was possible, that is) by imposing modern western sexual taxonomies on them.[8]

Though Foucault does not *explicitly* thematize this, I see in his work evidence that biodisciplinary power is channeled through what I call a fourfold made up of "Man," his raced and sexed others, his divine other, and his animal other. Man occupies the center, while his others surround him like a network of mirrors that reflect Man back to himself, thus securing his boundaries and his sense of mastery.[9] As biodisciplinary power's conduit, the fourfold affects how those subjected to that power (that is, thanks to colonialism and its heir, globalization, all of us) become, live, and die. We live out our lives, then—individually and collectively—by conforming to and/or resisting biodisciplinary power's normative demands. To live as, say, a straight white American woman or a gay Ugandan man is to take up one's place in the taxonomy of subject positions proffered us by biodisciplinary power as gendered, sexed, raced or ethnicized, and sexual subjects.

Photography is deeply imbricated in the establishment and circulation of biodisciplinary power—and biodisciplinary power, in turn, in photographic practice, including our assumptions about what I call photographic truth. Though we now assume it, photography's claim to simply re-present the photographed object (what I call, riffing off of Roland Barthes, its "that-there-then") was established by photography's use as an instrument of biodisciplinary power channeled through the fourfold.[10] In turn, photography was essential to realizing biodisciplinary power's drive toward normalization, manifest in and as the establishment of modern man's mastery over himself and his (animal, raced, and sexed) others.

Colonialism and racism, anchored by modern sexuality, were and are critical players here. Both casual snapshots (family and souvenir photographs) and professional photographs (by photojournalists, for example) circulate biodisciplinary power. Subjecting oneself to the camera—willingly or unwillingly, as its viewed object or viewing subject—(en)trains us in the modes of seeing and being seen that are integral to modernity as a way of knowing, doing, and therefore being.

But photography's role in the circulation of biodisciplinary power—and our ongoing subjection to it—involves more than a given photograph's that-there-then (or what photographs index). It also involves photographic *signifiance* (a term I get from Julia Kristeva via Roland Barthes), that is, what photographs open up and onto and how they move us (to feel certain emotions and/or to take action).[11] We speak of certain photographs as iconic, as able to stand in for the events they reference because they capture what is at stake with remarkable pathos and power. In their aptly titled study of iconic photographs, *No Caption Needed: Iconic Photographs, Public Culture, and Liberal Democracy*, Robert Hariman and John Louis Lucaites argue that iconic photographs are circuits of political affect that arise out of situations of social conflict or crisis. By "concentrat[ing] and direct[ing] emotions," they serve as "aesthetic resource[s] for performative mediation of conflicts."[12] And yet, as the photographic story lines I opened this essay with suggest, the same photograph can move us (as we say)—to feel emotion and to take action—in very different ways, a dynamic I call *photographic ambivalence*.

In *Signs and Wonders*, I use this framework to analyze four sets of photographs, the events they index, and what they open up and open onto. Two of those sets of photographs open up and onto colonialism and its legacy in ways that directly implicate religion, and Christianity in particular: the Abu Ghraib "archive" (per W. J. T. Mitchell) and the global crisis within the Anglican Communion that Rev. Gene Robinson's consecration as its first openly gay bishop unleashed.[13] Both reveal colonialism as a biopolitical *and theopolitical* system with formative asymmetrical effects on colonized and colonizer. Per anthropologist Ann Laura Stoler, the colonies were "laboratories of modernity" featuring experiments in managing and deploying biodisciplinary power.[14] One major project and product of these experiments, if you will, is what Stoler calls "the bourgeois subject."[15] Produced in part by properly managing his own sexuality, as well as that of his raced and sexed others, the organization of sexual, family, and affective life was essential to colonial man as project and projection.

Fortuitously for me, Stoler's books are sprinkled liberally with photographs from the colonial archive, including photographs taken *en famille*. On my read, these photographs (intentionally or not) reflect (or refract) that project's reliance on successfully managing the threat posed to it by living in close—sometimes too close—proximity to the colonized.

From *Signs and Wonders* to Seeing and Believing

THE PHOTOGRAPHS THAT ANCHOR *Signs and Wonders* and the events they index all come from 2003–5. A lot has changed in our photographic lives in the fifteen years since, thanks to innovations that we now take for granted but that were just becoming available then. The invention (2002) and widespread adoption of the (now-ubiquitous and video-capable) cell phone camera and the advent and spread of social media have changed the production and public circulation of photography in multiple ways. Two of the most popular social media platforms are specifically photographic (Instagram, founded in 2010, and Snapchat, founded in 2011). And virtually every post that I see on the social media behemoth, Facebook (founded in 2004 and now the owner of Instagram), is headlined by some kind of visual image—often a photograph taken with and uploaded by someone's cell phone.

The new media landscape has further democratized the making and circulating of photographs (already a widely available technology in analog form), thus leveling the playing field (to a degree) between amateur and professional media producers and curators. Indeed, both of the photographic story lines I cited at the outset took off first on social media before being taken up by legacy media. These online platforms enable story lines like these to extend and expand across time and space, giving photography an ever more prominent role in public events and political debate—for good or ill. Religion, too, has migrated online—including institutional and parainstitutional forms of Christianity. Not only do many brick-and-mortar churches have social media pages, but at least two denominations (the Metropolitan Community Church and the Anglican Communion) have virtual congregations on Second Life.[16] And photography and other forms of visual representation are as important to virtual religion—perhaps especially its parainstitutional forms (think of Christian influencers, for example)—as to other aspects of our virtual lives.[17] We call social media the new public square. What role is photography playing in and on it and thus in and on us—not only in our virtual lives but IRL (in real life)?

My preliminary research suggests that scholars of new media are divided about their social costs and benefits. Some (e.g., Clay Shirky) see new media—especially social media—as empowering communal action.[18] Others (e.g., Sherry Turkle) argue that our virtual lives are diminishing embodied capacities (empathy and emotional resilience) that are vital to living well together.[19] The same ambivalence appears in scholarship on virtual religion.[20] There is compelling evidence that virtual religion, when designed and managed well, can foster greater engagement between religious leaders and faith community members, say, but the jury is out on how fully it can substitute for IRL religion.[21]

The scholarship I've read to date that specifically addresses photography's role in the new-media landscape reflects a similar ambivalence.[22] That ambivalence is reflected in popular perceptions of the relationship among our virtual lives, our photographic lives, and our real lives and their impact on one another. We live (virtually) in social media bubbles, we're told, likely a reflection of the social bubbles that, scholars tell us, constitute our flesh-and-blood lives. What we see online tends to reinforce what we already believe, it seems, and what we already believe shapes what we see. To Trayvon Martin's killer, a young Black man walking through a white neighborhood wearing a hoodie was by default a threat. A black-and-white photograph of Martin in a hoodie placed contesting that stereotype at the visual center of the movement pursuing justice for Martin on social media and IRL.[23] That iconic image and the story line it anchored gave birth to the Black Lives Matter movement, but it also prompted a budding white supremacist named Dylann Roof—radicalized online, by the way—to try to start a "race war" by murdering nine worshippers at the historic Emanuel African Methodist Episcopal Church in Charleston, South Carolina.[24] Clearly, then, questions about photographic truth and significance remain deeply relevant to how we navigate our new public square.

From Photographic Subjection
to Photographic Insurrection

IF MY FOCUS IN *Signs and Wonders* was on photographic subjection, my interest in "Seeing Is Believing" is in photographic insurrection—something we will need if we hope to live well in this mediated world. By *photographic insurrection*, I mean pushing back against photographic subjection as a matter of seeing and believing. Rather than docile acquiescence, might we cultivate the ability to see through biodisciplined (photographic) normativity and what it would have us believe about ourselves, others, and the world we share?

I am particularly interested in mobilizing those wooed into photographic subjection by biodiscipline's carrots, if you will—a population that would include, for example, those "good white people" descended (socially if not necessarily biologically) from the colonizers rather than the colonized. ("Good cisgender heteronormative people" would constitute another such population, among others. And these populations would intersect, of course, though not overlap.) In her response to *Signs and Wonders*, the philosopher Shannon Winnubst asks about the impact of my Abu Ghraib chapter on precisely this population.[25] She worries that I risk getting mired in what she calls "liberal sentimentality," limned in Saidiya Hartman's work as liberal humanism in affective mode. Its affective repertoire includes outrage and empathy, shame and pleasure (among other feelings).[26] Spectacular instances of violence and violation (the tortures inflicted under chattel slavery in Hartman's work, spectacle lynchings after Emancipation and the torments inflicted by U.S. soldiers on Muslim detainees held at Abu Ghraib in mine) activate this affective repertoire, but its mobilization often trades on (and thus leaves in place) the logics underlying the very violence it aims to challenge. I think Winnubst is right; I do run that risk and am grateful to her for pointing it out and pointing me to Hartman. I read Hartman's analysis as illuminating liberal sentimentality as (white) mastery in affective form. Mastery manifests not only as domination *over* others but as moral goodness *to* others that makes "us" feel like "good [white] people" but maintains the hierarchy of us (whites, in this case) over them (people of color, in this case).

That risk, of course, does not simply attend academic analysis but has direct import for real life. Indeed, I would argue it tracks with the two (post)colonial photographic story lines that I referenced at the beginning of this essay. Both story lines illustrate photography's ability to move people in the direction of photographic insurrection—and potential limits to that ability. Aiding refugees rather than demonizing them, say, is morally laudable *and potentially but not necessarily* transformative, both personally and politically. That military veterans took the time, trouble, and expense to *be with* Native protestors—a being-with that included a formal apology for the military's role in colonization—is evidence of one kind of transformation that can occur. Yet neither story line has a happy ending (so far, at least), a sobering reminder of the limits of photographic insurrection when it confronts state sovereignty. We have evidence, then, of the promise (even if limited) of photographic insurrection. What can we do to nurture and cultivate that promise?

Might Christian theology, my home discipline, be helpful to us in that pursuit? It has, after all, been wrestling with the relationship between seeing and believing and its import for Christian formation for eons now. That we speak of iconic photographs at all references Christianity's own history with visual images, a history characterized by conflicts over the relationship between seeing and believing. The controversy over the relationship of icons to belief divided the Western Church from the Eastern Church long before the Reformation divided Catholicism from Protestantism. Were visual images of Christ and of Christian saints windows onto the divine (and thus worthy of veneration), or were they misrepresentations? Suspicions about seeing and believing also fueled the Protestant movement. Reformers stripped churches and cathedrals of visual media deemed idolatrous and thus dangerous to true belief and right practice. And yet Protestantism can hardly be accused of jettisoning seeing as an aid to believing. John Calvin, for example, exhorted Christians to look instead at nature, where they would encounter the glory of God.[27] As David Morgan has shown, modern Protestantism— both conservative and evangelical—went on to invest significantly in visual resources, especially with the advent of modes of their mechanical reproduction.[28]

To understand how Christian visual theo-logics might provide resources in support of photographic insurrection, though, we must also understand what stands in its way. In what follows, I outline some of the possibilities and problems attending the pursuit of photographic insurrection that arise from photography itself (as a medium and a practice) and from conceptions of photographic spectatorship (and its possible decolonization). I do so with the aid of recent work by scholars of photography whose earlier work proved particularly generative for *Signs and Wonders*: Hariman and Lucaites (referenced earlier) and Ariella Azoulay. That engagement will circle back around to liberal sentimentality, though it will not resolve that problem. My aim in this essay is to make some headway toward erecting a conceptual framework that can house attempts to work through that affective repertoire in the service of decolonizing spectatorship and encouraging photographic insurrection. I conclude with some reflections on Christian theology's possible contribution—as a discourse and a practice—to that goal.

IN *THE PUBLIC IMAGE: PHOTOGRAPHY AND CIVIC SPECTATORSHIP*, Hariman and Lucaites broaden their inquiry into the impact and import of photographs for our communal and political lives from iconic photographs to photography in general (particularly photojournalism). They seek to persuade their readers that photographs are essential "resources for thinking what it means to see and be seen," a task we need to undertake if we are to "live well in a world connected by lines of sight."[29] Our new media landscape and the technologies that undergird it (including digital photography) only raise the stakes of that endeavor, they (rightly) claim, even as this new reality heightens skepticism about photography as a medium able to help us see and be seen.[30] Photography may now bear what they call (per John Tagg) "the burden of representation," but the real problem isn't with it or any other medium but with those who use it, that is, with we the people and the society we inhabit, with what we expect from photography and from each other.[31]

That said, photography *as* a medium needs to be rethought, they argue, a task that will require a reboot of its scholarly discourse. We need a new paradigm (per Thomas Kuhn) for thinking about and with photography, one centered, on my read, on reframing the relationship between seeing and believing. At the heart of the old paradigm is a certain understanding of photographic truth as literal and unmediated, as nothing more (or less), recall, than a re-presentation of a certain "that-there-then." Photography's (allegedly unmediated) relationship to the real fueled its use as a "modern recording technology" deployed in the service of "science, industry, advertising, art, and most notably the press," which put all of its eggs in the literalist basket.[32] Journalism came to see its primary ethical obligation as simply to publish only photographs whose relationship to the real can be confirmed. (That said, editorial decisions about *which* photographs to publish are often considerably more complicated, especially where children are concerned. Newspaper editors debated whether to publish Kurdi's photograph, for example. And journalistic convention—at least until the iconic photograph from the Vietnam War, "Accidental Napalm," foregrounding an injured naked little girl running screaming away from a napalm attack—placed photographs of naked children off-limits.[33])

According to the old paradigm, seeing *should* trump belief—or be enough to inspire belief (in the truth of what is put before your eyes). Yet it's precisely that confidence in photographic literalism that skeptics (Hariman and Lucaites call them "iconoclasts") reject. Susan Sontag, their exemplar of photographic iconoclasm, observes that even though photographs can be staged or altered (more easily than ever in this digital era), "everyone is a literalist when it comes to photographs."[34] And yet the very same photograph can serve the political interests of opposing sides. Both sides in the Bosnian conflict, for example, claimed the same photograph of Bosnian children killed by bombs as evidence of the other's war crimes. Serbs and Croats both reproduced that picture to rally support— and likely both succeeded. "No 'we' should be taken for granted when the subject is looking at other people's pain," Sontag observes.[35]

Hariman and Lucaites are hardly naive when it comes to these realities, but they resist consigning photography to the dead end where literalism and iconoclasm meet. Significantly, given my interest in seeing and believing, they resort to a theo-logic of sorts to describe this dead end. Photographic literalism is a form of fundamentalism that flattens photography's relationship to reality, on their read. Instead, photography— literally "light writing"—embodies a complex relationship between "trace and artifact, reality and imagination," Hariman and Lucaites argue.[36] As light writing, it carries a trace *of* the artifact it re-presents (a constitutive element of its power to move us, on Barthes's read). But the photograph is also an artifact itself and, as such, takes on a life of its own (potentially an eternal one online).[37] But the biggest problem with photographic literalism is that it "sever[s] the most vital connections between the photograph and the world," which impoverishes our ability to have a critical ethical discussion about what we see.[38] Reckoning with that complicated relationship between the real and the re-presented—and with the re-presented as itself real—requires reconceiving the relationship between seeing and believing, vision and imagination. We must resist in no uncertain terms a radical split between realism and imagination. Indeed, Hariman and Lucaites urge us to think of photography as a "mode of extraordinary seeing," one that animates viewers' vision *and* imagination to expand their narrow understanding of reality.[39] "A photograph is both image and optic; a picture of some part of reality and a way of seeing that reality more extensively."[40] This is what makes photography a crucial resource for our civic and our political life. Mining that resource requires cultivating a more nuanced understanding of photographic truth, one that can acknowledge and work with conflicts of interpretation that (inevitably) arise—over the photograph itself as a re-presentation of reality *and* over the reality it re-presents.[41]

As the subtitle of Hariman and Lucaites's book indicates, that project also requires rethinking spectatorship as an element of civic life. That task is the focus of Azoulay's work in *The Civil Contract of Photography* and, more recently, in *Civil Imagination: A Political Ontology of Photography*. Both texts inform *The Public Image* and thus merit attention in their own right. Azoulay argues in *Civil Contract* that photography made possible a new and uniquely modern form of civic life, one that "modified the way in which individuals are governed and the extent of their participation in the forms of governance."[42] Photography is first and foremost neither a technology nor a form of seeing, she argues, but a tacit civil contract that binds viewers, photographed subjects and objects, and photographers together. To call this a contract bespeaks the social constitution of photographic practice that for all practical purposes obligates all of these parties, though often without their conscious consent. Especially given the ubiquity of the camera these days, any of us can (and most of us likely will) occupy any or all of those positions (photographer, photographed subject, viewer) at some point.[43] In doing so, we effectively sign on to the photographic contract and are made photographic citizen-subjects with all of the rights and responsibilities thereto appertaining, if you will.[44]

Citizenship in a photographic body politic can constitute an important counterweight to politics as usual—or not. *Civil Contract* is anchored in and by Azoulay's own political situation as an Israeli citizen at odds with Israeli policy and practice on Palestine. That context makes her work particularly relevant to a decolonial project like the one under consideration here. Of specific concern to Azoulay are the responses of Israeli citizen-spectators to photographs that document their government's mistreatment of Palestinians. The photographic civil contract enables Palestinian photographed subjects, though excluded from Israeli citizenship (or full citizenship, in the case of those who reside in Israel), to claim photographic citizenship with their Israeli spectators, a claim that registers as an ethical demand (that their suffering be seen, acknowledged, and addressed). That claim is honored by Israeli citizen-spectators as much in the breach as in the fulfillment. Photographs documenting mistreatment of Palestinians are (or were, at the time Azoulay wrote *Civil Contract*) a regular part of the daily news.[45] Yet, for every Israeli who responds to such photographs with outrage and compassion, there is another who responds with righteous triumph—and yet another with a shrug; this phenomenon trades on photographic ambivalence and reinforces the conventional relationship between seeing and believing. Not even the most arresting photograph can compel a given spectator to respond to it in a specific way. A viewer may pass over the photograph without blinking; they may question its truthfulness and dismiss it; or they may be moved to protest what they see.

For a time, Azoulay reports in *Civil Imagination*, she gave up on photography as a political resource. Its inefficacy lay, in her view, in the way photographs turn reality into art. Photographs of suffering aestheticize it, thereby anaesthetizing spectators against the (all-too-real) pain that the photographers aimed to capture. That is not the fault of the photographers, on her read, but of the mechanism at the center of the photographic contract: the camera. Unique among the various forms of documentation human beings employ, Azoulay argues, the photograph always contains more—and less—than the photographer intended. This reflects the camera's stubborn independence. "Possess[ing] its own character and drives," Azoulay writes, the camera might seem "obedient, but it is also capable of being cunning, seductive, conciliatory, vengeful or friendly." (It has not only agency but its own affective repertoire, note!) It is, moreover, "an opaque tool that does not expose anything of its inner workings."[46] What early adopters of the camera called "the pencil of nature," Azoulay notes, is "an inscribing machine that transforms the encounter that comes into being around it, through it, and by means of its mediation, into a special form of encounter," a "visual protocol" that confounds human visual sovereignty whether one is photographer, spectator, or photographed subject.[47] Even when the camera is pointed at someone or something (surveillance cameras, for example), those (potentially) caught in its view cannot tell whether the camera is on or off or whether or what it's registering. This "creates conditions under which the mere possibility of the existence of a photograph of us taken without our knowledge might come to affect us with as much potency as if we had encountered the photograph itself," Azoulay writes.[48] She offers the example of a Palestinian detainee threatened with the alleged existence of a photo that places the detainee in a certain unwanted situation (one use, by the way, to which the Abu Ghraib photographs were put by the U.S. military). The threat is effective without the photograph being shown (as is usually the case, she goes on to say); believing *is* (for all practical purposes) seeing, in such instances.

The camera-machine thus proves itself useful to the sovereign nation-state, itself "a kind of war machine" that promises its citizens safety via its security apparatus.[49] The price for this promise of safety is extracted primarily from those deemed threats, of course, but it also threatens democracy itself and thus the citizens the state aims to protect, Azoulay claims. The remedy to this problem is what she calls the civil imagination and the civil gaze that fuels it. Together, they can generate a different form of being-with that cuts across the lines of us versus them, of self versus other. Because it has the potential to animate the civil gaze, photography is uniquely able to jump-start the civil imagination. Photography's civil potential arises, she argues, from seismic shifts in political ontology generated by photography as a technology and a practice. Photography's advent inaugurates a change in human being-together with one another and with visual images. By creating a public place/space we share with everyone and everything, photography has created a visual culture that has transformed not only how people see images but how they see themselves and their surroundings. "Every gaze is always exposed to the gaze of the other and its sense changes in accordance with their reactions," Azoulay writes.[50]

The civil gaze, however, is anything but an automatic response to a given photograph. Our default response to our "culture of visual plenty" is what Azoulay calls the leisurely gaze. Reminiscent in many ways of Walter Benjamin's flaneur, the leisurely gaze wanders aimlessly through this visual landscape and its plethora of visual objects. In search of nothing in particular, it "skim[s] . . . the surface of the visible," largely undisturbed by what it sees.[51] Precisely this randomness, though, gives rise to the civil potential in the leisurely gaze. Once animated, the civil gaze requires much more of spectators than the leisurely gaze. Spectators must look more deeply into their visual landscapes and into themselves. To gaze civilly, the spectator must "transcend his or her own particular interests" to become "capable of judging in universal terms that which is on display."[52]

How well aligned are the civil gaze and the civil imagination with de-colonizing spectatorship and/as photographic insurrection? In evoking transcendence of self-interest in favor of universality, Azoulay seems to yoke the civil gaze to the very modern invention that her account of the camera's agency called into question, the (allegedly) self-sovereign subject. Knowing and applying universal principles—especially instead of taking the easy route of self-gratification—is the very essence of self-mastery and thus self-sovereignty. However, a more Foucauldian genealogy of that subject such as that on offer in *Signs and Wonders* would seem to question whether the civil gaze is up to the task of decolonizing spectatorship. Modern politico-visual culture and its sovereign subject are, in no small part, products of colonialism, I argue there. Man's status as sovereign is realized through achieving mastery over self and other, a project that photography helps realize. Per Stoler, the colonies were sites where colonizers practiced the (more benign) craft of self-mastery alongside—and indeed through—the (more brutal) exercise of mastery over colonized others. Photography aided and abetted both practices.

The civil gaze, however, is not (on my read, at least) a product of self-sovereignty as self-mastery; it is, rather, a (quasi-Levinasian and explicitly Arendtian) response to the gaze of the photographed other.[53] The civil gaze is, of course, one response among others that our participation in the civil contract of photography can prompt. Nothing can guarantee that a given spectator will respond to the photographs of Kurdi, say, with sympathy or outrage, much less that those who do will become advocates for refugees. And one can name certain universal principles, such as those embedded in human rights discourse, that could certainly be invoked as obligating us to others regardless of nationality or citizenship status.[54] Still, Azoulay's primary interest is in the civil gaze as a counterforce to visual capitulation to the sovereign nation-state that wants us to see things its way. However, the analysis I've offered of photographic subjection shows that the sovereign nation-state is not the only barrier to the civil imagination. And human rights discourse brings us back to liberal humanism (and its affective repertoire, liberal sentimentality), at whose center the modern sovereign subject resides, itself a product, I've argued, of biodisciplinary power. The path toward decolonizing spectatorship can't go around liberal humanism any more than it can go around liberal sentimentality. It must go through both, I would argue, and thus through their biopolitical milieu.

In its introduction, I frame *Signs and Wonders* as an exercise in photographic ascesis, a reference that exploits a convergence of the religious and the secular, theology and philosophy. Of Greek provenance, *ascesis* references practices of deliberate self-(re)formation undertaken under the aegis of philosophy (Stoicism, for example) or religion (including but hardly limited to Christianity). Those practices were aimed toward realizing the human being's proper end (telos): *eudaimonia* for the Stoic ascetics, union with God for Christian ascetics. In both cases, the practices engaged required looking both outward and inward for the effects of deformation and resources for reformation. In the introduction I suggest readers approach *Signs and Wonders* as a contemplative exercise of sorts, one that asks them to slow down and pay careful attention to the photographs that anchor it and what they open up and open onto—including their (our) own formation by biodisciplinary power.

While Azoulay's civil gaze is a start, it is insufficient on its own as a route toward decolonized spectatorship and the practices of photographic ascesis that could generate and sustain it. For one thing, Azoulay's visual repertoire—two gazes, essentially, the leisurely and the civil—seems impoverished taxonomically and ethically. We know from other scholarship on visual culture that the visual repertoire available to us includes ways of seeing that objectify, demean, and exoticize women (Laura Mulvey), people with disabilities (Rosemarie Garland-Thomson), and colonized people of color (Frantz Fanon).[55] Furthermore, it bypasses altogether questions of photographic affect: how photographs move us—to feel emotion and to take action. Yet these are questions that, I've argued, are deeply connected to seeing and believing. What resources might Christian theology—understood, recall, as a discourse and as a visual practice—offer instead or in addition?[56] On the one hand, theology's negotiations with seeing and believing have been embedded in (indeed, mostly in bed *with*) colonialism for virtually its entire history. Christianity's founding moment is arguably a crisis of embedded seeing and believing: what to make of the sight of an empty tomb intended to house the colonized Jew believed by his followers to be the Messiah but crucified by imperial Roman forces as a dangerous rebel. Within a few hundred years, however, the religion that ultimately emerged from that crisis was in bed with Rome, an alliance it would craft with subsequent western European colonial powers. Decolonization is not something that will come easily to Christianity, then.

But Christianity's history as what we might call a mediated religion, on the other hand, holds out some promise. Per the anthropologist Birgit Meyer, religions are forms of mediation in two senses. They claim to mediate the transcendent, and they do so in and through the media available to them.[57] Many of those are visual media (paintings, sculpture, or architecture; ordinary writing or calligraphy; the scroll, the book, the tract; film or television; Facebook or Second Life).[58] Likely because they seek to mediate transcendence, religions—including but hardly limited to Christianity—are extremely sensitive to visual mediation's complex relationship to seeing and believing, to the power of iconography and the danger of idolatry, for example.

David Morgan, a historian of religious visual culture, brings these insights to bear on Christianity in ways I find particularly productive. Citing written gospels, visual icons, and cathedral architecture as examples before focusing in on the British Evangelical tract, Morgan demonstrates that Christianity has been a mediated religion for virtually its entire history.[59] Indeed, navigating the relationship between seeing and believing has meant negotiating with one media revolution after another (e.g., the printing press, television, and now social media) and the visual cultures in which they are embedded. And Christianity's status as a global lingua franca, if you will (itself a reflection of its imperial and colonialist legacy), has impacted those visual cultures as well.[60] One example, I would argue, is the theological rhetoric (iconicity and iconoclasm, photographic literalism) repurposed so productively by the scholarly and popular discourse on photography I have engaged here.

I can only sketch some of them in rough outline here, but I see in Morgan's approach to seeing and believing important resources for curating (and hopefully cultivating) practices of photographic ascesis that could decolonize spectatorship, particularly in his recent book *The Embodied Eye: Religious Visual Culture and the Social Life of Feeling*. First of all, he explicitly addresses seeing *and* believing as complex and interrelated phenomena. For Morgan, seeing is much more than simply casting one's eye on a visual object, and believing is much more than mere intellectual assent to a proposition. Individually and together they are deeply *embodied*, *enculturated*, *interactive*, and *affective* practices. Religious seeing takes place in and on visual fields shaped as much by viewers' larger social context (family, nation, social location, etc.) as by their religious affiliation (or lack thereof). These visual fields generate multiple and multiform gazes, each of which disposes viewers to certain postures toward their world and the others who inhabit it with them. And Morgan argues that one cannot disaggregate religious seeing (and believing) from the full human sensorium and from the full range of human feeling.

Morgan limns as examples eight religious gazes drawn from Christian visual culture but present in other religions as well. Not only the gazes themselves as a visual repertoire but the larger framework he provides for them strike me as potentially generative. This particular set of gazes is not intended to be exhaustive but exemplary and invitational. Some may be ephemeral, while others endure. All will come and go and shape-shift—even shift into one another—depending on the context. Notably, given my interests, Morgan has an expansive notion of what can be objects for these gazes. In addition to explicitly religious visual objects (religious icons, say), these gazes are evoked by visual objects that invoke "a mythical past, a national destiny, a compelling narrative, a social order, a people, a totemic founder or hero, a place or a ritual enactment."[61] In certain cases, he also connects these gazes to other very mundane experiences of seeing. The occlusive gaze, for example, in which the viewer seeks to avoid being seen by the divine power (the evil eye, say), is analogous to the experience of closing one's eyes in shame to avoid another's judgmental gaze.[62] While making good on this promise is beyond the scope of this essay, Morgan offers a visual repertoire that I think could resource practices of photographic ascesis in support of decolonizing spectatorship.

I HAVE OFFERED HERE AT LEAST PRELIMINARY evidence that Christian theology—understood as a discourse and a visual practice—offers critical resources for wrestling with the ethical and social challenges posed by the convergence of digital technology, social media, and photographic practice that forms our current visual culture. Perhaps we should not be surprised by this. After all, well before photographs were embodied in silicon and binary code, Christianity was navigating the complicated relationships between (per the epigraphs at the start) the "real and [the] virtual," the "material and [the] symbolic," the "sensate and [the] mediated," as not simply "clouds of fancy" or "pellets of information" but routes to self-formation (deformation and reformation). To complicated and sometimes conflicting ends, of course, but with lessons to teach us as we do the same in our (not-so?) newly mediated world.

Notes

1 The photographs were taken by a Turkish professional photojournalist, Nilüfer Demir, of the Dogan New Agency and shared via Twitter by Peter Bouckaert of Human Rights Watch. Bryan Walsh and Time Photo, "Alan Kurdi's Story: Behind the Most Heartbreaking Photo of 2015," *Time,* December 29, 2015, http://time.com/4162306/alan-kurdi-syria-drowned-boy-refugee-crisis.

2   Andrew Anthony, "Accidental Activists: The British Women on the Front Line of the Refugee Crisis," *Guardian*, June 12, 2016, https://www.theguardian.com/world/2016/jun/12/help-refugees-calais-accidental-activists.

3   Jody Cantor and Katrin Einhorn, "Refugees Encounter a Strange Word: Welcome," *New York Times,* June 30, 2016. I have much more to say about this photograph and the issues it opens up and onto in "Justice for Alan Kurdi? Philosophy, Photography and the (Cosmo)Politics of Life and Death."

4   Spencer Ackerman, "Islamic State Uses Images of Alan Kurdi to Threaten Syrian Refugees for Fleeing," *Guardian,* September 9, 2015, https://www.theguardian.com/world/2015/sep/09/islamic-state-alan-kurdi-photo-magazine-dabiq-syrian-refugees.

5   Vanessa Willoughby, "U.S. Army Veterans Apologized to Native Americans at Standing Rock," *Teen Vogue,* December 5, 2016, https://www.teenvogue.com/story/us-army-veterans-apologized-to-native-americans-at-standing-rock; and Wes Enzinna, "I Witnessed Cops Using Tear Gas, Rubber Bullets and Sound Cannons against Anti-Pipeline Protestors," *Mother Jones,* October 31, 2016, https://www.motherjones.com/politics/2016/10/standing-rock-protests-pipeline-police-tasers-teargas/.

6   For more on Foucault's understanding of power, see Armour, *Signs and Wonders*, ch. 1.

7   See McWhorter, *Racism and Sexual Oppression in Anglo-America.*

8   For more on Christianity's imbrication in colonial biodiscipline (and the consequences thereof), see Armour, *Signs and Wonders,* chs. 3, 4.

9   For more on why I speak of a fourfold, see the Introduction to *Signs and Wonders,* 2–4. I am not claiming that only modern human beings divided the world along these lines. Rather, the specific modern taxonomies that the fourfold produces—and their effects—are distinctive.

10 In *Camera Lucida,* 115, Barthes speaks of the photograph's "that-has-been" (*ça-a-été*).

11 For Barthes' use of *significance* and its Kristevan roots, see Barthes, *Image-Music-Text,* 10–11. I develop the concepts of photographic truth and significance in chapter 2 of *Signs and Wonders.*

12 Hariman and Lucaites, *No Caption Needed,* 36, 37.

13 W. J. T. Mitchell, "The Abu Ghraib Archive," in *Cloning Terror,* 133–56. A third set of photographs, on Hurricane Katrina, also attends to (settler, in this case) colonialism as a geographic and ecological force, but that is not the chapter's primary focus.

14 Stoler, *Race and the Education of Desire,* 16; and Stoler, *Carnal Knowledge and Imperial Power,* 97.

15 Stoler, *Race and the Education of Desire,* 18.

16 See Lytle, "Virtual Incarnations."

17 I learned about Christian influencers from the students in my Theology, Visual Culture and New Media course. Christian evangelicals—cis men and women—are particularly prominent in this aspect of virtual religion, but so are LGBTQI folks using social media to connect with their spiritual kin in search of spiritual sustenance. Thanks to my students in the course for alerting me to these phenomena.

18 See Shirky, *Here Comes Everybody*.

19 See Turkle, *Alone Together*.

20 See the essays in Cheong et al., *Digital Religion, Social Media and Culture*. Communications scholar Heidi Campbell and theologian Stephen Garner sketch out some of the promise in what they call "networked theology" by examining some of the more creative ways that institutional Christianity shows up online. See Campbell and Garner, *Networked Theology*.

21 For example, the Anglican Cathedral of Second Life offers opportunities for worship and prayer on Epiphany Island (its online site) but does not offer any of the sacraments (baptism, Eucharist, or marriage) online on the grounds that they require and express "a real, physical and personal interaction" that simply isn't possible online (see their statement "Sacraments on Epiphany Island" on the Anglican Cathedral of Second Life website, accessed September 14, 2020, https://slangcath.wordpress.com/the-vision /sacraments-on-epiphany-island/. Nonetheless, Julie Anne Lytle argues— using the work of theologians Catherine LaCugna and Karl Rahner—that online religion provides "virtual incarnations" of divine presence that can indeed foster genuinely faithful communal and personal devotion. See Lytle, "Virtual Incarnations."

22 As with research on social media in general, most of the scholarship on this topic is ethnographic and focuses on particular issues and/or particular communities and attends to photography as a dimension of social media. Jessie Daniels's *Cyber Racism: White Supremacy Online and the New Attack on Civil Rights*, for example, explores briefly the role photographs play in how teenagers evaluate websites dealing with racial matters. Photographs get read as evidence; their presence enhances a website's credibility, while their absence calls it into question. An exception (in focus, though not in its sociological approach) is Edgar Gómez Cruz and Asko Lehmuskallio's edited collection *Digital Photography and Everyday Life: Empirical Studies on Material Visual Practices*, which combines research on the role digital photography plays in various communities with research on photographic practices writ large.

23 Appropriately, that photograph now adorns hoodies, T-shirts, and other paraphernalia sold to support the Trayvon Martin Foundation, a testimony to its iconic power. See the Trayvon Martin Foundation shop website,

accessed September 14, 2020, https://www.trayvonmartinfoundation.org
/shop.

24 See Keith O'Shea, Darran Simon, and Holly Yan, "Dylann Roof's Racist
Rants Read in Court," *CNN*, December 14, 2016, https://www.cnn.com
/2016/12/13/us/dylann-roof-murder-trial/index.html.

25 Winnubst, "After Modernity?"

26 See Hartman, *Scenes of Subjection*.

27 Calvin, *Institutes of the Christian Religion*, 95–96, quoted in Morgan, *Embodied Eye*, 73.

28 Morgan, *Protestants and Pictures*. The allusion to Walter Benjamin's famous
essay, "The Work of Art in the Age of Mechanical Reproduction" (1936),
is deliberate. Morgan endorses much of Benjamin's position but argues
that mechanically reproduced religious images, at least, retain their (actual,
not simply metaphorical, as applied to art) sacred aura. For the essay, see
Benjamin, *Illuminations*. I discuss Benjamin in my chapter on photography
in *Signs and Wonders*.

29 Hariman and Lucaites, *Public Image*, 28.

30 Hariman and Lucaites remind us that photography is hardly the first (or
the last, given critiques of social media) public medium to be accused of
doing us more harm than good. Indeed, every media revolution has aroused
concern about its deleterious effects on humanity—including writing. That
observation called to this reader's mind (via Jacques Derrida) the Platonic
view of writing as a *pharmakon*—cure and poison—for forgetting. Nor
is the most recent media revolution the first to enchant us, if you will.
William Gibson, author of *Neuromancer*, the sci-fi novel that presciently
envisioned our virtual reality today (and inventor of the term *cyberspace*),
observed recently that TV's advent in the 1940s likely meant fewer people
were hanging out on their front stoops in New York City, for example; a
change that went largely unremarked perhaps *because* those who might note
it were themselves inside watching TV. Laura Sydell, "The Father of the
Internet Sees His Invention Reflected Back through a 'Black Mirror'," *All
Tech Considered*, National Public Radio, February 20, 2018, https://www
.npr.org/sections/alltechconsidered/2018/02/20/583682937/the-father-of
-the-internet-sees-his-invention-reflected-back-through-a-black-mir.

31 Hariman and Lucaites, *Public Image*, 31. Tagg's game-changing text in the
study of photography, *The Burden of Representation: Essays on Photographies
and Histories*, is critical to my account of photographic truth in *Signs and
Wonders*.

32 Hariman and Lucaites, *Public Image*, 62.

33 "Accidental Napalm" features prominently not only in *No Caption Needed*
but in *Signs and Wonders'* account of photography. Photojournalists
(including Nick Ut, who took "Accidental Napalm") experience journal-

istic ethics in more fraught and complex ways, of course, as Hariman and Lucaites are well aware. For more on this issue, see Armour, *Signs and Wonders*, 82–84, and the associated endnotes. See also Armour, "Justice for Alan Kurdi."

34 Sontag, *Regarding*, 47.

35 Sontag, *Regarding*, 7.

36 Hariman and Lucaites, *Public Image*, 59.

37 In *Civil Imagination: A Political Ontology of Photography*, Ariella Azoulay speaks of the photographic event: the ongoing call-and-response between a given photograph and the various publics who view it. I have more to say about this book (though not this topic) later on.

38 Hariman and Lucaites, *Public Image*, 69.

39 Hariman and Lucaites, *Public Image*, 71.

40 Hariman and Lucaites, *Public Image*, 72.

41 The (subtle) reference to Hans-Georg Gadamer is intentional.

42 Azoulay, *Civil Contract*, 89.

43 But Azoulay notes that the disenfranchised and those on the bottom-most rungs of the social ladder are more often the photographed than the photographer.

44 For much more on this in relationship to what I call spectatorial responsibility, see chapter 2 of *Signs and Wonders*.

45 Some of the photographs Azoulay considers are acts of photographic insurrection taken by Israeli photographers who share Azoulay's political perspective with the goal of moving their fellow citizen-viewers toward insurrection, by the way.

46 Azoulay, *Civil Imagination*, 15–16.

47 Azoulay, *Civil Imagination*, 17.

48 Azoulay, *Civil Imagination*, 23.

49 Azoulay, *Civil Imagination*, 8.

50 Azoulay, *Civil Imagination*, 68.

51 Azoulay, *Civil Imagination*, 71.

52 Azoulay, *Civil Imagination*, 44.

53 Azoulay, *Civil Imagination*, 44.

54 This connects the civil gaze and civil imagination with another discourse, that of cosmopolitanism, which has its own conflicted relationship with sovereignty. I use that discourse (and that conflict) to analyze the response to Kurdi's photographs in "Justice for Alan Kurdi?"

55 Mulvey, an art historian, famously limned "the male gaze" in her 1975 essay "Visual Pleasure and Narrative Cinema." On ways of seeing disability, see Garland-Thomson, *Staring*. In *Black Skin, White Masks*, Fanon describes the objectifying effect of the white gaze. Of course, before all of these is Jean-Paul Sartre's analysis of the gaze (*le regard*) in *Being and Nothingness*.

56 That I turn to Christian theology is not an indication that resources exist *only* here. There are resources to be found in other scholarly disciplines (and interdisciplines) as well. Scholars (including but not limited to those cited in the previous endnote) have taken up the challenge of articulating ways of looking back, if you will, that resist objectification. Attending to that body of literature, however, is beyond the scope of this essay.

57 Meyer, "Religious Sensations."

58 That Meyer uses ethnography to study them and their impact reminds that all media are social media—even if put to use on occasion by an individual for their eyes only.

59 Morgan, "Mediation or Mediatisation." Morgan's larger aim (successfully realized, on my read, at least) is to contest perspectives on the relationship between religion and media distorted by the presumptive narrative of modernity as the gradual triumph of secularism.

60 Of course, these cultures are not only visual. Morgan's account of the tract tracks along the way its imbrication not only in print culture but in commerce, capitalism, and colonialism.

61 Morgan, *Embodied Eye*, 69.

62 Morgan, *Embodied Eye*, 72.

Bibliography

Armour, Ellen. "Justice for Alan Kurdi? Philosophy, Photography and the (Cosmo)politics of Life and Death." *Philosophy Today* 63, no. 2 (Spring 2019): 315–33.

Armour, Ellen. *Signs and Wonders: Theology after Modernity*. New York: Columbia University Press, 2016.

Azoulay, Ariella. *The Civil Contract of Photography*. New York: Zone Books, 2012.

Azoulay, Ariella. *Civil Imagination: A Political Ontology of Photography*. New York: Verso, 2015.

Barthes, Roland. *Camera Lucida: Reflections on Photography*. London: Vintage, 1990.

Barthes, Roland. *Image-Music-Text*. Translated by Stephen Heath. New York: Farrar, Strauss and Giroux, 1977.

Benjamin, Walter. *Illuminations: Essays and Reflections*. Edited by Hannah Arendt. New York: Harcourt, Brace, Jovanovich, 1968.

Calvin, John. *Institutes of the Christian Religion*. Translated by Henry Beveridge. Grand Rapids, MI: Eerdmans, 1989.

Campbell, Heidi, and Stephen Garner. *Networked Theology: Negotiating Faith in Digital Culture*. Grand Rapids, MI: Baker Academic, 2016.

Cheong, Pauline Hope, Peter Fisher-Nielsen, Stefan Gelfgren, and Charles Ess, eds. *Digital Religion, Social Media and Culture: Perspectives, Practices and Futures*. New York: Peter Lang, 2012.

Daniels, Jessie. *Cyber Racism: White Supremacy Online and the New Attack on Civil Rights*. New York: Rowman and Littlefield, 2009.

Fanon, Frantz. *Black Skin, White Masks*. New York: Grove, 1967.

Garland-Thomson, Rosemarie. *Staring: How We Look*. New York: Oxford University Press, 2009.

Gómez Cruz, Edgar, and Asko Lehmuskallio, eds. *Digital Photography and Everyday Life: Empirical Studies on Material Visual Practices*. New York: Routledge, 2016.

Hariman, Robert, and John Louis Lucaites. *No Caption Needed: Iconic Photographs, Public Culture, and Liberal Democracy*. Chicago: University of Chicago Press, 2007.

Hariman, Robert, and John Louis Lucaites. *The Public Image: Photography and Civic Spectatorship*. Chicago: University of Chicago Press, 2016.

Hartman, Saidiya. *Scenes of Subjection*. New York: Oxford University Press, 1997.

Lytle, Julie Anne. "Virtual Incarnations: An Exploration of Internet-Mediated Interaction as Manifestation of the Divine." *Religious Education* 105, no. 4 (2010): 395–412.

McWhorter, LaDelle. *Racism and Sexual Oppression in Anglo-America: A Genealogy*. Bloomington: Indiana University Press, 2009.

Meyer, Birgit. "Religious Sensations: Why Media, Aesthetics and Power Matter in the Study of Contemporary Religion." In *Religion, Media and Culture: A Reader*, edited by Gordon Lynch, 159–70. New York: Taylor and Francis, 2011.

Mitchell, W. J. T. *Cloning Terror: The War of Images, 9/11 to the Present*. Chicago: University of Chicago Press, 2011.

Morgan, David. *The Embodied Eye: Religious Visual Culture and the Social Life of Feeling*. Berkeley: University of California Press, 2012.

Morgan, David. "Mediation or Mediatisation: The History of Media in the Study of Religion." *Culture and Religion* 12, no. 2 (2011): 137–52.

Morgan, David. *Protestants and Pictures: Religion, Visual Culture, and the Age of American Mass Production*. New York: Oxford University Press, 1999.

Mulvey, Laura. "Visual Pleasure and Narrative Cinema." *Screen* 16, no. 3 (1975): 6–18.

Sartre, Jean-Paul. *Being and Nothingness*. New York: Washington Square, 1956.

Shirky, Clay. *Here Comes Everybody: The Power of Organizing without Organizations*. New York: Penguin Books, 2008.

Sontag, Susan. *On Photography*. New York: Picador, 1977.

Sontag, Susan. *Regarding the Pain of Others.* New York: Picador, 2003.

Stoler, Ann Laura. *Carnal Knowledge and Imperial Power: Race and the Intimate in Colonial Rule.* Berkeley: University of California Press, 2002.

Stoler, Ann Laura. *Race and the Education of Desire: Foucault's History of Sexuality and the Colonial Order of Things.* Durham, NC: Duke University Press, 1995.

Tagg, John. *The Burden of Representation: Essays on Photographies and Histories.* Minneapolis: University of Minnesota Press, 1993.

Turkle, Sherry. *Alone Together: Why We Expect More from Technology and Less from Each Other.* Rev. and exp. ed. New York: Basic Books, 2017.

Winnubst, Shannon. "After Modernity? Whose? Which? When? And, Perhaps Most of All, How?" In the *"Signs and Wonders"* symposium. Syndicate, December 12, 2018. https://syndicate.network/symposia/theology/signs-and-wonders/.

J. Kameron Carter

6 The Excremental Sacred

A Paraliturgy

Bidault, looking like a communion wafer dipped in shit . . .—Aimé Césaire, *Discourse on Colonialism*

There is so much the west is unable to digest / finds / unthinkable / does not wish to / perhaps cannot / assimilate without itself changing . . . / so perhaps ritual provides a way through the thicket of impossibles . . . / I am committed to retaining an ambivalence of the sacred object.—M. NourbeSe Philip, "Wor(1)ds Interrupted"

The ceremony must be found . . .—Sylvia Wynter

Indigestion: "There Is So Much the West Is Unable to Digest"

IN THE LATE 1930S, a group of "evolved" (*evolué*) francophone Black intellectuals gathered in France to express among themselves their disfavor of and resistance to French colonialism. Among them were Aimé Césaire and Suzanne Roussi (who would become partners), Léopold Sédar Senghor (future president of Senegal), and Léon-Gontran Damas of French Guiana. Convening them were "freedom dreams" for futures beyond the conventional notion and form of the human at the heart of the Western civilizing (that is, colonizing) project. *Negritude* is the name this itinerant group convened in Paris in the late 1930s gave what they were doing.

My concern in what follows is with a specific dimension of negritude that has gone underexamined. Internal to negritude as an aesthetic and political practice is an exposure of the logic of Christian political theology that was underwriting the nation-state of France and that, I claim, continues to underwrite and structure Western modernity as a practice of the political. Césaire's exposure of this has my attention in what follows, for his poetics reveals that the political as a concept and as one of Western civilization's key terms is, in fact, a "god term." Which is to say, Western modernity's concept of the political is a function of Western modernity's concept of the theological, even as the concept of the theological is a function of the concept of the political. Moving illegibly at the limits of political theology, negritude brings into view white supremacy—or, more simply, whiteness—as the performance of racial-imperial transcendence. What David Marriott has recently said in a definitive study of the thought of Frantz Fanon, a one-time student of Césaire's, regarding the philosophical and spiritual stakes of Fanon's anticolonial project can just as well be said of Césaire's project too. Césaire understood that (and suggested how) racial capitalism, at the heart of which is whiteness, operates as the "performance of [a kind of] spiritual power" whose ontology is organized around both the violent consumption (the incorporation) and the phobic expenditure (the excrementalization) of Blackness, even as something of that Blackness remains lodged in the innards of capitalism itself, an indigestible remainder that is capital's ongoing inner and unsettling disturbance.[1] As an indigestible excess that refuses institutional naming and ultimately falls out of representation, Blackness operates as varied and variegated practices of commoning and commune-ion-ing in the name of nonunitary community. This is an alternative practice of the social, a poetics of improvisational sociality under constraint. As such, Blackness signals others modes of aliveness or life-together in the world. Such a negritudinous or "black way of living" is bound up with a reimagination of matter and a reimaging of self—self or subjectivity in and as relation, in and as relational identifications—beyond the individuating and suffocating frameworks of identitarian and thus propertizing logics of the human.[2]

In many ways, unpacking this claim is what I pursue in the pages to follow. But before getting right to this, it is worth remarking ever so briefly that while Césaire's insight here was, to be sure, uniquely powerful, it was not singular. Indeed, his insight is in keeping with a strikingly similar one made by another radical intellectual of the first half of the twentieth century: W. E. B. Du Bois. In "The Souls of White Folk"—first published in 1910 for the *Independent* and then massively extended and republished in *Darkwater: Voices from within the Veil* in 1919, at the conclusion of the Great War, or World War I, just as the Treaty of Versailles, which formally brought the war to an end, was being signed—Du Bois spoke of that conflagration as the expression of *the religion of whiteness* in distress. He diagnosed the war as whiteness's incoherence, its conflict an intramural one coming violently into the open and taking the form of the Western powers struggling among themselves over who would lord it over which part of the planet. With this claim in place, Du Bois then puts a fine point on precisely what he means when he says that whiteness is religion. "I do not laugh," he says. "I am quite straight-faced as I ask soberly: 'But what on earth is whiteness that one should so desire it?' Then always, somehow, some way, silently but clearly, I am given to understand that whiteness is the ownership of the earth forever and ever, Amen!" As for the intramural unrest at that time, Du Bois speaks of this as wave upon wave, "dashing this new religion of whiteness on the shores of our times."[3]

Césaire also was onto this problem of what Du Bois called *the religion of whiteness* and what Césaire, in effect, will clarify as the coconstitutive nature of the concepts of race, religion, and the political as these converge on theology, though Césaire's immediate reference points in making the case for this are the island of Martinique and the wider Caribbean archipelago as gateway into the "New World." That is to say, Césaire understood that the imagination of the conventional human ("Man") and along with it the Western humanism that underwrites whiteness's trespassive transcendence or its practice of (phallic) sovereignty are sustained by the very notions of the political and the theological in their inseparable or coconstitutive convergence. That convergence is what I call *political theology*. The problem of the political and the theological, or of racial capitalism and colonialism as theological discourse, is what Césaire is getting at in the opening pages of *Discourse on Colonialism* when he speaks of the "Christian pedantry" and the "dishonest equations" of "Christianity = civilization, paganism = savagery" driving colonialism as discourse or as a mode of thought. From these equations, Césaire continues, "there could not but ensue abominable colonialist and racist consequences, whose victims were to be the Indians, the Yellow peoples, and the Negroes."[4] This concern over racial capitalism and colonialism as theological discourse also propels much of what Césaire works to articulate in *Cahier d'un retour au pays natal* (most recognizably translated as *Notebook of a Return to the Native Land*), his extended poem in which he advances the notion of negritude as a kind of anticolonial "countermyth" that subverts and dislocates Western civilization's terms of theologico-political order precisely "through a dislocation of language, through an assault upon the linguistic code itself in a sovereign disposal of its structural elements."[5] This sovereign—or, as I'm given to thinking about it, this insovereign—disposal and dispersal of the linguistic code, this scattering and scatting of language, is emphatically not of Christian or Western eschatology but is, shall we say, eschatology clipped. Not eschatology but scatology, the enactment of Black poetic knowledge precisely by thinking from that originary and excremental displacement, the abyssal descent associated with the Middle Passage, that is nothing less than the history of Blackness. That history, which also prompts the question of the status of the "archive" of slavery and its afterlives so valiantly and beautifully pursued in the work, for example, of Saidiya Hartman, is the history of a certain suspension.[6] More precisely, it is the history that eludes History (with a capital *H*), the history of what representation can neither capture nor hold but whose effects, like a black hole, are felt. This is a history of the hold, a history of what's "held-not-had."[7]

This is what is at stake when Césaire in his poem *Cahier* speaks of negritude not as an essence but as a certain kind of movement—a descending, which is a dissent, into hell, a falling. It is also what's at stake when in the same poem he invokes the Christian liturgical chant ("Alleluia / Kyrie eleison … leison … leison, / Christe eleison … leison … leison") in relationship to the Martinican landscape specifically but also more generally in relationship to the Caribbean archipelago and thus invites a consideration of Christian worship's relationship to the colonial script or to colonialism as a theosocial text. By way of these invocations, *Cahier* presents itself as a refusal or as the nonperformance of political theology's linguistic codes, codes that have corpsed Blackness and positioned Black life at the horizon of death. The refusal of which I speak *Cahier*'s poet calls *negritude*, the performance of an alternative spirituality or poetics of the sacred occasioned by the abyssal history of Blackness. From the abyss and thus in excess of the political and the theological, that is to say, in excess of what is called political theology, the poet approaches the Blackness of the sacred at the anamorphic limit of the Western political where possibilities not of "the world of Man" might be imagined.[8] Of the abyss, Blackness and the sacred operate liminally, as thresholds, vestibularly, as ellipses and thus as Silence—in short, as the (im)possibility of matter's reorganization without telos.

But I'm already getting ahead of myself. Allow me to trace the itinerary of the exploration to be undertaken here. In unfolding across this essay what I've just said in summary, I pause over a specific dimension of Césaire's critique of racial colonialism as political theology. More specifically, I want to think through the connection Césaire posits between the Christian sacrament of the Eucharist and his understanding of colonialism itself as a ritual. In thinking through this linkage, I want to follow Césaire's locating of racial colonialism inside of a long history of political theology *as sacramental performance* and as *ritual-qua-eucharistic event.*

Only recently has Césaire's early insight, developed in the mid-twentieth century as post–World War II decolonization efforts were getting into full swing, been picked up on or returned to in Black studies. Take, as an example, Denise Ferreira da Silva's arresting essay "Toward a Black Feminist Poethics: The Quest(ion) of Blackness toward the End of the World," which bears traces of Césaire's insight. There, Ferreira da Silva argues that the known and knowable world and, indeed, the very structures of our knowing the world draw on intellectual tools "modeled after the Category of Blackness."[9] Important in this formulation is what is meant by *category.* To confine Blackness to a rational category of racial knowledge about the people on whom the signifier "Black" has been imposed and thus to violently reduce Blackness to a rational category of the understanding is "[to arrest] Blackness's creative potential," its "capacity to signify otherwise." That is to say, in a kind of sleight of hand, racial knowledge recasts the violent "expropriation of the productive capacity of natives' lands and Black and African bodies" as but the "effects of the naturally (according to the notion of the survival of the fittest) violent encounter between racially different collectives."[10] This is all done to protect the (white) "Subject's claim to universality and transparency . . . and with this [tame] the radical potential Blackness hosts," that "creative potential . . . which slavery has never been able to destruct."[11] Interestingly, what Ferreira da Silva here explains as racial knowledge's would-be arresting and taming of the creative potentials that Blackness hosts by capturing Blackness within a sociology of race relations and a naturalized understanding of antagonistic racial difference, she earlier in the essay explains through the sacramental idea of transubstantiation, with the further implied notions of ritual, sacral eating, and religious sacrifice that work in relationship to that idea. "Because racial knowledge," she says, "transubstantiates (shifts them from the living to the formal register) what emerges in political relations into effects of efficient (scientific reason's) causality, its critical tools fail to register how the total (past, present, and future) value expropriated is in the very structures (in blood and flesh) of global capital."[12] Here, Ferreira da Silva suggests that the known and lived world, precisely as a *racially* known and lived world, is the result of a violent consuming of native lands and Black life and labor such that these become the inner substance or divine energy that powers or fuels global capital. All the more interesting here is that Ferreira da Silva understands this consumption as eating of "flesh and blood" or the "total value" in colonial expropriation. But my attention is particularly on the eating of flesh and blood inasmuch as it calls to mind the Christian sacrament of the Eucharist, the Communion ritual in which the bread and wine of the ceremony become or are, within the ritual terms of the ceremony, transubstantiated into the body and blood of the sacrificed God, Jesus Christ. Within the ceremony, matter is reorganized so as to establish an alternative order of things whose yield is a certain kind of community. That is to say, as communicants ceremonially eat and drink the bread and wine, the theopolitical community of the church, Christendom, comes into being and is sustained in being as a distinct kind of engulfing and yet exclusionary "we." Ferreira da Silva does not bear deeply into the symbolics of transubstantiation and thus into the colonial performance of religion that produces the world as we know it and as a scene of terror for those colonially "eaten" in this process. She simply deploys transubstantiation (clarifyingly so) within her explanation of the violent production of racial knowledge.

This is where Césaire comes in, for he approaches the eucharistic sacrament as a social text of the body (politic). Key for him on this is his insight into the European Middle Ages. Césaire contends that decolonization requires reckoning with how racial capitalism is lodged within, how it spatially expands to planetwide proportions, the sacrificial logics of the body (politic) as born out of the "eucharistic matrix" of the Middle Ages. More still, he proposes that effective decolonization requires contending with the linguistic codes or the operations of language upon matter that were a function of the eucharistic sacrifice of the Middle Ages. Césaire is keen in understanding how in the eucharistic ceremony, language operates upon matter in such a way as to ritually repeat the myth—the story that matters by conferring meaning, compass, direction, and a sense of home or orientation in the world—that structures Western culture.[13] I suggest here that in *Discourse on Colonialism* Césaire approaches the liturgy of the Eucharist not just as an empirically significant ritual in French culture and Western civilization; he approaches it at the level of myth, language, and, finally, matter. Indeed, he intuits that at the level of its symbolic codes, Western culture attempts to cohere itself by containing that which it deems the disorderly, chaotic, lawless, and even pathological and unregulatable energy or surplus that suffuses, surrounds, and is poised to anarrange, if not derange, Western order. The Eucharist functioned as part of a religious or politico-theological apparatus, indeed as part of a more general mythological apparatus in the Middle Ages, that sought to subdue this intolerable excess that is given to an alternative sociality. In *Cahier*, besides *negritude*, Césaire called this excess, which operates appositionally to what is called *religion* though ultimately it is distinct from it, *the sacred* (*sacré*, meaning both what is unique or holy and what is accursed and wretched). To further clarify its distinction from religion, I speak of this excess as *the pathological sacred*—that which deranges even as it, strictly speaking, is anterior to religion or theopolitical order.[14]

The religio-symbolic and even mythic machinations that I am describing here Césaire sees playing out through the imposition of certain eucharistic qua language protocols and operations onto matter itself—or more strictly speaking, onto our *imagination* of matter through which occurs the genesis or "imaginary institution of society."[15] These eucharistic-language protocols, tied as they were to the words uttered by the priest over the bread and wine to transubstantiate or change them into the body and blood of Christ ("Take and eat. This is my body. . . . This is my blood. . . ."), operate against the backdrop of a polymythic outside the normative (Christian) body (politic) presided over by priest and king, who together mediate divine sovereignty through churchly and royal or monopolitical sovereignty. The emergence of the body and indeed of the body politic points to a new mode of being, a new organization of matter, a new mode of approach to self-consciousness, where self emerges as an entity of individualized sovereignty. I'll hold off going further into this as I take up what happened in the Middle Ages in more detail later on. In time, and eventually with the opening up of the Black Atlantic toward the late Middle Ages and what comes to be periodized as early modernity, the medieval notion of a *homo christianus* and of the Christian body (politic) will through further symbolic feats transubstantiate into the body of modernity, that is, into the sovereign, individuated body of modern-colonial

Man. This body or Man's body will socially display itself as the demo-cratized body politic of modern civil society. This is the societal commu-nion or fraternity of Men as a certain extension of the logics of political theology born in the Middle Ages, which transformed from ecclesial and royal sovereignty into democratic sovereignty.

If colonial violence works ceremonially in this way, then decoloniza-tion, Césaire in effect proposes, must intervene in or contravene this cer-emony. It must enact an alternative ceremony, one that is extraceremonial to the racially gendered ceremony of coloniality. I propose to think with Césaire's extraceremonial poetics. More specifically, I key off of Césaire's statement in *Discourse on Colonialism* that the colonial administrator Georges Bidault, standing in the French National Assembly to give a pub-lic statement about how France was faring in the face of the anticolonial uprising in Madagascar in the late 1940s, was "looking like a communion wafer dipped in shit."[16] Here, Césaire invites an understanding of what we might think of as the *colonial sacrament of race*, a transubstantiating or extending of medieval political theology into globality. In taking up Césaire's invitation, I explore both racial capitalism as the inner grammar of modernity's colonial medievalism and political theology as the inner grammar of racially gendered capitalism.

The both-and of this last sentence highlights my effort to refuse the colonial temporality that structures the Western Christian symbolic uni-verse. Within this symbolic universe, a retrograde past progresses toward a secularized and thus more advanced modernity. However, as historian Kathleen Biddick has rigorously argued, "the purported 'secularization' of modernity" is built on a set of teleological and ultimately "supersessionary fantasies" about time.[17] Bound up with the sacrament of the Eucharist in the Middle Ages, those fantasies had to do with establishing a Christian "this is now" that supersedes a Jewish "that was then."[18] Moreover, this medieval form of Christian time entailed nothing less than a sacramen-tally enacted imagination of matter. Christ's sacramental presence in the matter of bread and wine worked toward Jewish displacement. I'll have more to say about this shortly. The point now is simply that Césaire intuits that this approach to the matter of time did not go away but rather tran-substantiated into a new, colonial organization of time wherein through the transatlantic circuit a Westernized "this is now" of History (with a capital *H*) constituted itself as the temporal overcoming of the "that was then" that Johannes Fabian has called "the time of the other."[19] The Jewish as "Semitic" other and Western Man's savage other become typologically yoked under a sacred canopy and within a singular symbolic universe of a still ritually enacted liturgical-as-ontotheological terror.[20] The terror of it all, at least as I investigate it here, has to do with the ecclesiastical ceremoniality of colonialism, how it plays out as a sacramental ritual that extends the medieval eucharistic matrix so as literally to organize matter into a violent and restricted economy of value, the basis of a phenomenology of colonial violence. Much of what I am trying to get at here has to do with my (following Césaire's) effort to read the theological idea of transubstantiation as enacting a social text and, in light of this, to ask what it might mean, in keeping with the epigraphs to this essay, to find a "new ceremony" and to be involved in a decolonial performance, an alternative ritual of Blackness that might "[provide] a way through the thicket of impossibles." I propose that within his critique of the colonial sacrament of race or the liturgy of Man, Césaire speaks to this issue of an alternative mythography of the possible through the impossibles.

This brings me to the second matter that I take up in this essay. Continuing to think with Césaire, I want to situate the insight about the co-constitutive nature of colonialism and/as Christian Communion against the wider backdrop from which Césaire's critique of this aspect of Western civilization emerges. This wider backdrop is Blackness or, in Césairean parlance, *negritude*, which for Césaire is emphatically not about an essential Blackness. If anything, for Césaire the essence of Blackness proves to be the performance of its nonessence or its abyssal and essential inessentiality. To say it yet one more time but with a slightly different inflection drawn from Fred Moten, Blackness is the performance of the "groundedness of an uncontainable outside," a founding groundlessness.[21] I thus want to argue for Blackness, under Césaire's provocation, as an anticolonial antisacrament or, to use Sylvia Wynter's language, as the practice of another ceremony that moves in extraceremonial apposition to the linguistic ceremony of race. Negritude, in short, functions in apposition to the priestly words of institution—words that aim to institute, or that house, a semiotics or (anti-Black?) grammar of the body proper. In making this case, I offer an exegesis or a midrash-like commentary on Césaire's statement "[Georges] Bidault, looking like a communion wafer dipped in shit." In so doing, I aim to position negritude as breaking the linguistic code of eucharistic bodily propriety with a view to exposing colonial discourse to an excremental, an extraceremonial, a fleshy outside. A decolonial poetics of remaindered, inconsumable, and indigestible life, negritude operates as extraceremonial performance.

More still, Césaire most forcefully stages his approach to negritude at the scene of the poem. Why the poem? Because it is there that certain mythographic operations take place. Those operations refuse language (in Césaire's case, the imperialism of the French language) as a hegemonically closed system through which society is imaginarily instituted around "God's phallus" or the (monotheistic as the monopolitical) One.[22] Hence, my attention toward the end of this essay on Césaire's *Cahier*, where I discuss the poem as mythographic performance from and of a nonrepresentable abyss, an abyss of nonknowledge or whose "rationality" is disordered or of an-Other arrangement. The poem cuts language as a supposedly closed system to expose the ruse of time and in this way have readers confront the gaps of a surreal and mythographic outside on the inside of language itself. The philosophical and in many ways theological subordination of mythos to Logos only violently represses mythos within Logos itself as an anterior aliveness. The wor(l)d thus is mythic, and the poem knows this. As does negritude inasmuch as negritude is a poem, an "aerialist narrative," Ed Roberson might say, in which Blackness exceeds (racial) categorical reduction to host varied psychical, cultural, mythographical capacities for creating new identifications at the scene of colonial mutilation. In artistic Wangechi Mutu–like fashion, negritude dwells with the *mu* in Mutu's cuts—which is to say, with the *mu* in mutilation, too. Poetics of negritude is "poetics of mu," wherein creating and making is Blackness is mythopoiesis.[23] This is what I'm trying to contemplate. A paraliturgy.

Eucharistic Violence: "A Communion Wafer Dipped in Shit"

I BEGIN MY ENGAGEMENT WITH Césaire's statement—"Bidault, looking like a communion wafer dipped in shit"—by noting that he situates it within a wider claim about modernity itself. This wider claim is that World War II reveals that modernity and Western civilization *are* a crisis and are not just *in* a crisis and thus not just in need of reform. This is why he begins the section of *Discourse on Colonialism* in which he makes his arresting Bidault statement by going out of his way to say that, notwithstanding that continental Europe, indeed the Western world, was yet reeling over the gas chambers and Europe itself was yet smoldering and reduced to rubble, it is not with "Hitler, or the SS, or pogroms, or summary executions" that one must begin if one is to understand the West as an ethical crisis. The ethical crisis that is Western civilization, its "barbarism," as Césaire calls it, started centuries back in "bringing to the Indies the example of Christian virtues" (47). That barbarism has now reached a profoundly high level of "progress," for "today," he says, "it is the possessor of the 'Christian virtues' who intrigues—with no small success—for the honor of administering overseas territories according to the methods of forgers and torturers" (47).

What moves Césaire to make this claim has its flash point in his first-hand observation of a scene he recalls from the early years of when he had become a representative of the island of Martinique (which had acquired departmental status) to the French National Assembly, France's legislative body. Césaire recalls a moment in the legislative body when a number of the politicians were addressing the question of what to do about the push for independence from many of France's colonies, indeed, given that some of those colonies had taken their anticolonial struggle to the level of armed resistance. Reporting on the Assembly's deliberations, Césaire tells us that the comments from the politicians were for the most part reactionary, if not downright cynical. Césaire understood that cynicism to be due to France's refusal to address the deeper logics of white supremacy and anti-Blackness that were at the core of the polity's understanding of itself as on a "civilizing mission" and indeed at the core of Western civilization writ large. Given this backdrop of France's belief in its civilizing mission and of the very project of Western civilization, it was not lost on Césaire that his claim that France is barbarous and that Western civilization as executed is a barbarity was a strong one. And so, to establish this claim, he produces for his readers as evidence a scene of cannibalism—or, in Césaire's own words, "a scene of cannibalistic hysteria that I have been privileged to witness in the French National Assembly" (48), the heart of French political culture. Showing a playfulness that only barely cloaks his moral and ethical outrage at the scene he's about to describe, Césaire prefaces what he is about to recount, one "cannibal" speaking to another, as it were, by saying, "By Jove, my dear colleagues (as they say), I take off my hat to you (a cannibal's hat, of course)" (48). He then lets loose his description:

> Think of it! Ninety thousand dead in Madagascar! Indochina trampled underfoot, crushed to bits, assassinated, tortures brought back from the depths of the Middle Ages! And what a spectacle! The delicious shudder that roused the dozing deputies. The wild uproar! Bidault, looking like a communion wafer dipped in shit—unctuous and sanctimonious cannibalism; Moutet—the cannibalism of shady deals

and sonorous nonsense; Coste-Floret—cannibalism of an unlicked bear cub, a blundering fool.

Unforgettable, gentlemen! With fine phrases as cold and solemn as a mummy's wrappings they tie up the Madagascan. With a few conventional words they stab him for you. The time it takes to wet your whistle, they disembowel him for you. Fine work! Not a drop of blood will be wasted. (48)

What Césaire describes here has all the hallmarks of religious sacrifice, both of a Christian and of a non-Christian sort, unified around the idea of cannibalism or the ritual eating of a sacred object. Indeed, Césaire's innovation is to understand colonialism as sacrifice, the violent offering up and consumption of an object. The sacrifice or consumption of that object confers a sacral status, a rightness of being on the one who consumes the sacrificial object. In the case of colonialism as sacrifice, as colonialism consumes lands and lives and in the process metabolizes them into resources and labor or, more simply, exchange value in the capitalist system, the colonies become that around which the imperial nation and civic, metropolitan humanness congeal or cohere themselves.

Consider how Césaire, in effect, interrogates Christian ritual practice as a kind of colonial text. He does this by drawing attention to the bread of the Eucharist, or the Communion wafer, while by way of this same reference he turns to the question of colonial temporality and thus to the issue of time itself. Césaire's interest is in how the time of Western (colonial) progress invites a consideration of how what is called *modernity* is somehow caught within a eucharistic temporality whose roots lie in the European Middle Ages. His claim is that the Middle Ages have not ceased, that (post-)Enlightenment modernity is but medievalism's extension. Modernity is a *medieval modernity*. (I'll have more to say about this shortly.) Furthermore, and still with respect to the Christian sacrament of Communion, Césaire singles out three specific French politicians of the late 1940s who in public pronouncements from the floor of the Assembly advocated that France should put down the anticolonial revolt in Madagascar (March 1946 to February 1947) and the all-out war for independence waged against French rule in Indochina (also in 1946) in a decisive and harsh way. Césaire figures these politicians (Georges Bidault, Marius Moutet, and Paul Coste-Floret; later in the passage he mentions other politicians) as religio-political or, if you like, theosecular communicants in a sacred rite. Indeed, the political and the theological bleed (a fitting term, as we will soon see) into each other. That is to say, precisely in their capacity as legislative and secular guardians of the state, the politicians were working to secure the state's transcendence or sovereign rule over the colonies. They were working to secure and maintain the body politic's life precisely as a life structured in and through a sovereignty that is never not colonial. In other words, Césaire understood what happened on the floor of the French National Assembly not simply as akin to what communicants do at an ecclesial-eucharistic ceremony when they eat the host, the symbol that is the life of Christ's body and blood. Rather, Césaire likens this politico-eucharistic feeding frenzy to cannibalism, a trope that the same politicians and the West more generally have applied to the colonized. He charges the politicians with cannibalism owing to their call to brutally put down anticolonial unrest, seeing this as akin precisely to what animals do when aroused to consume their prey. But ultimately Césaire turns to the language of cannibalism to hold together the reference to eucharistic consumption and animals stalking and then attacking their prey and to describe the "scene of cannibalistic hysteria that [he witnessed] in the French National Assembly" (48). Indeed, pressing further into the politico-religious dimensions of what he observed in the French legislative body, Césaire says that in the name of maintaining state order, the politicians were, in effect, mummifying the Madagascans, binding them in holy wrappings.

Key to all of this is the holy wounding, we might say, that Césaire sees at work in all of this and how that wounding entails a violence carried out first and foremost as grammar and discourse or through language. After all, and significantly, Césaire titles his little manifesto that is big in its analysis *Discourse on Colonialism*. It is an analysis of colonialism as *discourse*—as a wounding, a violence, a rupturing in and through and as language. The words of these politicians on the legislative floor of the National Assembly, in effect, as performance, ritualized the colonized by aligning them with death or figuring them as both a threat to the life of the state and a kind of source of the life of the state. Both repulsive and attractive to the state, the colonized carry the classic signature of what a number of thinkers, from Émile Durkheim to Georges Bataille, have called "the sacred," which Césaire, too, seems to be theorizing, albeit from the vantage point of racialization, colonialism, and a poetics of decolonization.[24] Hence, he claims that the words spoken about the revolt of the colonized in the French National Assembly in the scene he recounts were "sanctimonious" (48). They were ritualizing the colonized into the status of a sacred object, or, more precisely, into an object for slaughter and sacrificial death at the hands of the captor. That sacrificial death would maintain the colonies as a consumable or assimilable substance or resource or capital to maintain the life of the body politic, while also holding the difference that the colonies represent at bay in the face of the state's entanglement with the colonies.

Again, what has my attention here is both how Césaire sees this process in terms of a liturgy or a Western ceremony or a sacrament of race *and* how that ceremony operates by way of words or through the force of language. This last part about language cannot be understated, for the words of institution in the National Assembly, Césaire suggests, are not unlike the words of institution in the Communion liturgy the priest utters: "Here. Take and eat this. This is my body broken for you, my blood shed for you." Just as the ceremonial and performative words pronounce that the Communion elements of bread and wine are Christ's body and blood, so too the ceremonial and performative words carry the force of an ontologico-political pronouncement: the colonized are ritually transformed into a consumable object. They have been transubstantiated into a sacred substance into which the white Communion host is dipped, even as the violence that this dipping indexes is disavowed. I should also quickly say that what Césaire figures here as the white Communion wafer is itself a transubstantiated figure. As Frank B. Wilderson III has helped us understand, whiteness emerges within a framework of antagonism.[25] What Césaire presents is that this process of emergence is theologico-political or, more precisely, sacramental or eucharistic and generates patriarchal or phallic sovereignty as the form of self whose subjectivity the state recognizes as legitimate. That legitimacy, however, is predicated on a violent "dipping" that compromises any and every claim to purity. That is to say, the white (Communion wafer) is always dipped into a bruised Black-and-Brownness, and Blueness, born of and always affected by excremental substance. Dark matter. That dark matter moves in relationship to the word *le négre*, "the Negro," even though the force that this word is meant to contain is irreducible to racist nomenclature or naming.

What I am driving at is this: Césaire grasps that the state avows bloodlessness while being predicated on bloodletting. Further still, he understands that such bloodletting is religious, though to fully appreciate his insight requires letting go of how we've been generally schooled to think about *religion*. Césaire, in effect, asks that we not think about religion as first and foremost referring to personal spiritual practices or to personally chosen beliefs about the existence of a deity (or not). While not denying that there is something to be said about coming at religion in this way, he is working at another level. He in effect asks that we reckon with Western culture as a religiously suffused semiotic system, indeed as a system of signs "suffused with religious figures, myths, and symbols."[26] More still, he calls specific attention to how blood, sacrifice, and the shaping of matter itself are at the heart of the Western cultural symbolic structure. He is interested in how, in fact, blood, sacrifice, and the attempt to arrest matter by rendering it static or focalizing it around (Western) Man as determinative of human being ground Man's world, how these terms operate mythically both to colonize the earth in creating the world of Man and to hold at bay any threats to Man's world. That holding at bay is precisely the sacrificial or theopolitical bloodletting that Césaire sees and that I am trying to attend to. Put differently, Césaire is engaging the Western cultural symbolic system, and by extension colonialism itself, at the level of religion as it verges on myth. He's dealing with Western culture's mythic architecture, an architecture of bloodletting. Such bloodletting or disemboweling is a protocol of colonialism, done with a view to establishing and maintaining the world of Man against alternative imaginations of the sacred that host blasphemous numinosities, renegade corporealities, and the numinous flesh of anticolonial refusals. Now, if this procedure of mythic (and, for this reason, all the more real) sacrifice is what animates the state, then the state's verdict on this situation is, let "not a drop of blood be wasted . . . drink it straight, to the last drop" (48).

This reading of what was taking place on the floor of the French National Assembly provides Césaire's segue into the two paragraphs following where I left off in the earlier quotation that speaks of Bidault looking like a shit-covered Communion wafer. In the two paragraphs following this, Césaire figures the colonies as blood victims of the state, victims, to use a formulation from theorist of religion Gil Anidjar, of the modern "vampire state."[27] Having killed Madagascans on the fields as the sacrifice needed to maintain imperial power, the politicians, offering plans from the floor of the French National Assembly to quell anticolonial unrest and secure the state, are involved in so much bloodletting. Indeed, it is now, after invoking the Communion wafer, that Césaire becomes explicit about wine and blood. Adding more politicians to the list of those he has already mentioned, Césaire says that these politicians are those

who drink [the blood] straight, to the last drop. The ones like [Paul] Ramadier [the French prime minister in 1947], who smear their faces with [blood] in the manner of Silenus, [Jacques] Fontlup-Esperaber [a member of Parliament at the time], who scratches his mustache with it, the walrus mustache of an ancient Gaul; old Desjardins bending over the emanations from the vat and intoxicating himself with them as with new wine. Violence! The violence of the weak. A significant thing: it is not the head of civilization that begins to rot first. It is the heart.

I admit that as far as the health of Europe and civilization is concerned, these cries of "Kill! kill!" and "Let's see some blood," belched forth by trembling old men and virtuous young men educated by the Jesuit Fathers, make a much more disagreeable impression on me than the most sensational bank holdups that occur in Paris. (48–49)

Césaire's description here, both in its vividness and at the level of what he is conceptualizing, is arresting: both as a sign of violence and as a symbol in a ritual, blood drips from this passage. The politicians Ramadier, Jacques Fonlup-Espéraber, and Desjardins, in supporting France's militarized response to the Madagascan revolt, "drink [the blood] straight." They smear it on their faces as if in a cannibalistic ritual, Césaire says. Even a bespoke politician waxes his mustache with the blood of the colonized. Together they are drunk on this blood, which the passage speaks of as "new wine." Bottom line: blood irrigates this passage, a point that is all the more striking when we consider this passage in its totality. Indeed, by the time we get to its end, we are swimming in blood. If we recall the beginning of the passage, the part that speaks of Bidault as an excrement-covered Communion wafer, it does not start with blood. A kind of dissimulation is going on; the passage starts with excrement that stands in the place of blood or wine and ends with the politicians feasting on and engorging themselves with blood and "new wine," whose indigestible remains will, after consumption, be excreted. These remains will then presumably become (spilled) blood and "new wine" again. A ritual repetition is at play here.

At this point, I cannot help but think of the notion of transubstantiation, a key concept in Christian theology as developed in the European Middle Ages. I brought up this term earlier, but it is worth thinking about more intentionally now. Doctrinally speaking, and at the level of medieval ontology and metaphysics, transubstantiation is the idea within eucharistic theology that at the level of substance or essence, the wine and bread of the sacrament changes into the body and blood of Jesus Christ, while in species, that same wine and bread remain materially unchanged and are metabolized by communicants as such. In this way, and again staying within the domain of eucharistic ontology and metaphysics, the bread and wine undergo a becoming; they now *are* the body and blood of Christ. Therefore, as the communicants eat the bread and wine, thereby taking in through ritual consumption Jesus's flesh and blood, the communicants themselves become proper, which is to say "saved," bodies, the body of Christ. This ritual is the template for what I call *the liturgy of Man*. It is the ceremony in which Man through linguistic injunction enters into sociopolitical intelligibility or semiotic legibility as a *body*, where *body* here is precisely that which is endowed with sovereign, individual integrity. Within the framework of the Eucharist, the sovereign and individualized integrity of a body results from taking in divine-as-messianic blood. A certain blood that makes possible a certain body (politic) courses through (Christian, who will then become Western,) Man to establish his individuality and integrity, his sense of inward subjectivity. But this inwardness is not just a sense of individuality (the [idea of a] body figuring as a supposedly coherent individual thing); it also contains a sense of the unitary and universal human, the unity that is the community of Man under the rubric of the body politic of Christendom (eventually refigured under the idea of Europe and further still the West). I am thinking through the liturgical ecclesiasticism that generates the body (politic). And so, to state it again, this unitary human as the unitary body (politic) is predicated on consuming Christ's body and especially his redeeming blood (more on this in a second) in the form or under the aspect of bread and wine. What fundamentally occurs in the Eucharist is this: under the force of the priest's words of institution ("Here, eat, this is my body; here, drink, this is my blood. Do this in remembrance of me . . ."), matter is transubstantiated, organized in such a way that the potentials inherent in matter, which at its most base level might be organized in any number of ways, are in this ceremony ritually activated in a particular direction, the direction of the *body* as a unit of sovereignty. But this eucharistic body emerges only by disavowing, while siphoning energy from, matter's rawness, from the erotic reserve that enlivens matter or renders it what might be called, after R. A. T. Judy and with Hortense J. Spillers, "sentient flesh."[28] That is to say, in the eucharistic ceremony of the Middle Ages and through transubstantiation, matter's potentials are ritually activated in the direction of the sovereign individuality of Man's ruling body (politic), even as there remains an insovereign or negritudinous excess, an erotic reserve or reservoir of possibilities. In producing a constricted and restrictive vision of community, the ceremony contains something that is ingested but not fully digested, something that the ceremony violently apprehends on some level but cannot utterly obliterate.[29] That something is precisely what falls out of representation, though in its surreal nonrepresentability exerts black-hole-like effects back on the field of representation.[30]

In the final part of this essay, I will return to negritude as an insovereign or excreted remainder and as an erotic reserve that pushes language back toward the mythic abyss, or the abyssal Blackness, from which it arises. Approaching it in this way, I engage Césairean negritude as performance of an alternative rituality, a ritual virtuality, that, as M. NourbeSe Philip might say, harking back to one of the epigraphs to this essay, "provides a way through the thicket of impossibles." But before getting to that, I want to elaborate a bit more about what I see as Césaire's insight into the Eucharist, blood, and the problem of community.

The previously quoted blood-soaked passage brings the import of Césaire's earlier invocation of the Middle Ages in connection with the Communion wafer powerfully into relief, for it was in what is now periodized as the Middle Ages that the Eucharist became the basis for a new conception of the very notion of community. This new conception came to be rooted in blood such that, as a significant body of scholarship has now well established, the Middle Ages saw the establishment of Christianity as a kind of cult of blood.[31] And again it all turned on the Eucharist: through this liturgical ceremony, Christianity became a restrictive polis, the community of the *populus christianus*, where the very notion of the Christian people, sometimes called the *corpus mysticum*, comes online as a "hematological" body construct, a construct of the individuated body as the basis of thinking the body politic.[32] Césaire has his keen poetic eye on this problem and is in effect positioning negritude as an insurgency through it, an alternative sociality. But let us stay for the moment with the problem of the populus christianus as part and parcel of the problem of blood.[33]

In the Eucharist of the Middle Ages, the idea of the populus christianus connoted a people bound together by blood or in a ceremony of blood. Blood, or rather Christian blood, is what "the community [came to be seen as] made of," its "one shared substance," as noted by Anidjar, whose recent study of the topic of blood is essential in its theorization and clarification of the issues at hand.[34] More still, under the presumption of blood, or under the presumption of the ceremonial blood of Christ as what *makes* the Christian community what it is, there is the implicit understanding that other, non-Christian communities are also blood communities, though their blood is not of "our" Christian blood. Coagulating between the tenth and the thirteenth centuries CE, this change in the Eucharist as a doctrinal and social institution, indeed as a system of signification, was revolutionary. Blood, along with the ongoing need to replenish it, to infuse and reinfuse it, to repeatedly, ceremonially, performatively transfuse it back into a corpus mysticum, came to sustain Christendom as a community of distinction, as a body (politic). Additionally, entailed within a Christianity that during this time was coming to distinguish itself through blood was the need to keep its blood, which is to say the blood community, pure or uncontaminated even as this community disseminates its universal blood by spreading the Christian message. This dissemination through the missionary spreading of blood risks contaminating Christendom's own blood with other bloods. This is the danger of the community becoming impure. In light of this danger, the Eucharist also, then, had to do the work of providing a kind of ongoing dialysis for the community so as to ensure its hematological integrity, keeping the Christian bloodstream and thus the Christian community pure. In other words, in the Middle Ages, through the Eucharist, blood is invented as a disciplinary technology. It becomes the basis for an understanding, according to Roberto Esposito, of "Christianity not as a source of religious doctrine but as a form of understanding of self and community."[35]

What I want to suggest here is that in invoking the Middle Ages, Césaire has gone to the moment when the ecclesial ceremony of the Eucharist became the basis for a Western imaginary of politicality, a way of thinking and practicing community on the basis of a blood logic; that is, on the basis of the idea of a blood-based, inwardly determined, soon to be self-determined (Enlightenment) Subject. Arguably, "race" as we now live and suffer it arises out of this medievalism. Indeed, Césaire has tapped into the problem of what Anidjar has called a *eucharistic matrix*, that "massive enterprise of 'social disciplining' ... which took the 'flesh and blood' individual and the community (later, communities) as its aims and refashioned them in hematological terms."[36] Hematology sets what Cedric J. Robinson calls the "terms of order" for Western politicality.[37] That is, theological hematology opened onto a "political hematology" of globality that as such is political theology, for, as Anidjar further says, "[everywhere] in Western Christendom (and its later national divisions), blood became an essential element investing (and invested by) embryology and genealogy, belief and ritual, laws and habits, person and collectives, the state and the church."[38] In other words, the reach of the eucharistic sharing of blood was far and wide. It became "the fundamental, legal concept for inheritance, family, and kinship."[39] With blood sacrificially and ritually in place in this way, the medieval state had not only taken on a theologico-bio-juridical and biopolitical form that in *Black Marxism: The Making of the Black Radical Tradition* Cedric J. Robinson had already announced as the origins of race in the Middle Ages.[40] But even more, the eucharistic ceremony now operating as a blood liturgy set the conditions, Anidjar explains, for the "later metamorphosing [of the medieval consanguineous state] into the modern state," or into an extractive "vampire state" of global proportions.[41] What Anidjar says from here in further elaboration of the vampiric nature of the modern state as it grew from or represents an expansion of the eucharistic matrix is worth quoting for its relevance to the reading I am advancing here of Césaire's own critique of the eucharistic matrix as he carries out that critique from the decolonial and anticolonial vantage of a negritudinous or Blackpoetics:

> Henceforward [from the mystical body of Christ's expansion into the Westphalian system of modern, extractive states], the vampire state partakes of and refigures money (later political economy) as the blood of the state, the family (and kinship) as a sexual community of blood, the nation as a political community of blood, and race as the theological, later juridico-medical, community of blood. But the distinction between these forms or modalities of the community of blood should be understood, such is my contention, within the complex unity of the vampire state, the blood of which is constituted as an indispensable exteriority ("extravasat"), a set of exteriorities, the sources of its existence and nourishment. Representations of the social as the biological or physiologic (feeding) ground of the administrative (or, to follow Hobbes, the fictional and legal) machinery of the state might find here one of their sources and explanations.[42]

A central point of Anidjar's analysis of blood as a central category for any analysis of Western civilization and as bound up with the eucharistic liturgy in the Middle Ages is to trace the emergence of a new and distinctive type of "collective self-fashioning," the production of a blood-based and exclusionary "we."[43] By way of Césaire, I here am surfacing a complementary dimension to what Anidjar has powerfully displayed, namely, that the eucharistic matrix of the Middle Ages, which must be understood as an incipient racial matrix central to the production of that geographic entity called Europe, expands into a matrix of extraction from and consumption of exterior zones. Noting the indispensability of exteriority, Anidjar points in this direction but does not per se take it up in his analysis. Indeed, by his own admission, he grants "hermeneutical primacy" to the "inner and inward-directed activity [of the] collective self-fashioning" through Christological blood to cohere Western Christendom and eventually to cohere, despite national divisions, the West.[44] This hermeneutical primacy leads Anidjar to "not pronounce on ontological entanglements."[45] My contention is that Césaire is indeed speaking to those entanglements by way of his image of a Communion wafer dipped in excrement and by way of the further representation of excrement and blood as constantly transubstantiating into each other, wherein the state congeals through violent plunder from "extractive zones."[46] That plundering entangles colonizer and colonized. Césaire's imagery of the eucharistic matrix from the Middle Ages registers and is meant to establish that metropolitan humanness is predicated on extraction and points to the state's imbrication, its ontotheological entanglement, with colonialism. It is his way of advancing a claim that colonialism is nothing less than the colonizer eating us, consuming and then excreting us, in a process that like the Eucharist is then ceremonially repeated. As bell hooks will say some years after Césaire to make a similar point: "White racism, imperialism, and sexist domination prevail by courageous consumption. It is by eating the Other . . . that one asserts power and privilege."[47] Other lands and other lives converted into labor power mark both an attraction and a repulsion, the poles of a kind of feedback loop through which the body politic—that is, the state and civil society—establishes and sustains itself even as the state advances the violent fiction of sovereignty and untainted self-determination. Blackness figures within this feedback loop of consumption and expulsion as something both needed and resisted, something to be consumed and yet associated with "death and decay" or with what registers as a threat to the state and to its form of we-ness.

Negritude and the Witch:
The Dissident Middle Ages

TO THIS POINT IN THIS ESSAY, my attention has been on Césaire's *Discourse on Colonialism* and on the significance of his arresting representation of a moment he recalls from the French National Assembly. Seeing their sovereignty under attack in the anticolonial uprisings in Madagascar and other colonial outposts—that is, seeing the modern political state, the hierarchical arrangement of proper humanness that anthropologically underwrites the conception of the political community of Man, and finally the imperial-colonial order itself as together threatened—certain politicians took to the legislative floor in defense of France and ultimately in defense of Western civilization. Among those politicians was Bidault, who, Césaire said, as he observed him in action on the Assembly floor, was "looking like a communion wafer dipped in shit." Césaire went on to say that the war violences that this company of politicians were defending conjured "tortures brought back from the depths of the Middle Ages."

This excrementalized Communion wafer reference was for Césaire no mere throwaway line. And I've made the case that his invocation of the Middle Ages was no mere rhetorical flourish either. Rather, these formulations point us to a little-considered aspect of the genealogy of colonial humanization and the history of the body and blood embedded within it. That aspect concerns the machinery of political theology. More specifically, it concerns the transformations around the Christian eucharistic liturgy in the European Middle Ages that brought online the very notion of a body and the body politic, or the populus christianus, as animated by an inward substance that is taken in from the outside. This is the advent of hematological-as-biopolitical life, wherein life in its propriety is realized as an incarnation or corporealization that has been extracted. Here, proper life comes to be through the ritual eating of an animating and energizing, transcendent substance (i.e., Christ's blood and then total value from "extractive zones").[48] Through this communal consuming of an outside or external substance, the body (politic) coheres itself as a singular unity of purity, theopolitically inoculating itself, as it were, against pathogens or contaminants. This was all keyed to the ritual, cannibalistic ingestion of the Communion wine transubstantiated into Christ's actual blood as the inner substance of the Christian (eventually to become Western) body (politic).

This transformation of the liturgy of the Eucharist in the Middle Ages in the direction of conceiving it as the communal intake of an all-defining, untainted blood was not just a philosophico-theological concern at this pivotal moment in the history of (the very idea of) a body and of the body politic, though surely it was that. Rather, it was a sociohistorical concern too. The new imagination of the body rooted in a theological reorganization of matter by way of the notion of transubstantiation (what I addressed in the prior section) was just as much a response to cultural crises and related anxieties in the reproduction of the order of things beginning in the early Middle Ages. That is to say, the transformation of the Eucharist with the invention of the idea of theological blood secured by the doctrinal idea of transubstantiation, in order to establish the body as a construct predicated on boundaries that secure purity, occurred as part of a response to dissident and alternative social movements of anarcho-heresy and rebellion. I use *anarchy* here in something close to its etymological sense from Greek as being without (*an-*) foundation, founding principle, origin, telos, or stasis (*archē*). The anarchic is some other mode of genesis. A genesis without beginning, exceeding each and every natal occasion. More than heresy, such anarchic movements threatened the boundaries and thus the cohesion of the medieval *populus christianus*. Before turning to Césaire's poem of negritude, his *Cahier*, I want to say a bit about these movements of anarcho-heresy and syndical-rebellion, we might say. I contend that negritude as excremental excess is in keeping with these fugitive, mystical, esoteric, and often female-driven movements of rebellion against and refusal of political theology.

But let us stay within the historical scene of the Middle Ages for the moment. There were two general groups of potential social dissidence against the theological-political order of Christendom. The first group that Christendom perceived as a threat to the political order comprised the two other theological peoples of the book: the Jews (a threat within Christendom) and the Muslims (an impure presence in the Holy Land, so the understanding went). Together but in distinct ways, Jews and Muslims were seen as potential pathogenic taints against which Christ's transubstantiated blood was to inoculate Christendom, or "the king's two bodies."[49]

The second general group of social dissidents showed up in the Middle Ages in the form of popular heretical sects and social movements such as the Cathari, the Waldenses, the Poor of Lyon, the Spiritualists, the Apostolics, and the Albigenses, among others. It is this group that I want to reflect on a bit as they are particularly interesting when thought about in relationship to the problem of the eucharistic matrix. In the aggregate, as Silvia Federici notes in her pathbreaking book *Caliban and the Witch: Women, the Body, and Primitive Accumulation*, the heretical movements expressed "the search by the medieval proletariat for a concrete alternative to feudal relations and its resistance to the growing money economy," an economy based in property ownership and land enclosure by the church.[50] The effort to enclose flesh, which entailed in the liturgical sphere the emergence of the theological body as a site of enclosure and as a figure of foreclosed-on matter, was central to the general logic of enclosure that marked feudal relations. Hence, these movements were "persecuted by the church . . . to erase every trace of their doctrines."[51] To the question, What was the heresy these movements, again in the aggregate, tended to promulgate and to which the eucharistic matrix may be understood as a response? Federici responds:

> Popular heresy was less a deviation from the orthodox doctrine than a protest movement, aspiring to a radical democratization of social life. Heresy was the equivalent of "liberation theology" for the medieval proletariat. It gave a frame to the peoples' demands for spiritual renewal and social justice, challenging both the Church and the secular authority by appeal to a higher truth. It denounced social hierarchies, private property and the accumulation of wealth, and it disseminated among the people a new, revolutionary conception of society that, for the first time in the Middle Ages, redefined every aspect of daily life (work, property, sexual reproduction, and the position of women), posing the question of emancipation in truly universal terms.[52]

Dissenting from the seizure of the erotic as mystical power by clerics in collusion with the crown, these renegade heretical forces refused social hierarchies and "provided an alternative community" and indeed an alternative cosmological imaginary.[53] The more the church advanced its eucharistic protocol of seizure and enclosure so as to cohere by disciplining the body into an obedient work machine meant to sustain the feudal order—all through a repetitive ritual event that was as well a feat of language, or a rhetorical if not homiletic declaration ("Take and eat . . . This is my body, this is my blood . . .")—the more heretical and mystical movements of flesh propagated. Indeed, they propagated to the point that

> even after the 1215 crusade against the Albigensians . . . heresy (together with Islam) remained the main enemy and threat the Church had to face. Its recruits came from all walks of life: the peasantry, the lower ranks of the clergy (who identified with the poor and brought to their struggles the language of the Gospel), the town burghers, and even the lesser nobility. But popular heresy was primarily a lower class phenomenon. The environment in which it flourished was the rural and urban proletariat: peasants, cobblers, and cloth workers "to whom it preached equality, fomenting their spirit of revolt with prophetic and apocalyptic predictions."[54]

My point here is that across her vast study, Federici tracks how the forces of feudal power—the nobility, the bourgeoisie, and, the main ideological pillar of it all, the church in its clerical and hegemonic form—engaged in extraction of life and land and thus antagonized flesh and the earth itself. Such antagonism represented a kind of "bundling of organic and inorganic masses, matters, and potentials," resulting in the establishment of a new sociogenic code of existence.[55] This new code is the biological or, more precisely, biopolitical code of Man, the code of *his* body (politic). Through this liturgical encoding of life as an overcoding of matter—a code that is repetitively and ritually enacted through the eucharistic taking in, bundling, and then repacking of matter that amounts to a would-be theft of the energies of spirit that reside within all matter—the body comes into being as a kind of productive force. Henceforth, to be a body is to be a productive unit within the eucharistic matrix; it is to be of the body politic. At stake here is the political ontology and political theology—indeed, the violent metaphysics of matter that the eucharistic matrix installs—in contrast to the heretic movements' alternative cosmology and imaginary of matter, one that exceeds how matter is organized within the terms of the eucharistic matrix. For this reason Federici's principal interest is in tracking those nonproductive forces of refusal represented by heretical movements of rebellion. Such heretical movements, like the female-dominated Beguine movement, which in the late Middle Ages and in the transition to colonialism and racial capitalism came to be seen as harboring witches, were thought about as a threatening counterchurch—a dark church, as I am given to thinking about it—that practiced occult arts around life without, outside, beyond, or otherwise excessive to the eucharistic matrix, modes of ecstatic-erotic vitality that are excremental to theopolitical order.[56]

At this point, we can blend what I have summarized here about Federici's research on the history of the body, which contains an opaque or shadow history of resistant flesh in the form of heretical social movements that by the late Middle Ages would come to be aligned with witchcraft and wayward women or actually existing witches, with Césaire's critique of the violent colonial liturgy of eucharistic, even cannibalistic, consumption, which is the principal focus of this writing. Upon so doing, we come to understand that Césaire's decolonial poetics, or what I more specifically frame as his excremental poetics, or fecopoetics, is in the lineage of the heresy of fugitivity in the Middle Ages, the lineage of those alternative social experiments that, in effect, represent a sullying of the sacrament and an attempt to foreclose the uncanny and unforeseeable realm of spirit. That is to say, Césaire's anticolonial poetics, his Blackpoetics, is, I want to say, in the lineage of antifeudal or anarcho-heretical social movements of the Middle Ages, though now detoured or routed through the Middle Passage and the plot that was on but not of the plantation. Such a poetics cuts open the "natural" order of racial life so as to reritualize or enact another ceremony of Black life beyond the violent ritual of engulfment. The reritualizing of Black life, or the extraceremonial, alternative ritual, opens the supposedly natural order of racial life to what exceeds racial order and to what exceeds racist signification—most especially, to what exceeds but moves in relationship to the signifier or symbol le négre. Cutting open this hieroglyph to expose the dark interior that surrounds it, Césaire's fecopoetics stages an experimental spirituality, a ritual of healing, we might say, that takes place on the plane of the indigestible or the excremental. The plane of the indigestible, which allows for what Stefano Harney and Fred Moten have called "fugitive planning," is the domain of spirit, where spirit is here conceived of as "a plan(e) of composition for symbolic interaction with" and study of "the as yet unknown."[57] Entailed in such compositional study in and on the plan(e) of spirit is the overturning of speech through an insurgent rhetorics, a counterhomiletics, we might say, that alchemizes language to shift its codes. Not understood as housing a singular or static meaning (as came to be the case in the eucharistic matrix with the injunction "Take, eat. This is my body. This is my blood . . ."), within these heretical social movements, and again I read Césaire's poetics in this lineage, signs become wonders, enigmatic symbols through which other realities may be brought to light. More like hieroglyphs than a univocal Logos (a term that in Greek and in its most basic sense means a "coherent account" or a "cohesive tale"), signs or words and indeed matter may be understood as "[sheltering] . . . obscure multiplicity," heavy with opaque, "complex density" that returns matter, indeed the earth, to us in relational virtuality and as infinite "Plenum."[58]

Housing an alternative imagination of the universe, a cosmology of unforeseen collectivities, insovereign gatherings, a counter- or "dark church," the heretical and esoteric experiments of the Middle Ages were involved in a "spiritual ordeal" that staged lines of flight from the liturgical or eucharistic semiotics of the body (politic).[59] As excess, these experiments of spirit indicate social "productions, conceptions, growths that go counter" to the liturgico-colonial process of bodily subjectification by both falling short of and going beyond it.[60] In short, such movements point to "counter-natural generations" or monstrous degeneracies that circulate within the innards of capitalism and that show up in Césaire's *Discourse on Colonialism* under the symbol both of le négre and then, as if out of nowhere, of excrement and in this way form a paraliturgical surplus.[61] Moreover, in the poem *Cahier*, the text to which, as I read it, *Discourse* is an intertextual companion, Césaire's collective anticolonial poet is involved in a decolonial experiment, an experimental form of belief. The experiment entails a serial venturing, a circling into the depths of the dark symbol, le négre. Indeed, the anticolonial poet is of this experiment, of this experience, of this excess, this Black rapture that turns out to be a lapsarian condition, a fall or a Black descent into, the dissent of, a decolonial remainder, "remaindered life under empire."

Another Ceremony: Paraliturgical Blackness

WITH THIS SAID, I would now like to move into the final part of this essay and offer a few notes toward an understanding of Césaire's *Cahier* (and by extension the aesthetics of the Black radical tradition) as operating at the level of spiritual ordeal and experiment and thus exemplifying a practice of spirit as bound up with a certain hidden, if not uncanny or even gnostic, experience of the self beyond the ego. Such an experience *Cahier* figures as corpsed within and yet as such remaindered beyond capitalism's ritual of the human, within and extraceremonially beyond modernity's ceremony or liturgy of race. Borrowing from M. NourbeSe Philip, whose poem *Zong!* operates in a way similar to what I am suggesting here about Césaire's *Cahier*, we might think of the latter's poem as an alternative "island liturgy," an experimental spirituality or an experimental-as-improvisational poetics operative on the plane of spirit.[62] In this way, I see Césaire's poem as an expanded consideration of the excremental as only hinted at in his Bidault statement in *Discourse on Colonialism*.[63] More specifically, I read *Cahier*'s collective poet as engaged in a performance wherein the poet moves around the signifier *le négre* for what is excrementally remaindered within it and for this reason always already exceeds the term as such. That is to say, *le négre* both succeeds and fails in translation inasmuch as it hosts an unknown and strictly speaking unknowable remainder, which is also a reminder of a rapturous excess that is always present. It shelters what might be thought of as material intensities and cosmic vitalities that exceed capitalism but that capitalism nevertheless leeches upon in its would-be stealing of total or native value. That *le négre* as a term is never fully adequate to its referent signals that the intensities and vitalities hosted within this term cannot be reduced to commodity exchange or, as Hortense J. Spillers has put it, to being that is strictly for the captor.[64]

I think of what is leeched upon as spirit, by which I mean matter's infinite and quantum depth, its inexhaustible and protean reservoir. And what I am saying here about the quantum infinity of matter includes language, for in its infinite depth language is vibratory, sonic matter, a resonating or "sonic substance" full of recombinative possibilities, omens and portents.[65] The matter of language, which is to say sonic substance as a spirit-imbued reservoir, is precisely what the poet circles around throughout the poem. Inspirited, the poet recursively turns and overturns the word *le négre*, tweaking, twisting, and torquing it so as to release its codes from the imperial and racial accretions imposed on it. To speak of the poetic or of poiesis is to speak of the release of words, their veritable recommissioning, in search of alternate fantastic and marvelous (non)worlds buried or imperially corpsed within words, though equally convulsing and surging through and in excess of them as out of an abyssal wellspring that harbors volatile and sociopoetic energies of refusal that testify to the entanglement of all things. This ritual, not of a univocal Logos but of an ante-Logos, this incantatory and extraceremonial circling around matter's protean and inspirited depth, the poet-oracle names *negritude*, which the poet also insists, just in case it was not clear, is not an essence. Which is to say, the circling is not of the order of Western philosophy's approach to being. Indeed, says the poet, negritude simply "is not" ("My *negritude is not* a stone, its deafness heaved against the clamor of the day / my *negritude is not* a film of dead water on the day eye of the earth / my *negritude is neither* a tower *nor* a cathedral . . .").[66] The "is not" or, as I want to write it, the "is-not" of negritude indicates a "[delving] into the flesh of the soil / [a delving] into the burning flesh of the sky / [a digging] through the dark accretions that weighs down its righteous patience" (st. 115, 125–26).[67] This amounts to a nonegoic reritualizing of self, the performance of a self in excess of the sovereign subjecthood of the racially individuated ego and the imposition of a body of singular, bordered meaning. Negritude's is-not-ness does not mark it even as the negation (dialectical or otherwise) of traditional ontology; rather, negritude's is-not-ness points to Blackness as a transindividual reservoir of metamorphic possibilities, a black hole or a dark churchical reserve for fungible mutations, a collective "potential to be otherwise, including refusal and/or not to be as such."[68] To operate on spirit's plan(e) or to move into the zone of this hidden but open (sur)reality is to move into a region just beneath ontology's threshold where the link between all things, including between mind and protean matter, is known and experienced as having never been severed. Here connection is (re)discovered through what Joshua Ramey has called "spiritual ordeal."[69] Indeed, *Cahier*'s poet is engaged in, and by the end of the poem is seen as spiritually devoted to, a practice of spirit marked by devotion to the irregular or to language's infinite depth as that which colonial discourse cannot digest. That is to say, *Cahier* meditates on the excremental remainder in its own right and in so doing offers a *fecopoetics*.

Consider how this plays out in *Cahier* itself, whose concern, as I read it, is not just, as is the case in *Discourse*, with the discursive problem of the eucharistic-now-become-colonial matrix or with how racial capitalism functions as a liturgy that underwrites white supremacy as a political-economic system of consumption, excrementalization, and mortification. Its concern is with what freedom might even mean given that this very liturgy, the liturgy of Man as a liturgy of racial capitalism, solicits the attachment of the colonized themselves to their own mortification. In eucharistic terms, the colonized are invited to participate in the liturgy of Man, as it were, by eating up or eating away at what is deemed improper, what is racially designated as le négre, about themselves. Through a ritualized self-eating that manifests being shaped into racial obedience to the colonial order, the colonized in effect participate in, in a sense cooperate with, Man's or the colonizer's appropriative consumption of the life of the colonized and indeed of the earth itself. As an alternative ritual or a paraliturgy, the poem is very much about intercepting and interrupting this self-eating, or the colonized's own attachment to the eucharistic matrix of coloniality, this attachment to the self-corpsing that is part and parcel of colonial ontology's operation of corpsing through incorporation.

Cahier unfolds against the backdrop of this problem. Indeed, this is what the poem seems to be pointing to when the collective poet-oracle makes explicit reference fairly early on to the communal consumption of the body and the blood of Christ on the part of the colonized and the way that communal consumption operates as a form of self-consuming, self-annihilating attachment. Referring to the people of the island, the poet speaks of "our idiotic, insane gestures," our genuflections before the altar as we partake of "the bread, and the wine of collusion" (st. 20, 85). Collusion in what? It is collusion with coloniality, with the codes of "saved" and proper humanness, codes that necessarily corpse or "mortally wound" (st. 42, 97) those who are made to carry the designation of "nigger" (*le négre*). A little further into the poem, the poet explicitly connects the

Western project of the human with the inhumanity of slavery and plantation life and finally with theological claims about the "will of God":

> And this country broadcast for centuries that we are brute beasts; that the pulse of humanity stops beating at the entrance to the black slave quarters; that we are a walking dunghill, a hideous harbinger of tender canes and silky-smooth cotton, and they branded us with red-hot irons, and we slept in our excrement, and they auctioned us off in the public squares, and a measure of English cloth and Irish salt meat were cheaper than we were, and this country was unfazed and tranquil, declaring that its deeds reflected the will of God. (st. 94, 115)

The poet suggests we understand slavery and its afterlives—from the transatlantic slave trade and imposition of the plantation onto the landscape to the present in which the poet was writing—as a ritual of violent corpsing that has come to be called "social death."[70] Perplexing, however, in all of this, says the poet, is "our idiotic, insane" participation in, or rather attachment to, this liturgy of colonization. That is to say, the poet starts to meditate on how the colonized themselves in this racial capitalist process of being devalued in the accumulation or production of Western value(s) have been ritualized or liturgized, ceremonially corpsed as "nigger," in establishing the terms of being or the terms of order. In other words, nigrification and "theologization," to borrow Wynter's formulation, is a singular, identical process.[71] The poet is interested in the liturgical formation of colonized consciousness as it emerges at the back end of this very process and in relationship to the very language or theologico-juridical grammars that rationalize or otherwise naturalize the process. But closely related to this, the poet, it seems to me, is also interested in what it might mean to enter into a kind of madness with respect to this process, to tap into the frenzy that even the liturgico-colonial imposition of racial consciousness cannot arrest but that still convulses as a volatile and destabilizing charge within liturgical corpsing. What, indeed, would it mean to break with, if not be "in the break" of, the phenomenology of human consciousness and enter into a mode of collective and incoherent subjectivity, to consent to a practice of subjectivity that is at the edge of coherent subjecthood?

Let's bracket this question for just a moment longer in order to stay with the issue of the formation of colonized consciousness or colonized attachment as part and parcel of the ritual of racial capitalism itself. In developing this point, the poet turns to two metaphors to further reflect on how the eucharistic matrix now functions as a colonial matrix and to clarify how it is ritual itself that needs to be decolonized. The first meta-phor suggests that the eucharistic matrix effects a wider umbilical-like, though fragile, attachment along the lines of a uterine tie between mother and fetus, though here the attachment is between the colonized and the colonial order as such ("the umbilical cord restored to its fragile splendor, the bread, the wine of collusion . . ."; st. 20, 85). The poet suggests that at an embryonic level, colonized consciousness feeds on the very political order that violently consumes and excretes it. Following from this but still within the same stanza, the poet shifts to another metaphor with a view to extending this idea of the biopolitical attachment of the colonized to the colonial order. The metaphor is now of a (hetero)sexual blood union on the wedding night. Regarding the latter, the poet says that the Com-munion wine is "the bloodstain of true nuptials," the trace, as it were, of a stained attachment that operates at the level of desire. That is to say, the poet's language here suggests that the ritual attachment between the colonized and the colonial order in the eucharistic-now-become-colonial matrix is the would-be or attempted arrest of desire, a kind of comman-deering of the energies of the erotic as itself bound up with sacred.

The point here is that between these two metaphors—a blood connec-tion between mother and fetus, on the one hand, and a blood connection enacted through penetrative sexual union, on the other—the poet lever-ages the imagery of blood to point to the connection between theologi-cal blood and the blood erotics of racial capitalism, with both involving transubstantiation, or a reorganizing of matter. In the case of theologi-cal blood, transubstantiation establishes that Christ's blood as spilled in death becomes the inner or defining "whatness" of Christendom's and the church's theological purity as well as the theological basis of differ-ence, or what is outside that purity. This general logic comes to fuel racial capitalism as the purity of Christendom and the church mutates or tran-substantiates to fuel the "ontological terror" that emerges in the colonial contact between Europe and its others.[72] The consumption and ingestion of Christ's blood as the inner whatness that establishes Christendom and the church in theologico-cultural purity within itself and in theological difference from medieval others becomes the consumption and inges-tion of those whom Europeans meet in transatlantic and settler colonial contact. The ongoing ritual and violent consumption of this other is now the disavowed but consumed whatness through which Westernness con-geals itself. In this way, we can think of the ocean of the Middle Passage as both metaphorically and literally a shark-infested pool of blood, a nuptial meeting place as well as a kind of birth canal whose offspring is the master as white and the slave as caught within a violent system of language, a system of signification, in which they are le négre, Negro.[73]

But already literally with *Cahier*'s first, dreamlike words, words that announce within the same breath the closing of something and, through an ellipsis, its uncloseability ("At the close of foreday . . ." is how the poem starts), one discerns that something else is never not always already in play or operative for the poet. This "something else," which is in many respects what the theater of this poem is all about, is perhaps less a thing than a mood, a magical or hermetic mood, out of which arises another sense of existence, one that in fact exceeds all meaning or sense making, including every racial common sense. Like perfume perhaps emanating from a broken bottle (in this case the broken bottle is both imagination broken over the anvil of racial capitalism and a renewed, perfumed sense of the imagination), this mood is like a fragrance or a smell whose whence and when cannot be pinned down, for it operates on the terrain of what might perhaps be called the surreal, perhaps the uncanny, or simply the fantastic. Which is to say that, fantastically, *Cahier*'s shamanic poet journeys into the elsewhere and elsewhen of Blackness by experimenting with various totemic or racial masks and scripts that the dramaturgy of race compels those made to carry the negative appellation *le négre* to wear as part of the theopolitical and anti-Black ceremony or liturgy of racial world making. At one point, the poet imagines himself as global spokesperson of the oppressed (st. 33). At other points, the poet experiments with the role of "Madman" (st. 47) and then of being a man of "Reason and Beauty" (st. 48) and then of impersonating a Caribbean "witch doctor" (sts. 60–65), only to have each fail or reach a limit, unable to realize the ritual or, as Gregson Davis has put it, "conjure the escape . . . from the shackles of postcolonial subjugation."[74] These failures of the masked performance or of personhood eventually lead the poet to the poem's final scene (more about that shortly).

In dramatizing these masks or roles and showing their performative inadequacy, the poet is not so much trying to dramatize Black alienation from the liturgy of race or the liturgy of Man as aiming to show how le négre is all at once corpsed within the liturgy of colonial modernity, policed by it, and in a state of wandering flight or fugitivity through it. That is to say, in establishing that le négre is caught within Western political theology's liturgy of race as its negatively sacral object, the poet's objective is not to hold in place the sacrificial act of corpsing. The aim, in other words, is not to do (Christian?) sacrifice better.

I propose that in performing out of a negatively sacrificial or sacral condition, the poet aims toward an alternative ritual of self that, strictly speaking, is irreducible to a sacrifice needed to establish that self. That is to say, Césaire's poem "fails" in that it does not satisfy the demands of human propriety. This is because its action occurs in a liminal zone that is nothing less than the break/down of the world of (the hu)Man. The poet's attention is on what is unknowable and unclassifiable to Man and within his world. Indeed, the poet's intention is toward what is "unknowable" in what David Marriott has called "the history of racial parable."[75] This buried and unknowable and fundamentally untranslatable history points to another totality that is irreducible to racial colonialism's structuring of reality, its claim on the real or to being itself. An open or unforecloseable totality "[carried] in [the poet's] inmost being at a depth inverse to the height of the twentieth floor of the most supercilious edifices," this totality, the poet tells us, bespeaks an alternative architecture that "[arises] from the shore of catastrophe" and that is nothing less than (and here the language of Davis's recent translation is quite significant) "*a talisman against the putrefying power of crepuscular settings*" (st. 1, 77; emphasis mine).

What the poet communicates by the end of the first stanza is that what is being addressed through and as performance and under the name *negritude* is an alternative manifestation of the sacred. Indeed, what comes into view by the stanza's end is that negritude is engaged in a spiritual ordeal, a struggle over ritual itself. I take it that this is what is at stake in the poet's serial insistence at the level of ontology on negritude's is-not-ness, on the one hand, and at the level of performance on negritude as a telluric delving into the ether, into the flesh of the sky and the earth (see st. 115, 127–29), on the other. Black performance here is not liturgical but paraliturgical. It is that *ana*liturgical, that *a*theological, ritual that circles around a "secret and sacral blackness."[76] The poem carries the mood of this irregular sacrality, a kind of fecality, that operates apart from the atoning or sacrificial logics of "the white world" and that is bound up, the poet says, with "the unyielding stars" and with "mystic flesh" (st. 119, 127). This is an alternative cosmology, a negritudinous Black (and, as we will see in a moment, feminist) metaphysics. Enough of my feeble attempts to describe this. Here's how the poet puts it:

At the close of foreday . . .

Buzz off, I told the man, the pig-snout, homie-snout, buzz off! I despise your law-and-order lackeys, your hope-infesting termites. Buzz off, foul grigri, vile specimen of a cleric. Then, more composed than the face of a woman telling a lie, I turned toward paradises lost to him and his kin, and there, lulled by the ebb and flow of a tireless thought, I nurtured the wind, I unloosed the monsters and I heard rising from the other shore of the catastrophe, the river of turtledoves and savannah clover that I always carry in my inmost being at a depth inverse to the height of the twentieth floor of the most supercilious edifices and as a talisman (*par précaution*) against the putrefying power of crepuscular settings, patrolled night and day by an accursed venereal sun (*un sacré soleil vénérien*). (st. 1, 77)

Here, the poet announces the orientation that propels the poem's performance. Interestingly, that orientation breaks from a world or a Western civilizational order structured by "law-and-order lackeys" and ultimately by the figure of the police, whom the poet interprets as in the lineage of the cleric or priest. That is to say, the poet announces that this meditation operates out of a mood or orientation or structure of feeling that moves in the break of a world organized through the clerical ritual of policing. To operate out of the break of such a world is, for the poet, to enter into a sexual and gendered break. "More composed than the face of a woman telling a lie," the poet not so much becomes woman as cites woman in her opacity and through citation registers a transformation of self that takes place in and through what Amber Jamilla Musser, building on and extending Spillers, speaks of as "fleshiness," in and through the history of a matrilineal, a *mater*-ial Blackness.[77]

Precisely because this move on the poet's part is poised on a knife-edge of possibly reproducing a set of gendered assumptions that are not entirely positive and thus risks reproducing a feature of the colonial order of racially gendered capitalism, and because I am here reading the poem for its potentials beyond Césaire's own gender politics, I want to linger with the poet's statement of being "more composed than the face of a woman telling a lie," doing so with assistance from Musser's recent work, *Sensual Excess: Queer Femininity and Brown Jouissance*. I am taken with the themes of flesh, excess, and hunger that propel Musser's work, for I believe her insights open up the stakes of what *Cahier*'s poet is here saying as well as the general stakes of a negritudinous poetics or fecopoetics. In other words, I am interested in how Césaire's Afrosurrealist poetics in many ways exceeds Césaire himself. In first thinking through the poet's statement, I was inclined to interpret the poet as positioning himself as "becoming-woman." However, in thinking with Musser, I retreated from this or at least came to understand that this required a Black feminist and queer theoretical nuance and orientation. I am taken with Musser's elaboration of Gilles Deleuze and Félix Guattari's notion of "becoming-woman" and how her development of "brown jouissance" relates to and differs from it. Commenting on Lyle Ashton Harris's photo portrait *Billie #21*, in which Harris presents himself in the photo as and in the iconic pose of Billie Holiday, Musser notes that "Holiday's voice can never emerge from this photograph—not because of a failure of imagination, but because the self on display is Harris, not Holiday. Even as it recalls one of Holiday's more iconic images, it is Harris who performs this homage to the famous jazz singer. . . . It is Harris's head that tilts back. Through posture, make-up, and props, Harris allows us to conjure Holiday as a mode of dual embodiment, a citation, if you will."[78] Musser goes on to remark that "Harris's transformation [into Holiday] exists on the surface—enacted through gloss, make-up, and surgical tape."[79] Finally, Musser says pointedly that "this is not a performance of becoming. Harris does not become-Holiday; he cites her—positioning his body alongside hers" with his head tilted, mouth somewhat agape, and eyes closed in ecstasy.[80] Harris's being-beside-himself in being-beside-Holiday is a being in the flesh. This is a matter of ontology, but it is an alternative ontology, arguably, not an ontotheology. More specifically, Musser shows that Harris's being-besides-himself in being-beside-Holiday is being in a certain state of hunger, yearning, and desire. This is a state that "combines multiple incoherent states—insatiability, joy, and freedom."[81] Referencing Alexander G. Weheliye's *Habeas Viscus: Racializing Assemblages, Biopolitics, and Black Feminist Theories of the Human*, Musser says that "hunger . . . is not about the possibility of fulfillment or nurturance; there are no objects" to sacrificially consume. There are "just cravings"—cravings emanating from an opaque interior and a sensual excess. "[This] act of craving is part of survival."[82] It is the action of a "plural self" that in "feeling the limitlessness of insatiability . . . reveals a sensuality or mode of being and relating that prioritizes openness, vulnerability, and a willingness to ingest without necessarily choosing what one is taking in."[83] This is "an embodied hunger that takes joy and pain in this gesture of radical openness toward otherness. This, this fleshy mixture of self-production, insatiability, joy and pain, is brown jouissance" and stands in contrast to the sacrificial eating that I have detailed in what Césaire describes in *Discourse on Colonialism*.[84] The form of hunger that marks fleshiness and that Musser is interested in "is constitutive of a type of selfhood that coalesces—even as it gnaws at the edges—in [a] state of openness and insatiability." Thus, "the self that Harris presents, the self who hungers, cannot be understood through the matrix of sovereign subjectivity."[85] Which is to say, it cannot be understood through what I have been describing as the eucharistic-become-colonial matrix, which Césaire's poet is dealing with.

We now arrive at a place to understand why what *Cahier*'s poet performs in donning a face "more composed than the face of a woman telling a lie" is not merely a variant of Deleuze and Guattari's notion of "becoming-woman" but rather is better understood within the terms of a Blackness beyond racial category whose traits are that of a "brown jouissance," a mode of rapturous desire and study that marks a hunger in and for multiplicity, or what Édouard Glissant called "Relation" and also, with Moten after him, called "consent not to be a single being."[86] For if becoming-woman "seeks to displace traditional humanism through the disruption of patriarchy and the embrace of the disempowered, it does little to think about the transformations of self that can take place in and through fleshiness. In Harris's explicit manipulation of his body, we see that pleasure and pain emerge from the history of Black female fleshiness. This is summoned by the citation of Holiday" and is made possible by virtue of the "multiple dimensions of fleshiness" of which Holiday herself is a citation and which "shape the possibilities that we can imagine and those that we cannot."[87] I want to read Césaire's poet as performing something akin to Harris's performance of hunger, desire, and appetite without object in relationship to Holiday and the history of flesh and radical openness. The poet's performance is a paraliturgy of flesh that reritualizes desire, pain, and pleasure into an insatiable yearning toward and into sheer openness. Such desire, such performance, is fundamentally and *mater*-ially matrilineal. This is a paraliturgical aesthetics of flesh where flesh is a kind of scripture, bearing an unfinished and unfinishable writing that exceeds the ontopolitical-theology of the body of singular meaning, normed around heterosexual and patriarchal whiteness. What the poet points to is the feeling of "a hunger," as Weheliye has put it, "outside of the world of Man," sacrilegiously outside of the precincts of colonial gender.[88]

This Black (feminist) hunger of the flesh transforms the violent consumption that is constitutive of the eucharistic-become-colonial matrix, opening up what Avery Gordon and José Muñoz might call a utopian vantage but that the poet here simply calls "paradises" (which importantly is not a singular *paradise*). The poet's paradises might be thought of as plan(e)s of multiplicity, which is a plan(e) of spirit, where corpsed vitalities persist and are yearned for but which settler colonial and racial capitalism disciples and disciplines us not to see or to see only as assigned to a region of death. Out of paradises (not) (lost), the poet glimpses another "materialism"—raw, protean organizations of matter, matter in the raw, ethereal mat(t)er before and beyond and at the end of matter as organized into and around the fetish.[89] What obtains from paradises are modes of performance that yield alternative modes of life together, unforecloseable horizons of care and commune-ion.

But along with this, there's another side to the poet's Black feminist *mater*ialism or imagination of paradises. This has to do with how these paraliturgical paradises involve a revisioning of landscapes. The poet's discourse of paradises and my interest in linking this to a language of spirit and an understanding of the sacred, albeit a dissident one, is not a refusal of matter. To the contrary, there is a serious and rigorous tellurism, we might say, to Césaire's poetics and to what the poet has in view when the poet says that from paradises, "lulled by the ebb and flow of a tireless thought, I nurtured the wind, I unloosed the monsters and I heard rising from the other shore of the catastrophe, the river of turtledoves and savannah clover that I always carry in my inmost being." The poet's statement is of a piece with what F. Abiola Irele notes generally about the ecopoetic sensibility that courses through Césaire's thinking, in which Césaire's dislodging of self from the structures of modern racial consciousness is of a piece with his efforts to reimagine the Caribbean landscape itself beyond the imposition of plantation logics of property. Such a reimagining of self as part and parcel of reimagining the earth "represents a dynamic process, a growing with and into the natural environment," such that, as the poet puts it, "by dint of gazing upon trees I have become a tree and my long-rooted feet have dug into the ground huge pouches of toxin"(st. 52, 101).[90] A kind of "becoming-woman" in what I quoted earlier from the first stanza of the poem meets a "becoming-tree" later in the poem, which in its own way remixes the revising of landscape that already appears in the poem's first stanza. Arguably, the poet ruptures the imagination of the political theology of "Genesis," or Creation, so as to perform what Glissant will later think about under the rubric of "Digenesis" and so as to enact Ursa's injunction in Gayl Jones's *Corregidora* that "everything said in the beginning must be said better than in the beginning."[91] Just as *Discourse on Colonialism* begins with the excremental, *Cahier* also begins otherwise, with the red flesh of the earth itself. Thus, it seems to me that there's something to Irele's suggestion that there is "a wider mystic significance," if not a mysticism without colonial modernity's god terms, that is bound up with the Caribbean landscape and with Césaire's poetics.[92] That is to say, by way of the mystery of Blackness, if not the mysticism of negritude, the Caribbean itself provides the basis for a new imagination of matter and a reimagining of self. For the Caribbean's symbolic significance has to do with what the Caribbean incites for the poet; it incites "a creative animation of Caribbean consciousness through an invocation of the forces of the land in which it is lodged."[93] Irele concludes, and I agree with his reading of the matter, that "the Caribbean landscape is spiritualized in *Cahier*, transformed into the living symbol of a collective passion, in the religious sense of the word."[94]

This simultaneous "becoming-woman" in stanza 1 (with the drastic qualifications just noted) and "becoming-tree" in stanza 52, which is but a return to how landscape figures in the opening lines of the poem, where the landscape stands apart from imposed and civilizing architectures, indicates the direction of the poet's utopian performance of paradises (not) (lost), wherein that performance takes the form of a pariah and an incantatory poetics, a spiritual ordeal that surges through or otherwise refuses the priest's language act of transubstantiation as it obtained within the eucharistic matrix spoken of earlier and as it persists in what is now a colonial matrix. Dwelling with vitalities corpsed within and as Blackness or otherwise remaindered by the racially gendered codes (that are, in fact, transubstantiated, juris-theological "law-and-order" codes) of the human, codes ritually branded on flesh and imposed on the earth through language, the poet works with language at another level. More specifically, the poet experiments with language by descending into it as a shaman might do through incantation in order to (re)touch and be touched by the earth and the cosmos, by spirit or the Absolute. By way of descent "into language as some kind of original and founding mythic violence," the poet dissents, refusing clerical colonial rule(s), insovereignly refusing sovereignty.[95] I want to suggest here that *Cahier*'s shamanic poet does not so much claim or accept the language of *le négre* as perform differently the codes of race *and what those codes corpse*.[96] In what is less an Odyssean (though to be sure echoing Odysseus) and more a Dionysian adventure of Black rapture and an "unloosing of the monstrous" (st. 1, 77), the collective poet conjures not so much (Western) being as the Blackness that being intestinally buries or that an anti-Black world aims categorically to arrest or consume in order to establish, even if incoherently, "the world" (of Man) on top of the earth. In this way, *Cahier*'s poet "transforms the philosophical question that blackness represents in both thought and politics."[97] This is a performance within and of dispossession itself.

In a moment, as I move toward concluding this essay, I will offer comments on what Black performance performs or more precisely what Blackness as performance approaches and what the theopolitical and racial-liturgical codes of the human semiotically corpse. But first I must note one last thing about the first stanza on which I have been meditating here. It concerns specifically the stanza's quite significant ending. When the stanza concludes by saying that the "paradises" that give the poem its sociopoetic or talismanic force are "being patrolled night and day by an *accursed venereal sun* [sacré soleil vénérein]" (emphasis mine), what is being said? In answer, I propose that if the reference at the beginning of the poem to the police as the new cleric were not enough to clarify that the terrain on which the poet's performance of negritude operates is political theology's racialized regulation of the plane of the sacred, then this phrase at the end of the stanza ("an accursed venereal sun . . ."), which explicitly invokes in the French the word *sacred*, makes this quite clear. Attuned to the ambiguity within the very notion of the sacred (the French Latinate word *sacré* can refer to what is "holy" or "pure" or more colloquially can mean "accursed," "damned," or what is off-limits as "taboo"), *Cahier*'s poet says that the paradises or potentials for new ecologies or organizations of matter and new inhabitations of the earth are always, night and day, being patrolled or are under theopolitical or ontotheological surveillance. Davis has observed that the use of *sacré*, or *sacred* (in the sense of something being cursed), gives a sense of the poet's perception of the West: in its practice of civilizational holiness or the colonial enactment of its "rightness of being," a holiness and right(eous)ness carried out in the name of the holy (*sacré*), even if the holy has been secularized into democracy and markets, the West has cursed (*sacré*) the earth, subjected it to affliction or damnation.[98] Indeed, it has gone so far as to naturalize its damning of the earth by imposing that damnation onto the temperate zone itself. And if the weather and indeed the atmosphere are damned, so goes the logic of a colonizing West, so too are the people of these zones wretched or sacredly accursed.[99] What I want to emphasize about what the poet is saying regarding the West and its version or genre of the sacred is this: the poet sees the colonizing West, in its devastation of the Caribbean landscape, as performing both sides of the sacred-sacré as a dialectic of the pure and the holy, on the one hand, and the impure and the accursed, on the other, with the opposition between them resolved through social rituals of sacrifice that cohere society.[100]

And yet, as I have argued elsewhere (and I think that the Césairean poet is keen on this), there is another imaginary of the sacred, one that is tied precisely to the kind of performance that the poet carries out and that is irreducible to the pure or impure poles within an ontotheological dialectics of coloniality. This dialectics is constituted in a binary opposition, managed through sacrifice, between what is called the sacred and what is called profane.[101] Indeed, there is another sense or mood of the sacred that makes Blackpoetic performance excremental to political theology's restricted economy of sovereignty. The poet is all up in this, excrementally sullied within a paraliturgical ecology beyond Western political theology's restricted economy of liturgical sacrifice. In stanzas 117–18, the poet speaks to what I would call a general ecology of Black sacral excess:

> Hurray for those who have never invented anything
> for those who have never explored anything
> for those who have never vanquished anything
> but they surrender, possessed . . .
> by the movement
> of every thing . . .
>
> spark of the sacred fire of the world [*étincelle du feu sacré du monde*]
> flesh of the very flesh of the world, palpitating with the very movement of the world! (127)

The "spark of the sacred fire of the world" of which the poet speaks and which the poet relates to negritude, I submit, is not simply bound to one pole or the other within a dialectic that swings between the pure and the impure or between the holy and the profane and where negritude as a spark of the sacred is a necessary though negative moment within the dialectical unfolding of Western consciousness and History (with a capital *H*). Rather, the poet has tapped into some other still or silent movement, some other force or mood that is on the far side of philosophical dialectics, that indeed negates negation and resolution because its protocol is not of the order of the restricted economy of sacrifice and meaning. The poet's intention is of a mo(ve)ment that is extradialectical and extraceremonial.

Occupying the abyssal breach between language and racial sense or world making, negritude emerges as a resonating force that surges through both language itself and "the flesh of the world" (*chair de la chair du monde* ...), through but altogether anterior to dialectic.

The poet dwells with this force, is under its sway. Indeed, toward the end of the poem, the poet works to imagine this mood as suffusing the belly of a slave ship. This force of the sacred otherwise that the poet aligns with negritude renders an imagined slave ship a "spastic" scene of the fantastic (st. 162, 143). That is, the poet's imagined ship, under the sway of an unnameable and unknowable force or mood, carries an inspirited and conspiring, ancestral "nigger cargo" (st. 164–66, 143), a cargo of spirits, which claims an uprightness from the hold to take over the slave ship. These spirits of the dead who are alive in and beyond death, ghosts in effect, indicate vitalities beyond the opposition between life and death that has come to be racialized in such a way as to align whiteness with life and Blackness with death or with what in the movement of thought called *Afro-pessimism* has been called "social death." Now standing "upright," the cargo in this imagined poetic scene seizes the boat so as to turn the slave ship into a "lustral vessel" (st. 166–67, 145), the dead into a lustral cargo. Could uprising figured as uprightness or as the racial reclamation of life be what negritude finally means (which is certainly how Jean-Paul Sartre in "Black Orpheus" interprets it)?[102]

This is where the final scene of the poem becomes absolutely significant. Precisely in staving off such an interpretation of negritude that risks resolving it into a final meaning, or *sens*, and in this way risks keeping the poem within a racial economy of sacrificial world making, the poet delves further, coming to see even this gesture—negritude as the performance of uprightness or standing—as itself already corpsed. Not a singular uprightness or the claiming of standing but rather an ongoing fallenness where ascension and descent meet in an oceanic and cosmic abyss—this is where the poet goes in the last lines of the poem to effectively play out the ellipsis from the first line of the poem. Here's how the poet puts it:

> ascend to the lick the sky
> and the great black hole [*le grand trou noir*] where I longed to
>   drown myself the other moon
> that's where I now long to fish out the night's malicious tone in
>   its sweeping stillness [*la langue maléfique de la nuit en son
>   immobile verrition*]! (st. 174, 149)

Coming close, as Marriott I think suggestively observes, to "a sacral religious concept of black experience and history," the poet here offers what amounts to an abyssal theory of Blackness, if not of Black religion, staged as an alternative ritual of celebration.[103] Here the dead arrive not so as to claim standing in the world of Man but "from a time without us, from a past not our own, from a time that is not historical" or that is not of the history of Man. We are back at what Biddick calls unhistorical histories and uncanny temporalities.[104] These nameless revenants "arrive without sense or life" precisely because they are from a dark (non)place, a place of fundamental dislocation and dispossession, the central metaphor of which (which, in truth, is so much more than a metaphor) is the Middle Passage.[105] Being of "no-bodies" and from an abyssal no-place, in short, being of passage as such, these revenants do not just make possible an understanding of the racial-colonial condition of history but point to abyssal im/possibilities for being on and with the earth that nevertheless saturate history with new modes of relation, with indeterminate becoming.[106] This is the abyssal Blackness (*le grand trou noir*) spoken of in the final lines of the poem, that plane of spirit that announces the metaphysical end of race, which is nothing less than the end of the world as we know it.[107] Here the Blackness of racial category, which gets aligned with the Black body, might be constantly set ablaze, though the corpse of Blackness within, which thus exceeds categorical capture, is never immolated or consumed. The poet is given to hearing spirits or other revenant vitalities as they speak through a dead zone; from an abyssal plane, that is, wherein Black life and death literally mean nothing—and everything.[108] "All black everything."[109] Negritude speaks after and with what is corpsed to the abyss but can do so only insofar as its language is abyssal and thus involved in a constant aesthetic and ritual exploration of the heights and the depths of becoming: the abyss. Negritude is an abyssal ritual. Black-poetics. A Paraliturgy.

Notes

I express deep gratitude to Eleanor Craig and An Yountae for the care with which they edited this manuscript and helped me get it better than it was. I am also grateful to Colin Dayan, Denise Ferreira da Silva, Sora Han, Lenora Hanson, Laura Harris, David Lloyd, Fred Moten, Dylan Rodríguez, Atef Said, and Dorothy Wang for reading a version of this essay and offering invaluable comments. Where it yet falls short falls fully upon me.

1 Marriott, *Whither Fanon?*, xii.

2 I borrow the phrase "a black way of living" from Moten, *Universal Machine*, 235.

3 Du Bois, *Darkwater*, 56. For further reflections on this, see Carter, "Unlikely Convergence."

4 Césaire, *Discourse on Colonialism*, 33. Hereafter cited parenthetically in the text.

5 Irele, introduction, 60

6 See, Hartman, "Anarchy of Colored Girls"; Hartman, "Belly of the World"; and Hartman, *Wayward Lives, Beautiful Experiments*.

7 "Held-not-had" is from the poem "A Night in Jaipur ("mu" sixty-fifth part)" in Mackey, *Blue Fasa*, 4.

8 Across her vast oeuvre, Sylvia Wynter details the "problem of Man," at the heart of which is how colonialism overdetermined the very meaning of the human. See Wynter, "Unsettling the Coloniality." Another rubric under which to speak of this problem, wherein some are properly human while others exist under the colonial imperative to become human, is Denise Ferreira da Silva's notions of the "global idea of race" and the imposition of the "patriarch form." See Ferreira da Silva, *Toward a Global Idea of Race*; and Ferreira da Silva, "Hacking the Subject." Finally, Charles H. Long has for quite some time spoken of the "problem of Man" as bound up with the notion of the fetish, a notion whose origins are in the transatlantic slave trade. Long establishes how what is called "the human" emerged through a violent penetration into and transformation of matter. That is to say, the human is the yield of the violent imposition of certain logics of value onto matter itself. Long argues that this material violence or violating of matter established a new modality of religion predicated upon and exploitative of the "laws" of physics. This new modality of religion is whiteness. A metaphysical experiment from and on the slave ship, on and through transatlantic passage, for the genesis of modern society, Whiteness emerges through sociohistorical processes that violently seize upon the open-ended and unsettled structures of matter. See Long, *Ellipsis*. Thinking with this poetic trio, I deal with the problem of Man or what we might also think of as the colonial genre of the human as an issue of matter itself as that issue manifests in the sacramental, liturgical, or eucharistic structures of the world that Man has "worlded" for himself. In many respects, this is what I take up in this essay.

9 Ferreira da Silva, "Toward a Black Feminist Poethics," 84.

10 Ferreira da Silva, "Toward a Black Feminist Poethics," 84.

11 Ferreira da Silva, "Toward a Black Feminist Poethics," 84.

12 Ferreira da Silva, "Toward a Black Feminist Poethics," 83.

13 Informing my understanding of myth here are Barthes, "Myth Today"; Brisson, *Plato the Myth Maker*; Gourgouris, *Does Literature Think?*; Long, *Alpha* and *Significations*; and Tatman, *Numinous Subjects*.

14 Moten, *Stolen Life*, 55–56.

15 Castoriadis, "Institution of Society and Religion"; Castoriadis, *Imaginary Institution of Society*.

16 Aimé Césaire, *Discourse on Colonialism*, 48.

17 Biddick, *Typological Imaginary*, 1, 2.

18 Biddick, *Typological Imaginary*, 1. See also Carter, *Race*, where I deal extensively with the problem of Christian supersessionism against Jews as the basis of the production of an anti-Black world.

19 Fabian, *Time and the Other*.

20 The echo here of Calvin L. Warren's *Ontological Terror: Blackness, Nihilism, and Emancipation* is intentional.

21 Moten, *In the Break*, 26.

22 Mbembé, *On the Postcolony*. See particularly chapter 6 of this book, "God's Phallus," for an elaboration of the problem of the One in relationship to the "postcolony." My only supplement to Mbembé's insightful argument is that whereas he frames the relationship between discourses of Christian missionary conversion in Africa as powered by a logic of the imperial, monotheistic One (chapter 6 of *On the Postcolony*) and the phenomenology of colonial violence (chapter 5 of *On the Postcolony*) as analogy or allegory of each other, I contend in there relationship is not merely analogy or allegory; they are mutually constitutive. They are each other's inner logic or grammar. As discourse of the One (and Only and Unitary One), political theology is coloniality.

23 Han, "Poetics of Mu." "Mu-" is the title of one of poet Nathaniel Mackey's ongoing poems, which he sees as braided in serial difference from and with his other ongoing poem sequence, "Song of the Andoumboulou." For his own reflections on his poetry and poetics as a practice of "myth" or what I call "mythography," see the preface to Mackey, *Splay Anthem*.

24 See Durkheim, *Elementary Forms of Religious Life*. See also the essays collected in Bataille, *Visions of Excess*.

25 Wilderson, *Red, White and Black*. Charles H. Long and Katharine Gerbner also make this point from within the sphere of religious studies. Whiteness emerges in the scene of contact/conquest. See particularly Long, *Ellipsis*, chs. 1–2; and Gerbner, *Christian Slavery*. Finally, I take up this topic in a just completed manuscript, "The Religion of Whiteness: An Apocalyptic Lyric."

26 Tatman, *Numinous Subjects*, 2. The account of religion that I offer in this paragraph is deeply informed by Lucy Tatman's theoretically sophisticated and poetic, lucid work.

27 Anidjar, *Blood*. Anidjar's chapter 2, whose subtitle is "The Vampire State," develops the idea of the vampiric blood-sucking and bloodletting nature of the state. I should also note that Fanon employs the notion of the vampire in *The Wretched of the Earth*, doing so in a way that differs from Anidjar's development of the idea. Whereas Anidjar works from the idea of the vampire as consuming blood (hence the amenableness of Anidjar's analysis

to this stage of my own argument), Fanon employs the term more in keeping with the idea of a ghostly and uncanny disturbance that interrupts the reality of the colonial landscape. Summing up Fanon on this point, Samira Kawash says, "Where the settler seeks to determine the native as dead, inert matter, the persistence of a spectral remainder of [what's] undead disturbs this static division between settler and native. Beyond the living subject of the settler and the dead object of the native is this void which is not-empty, a no-place and a no-thing which cannot appear as positive being but which nonetheless interrupts the reality of the colonial landscape. This disturbance is what I am calling the vampire, not-living and not-dead, not-settler and not-native. The vampire thus simultaneously exceeds and interrupts the opposition between the living being of the settler and the dead matter of the native. The vampire is not the native; but the vampire comes from the native in a certain sense, insofar as it figures the living being of the native which cannot appear in colonial reality, and which therefore re-emerges in spectral form. Colonial reality is haunted by the real of the native that cannot be recognized as living being . . . a haunting remainder." Kawash, "Terrorists and Vampires," 253–54. What Kawash says here about a vampiric remainder that within the terms of Western being and within the ontotheological framework of coloniality-modernity is neither living nor dead but is something akin to ghostly foreshadows where I am going later in this essay's interpretation of Césaire's poetics of the excremental, his fecopoetics of negritude, as an abyssal, decolonial paraliturgy. Beyond racial category, Blackness operates in a ghostly, Sycoraxian, sorceress- or witch-like way. Such is the extraceremonialism, the paraliturgical stylistics, of Césaire's poetics and more generally of Blackpoetics.

28   Judy, "Sentient Flesh."
29   Besides bearing the traces of my ongoing thinking with Ferreira da Silva (see her *Toward a Global Idea of Race* for the notion of apprehension without obliteration), this paragraph is also indebted to what I continue to learn in thinking with Kara Keeling's *Queer Times, Black Futures*.
30   I am here thinking with Hammonds, "Black (W)holes."
31   Besides Anidjar's *Blood: A Critique of Christianity*, see the standard and fairly exhaustive text on this topic, Caroline Walker Bynum's *Wonderful Blood: Theology and Practice in Late Medieval Northern Germany and Beyond*.
32   On the idea of the corpus mysticum from the Middle Ages, see Lubac, *Corpus Mysticum*; and Kantorowicz, *King's Two Bodies*.
33   Anidjar's *Blood* deeply informs much of what follows.
34   Anidjar, *Blood*, 34.
35   Esposito, quoted in Anidjar, *Blood*, 38.
36   Anidjar, *Blood*, 39.
37   Robinson, *Terms of Order*.

38 Anidjar, *Blood*, 39.

39 Anidjar, *Blood*, 122.

40 See particularly Robinson, *Black Marxism*, ch. 1. But also see Robinson, *Anthropology of Marxism*. In this understudied text, Robinson rigorously engages the ontotheological medievalism that grounds what we call modernity. Additionally, he glimpses the fugitivity in the form of heresy and rebellion that is there as well and that I, drawing on Silvia Federici's work, will speak to shortly so as to connect that fugitivity and rebellion to Césaire's excremental poetics of negritude.

41 Anidjar, *Blood*, 122.

42 Anidjar, *Blood*, 122.

43 Anidjar, *Blood*, 39.

44 Anidjar, *Blood*, 39.

45 Anidjar, *Blood*, 39.

46 See Gómez-Barris, *Extractive Zone*.

47 hooks, *Black Looks*, 36.

48 See Gómez-Barris, *Extractive Zone*.

49 In addition to Anidjar's *Blood*, see Winner, *Dangers of Christian Practice*, particularly the chapter "Eucharist," and Kantorowicz, *The King's Two Bodies*.

50 Federici, *Caliban and the Witch*, 32.

51 Federici, *Caliban and the Witch*, 33.

52 Federici, *Caliban and the Witch*, 33.

53 Federici, *Caliban and the Witch*, 33.

54 Federici, *Caliban and the Witch*, 40.

55 I borrow this language from Tadiar, "Decolonization," 136.

56 See Federici, *Caliban and the Witch*, 179.

57 Harney and Moten, *Undercommons*; and Ramey, *Hermetic Deleuze*, 216.

58 See Ramey, *Hermetic Deleuze*, 216, 143, 144, 146. On virtuality and Plenum, see Ferreira da Silva, "Toward a Black Feminist Poethics."

59 Donahue, *Dark Church*; and Ramey, *Hermetic Deleuze*, 3.

60 Cooper, "The Living and the Dead," 91. See also Ferreira da Silva, "Hacking the Subject."

61 The language of "counter-natural generation" I specifically borrow from Melinda Cooper ("The Living and the Dead"). The general argument here represents a thinking with Nunes's *Cannibal Democracy* and Bianchi's profound meditation on the excessive in Aristotle's *De Anima* in *The Feminine Symptom*. Finally, I am indebted to Neferti X. M. Tadiar's thinking about the remainder for helping me think about Césaire's fecopoetics as an excremental experiment.

62 See Philip, "Island Liturgy I"; and "Island Liturgy II."

63 The lines of inquiry I start to develop here I expand on in my manuscript in progress, "Black Rapture: A Poetics of the Sacred."

64 "Being for the captor" is a formulation from Spillers, "Mama's Baby, Papa's Maybe," 67.

65 On "sonic substance," see Moten, *In the Break*. See also the general oeuvre of Nathaniel Mackey, though I find the essays in *Discrepant Engagement*, the letters collected in *Bass Cathedral*, and his interview with Sarah Rosenthal, "The Atmosphere Is Alive," particularly resonant for what I am saying here.

66 Césaire, *Journal*, st. 115, 125 (emphasis added). Hereafter cited parenthetically in the text with the stanza (st.) followed by the page number.

67 For more on Césaire's use of "is not," see Davis, "Negritude-as-Performance."

68 My thinking here is indebted to Keeling's exquisite *Queer Times, Black Futures*, 73. I have learned so much from Keeling's creative extension of Gilbert Simondon's philosophy into Black studies.

69 Ramey, *Hermetic Deleuze*.

70 Sexton, "Social Life of Social Death."

71 Sylvia Wynter, "Black Metamorphosis: New Natives in a New World," n.d., Institute of the Black World Records, MG 502, Box 1, Schomburg Center for Research in Black Culture, New York Public Library, New York. See my engagement with Wynter on theologization in "Black Malpractice (a Poetics of the Sacred)."

72 Warren, *Ontological Terror*.

73 I have in mind here Sharpe's account of the Middle Passage as a kind of birth canal and the relationship of this to how Black woman is positioned as the liminal threshold of racial-colonial modernity through slavery. See Sharpe, *In the Wake*.

74 For more on Césaire's wearing of these masks and the way a certain conjuring practice is going on here, see Davis, "Negritude-as-Performance," 150.

75 Marriott, *Whither Fanon?*, 332.

76 Marriott, *Whither Fanon?*, 332.

77 Musser, *Sensual Excess*.

78 Musser, *Sensual Excess*, 2.

79 Musser, *Sensual Excess*, 3.

80 Musser, *Sensual Excess*, 3.

81 Musser, *Sensual Excess*, 5.

82 Musser, *Sensual Excess*, 5.

83 Musser, *Sensual Excess*, 5.

84 Musser, *Sensual Excess*, 5.

85 Musser, *Sensual Excess*, 5.

86 Glissant, *Poetics of Relation*. Glissant offers the phrase "consent not to be a single being" in "One World in Relation: Édouard Glissant in Conversation with Manthia Diawara." Across a three-volume series bearing the unifying title Consent Not to Be a Single Being, Moten takes up this Glissantian notion. See Moten, *Black and Blur*; Moten, *Stolen Life*; and Moten, *Universal Machine*.

87 Musser, *Sensual Excess*, 3.

88 Weheliye, *Habeas Viscus*, quoted in Musser, *Sensual Excess*, 4.

89 My understanding of the fetish is indebted to Long's engagement with this idea. See Long, *Ellipsis*. See also Pietz, "The Problem of the Fetish, I," "The Problem of the Fetish, II," and "The Problem of the Fetish, IIIa"; and Matory, *Fetish Revisited*. I addressed the issue of theology and the racial fetish in a talk given in June 2019 on Karl Barth's *Römerbrief* at the University of Geneva.

90 Irele, introduction, 63.

91 "Digenesis" is from Glissant's *Introduction à poétique du divers* and is beautifully elaborated in Drabinski, *Glissant and the Middle Passage*. Jones, *Corregidora*, 54.

92 Irele, introduction, 63.

93 Irele, introduction, 63.

94 Irele, introduction, 63.

95 Marriott, *Whither Fanon?*, 332.

96 Marriott, *Whither Fanon?*, 329–41. The reading of Césaire's *Cahier* that I am working out here owes a significant debt to Marriott.

97 Marriott, *Whither Fanon?*, 329.

98 For "rightness of being," see Wynter, "Unsettling the Coloniality."

99 Might this be what Fanon intuits in the very title of his final work, *The Wretched of the Earth*?

100 It was Émile Durkheim who formulated a sociology of religion that rigorously analyzed this. See Durkheim, *Elementary Forms of Religious Life*.

101 For more on this, see Carter, "Black Malpractice," 73.

102 Sartre, "Black Orpheus."

103 Marriott, *Whither Fanon?*, 331.

104 Biddick, *Typological Imaginary*, 3, 21.

105 Marriott, *Whither Fanon?*, 331.

106 Ferreira da Silva, "NO-BODIES"; and Moten, "Notes on Passage."

107 Marriott, *Whither Fanon?*, xix.

108 Marriott, *Whither Fanon?*, 331.

109 Sexton, "All Black Everything."

Bibliography

Anidjar, Gil. *Blood: A Critique of Christianity*. New York: Columbia University Press, 2014.

Barthes, Roland. "Myth Today." In *Mythologies: The Complete Edition, in a New Translation*, translated by Richard Howard and Annette Lavers, 215–74. 2nd ed. New York: Hill and Wang, 2013.

Bataille, Georges. *Visions of Excess: Selected Writings, 1927–1939*. Edited by Allan Stoekl. 1st ed. Minneapolis: University of Minnesota Press, 1985.

Bianchi, Emanuela. *The Feminine Symptom: Aleatory Matter in the Aristotelian Cosmos*. 1st ed. New York: Fordham University Press, 2014.

Biddick, Kathleen. *The Typological Imaginary: Circumcision, Technology, History*. Philadelphia: University of Pennsylvania Press, 2003.

Brisson, Luc. *Plato the Myth Maker*. Translated by Gerard Naddaf. Chicago: University of Chicago Press, 2000.

Bynum, Caroline Walker. *Wonderful Blood: Theology and Practice in Late Medieval Northern Germany and Beyond*. Philadelphia: University of Pennsylvania Press, 2007.

Carter, J. Kameron. "Black Malpractice (A Poetics of the Sacred)." *Social Text* 37, no. 2 (2019): 67–107.

Carter, J. Kameron. "Black Rapture: A Poetics of the Sacred." Unpublished manuscript. January 2020.

Carter, J. Kameron. *Race: A Theological Account*. New York: Oxford University Press, 2008.

Carter, J. Kameron. "The Religion of Whiteness: An Apocalyptic Lyric." Unpublished manuscript. October 2020.

Carter, J. Kameron. "The Römerbrief and the Racial Fetish." Keynote lecture at the International Barth Conference at the University of Geneva, Switzerland, June 19, 2019.

Carter, J. Kameron. "An Unlikely Convergence: W. E. B. Du Bois, Karl Barth, and the Problem of the Imperial God-Man." *CR: The New Centennial Review* 11, no. 3 (2012): 167–224.

Castoriadis, Cornelius. "Institution of Society and Religion." In *World in Fragments: Writings on Politics, Society, Psychoanalysis, and the Imagination*, translated by David Ames Curtis, 311–30. Stanford, CA: Stanford University Press, 1997.

Castoriadis, Cornelius. *The Imaginary Institution of Society*. 2nd ed. Cambridge: Polity, 1997.

Césaire, Aimé. *Discourse on Colonialism*. 1955. Translated by Joan Pinkham. New York: Monthly Review Press, 2000.

Césaire, Aimé. *Journal of a Homecoming/Cahier d'un retour au pays natal*. Translated by Gregson Davis. Bilingual ed. Durham, NC: Duke University Press, 2017.

Cooper, Melinda. "The Living and the Dead: Variations on *De Anima*." *Angelaki* 7, no. 3 (2002): 81–104.

Davis, Gregson. "Negritude-as-Performance: The Interplay of Efficacious and Inefficacious Speech Acts in *Cahier d'un retour au pays natal*." *Research in African Literatures* 41, no. 1 (2010): 142–54.

Donahue, Joseph. *Dark Church*. Chicago: Verge, 2015.

Drabinski, John E. *Glissant and the Middle Passage: Philosophy, Beginning, Abyss*. Minneapolis: University of Minnesota Press, 2019.

Du Bois, W. E. B. "The Souls of White Folk." 1919. In *Darkwater: Voices from within the Veil*, 55–74. Amherst, NY: Humanity Books, 2002.

Durkheim, Émile. *The Elementary Forms of Religious Life*. Translated by Karen E. Fields. New York: Free Press, 1995.

Fabian, Johannes. *Time and the Other: How Anthropology Makes Its Object*. New York: Columbia University Press, 1983.

Fanon, Frantz. *The Wretched of the Earth*. 1961. New York: Grove, 2004.

Federici, Silvia. *Caliban and the Witch: Women, the Body and Primitive Accumulation*. New York: Autonomedia, 2004.

Ferreira da Silva, Denise. "Hacking the Subject: Black Feminism and Refusal beyond the Limits of Critique." *PhiloSOPHIA* 8, no. 1 (2018): 19–41.

Ferreira da Silva, Denise. "NO-BODIES: Law, Raciality and Violence." *Griffith Law Review* 18, no. 2 (2009): 212–36.

Ferreira da Silva, Denise. "Toward a Black Feminist Poethics: The Quest(ion) of Blackness toward the End of the World." *Black Scholar* 44, no. 2 (2014): 81–97.

Ferreira da Silva, Denise. *Toward a Global Idea of Race*. 1st ed. Minneapolis: University of Minnesota Press, 2007.

Gerbner, Katharine. *Christian Slavery: Conversion and Race in the Protestant Atlantic World*. Philadelphia: University of Pennsylvania Press, 2018.

Glissant, Édouard. *Introduction à une poétique du divers*. Montreal: Presses de l'Université de Montréal, 1995.

Glissant, Édouard. "One World in Relation: Édouard Glissant in Conversation with Manthia Diawara." Edited by Manthia Diawara. *Nka Journal of Contemporary African Art* 28 (2011): 4–19.

Glissant, Édouard. *Poetics of Relation*. Translated by Betsy Wing. Ann Arbor: University of Michigan Press, 1997.

Gómez-Barris, Macarena. *The Extractive Zone: Social Ecologies and Decolonial Perspectives*. Dissident Acts. Durham, NC: Duke University Press, 2017.

Gourgouris, Stathis. *Does Literature Think?: Literature as Theory for an Antimythical Era*. Stanford, CA: Stanford University Press, 2003.

Hammonds, Evelynn. "Black (W)Holes and the Geometry of Black Female Sexuality." In *The Black Studies Reader*, edited by Jacqueline Bobo, Cynthia Hudley, and Claudine Michel, 301–14. New York: Routledge, 2004.

Han, Sora. "Poetics of Mu." *Textual Practice*, 34, no. 6 (2020): 921–48.

Harney, Stefano, and Fred Moten. *The Undercommons: Fugitive Planning and Black Study*. New York: Minor Compositions, 2013.

Hartman, Saidiya. "The Anarchy of Colored Girls Assembled in a Riotous Manner." *South Atlantic Quarterly* 117, no. 3 (2018): 465–90.

Hartman, Saidiya. "The Belly of the World: A Note on Black Women's Labors." *Souls* 18, no. 1 (2016): 166–73.

Hartman, Saidiya. *Wayward Lives, Beautiful Experiments: Intimate Histories of Social Upheaval*. New York: Norton, 2019.

hooks, bell. *Black Looks: Race and Representation*. New York: Routledge, 2014.

Irele, F. Abiola. Introduction to Césaire, *Journal of a Homecoming*, 1–73.

Jones, Gayl. *Corregidora*. Boston: Beacon, 1987.

Judy, R. A. *Sentient Flesh: Thinking in Disorder, Poiesis in Black*. Durham, NC: Duke University Press, 2020.

Kantorowicz, Ernst H. *The King's Two Bodies: A Study in Mediaeval Political Theology*. Princeton, NJ: Princeton University Press, 1985.

Kawash, Samira. "Terrorists and Vampires: Fanon's Spectral Violence of Decolonization." In *Frantz Fanon: Critical Perspectives*, edited by Anthony C. Alessandrini, 235–57. New York: Routledge, 1999.

Keeling, Kara. *Queer Times, Black Futures*. New York: New York University Press, 2019.

Long, Charles H., ed. *Ellipsis . . . : The Collected Writings of Charles H. Long*. New York: Bloomsbury Academic, 2018.

Long, Charles H. *Alpha: The Myths of Creation*. Atlanta: Scholars Press, 1963.

Long, Charles H. *Significations: Signs, Symbols, and Images in the Interpretation of Religion*. Rev. Series in Philosophical and Cultural Studies in Religion. Aurora, CO: Davies Group, 1995.

Lubac, Henri de. *Corpus Mysticum: The Eucharist and the Church in the Middle Ages*. Notre Dame, IN: University of Notre Dame Press, 2007.

Mackey, Nathaniel. *Blue Fasa*. New York: New Directions, 2015.

Mackey, Nathaniel. "The Atmosphere Is Alive: Nathaniel Mackey Interviewed by Sarah Rosenthal." In *A Community Writing Itself: Conversations with Vanguard Writers of the Bay Area*, edited by Sarah Rosenthal, 137–66. Champaign, IL: Dalkey Archive Press, 2010.

Mackey, Nathaniel. *Bass Cathedral*. New York: New Directions, 2008.

Mackey, Nathaniel. *Discrepant Engagement: Dissonance, Cross-Culturality, and Experimental Writing*. Tuscaloosa: University of Alabama Press, 2000.

Mackey, Nathaniel. *Splay Anthem*. New York: New Directions, 2006.

Marriott, David. *Whither Fanon? Studies in the Blackness of Being*. Stanford, CA: Stanford University Press, 2018.

Matory, J. Lorand. *The Fetish Revisited: Marx, Freud, and the Gods Black People Make*. Durham, NC: Duke University Press, 2018.

Mbembé, Achille. *On the Postcolony*. Berkeley: University of California Press, 2001.

Moten, Fred. *Black and Blur*. Durham, NC: Duke University Press, 2017.

Moten, Fred. *In the Break: The Aesthetics of the Black Radical Tradition*. Minneapolis: University of Minnesota Press, 2003.

Moten, Fred. "Notes on Passage (The New International of Sovereign Feelings)." *Palimpsest: A Journal on Women, Gender, and the Black International* 3, no. 1 (2014): 51–74.

Moten, Fred. *Stolen Life*. Durham, NC: Duke University Press, 2018.

Moten, Fred. *The Universal Machine*. Durham, NC: Duke University Press, 2018.

Musser, Amber Jamilla. *Sensual Excess: Queer Femininity and Brown Jouissance*. New York: New York University Press, 2018.

Nunes, Zita. *Cannibal Democracy: Race and Representation in the Literature of the Americas*. Critical American Studies. Minneapolis: University of Minnesota Press, 2008.

Philip, M. NourbeSe. "Island Liturgy I." *Callaloo* 37, no. 1 (2014): 30.

Philip, M. NourbeSe. "Island Liturgy II." *Callaloo* 37, no. 1 (2014): 32.

Philip, M. NourbeSe. "Wor(l)ds Interrupted: The Unhistory of the Kari Basin." *Jacket2*, September 17, 2013. http://jacket2.org/article/worlds-interrupted.

Philip, M. NourbeSe. *Zong*! Middletown, CT: Wesleyan University Press, 2011.

Pietz, William. "The Problem of the Fetish, I." *RES: Anthropology and Aesthetics*, no. 9 (1985): 5–17.

Pietz, William. "The Problem of the Fetish, II: The Origin of the Fetish." *RES: Anthropology and Aesthetics*, no. 13 (1987): 23–45.

Pietz, William. "The Problem of the Fetish, IIIa: Bosman's Guinea and the Enlightenment Theory of Fetishism." *RES: Anthropology and Aesthetics*, no. 16 (1988): 105–24.

Ramey, Joshua. *The Hermetic Deleuze: Philosophy and Spiritual Ordeal*. Durham, NC: Duke University Press, 2012.

Robinson, Cedric J. *An Anthropology of Marxism*. Aldershot, UK: Ashgate, 2001.

Robinson, Cedric J. *Black Marxism: The Making of the Black Radical Tradition*. Chapel Hill: University of North Carolina Press, 2000.

Robinson, Cedric J. *The Terms of Order: Political Science and the Myth of Leadership*. Albany: State University of New York Press, 1980.

Sartre, Jean-Paul. "Black Orpheus." 1948. In *Race*, edited by Robert Bernasconi, 115–42. Malden, MA: Blackwell, 2000.

Sexton, Jared. "All Black Everything." *E-flux* 79 (2017). https://www.e-flux.com/journal/79/94158/all-black-everything/.

Sexton, Jared. "The Social Life of Social Death: On Afro-Pessimism and Black Optimism." *InTensions*, no. 5 (2011): 1–47.

Sharpe, Christina. *In the Wake: On Blackness and Being*. Durham, NC: Duke University Press, 2016.

Spillers, Hortense J. "Mama's Baby, Papa's Maybe: An American Grammar Book." *Diacritics* 17, no. 2 (1987): 65–81.

Tadiar, Neferti X. M. "Decolonization, 'Race,' and Remaindered Life under Empire." *Qui Parle* 23, no. 2 (2015): 135–60.

Tatman, Lucy. *Numinous Subjects: Engendering the Sacred in Western Culture, an Essay*. Canberra: ANU Press, 2007.

Warren, Calvin L. *Ontological Terror: Blackness, Nihilism, and Emancipation.* Durham, NC: Duke University Press, 2018.

Weheliye, Alexander G. *Habeas Viscus: Racializing Assemblages, Biopolitics, and Black Feminist Theories of the Human*. Durham, NC: Duke University Press, 2014.

Wilderson, Frank B., III. *Red, White and Black: Cinema and the Structure of U.S. Antagonisms*. Durham, NC: Duke University Press, 2010.

Winner, Lauren F. *The Dangers of Christian Practice: On Wayward Gifts, Characteristic Damage, and Sin*. New Haven, CT: Yale University Press, 2018.

Wynter, Sylvia. "The Ceremony Must Be Found: After Humanism." *boundary 2* 12/13 (1984): 19–70.

Wynter, Sylvia. "Unsettling the Coloniality of Being/Power/Truth/Freedom: Towards the Human, after Man, Its Overrepresentation—an Argument." *CR: The New Centennial Review* 3, no. 3 (2003): 257–337.

7 On Violence and Redemption

Fanon and Colonial Theodicy

THEODICY IS ORIENTED toward the question of justice. It raises theological and philosophical questions regarding the unjust situation that overwhelms the human subject. Traditional accounts of theodicy, however, tend to suggest justifications based on redemptive theological paradigms managed by sacrifice and exclusion. They gravitate toward notions of punishment, providence, or mystery.

These accounts commonly assume sacrifice/exclusion as a necessary component of the divine salvific plan.[1] The more recent model of divine suffering advanced by political theologians such as Jürgen Moltmann, James Cone, and Jon Sobrino shows an increased sensibility toward the injustices done to marginalized communities, but it does not fully divorce itself from the paradigm of redemptive sacrifice as it rests on the idea of self-sacrificial suffering. Similarly, the story of Job is often read through the lens of redemptive theology, in which the sacrifice of many lives, including those of his loved ones, is justified by redemptive ends. Job earns honor as the faithful servant who speaks the truth about divine justice, for he has endured what seemed to be unjust suffering in good faith. The many sacrifices incurred in the process (physical pain, emotional agony, the deaths of his children) pay off, as he is blessed with more wealth and children than before.

The biblical story of Job is often used to highlight enduring faith and the mystery of divine justice. The narrative culminates with the highly enigmatic scene often dubbed as Job's epiphany. God appears out of the whirlwind and delivers a long monologue in which God neither addresses Job's questions nor defends divine justice. The scene is followed by Job's sudden epiphany. He confesses his ignorance and God's almightiness. The ancient drama of human suffering ends with a happy tone of restitution in which Job's losses are restored while divine sovereignty and justice are reaffirmed. The abstruse nature of Job's drastic epiphany, however, has puzzled readers through time. Why do innocents suffer? What kind of lessons does one draw from such atrocity? In the face of the outcry of the agonized, the ancient text offers no answer, yet lessons on absolute sovereignty and enduring faith are drawn from the puzzling text, which purportedly upholds divine justice.

Theodicy, the philosophico-theological articulation of the question of divine justice in the face of the prevalence of evil, is inevitably enigmatic. Rational explanations are bound to fail. The demand for an explanation of the prevailing violence is usually met by another form of violence: either absolute silence or the justification of a higher form of violence (divine violence) as a response to violence. The silence on the question of justice leads to another question: What does such silence say about God? Theologians and philosophers of religion who wrestle with this question have attempted to rationalize the traditionally established concepts and attributes commonly associated with the figure of the divine. Yet, for others, no concept of God can justify the atrocities of violence experienced in human reality. They claim the irrelevance of the notion of God, if not the death of God.

In the colonial context, the problem of theodicy is inseparable from everyday reality. The theological interrogation of divine justice is imbricated in the daily fabric of colonial reality. For the Martinican psychiatrist and revolutionary Frantz Fanon, the analysis of violence in (de)colonial politics is, in a way, a theological endeavor. A theological worldview underpins the construction and the governance of the colonial world: a Manichaean worldview. As Lewis Gordon suggests, Fanon's analysis of colonialism can be viewed as a kind of theodicy, a Manichaean theodicy.[2] Colonialism, for Fanon, does not work through coercion alone. It operates through a worldview that makes the colonized accept a certain set of values and norms. Manichaean theodicy justifies the existing social order in which the colonizer represents the good, while the colonized embodies the evil.

Manichaean theodicy offers a simplistic answer to the complex question of divine justice: redemption through violence and sacrifice. Existing forms of evil and violence are atoned through redemptive (divine) violence, an economy of redemption that operates through the currency of sacrifice, an economy of redemption mediated by the sacrifice of the unworthy. Violence is neither removed nor fundamentally altered by this theodicy. Rather, it is managed and controlled by the sovereign. Against the colonial Manichaean theodicy managed by violence, Fanon articulates a form of countercolonial (countertheological) violence. However, Fanon's notion of violence breaks from the Manichaean binary of violence/nonviolence, a binary that reproduces a narrow understanding of violence. Rejecting the instrumentalist understanding of violence, Fanon views decolonial violence as intrinsic and absolute.

In what follows, I rethink the problem of violence from the colonial point of view. The main goal here is to upset the simplistic articulation of violence as the binary opposite of nonviolence. Interrogating existing forms of violence from the standpoint of colonial governmentality discloses the complexities looming underneath the concept of violence, which are often truncated in the discourse of (non)violence. The dominant narratives of (non)violence often obscure the mechanism of violence operative in the fabric of social reality within which critiques of violence are articulated.

In conversation with Fanon, I reflect on the ways violence operates in the theologico-political logic of redemption. I read Fanon's "Concerning Violence" as an analysis of colonial theology, that is, Manichaean theodicy, operating through the economy of redemption and sacrifice. Against the common misleading caricature of Fanon as an advocate of violence, I read Fanon as a staunch critic of violence. His analyses point at various manifestations of violence that constitute the ordinary reality of colonial existence. Reading Fanon alongside Walter Benjamin and Antonio Negri offers insights for understanding his critique as a form of secular theology that denounces the theological violence operative in colonial governance, a theology that legitimizes—by way of sacralizing—certain mechanisms of violence while condemning others.

In contrast to theodicy that demands sacrifice, Fanon claims the end of theodicy, or, rather, the abolition of the world and of the theology that gives birth to colonial theodicy, thus suggesting a way out of the Manichaean dialectic that feeds itself through an endless loop of sublation and sacrifice.

Colonial Theodicy

COLONIALISM CANNOT BE REDUCED to either the problem of material control of resources or epistemic domination. Rather, it operates through a worldview that requires a metaphysical foundation. It necessitates a theology that rationalizes the existing order of norms and values. From its initial stage, colonialism was inaugurated on a metaphysical platform that ratified its enterprises, as demonstrated in the sixteenth-century Valladolid debates. As Eleanor Craig's chapter in this volume demonstrates, the agenda of the philosophical and juridico-theological debates among Spanish Renaissance humanists was to address the ethical issues regarding the Spanish crown's activity in the New World. Central to the debates was the question of the humanity of Indians. The debates mark the inception of a new theology that established clear hierarchies demarcating the division between humans and less-than-humans or between rational humans and humans who were lacking.

Colonial theology drives not only overt missionary activities aiming at converting the natives but also the gospel of secular rationality, the "sacred principle" of the modern Enlightenment Europe. The born-again colonial subjects are urged to abandon their outmoded theological worldview and become citizens of the newly inaugurated secularized order regulated by impartial rationality. Such an order, according to Sylvia Wynter, is inscribed in the very modality of being that was imposed by Europe. Wynter uses the term *Man* for the bourgeois and Eurocentric ideal of the human, the secular, rational political subject who is erected over against the enchanted subjects of colonial cartography. For Wynter, Europe's colonial expansion cannot be separated from the reinvention of its selfhood in terms of a secularist-humanist statehood, as opposed to the theocratic hegemony of the church. In this sense, colonial religion and secularism are coconstitutive. Colonial religion (Christianity) removes itself from the realm of religion by associating itself with universalizing values of secularist rationalism, a normative ideal informed by its own Christian worldview.

Wynter excavates the theology structuring the secularist-colonial enterprise of Europe by reading the ontological lack of the native/Black as the transference of original sin; that is, as the other of the secular-rational self, the native/Black became the repository of original lack, the lack of being. The theological Adamic lack (original lack) is transferred in scholastic theology to the laity, who are subject to lower sensory nature. With secular humanism, it is then transferred to those outside of Europe: the Natives/Blacks of the New World.[3]

The dialectical dualism grounding colonialism is a Manichaean worldview of good and evil: a world compartmentalized by different species. Such a worldview, according to Fanon, cannot be sustained by physical control alone: "a reference to divine right is needed to justify [the] difference," that is, the fundamental ontological difference between the serf and the knight.[4] The disturbing injustice of colonial reality is rigidly dualistic. He adds:

> The colonized's sector, or at least the "native" quarters, the shanty town, the Medina, the reservation, is a disreputable place inhabited by disreputable people. You are born anywhere, anyhow. You die anywhere, from anything. It's a world with no space, people are piled one on top of the other, the shacks squeezed tightly together. The colonized's sector is a famished sector, hungry for bread, meat, shoes, coal, and light. The colonized's sector is a sector that crouches and cowers, a sector on its knees, a sector that is prostrate.[5]

Fanon denounces the infernal cycle of endless misery as a predestined reality for those whose ontological difference is indelibly marked by their racial difference. Colonial metaphysics offers an answer to the problem of theodicy by reinforcing the theological difference between the colonizer and the colonized, thus endorsing the existing social order as just. The former represents the good, while the latter embodies absolute evil. The colonized lacks spiritual value, "impervious to ethics, representing not only the absence of values but also the negation of values."[6] The question of divine justice is no longer in peril; it is affirmed by the colonial reality. The irreparable (original) sin of the native/Black can be expiated only by confession and penance: recognition of their inferior (sinful) nature, acceptance of their material-ontological reality.

Redemption is open to all. Yet it is not for all. Redemption requires sacrifice, that is, exclusion: "Many are called but few are chosen."[7] Fanon saw the theological logic of redemption and sacrifice operating in the Manichaean theology that organizes the colonial order. The role of religion (Christianity) in colonial governance is comparable to that of a powerful insecticide: "This is why we should place DDT, which destroys parasites, carriers of disease, on the same level as Christianity."[8] Natives' customs and myths are signs of lack, whereas Christianity "roots out heresy, natural impulses, and evil."[9] Redemptive theology requires an enemy, the damned through whom the chosen ones can be identified.[10] The precondition of sacrifice is the sacred. As Paul Kahn writes, "Neither the quest for justice nor the calculation of costs and benefits will bring us to sacrifice. Only the sacred can do that."[11] Violence is constitutive of the mechanism of redemptive theology in which confession and penance can be completed only by sacrifice and absolution.

If Job's theodicy highlights the interrogation of divine justice in the face of suffering, the theodicy at work in the Manichaean construction and management of the colonial world is not so much a challenge to the divine order as the justification of the existing social reality: that the good always triumphs over evil in the end. Justifying violence is key to the operations of sovereignty.[12] Being a subject means being subject to biopolitical violence. Biopower, however, is not color-blind. Manichaean dualism draws a clear line separating the saved from the damned. Colonial theodicy fuels the necropolitical theology that redeems the few at the expense of the sacrifice of others.

The highlight of Job's story, which is, ironically, also the most perplexing part of the narrative, involves the apparition of God from a whirlwind and a long monologue in which God evokes the grand narrative of the cosmological origin of the universe without addressing Job's pressing questions. This strange encounter somehow turns into a revealing moment for Job. Suddenly he experiences an epiphanic vision. He confesses his sin of ignorance: "My ears had heard of you but now my eyes have seen you. Therefore I despise myself and repent in dust and ashes" (Job 43:5–6). The scene is commonly understood as highlighting the immeasurable asymmetry of power between human beings and the sovereign God. Instead of answering Job's questions, God points at the foundation of the universe, revealing the unfathomable depths of his infinite power. Job's confession reflects his realization of his finite nature before the all-powerful sovereign, a great lesson that emphasizes the virtues of sacrifice and patience and the power of the sovereign, who transcends the parameters of ethics, whose very ends (redemption) justify the means (violence/sacrifice).

In *The Labor of Job*, the Italian Marxist Antonio Negri proposes a materialist reading of Job. In contrast to traditional readings, he views Job's indignation against God as a moment of strong defiance. For Negri, Job's frustration is not a passive form of self-loathing but a direct confrontation with the sovereign. By accusing God of being unjust, Job turns God into a mere adversary, raising himself up "as power standing before divine power."[13] Job's insistence, Negri adds, knows no resignation. He is determined to seek justice, as justice has been violated beyond measure. In Negri's reading, the story of Job's epiphany is not so much a story of Job seeing the divine out of his own wretchedness as it is the proclamation of the death of God.[14] Job's epiphany proclaims the end of transcendence: "I have seen God, thus God is torn from the absolute transcendence that constitutes the idea of him. God justifies himself, thus God is dead."[15]

Following Negri's reading of Job, it is perhaps possible to read Fanon's outcry along the same lines as Job's confrontation with the tyrannical sovereign, as a Fanonian proclamation of the end of transcendence. Fanon offers an answer to theodicy that differs from traditional measures. Instead of seeking the answer to the problem of divine justice, he demystifies the colonial order and its theology by proclaiming the death of God. In this sense, decolonization is not a measurable formula of balance and negotiation with predictable outcomes. Rather, decolonization goes beyond measure: absolute and perhaps violent. Decolonization cannot be reduced to a reconfiguration of social order, the epistemic system, or socioeconomic structure. For Fanon, decolonization signifies rejection or destruction of the world and the metaphysical foundation that has created and maintained its Manichaean regime. The decolonial violence at play in Fanon's thought hints at both the particular and the universal. In its particular form, it points at its specific and strategic employment as a concrete tool for confronting colonial violence. However, Fanonian violence refuses to be reduced to the particularity in which violence is conceived solely in teleological terms. Fanon suggests decolonial violence as an absolute and eschatological notion.

The ontological grammar of colonial existence makes the genuine description of being impossible for the colonized since the colony exists only as the dialectical negativity that makes the being-there-of-Man possible. Decolonization, in this sense, is eschatological. It is a theological confrontation that involves the killing of God. It aims at bringing an ultimate end to the colonial order and its metaphysics. For many skeptics, the overly belligerent tone Fanon employs in his attempt to reappropriate the notion of violence may seem questionable, as those who charge him with hypermasculinist fantasy have pointed out already. At times, he seems caught in the sovereign imaginary and the anxious illusion of mastery.[16] I come back to this question later and identify the ambiguities around his understanding of his own agency and thus his complex view, often obscured by the language of certainty.

On Violence

FANON'S REFLECTION on violence in the provocative first chapter of *The Wretched of the Earth* has been a constant subject of controversy since its publication. The most well-known critique comes from Hannah Arendt, who found the relationship between violence and politics problematic. She rejects the association between the two by emphasizing the unpredictability of human behavior, which often fails to control the means, thus eclipsing its putative ends.[17] Arendt separates violence from politics by suggesting that violence fails to generate power, which is constitutive of politics.[18] She considers Fanon someone who glorifies violence for its own sake. But as many have pointed out already, Arendt's critique of Fanon reveals that she views violence in purely instrumentalist terms, that is, as a means to political ends (action).[19] More important, Arendt's critique demonstrates her lack of understanding of the epidemic nature of violence that constitutes the mechanism of colonial governance.

Fanon's chapter "Concerning Violence" analyzes how the subject is constituted by violence in the colonial context. The starkly dualistic world of colonialism is sustained by violence, physical and symbolic. The colonial sovereign operates through exclusion and violence, without which it cannot exist. Fanon observes that colonial violence relegates the colonized to nonbeing, nothingness, forcing "the colonized to constantly ask the question: 'who am I in reality?'"[20] The biopolitical manifestation of colonial violence is ubiquitous. The colonized is free only when asleep.[21] Everyday life becomes an impossibility in the colony: "Being a fellow, a pimp, or an alcoholic is no longer an option."[22] The colonized, dehumanized, becomes a thing, a no-thing. At best, he or she becomes the disposable offering for sacrifice through which the redemptive economy of necropolitical theology operates. How is violence in such a situation avoidable? What does it mean to resort to nonviolence when the discourse of nonviolence already operates within the orbit of violence?[23]

The discourse of nonviolence, Fanon remarks, is introduced to the colony by the colonialist bourgeoisie: "an attempt to settle the colonial problem around the negotiating table before the irreparable is done, before any bloodshed or regrettable act is committed."[24] In the "war-paradigm" dictated by the ethics of death/violence, living means merely surviving. As Nelson Maldonado-Torres observes, the colonial world is a world in which extraordinary forms of violence become normalized as ordinary life.[25] Fanon adds, "For the colonized, living does not mean embodying a set of values, does not mean integrating oneself into a coherent, constructive development of a world. To live simply means not to die. To exist means staying alive."[26] Should not his reflection on violence in such a context be read as a critique of violence instead of a promotion of violence?

The liberal understanding of violence, Ghassan Hage writes, "involves a form of symbolic violence that forces us to normalize certain forms of violence and to pathologize others."[27] The denouncement of certain forms of violence takes place alongside the simultaneous legitimation of other forms of violence. The legitimation of violence often takes on a theological character when it is conjoined with the double rhetoric of democracy and patriotism, sacralizing the violence sanctioned in the name of the state. It indicates a form of theodicy in which one form of violence (western, colonial, democratic, secular, state-sanctioned) represents absolute good, while the other (anticolonial, nonwestern, non-state-sanctioned, religious) embodies absolute evil. Along these lines Talal Asad asks, commenting on the western liberal attitude toward Islam and terrorism, "Why is it that aggression in the name of God shocks secular liberal sensibilities, whereas the art of killing in the name of the secular nation, or of democracy, does not?"[28]

When articulated from the instrumentalist perspective, violence is conceived as pure means. It is a tool to be employed to reach certain ends. Fanon's notion of violence begs a distinction from this understanding. Decolonial violence is absolute. It aims at replacing one world with another, yet this is not a substitution of one system with another in which violence works as a means to bring an end (a particular political order). Rather, "the substitution is unconditional, absolute, total, and seamless."[29] Absolute violence is irreducible to particular actions or moments; it cannot be captured by terms of negotiation, transformation, or reconfiguration. Rather, it "is always in excess and elsewhere to the instrumental violence of the colonized in struggle."[30] Absolute violence signals the total destruction of the world, a complete rejection of its metaphysics: "To dislocate the colonial world does not mean that once the wall collapses, there will be equal rights between the two. To destroy the colonial world means nothing less than demolishing the colonist's sector, burying it deep, vanishing it from territory."[31]

In many ways, Fanon's notion of violence resonates with Walter Benjamin's distinction between mythical and divine violence. For Benjamin, mythical violence preserves law, while divine violence destroys it. The former happens in the present age, while the latter is indiscernible in history.

If the former operates under the principle of power, the latter is grounded in justice. Bringing together his Marxist revolutionary vision with a messianism inflected with Jewish mysticism, Benjamin suggests the notion of divine violence as a form of absolute rupture that lies beyond the terms of means and ends. If mythical violence destroys law with the end of founding a new law, divine violence is actualized in law's very demise.[32] Divine violence refuses closure. It creates a perennial crack in the seemingly impenetrable fabric of reality.

Benjamin views absolute (divine) violence as rejecting the substitutionary logic constituting law, namely, mythical violence. Mythical violence demands sacrifice and destruction; divine violence does not cause destruction in the world but assumes it.[33] Divine violence engages and transforms the destructive force of violence. In this sense, divine violence is a critique of violence. Similarly, Fanon's notion of absolute violence can be read as a critique of violence as it seeks to engage and transform the prevailing destructive force of colonialism. This is why countercolonial violence is not derivative of the colonizers' violence. Fanon rejects Jean-Paul Sartre's commentary on revolutionary violence, which renders the European colonizer the true agent of violence while the colonized's violence becomes an effect, reactionary to the original.[34]

The Fanonian countercolonial violence leads to a fundamentally different understanding. It goes beyond the rational calculation of means and ends. It cannot be apprehended by the teleological temporality: "Challenging the colonial world is not a rational confrontation of viewpoints ... but the impassioned claim by the colonized that *their world is fundamentally different*."[35] Absolute violence refuses the instrumentalist grammar with which violence is articulated. It cannot be contained within the social reality dictated by a particular economy of signification. Rather, Samira Kawash writes, "it interrupts and erupts into history and wrests history open to the possibility of a justice radically foreclosed by the colonial order of reality."[36]

Theodicy takes an interesting form in Benjamin, whose term *divine violence* perplexes readers. If we assume that Benjamin is hinting at proletarian revolution in his writing, the reference to the divine becomes all the more enigmatic.[37] The politico-theological character of his mystical messianism overrides the notion of divine violence, a force that purifies and expiates, not from sin/guilt, but from law. One might wonder whether the all-transcending character of divine violence can be viewed as the reification of sovereignty: the absolute authority who can decide on the state of exception and whose existence warrants the creation of the enemy as well as justifying violence. Indeed, Benjamin calls divine violence sovereign: "Divine violence, which is the sign and seal but never the means of sacred dispatch, may be called sovereign."[38] However, numerous interpretations of the meaning of Benjamin's *sovereign* (*die waltende*) commonly point at the polysemic nature of the term, leading to the conclusion that Benjamin's *die waltende* clearly differs from the Schmittian *sovereign*.[39] This is why, for Benjamin, divine violence works for the sake of the living and not at their expense, unlike mythical violence. Unlike mythical violence or the Schmittian sovereign, whose decision draws boundaries, sheds blood, and creates/uncreates citizens of the state, divine violence destroys boundaries and laws and is bloodless. As Jacques Derrida articulates with regard to Benjamin's divine violence: "Instead of founding droit, it destroys it; instead of setting limits and boundaries, it annihilates them; instead of leading to error and expiation, it causes to expiate; instead of threatening, it strikes; and above all, this is the essential point, instead of killing with blood, it kills and annihilates without bloodshed."[40] Theodicy becomes in Benjamin's schema the central tenet of history, since God is viewed not as the sovereign in control of the status quo but as the constant interrogator of it. Justice can be fulfilled only through divine violence, yet it (divine violence) is not discernible by human beings. All forms and representations fail; they fail to mediate what is eternal—irreducible to transient forms. Divine violence manifests only as an eternal promise, an eternally recurring rupture of the transient. Even the very notion of sovereign God can itself be challenged. Theodicy becomes the driving force of history by rupturing rigid boundaries of closure. As Luis Guzman puts it, divine violence "takes place not in the bloody, physical manifestations of mythical violence exercised at particular historical junctures, but in the purity of the thirst for justice that leads humans to attempt to change their conditions."[41]

In contrast to the mystico-theological vision of Benjamin, Fanon suggests a secular-theological vision of rupture. Like the imagery of absolute exteriority characterizing Benjamin's divine violence, Fanon's absolute violence too is susceptible to the accusation of reifying a sovereign imaginary. The eschatological tone of total destruction coupled with his hypermasculinist desire might be viewed as a resort to a sovereign imaginary. Does not the notion of total destruction of the colonial world replicate the eschatological temporality of redemptive theology in which the present is subsumed (sacrificed) to the linear temporality of future?

While he addresses the specific struggle of the Algerian revolution, a case with clear end goals, his articulation of violence in *The Wretched of the Earth* points beyond the particular. Fanon's notion of violence as absolute is both an endorsement of the armed struggle that suspends colonial violence and an indication of its distinct nature from colonial violence. Here Georges Sorel's distinction between the political general strike and the proletarian general strike—to which Benjamin refers in his conceptualization of mythical violence and divine violence—might be helpful for illustrating the two different notions of violence in Fanon. Sorel's distinction between the two types of violence rests in their relation to prevailing forms of (state) violence. The political general strike operates within the orbits of (state) violence as it seeks to invert the power relation. It leaves the modus operandi of violence and the social logic of domination intact. In contrast, the proletarian strike aims at abolishing the order in which social relations of power and domination are constituted.[42]

Similarly, both Benjamin's divine violence and Fanon's countercolonial violence are oriented toward overthrowing the social order that operates on the mechanism of violence and dominion. Whether Benjamin conceived pure violence as a form of nonviolence or not is an ongoing point of scholarly debate that is beyond the scope of this essay.[43] From Fanon's perspective, the problem of violence begs a different set of questions, beyond the simplistic binary of positions for or against violence. It seems clear that he does not object to the use of violent force in the particular revolutionary situation in which he was involved. However, the main agenda of Fanon's chapter is not so much theorizing the mechanism of the anticolonial armed revolution as analyzing the mechanism of colonial violence. Decolonial struggle does not exclude violent means, as its ultimate goal is to extinguish the world by any means. Here, the focus is not on the means, as it is in the instrumentalist understanding. Rather, the movement is geared toward putting an end to the world and its theology that sustains itself through blood and violence.

In the same way, Fanon rejects the teleological sense of progression. Decolonial vision and absolute violence are not steered toward a known, fixed point. Rather, they are driven by the unknown and the uncontainable, which exceed the normative grammar of political ontology: "Decolonization is truly the creation of new men. But such a creation cannot be attributed to supernatural power: The 'thing' colonized becomes a man through the process of liberation."[44] The inauguration of the new human is not a fixed objective that can be achieved by a linear progression.

Rather, it happens *in* and *through* the process. Fanon redefines the human in terms of action, as a praxis.

Theodicy and Redemption, Reconsidered

WOMANIST THEOLOGIANS HAVE ALREADY pointed out the problem with the substitutionary theology of redemption. Delores Williams uses the biblical story of Hagar as a story of surrogate motherhood in order to critically examine the substitutionary logic engraved in theologies of redemption. The story of Hagar, the surrogate mother and slave of African origin, is an important constituent of the grand narrative of Abraham's journey in faith, which despite its dramatic plots of doubt, agony, and conflict leads to the fulfillment of God's promise: the birth of Isaac. In the plot, Hagar plays the sacrificial role; through her, Abraham's and Sarai's faith journey comes to its culmination. Meanwhile, Hagar's (and her son's) well-being is far from the main concern of the narrative. The story of coerced surrogacy, the maltreatment from the master (Sarai), and the flight to the desert with her baby son leads not to interrogation but justification of divine justice. Williams finds problematic the logic of substitutive atonement undergirding the dominant models of redemptive theology, as the sacrificial role has historically been imposed on the most vulnerable communities—African American women, in her context.[45] The colonial theology in play here manifests itself in the form of a sovereign power who decides who is good and who is evil, who is worthy of life and who is disposable. Thus, Achille Mbembe famously defines the sovereign as "the power and the capacity to decide who may live and who must die."[46] The ultimate expression of the colonial sovereign's power manifests in the state of exception: a judicial suspension that allows the exercise of violence beyond the boundaries of law. Divine order and justice—be that punishment, providence, or mystery—surpass the realm of rationality. Violence sanctioned by the sovereign is always justifiable since it is deemed the necessary sacrifice constitutive of redemption. For Mbembe, too, violence is key to the management of the neocolonial global order constituted by a dualistic worldview of a Manichaean kind: the savages inhabiting the warlike zones are administered by lawless violence, which is key for guaranteeing life for the few who are deemed worthy of life: "Here, the fiction of a distinction between 'the ends of war' and 'the means of war' collapses."[47] *Necropolitics* is another name for Manichaean colonial theodicy.

In a way, Fanon too seems to suggest a form of substitutionary dialectic. He defines decolonization as "the substitution of one species of mankind by another."[48] However, this replacement is absolute and unconditional. Its goal is not to replace one system with another; rather, it rejects the world that gives rise to such systems and aims to bring an end to the metaphysical and theological foundations of the Manichaean world that creates and sustains the theodicean management of the world. This is why Fanon finds the decolonial desire for replacement to be the wrong solution. While he feels sympathetic to such a desire, it perpetuates the infernal cycle that reproduces its logic of substitutionary dialectic: a hell and a paradise for the colonized at the same time.[49] Such a measure amounts to accepting the normative offering of redemption; it reproduces the colonial order of knowing/being and operates within the paradigm of redemptive violence that governs the colonial reality, a violence that has acquired divine status and rules beyond the measure of the law, a violence that enacts retribution, punishes, and executes justice.

Decolonization is not the contestation of two different perspectives; the colonized's world, both the lived reality and its vision of the future, is "fundamentally different," hence Fanon's proclamation of the end of the world. In the same breath, he discusses the Manichaean worldview and the colonial theodicy. Fanonian theodicy rejects the Manichaean good-and-evil paradigm, the life-and-death cycle in which the triumph of good over evil involves sacrifice and exclusion or the replacement of one world by another.

The utterly negative terms with which he describes the colonial existence as well as the antagonistic language of rejection and destruction might raise questions as they seem to foreclose any constructive vision of life, any possibility of a world. Does coloniality determine life so fully and completely that it sweeps out all possibilities of resistance, life, and agency? As an active member of the revolutionary struggle, Fanon often signals a pessimistic answer. At times, a fatalism seems at play in Fanon's view that displaces the possibility of any type of meaning-making activities for the colonized. And perhaps this is why he often fails to acknowledge the political potential that diverse religious and cultural practices in the colony have to offer to the anticolonial resistance. However, precisely this sense of urgency and this uncompromising political vision make Fanon's analysis relevant for theorizing anticolonial resistance. What often seems an overly pessimistic, overly dramatized depiction of colonial existence aims at highlighting the profound power of the symbolic signifying the colonial worldview—which often goes unacknowledged. In this sense, absolute violence is not about the destruction of the current order, to be followed by a new order. Rather, the emphasis lies on the present act of praxis, the absolute singularity of the act (of refusal/rejection/destruction) itself.

Conclusion

THE PROBLEM OF COLONIALISM exceeds the modern binary framework of religion and the secular. Colonialism is coconstitutive not only with religion but also with the secular. While Fanon draws his inspiration mainly from secular sources, he sees religion as the metaphysical backbone of colonialism. Colonial order is grounded in a redemptive theology that normalizes the infernal reality dictated by the Manichaean dualism: a politico-theological order administered through the ubiquitous sanctioning of violence by the colonial sovereign whose rule surpasses the realm of law, a sacred violence that serves redemptive ends, executing justice by absolving the guilty and damning evildoers. Redemption requires sacrifices.

Traditional theodicies are largely oriented toward justifying divine sovereignty in the face of injustice. Fanon's take on the problem of theodicy is far from a justification of divine justice, instead confronting it. He denounces the reification of the transcendent God, a signifier that consecrates western Man and demands sacrifice. Theodicy for Fanon is not so much an unanswerable question that highlights patience, endurance, and the mystery of divine justice. Rather, it is the denouncement of various forms of violence inseparable from the everyday reality of the wretched of the earth. His position on violence articulates a charge against the colonial theology that legitimizes certain forms of violence while condemning others. Reflecting on political theology, Kahn observes that politics refers to "an organization of everyday life founded on an imagination of the sacred."[50] The secular-theological imagination of the sacred engraves violence into the lexicon that organizes political life: a political life sustained by the necropolitical management of life and death, good and evil.

Fanon envisions the notion of absolute violence, a violence that cannot be contained in social reality and its colonial theology. Absolute violence reveals the cartography of violence. It exceeds the economy of exchange inscribed in the instrumentalist understanding in which the ends justify the means. It presents an indictment of the theodicean organization of the colonial order that operates through a substitutionary theology that assumes sacrifice as a constitutive element of divine justice, a social order that enacts a particular modality of being as the normative ideal of the human.

Fanonian countercolonial violence signals the total and absolute abolition of the world. The abolition of the world is not oriented toward a teleological end. Rather, it signals a refusal to operate within the parameters of what is offered. Fanon has consistently insisted on the inadequacy of ontology for Blackness. Being corresponds to white European Man, while the Black person signifies nonbeing. The grammar of ontology already excludes the being of Blackness. Fred Moten observes that Blackness as articulated by Fanon points at that which escapes enframing: it signals an escape, a stolen life, a break, a hold that can only be "understood in its relation to the inadequacy of calculation to being in general."[51] In this sense, the excess of the new order, be that Blackness or the decolonized mode of being, is extraontological: it rejects the sanctioned mode of being, which offers the binary options of either existing as nothing or being recognized as a human who conforms to the normative ideal set by colonial theology.

The existential agony of Job's suffering is centered around his own (individual) suffering. The central question afflicting Job as presented by the narrator is not oriented toward other victims of suffering. Rather, his struggle is focused on the unbearable weight of his own suffering and the ever-incomprehensible mystery of the sovereign's arbitrary decisions. Unlike Job's struggle, Fanon's decolonial philosophy is driven by an ethical concern for the other. At the center of his reflection lies the self. But the self is conceived only through social relations, which give it its form. His interrogation of the (constitution of the) self is driven by an ethical concern born out of phenomenological reflection on the lived experience of the being in its bare materiality of the flesh, in which the other is not a mere object of perception but a constitutive element of the subject's self-formation that nevertheless is never fully given to the self. The self is conditioned by social relations, inescapably shaped in its very corporeality by others who constitute the world. He or she is always already given to the other: "It does not impose itself on me; it is, rather, a definitive structuring of the self and of the world—definitive because it creates a real dialectic between my body and the world."[52] The scorching outcry illustrated in Black Skin, White Masks does not signal the rage of a single individualized self. Rather, it is an indictment of the colonial metaphysics that dictates the (im)possibilities of collective existence, of shared survival; it is a decolonial vision driven by "a desire to evade death, one's own but even more fundamentally that of others."[53]

On the same note, one finds in Fanon's texts not only a hypermasculinist sense of violence but also a vulnerable openness to alterity and the unknown, as reflected in the closing prayer of *Black Skin, White Masks*. Reflecting on the charges of hypermasculinist fantasy often directed at Fanon, Judith Butler pays attention to the fact that Fanon "understands the fantasmatic dimension of hypermasculinity."[54] In other words, when Fanon talks about the hypermasculinist fantasy of the colonized, he is not arguing for it but describing it, acknowledging its compensatory nature, which serves as "a motivational component in the struggle" but "not a moral ideal toward which the decolonized should strive."[55] The complex question of hypermasculinity and violence in Fanon has been a constant subject of discussion—and I do not intend to reproduce the extensive conversations here.[56] Neither is it my intention to argue for an either/or position regarding the question, as that would indicate falling back into the simplistic frame that I have been attempting to deconstruct in this essay. While acknowledging the presence of Fanon's problematic view on gender and sexuality, I follow Butler's reading and insist on the complex ambiguities present in his works.

Fanon's prayer presents not a doctrinal manifesto of a hypermasculinist revolution but an openness directed to the body, to the other, to the unknown future he does not yet know: "O my body, make of me always a man who questions!"[57] The body is a contested site of subject formation, conditioned by the myriad web of social relations. The self is oriented toward the other: "Why not the quite simple attempt to touch the other, to feel the other, to explain the other to myself? Was my freedom not given to me then in order to build the world of *you*?"[58] Such openness to the unknown is also re-created in the final paragraphs of *The Wretched of the Earth*, in which Fanon acknowledges that the question of the "new man" is an ideal that refuses closure.[59] Fanon's anticolonial theology is oriented toward alterity and a new order that goes beyond the boundaries of nationalism, ethnocentrism, and colonialism/anticolonialism: "We want an Algeria open to all, in which every kind of genius may grow."[60]

In a world in which being a human is an impossible task, Fanon's decolonial politics refuses to be reduced to a passive act of nonintervention, thus breaking from the dialectical binaries of violence/nonviolence, self/other, good/evil, and redemption/exclusion. This refusal reveals the incoherence of power. It indicates *not* conforming to the normative ontological and political choices as offered. The totalitarian narrative of colonial theod- icy legitimizes the dualistic theological formula of redemption enacted through violence while prescribing the grammar that constitutes the terms of political action and imagination. The vision of the new world and the new human that Fanon proposes disrupts the theologico-political machine of sovereignty that subjects modalities of subjectivity and politi- cal agency to the sovereign imaginary.

Rather than questioning the source of suffering, Fanon demystifies vio- lence and the colonial sovereign by denouncing the redemptive theology that sustains the Manichaean order. This is how Fanon's secular humanism distinguishes itself from the modern western notion of secularism that has been coconstitutive of colonialism. The secularist project of colonial- ism operates through the theologico-political apparatus. But denouncing the theologico-political apparatus of colonialism need not be conducive to the reinstatement of secular rationality. Rather, the end of transcen- dence, the decolonial epiphany, is oriented toward disenchanting from the necropolitical sovereign and its theodicean governance that promises redemption to some and demands sacrifice from others.

Notes

I thank Lena Zuckerwise, Anthony Neal, Vinicius Marinho, Stephanie Rivera Berruz, Nikolay Karkov, and Eleanor Craig for reading an earlier draft of the chapter and providing critical feedback.

1 The most well known of these is Irenaean theodicy, espoused by John Hick. See Hick, *Evil and the God of Love.*
2 Gordon, "Fanon and Development," 72; and Gordon, "Through the Zone of Nonbeing," 1.
3 Wynter, "Beyond the Word of Man," 641–42.
4 Fanon, *Wretched of the Earth*, 5.
5 Fanon, *Wretched of the Earth*, 4.
6 Fanon, *Wretched of the Earth*, 6.
7 Fanon, *Wretched of the Earth*, 7.
8 Fanon, *Wretched of the Earth*, 7.
9 Fanon, *Wretched of the Earth*, 7.
10 Shulman, "From Political Theology to Vernacular Prophesy," 243.
11 Kahn, *Sacred Violence*, 115.
12 Vardoulakis, *Sovereignty and Its Other*, 2.
13 Negri, *Labor of Job*, 43.

14 Negri parallels Job's suffering with the place of labor (forced labor) in contemporary capitalist production. Just as Job's suffering finds no form of equivalence, labor does not operate under the theory of value as it functions on the basis of an unequal exchange of value. Labor that has ceased to be a value becomes evil—it becomes labor without an end, "a senseless instrumentality that does not reveal value." The solution Negri finds in Job is the turn to creative labor that emerges out of pain: "When power opposes Power, it has become divine." Negri, *Labor of Job*, 9–12, 75.

15 Negri, *Labor of Job*, 96.

16 Singh, *Unthinking Mastery*, chs. 1 and 2.

17 Arendt, *On Violence*, 4.

18 Arendt, *On Violence*, 56.

19 Frazer and Hutchins, "On Politics and Violence," 103.

20 Fanon, *Wretched of the Earth*, 182.

21 Fanon, *Wretched of the Earth*, 15.

22 Fanon, *Wretched of the Earth*, 46.

23 Dodds, "Violence and Nonviolence," 145.

24 Fanon, *Black Skin, White Masks*, 23.

25 Maldonado-Torres, *Against War*, 3, 95.

26 Fanon, *Wretched of the Earth*, 232.

27 Hage, "'Comes a Time,'" 72.

28 Asad, "Freedom of Speech," 295.

29 Fanon, *Wretched of the Earth*, 3.

30 Kawash, "Terrorists and Vampires," 237.

31 Fanon, *Wretched of the* Earth, 6.

32 Guzman, "Benjamin's Divine Violence," 53.

33 Friedlander, "Assuming Violence," 160.

34 Butler, *Senses of the Subject*, 182–83.

35 Fanon, *Wretched of the Earth*, 6 (emphasis mine).

36 Kawash, "Terrorists and Vampires," 240.

37 This is one of the reasons some suggest that the reference to the divine indicates an appeal to a transcendent authority, which contradicts its connection to proletarian revolution. See McNulty, "Commandment against the Law," 42.

38 Benjamin, "Critique of Violence," in *Selected Writings*, 252.

39 McNulty, "Commandment against the Law." 50.

40 Derrida, "Force of Law," 52.

41 Guzman, "Benjamin's Divine Violence," 58.

42 Benjamin, "Critique of Violence," in *Reflections*, 291; Sorel, *Sorel*, 161.

43 See Sinnerbrink, "Violence, Deconstruction, and Sovereignty"; Derrida, "Force of Law"; Hamacher, "Affirmative Strike"; and Agamben, *State of Exception*.

44 Fanon, *Wretched of the Earth*, 2.

45 Williams, *Sisters in the Wilderness*, ch. 3.

46 Mbembe, "Necropolitics," 11.

47 Mbembe, "Necropolitics," 25.

48 Fanon, *Wretched of the Earth*, 1.

49 Fanon, *Wretched of the Earth*, 16.

50 Kahn, *Sacred Violence*, 23.

51 Moten, "Case of Blackness," 187.

52 Fanon, *Black Skin, White Masks*, 111.

53 Maldonado-Torres, "On the Coloniality of Being," 251.

54 Butler, *Senses of the Subject*, 192.

55 Butler, *Senses of the Subject*, 192.

56 Bergner, "Who Is That Masked Woman?"; McClintock, *Imperial Leather*; Fuss, *Identification Papers*; Chow, "Politics of Admittance"; Sharpley-Whiting, *Frantz Fanon*; Dubey, "'True Lie'"; Seshadri-Crooks, "I Am a Master"; and Singh, *Unthinking Mastery*.

57 Fanon, *Black Skin, White Masks*, 232.

58 Fanon, *Black Skin, White Masks*, 232.

59 Fanon, *Wretched of the Earth*, 235–39. See also Butler, *Senses of the Subject*, 192–93.

60 Fanon, *Dying Colonialism*, 32.

Bibliography

Agamben, Giorgio. *The State of Exception*. Translated by Kevin Attell. Chicago: University of Chicago Press, 2005.

Arendt, Hannah. *On Violence*. New York: Harvest Book, 1969.

Asad, Talal. "Freedom of Speech and Religious Limitations." In *Rethinking Secularism*, edited by Craig Calhoun, Mark Juergensmeyer, and Jonathan VanAntwerpen, 282–97. Oxford: Oxford University Press, 2011.

Benjamin, Walter. "Critique of Violence." In *Reflections: Essays, Aphorisms, Autobiographical Writings*, translated by Edmund Jephcott, 277–300. New York: Schocken, 1986.

Benjamin, Walter. "Critique of Violence." In Walter Benjamin, *Selected Writings*, edited by Marcus Bullock and Michael W. Jennings, 1:236–52. Cambridge, MA: Belknap Press of Harvard University Press, 1996,

Bergner, Gwen. "Who Is That Masked Woman? Or, The Role of Gender in Fanon's *Black Skin, White Masks*." *PMLA* 110, no. 1 (1995): 75–88.

Butler, Judith. *Senses of the Subject*. New York: Fordham University Press, 2015.

Chow, Rey. "The Politics of Admittance: Female Sexual Agency, Miscegenation, and the Formation of Community in Frantz Fanon." In *Frantz Fanon: Critical Perspectives*, edited by Anthony Alessandrini, 34–56. London: Routledge, 1999.

Cone, James. *God of the Oppressed*. New York: Seabury Press, 1975.

Derrida, Jacques. "Force of Law: The Metaphysical Foundation of Authority." In *Deconstruction and the Possibility of Justice*, edited by Druscilla Cornell, Michel Rosenfeld, and David Carlson, 3–67. London: Routledge, 1992.

Dodds, James. "Violence and Nonviolence." In *Philosophy and the Return of Violence*, edited by Nathan Eckstrand and Christopher Yates, 137–53. New York: Continuum, 2011.

Dubey, Madhu. "The 'True Lie' of the Nation: Fanon and Feminism." *Differences: A Journal of Feminist Cultural Studies* 10, no. 2 (1998): 1–29.

Fanon, Frantz. *Black Skin, White Masks*. New York: Grove, 1967.

Fanon, Frantz. *A Dying Colonialism*. New York: Grove, 1965.

Fanon, Frantz. *The Wretched of the Earth*. New York: Grove, 1963.

Frazer, Elizabeth, and Kimberley Hutchins. "On Politics and Violence: Arendt contra Fanon." *Contemporary Political Theory* 7, no. 1 (2008): 90–108.

Friedlander, Eli. "Assuming Violence: A Commentary on Walter Benjamin's 'Critique of Violence.'" *boundary 2* 42, no. 4 (2015): 159–85.

Fuss, Diana. *Identification Papers: Readings on Psychoanalysis, Sexuality, and Culture*. New York: Routledge, 1995.

Gordon, Lewis. "Fanon and Development: A Philosophical Look." *Afrique et Developpement* 29, no. 1 (2004): 71–93.

Gordon, Lewis. "Through the Zone of Nonbeing: A Reading of *Black Skin, White Masks* in Celebration of Fanon's Eightieth Birthday." *C. L. R. James Journal* 11, no. 1 (2005): 1–43.

Guzman, Luis. "Benjamin's Divine Violence: Unjustifiable Justice." *CR: The New Centennial Review* 14, no. 2 (2014): 49–64..

Hage, Ghassan. "'Comes a Time We Are All Enthusiasm': Understanding Palestinian Suicide Bombers in Times of Exighophobia." *Public Culture* 15, no. 1 (2003): 65–89.

Hamacher, Werner. "Affirmative Strike: Benjamin's Critique of Violence." In *Walter Benjamin's Philosophy: Destruction and Experience*, edited by Andrew Benjamin and Peter Osborne, 110–38. London: Routledge, 1994.

Hick, John. *Evil and the God of Love*. New York: Harper and Row, 1966.

Kahn, Paul. *Sacred Violence: Torture, Terror, and Sovereignty*. Ann Arbor: University of Michigan Press, 2008.

Kawash, Samira. "Terrorists and Vampires: Fanon's Spectral Violence of Decolonization." In *Frantz Fanon: Critical Perspectives*, edited by Anthony Alessandrini, 235–57. New York: Routledge, 1999.

Maldonado-Torres, Nelson. *Against War: Views from the Underside of Modernity*. Durham, NC: Duke University Press, 2008.

Maldonado-Torres, Nelson. "On the Coloniality of Being: Contributions to the Development of a Concept." *Cultural Studies* 21, nos. 2–3 (2007): 240–70.

Mbembe, Achille. "Necropolitics." *Public Culture* 15, no. 1 (2003): 11–40.

McClintock, Anne. *Imperial Leather: Race, Gender, and Sexuality in the Colonial Conquest*. New York: Routledge, 1995.

McNulty, Tracy. "The Commandment against the Law: Writing and Divine Justice in Walter Benjamin's Critique of Violence." *Diacritics* 37, nos. 2–3 (2007): 34–60.

Moltmann, Jurgen. *The Crucified God: The Cross and Christ as the Foundation and Criticism of Christian Theology*. Minneapolis, MN: Fortress Press, 1972.

Moten, Fred. "The Case of Blackness." *Criticism* 50, no. 2 (2008): 177–218.

Negri, Antonio. *The Labor of Job: The Biblical Text as a Parable of Human Labor*. Durham, NC: Duke University Press, 2009.

Sartre, Jean-Paul. Preface to Fanon, *Wretched of the Earth*, xliii–lxii.

Seshadri-Crooks, Kalpana. "I Am a Master: Terrorism, Masculinity, and Political Violence in Frantz Fanon." *Parallax* 8, no. 2 (2002): 84–98.

Sharpley-Whiting, T. Denean. *Frantz Fanon: Conflicts and Feminisms*. Lanham, MD: Rowman and Littlefield, 1997.

Shulman, George. "From Political Theology to Vernacular Prophesy: Rethinking Redemption." In *Race and Political Theology*, edited by Vincent Lloyd, 234–48. Stanford, CA: Stanford University Press, 2012.

Singh, Julietta. *Unthinking Mastery: Dehumanization and Decolonial Entanglements*. Durham, NC: Duke University Press, 2017.

Sinnerbrink, Robert. "Violence, Deconstruction, and Sovereignty: Derrida and Agamben on Benjamin's 'Critique of Violence.'" In *Walter Benjamin and the Architecture of Modernity*, edited by Andrew Benjamin and Charles Rice, 77–91. Melbourne: Re.press, 2009.

Sobrino, Jon. *Christology at the Crossroads: A Latin American Approach*. London: SCM Press, 1978.

Sorel, Georges. *Sorel: Reflections on Violence*. Edited by Jeremy Jennings. Cambridge: Cambridge University Press, 1999.

Vardoulakis, Dimitris. *Sovereignty and Its Other: Toward the Dejustification of Violence*. New York: Fordham University Press, 2013.

Williams, Delores. *Sisters in the Wilderness: The Challenge of Womanist God-Talk*. Maryknoll, NY: Orbis, 1993.

Wynter, Sylvia. "Beyond the Word of Man: Glissant and the New Discourse of the Antilles." *World Literature Today* 63, no. 4 (1989): 637–48.

8 Alter-Carnation

Notes on Cannibalism and
Coloniality in the Brazilian Context

And I found myself far from you . . . and heard as it were your voice from on high: "I am the food of the fully grown; grow and you will feed on me. And you will not change me into you like the food your flesh eats, but you will be changed into me."—Augustine, *Confessions*

The Carib instinct. Death and life of all hypothesis. From the equation "Self, part of the Cosmos" to the axiom "Cosmos, part of the Self." Subsistence. Experience. Cannibalism.—Oswald de Andrade, "Cannibalist Manifesto"

THIS IS NOT A STORY FOR THE FAINT OF STOMACH. For this is a story about stomachs and that which lies therein. I apologize for telling it so crudely, but this is the story you are about to read: the first bishop ever appointed to a Brazilian see was devoured by a Caeté warrior in an anthropophagic ritual. This essay narrates this story while also suggesting this event is an originary myth of sorts that we can savor to consider the relationship between religion and coloniality in the Brazilian context. Cannibalism, as we shall see, has its own genealogy tangled up in colonial discourse. The word *cannibal* itself probably comes from the term *carib*, used by the Arawak as a derogatory term for a rival tribe, the Caribs, who allegedly practiced anthropophagic rituals.[1] Fatefully, the term was first recorded in one of Christopher Columbus's journals, inscribing cannibalism at the inception of the colonial invasion of the Americas. In the Brazilian case, the cannibal haunts Portuguese colonial efforts from the start. It is so ubiquitous that for philosopher and poet Oswald de Andrade, anthropophagy is the signature recipe of Brazilian culture. We shall ruminate on this in the pages to follow.

What becomes of the Caeté warrior who swallows the bishop at the inception of Brazil? As I show in the following pages, the eucharistic encounter between a Portuguese bishop and his Caeté capturer offers a pathway to theorize cannibalism as a mode of relation that resists coloniality precisely by incorporating it. In theological terms, what concerns us here is the theme of incarnation, not the incarnation of a soul into a body, but the incarnation of a body assuming the other's flesh.

First, this essay offers a brief account of the life and swallowing of Bishop Pero Fernandes Sardinha (1495–1556), the first priest to occupy the episcopal office in Brazil, alongside some notes on anthropophagy in the Tupi social imagination. As a war ritual, cannibalism maintains that the other, even the enemy, cannot be extinguished by death but must be incorporated. The constitution of the cannibal self is mediated by the swallowing of the other. Second, this same logic intrigued Sigmund Freud in his analysis of "primitive" societies in *Totem and Taboo*, a book also haunted by the shadows of the cannibal. I then offer a reading of Andrade's "Cannibalist Manifesto" as a way to speak of cannibalism as a foretaste of the Brazilian experiment with resisting coloniality.[2] In his poem, Andrade humorously argues that the devouring of Bishop Sardinha is the founding story of Brazil: a cultural construct that emerges out of the digesting of the Portuguese colonizer in the belly of a Caeté warrior. For Andrade, this is what colonial Brazil has engendered: a hybridity that takes shape in the anthropophagic moment.

The closing moment of the essay is a theological reading of the cannibal scene and its fleshly meanings for thinking about eucharistic mysteries. *Alter-carnations* is the name this essay offers for thinking about how every act of incarnation—of becoming flesh—is indeed an act of incorporating the other. That is, to be incarnate is to become the flesh of others.

The Bishop, Eaten

WHEN BISHOP SARDINHA first landed in the Bay of All Saints in Bahia on June 22, 1552, he arrived in a land already filled with a controversial legacy. Not far from there was the beach where Captain Pedro Álvares Cabral had landed the first Portuguese fleet in the New World, half a century before. Portugal, however, would invest few resources in its new Atlantic colony, devoting greater attention to its more profitable colonies in India.[3] The Portuguese crown instead delegated the colonization of the land to twelve noble families.[4] The captaincy of Bahia, the place of the "discovery" of Brazil and the future diocese of Bishop Sardinha, was given to the nobleman Francisco Pereira Coutinho, known as "the Rustic."[5] Troubled with precarious investments and great tensions resulting from Indigenous attacks and internal conflicts with the settlers, the Rustic's mission soon failed: he was captured and killed by the natives in 1546.[6] Reports of cannibalism were already reaching the ears of the Portuguese monarch. King John III reacted by calling for a more centralized approach to colonization, reclaiming the captaincy of Bahia for the crown, and appointing Tomé de Sousa as governor-general of the colony on January 7, 1549.[7]

Centralizing the colonial efforts in the hands of the crown ignited a stronger push for the evangelization of Brazil. Led by Father Manoel da Nóbrega, six Jesuits joined Sousa's expedition and landed in Bahia "with a great cross on the back of one of them, followed by many tears that caused devotion in the Christians, and among the Gentiles not little admiration for what they did not understand."[8] Yet Father Nóbrega's first impressions of his new mission field appalled him: "[The settlers] of the land live in mortal sin, and there is none of them living without many black [Native] women from whom they have too many children, and there is great evil."[9] In spite of the negative impression, Nóbrega's focus and passion was the evangelization of the Tupinamba, the tribe that inhabited the Bay of All Saints. One of the friars, Father Juan de Azpicuelta Navarro, was reportedly fluent in the Tupi language within six months of his arrival.[10] According to Nóbrega's correspondence with his superior in Portugal, the mission flourished rapidly.[11] Yet Father Nóbrega urged that the arrival of a bishop was necessary to "punish and heal great ills."[12]

This appeal was answered by the Portuguese and Roman Catholic authorities with unusual speed. Following the advice of the Portuguese Jesuits, on February 25, 1551, Pope Julius III created the first Brazilian see and appointed Pero Fernandes Sardinha to it. Bishop Sardinha, who had a strong academic foundation and connections to the Portuguese nobility, seemed like the right man for the mission. Born in 1495 in the city of Évora, Sardinha had strong ties to the king, including a brother, Álvaro Gomes, who served as King John III's confessor and was notorious for writing a treatise against British King Henry VIII and his divorce from Catherine of Aragon.[13] Sardinha had studied in Salamanca and Paris and had taught at the University of Coimbra, places where he was in touch with important figures of the Catholic world in the years before the Council of Trent. In Paris, Sardinha had studied together with Francis Xavier, and later, at the College of Santa Barbara, he was a tutor to Ignatius of Loyola, founder of the Society of Jesus. After his return to Portugal, Sardinha was called to supervise the Portuguese colony of Goa in India, where he stayed from 1546 until 1549.

In spite of his impeccable record, Bishop Sardinha's time in Brazil was marked by controversy.[14] Nóbrega initially described the bishop as "benign and zealous" and praised the "authority and majesty" of the episcopal office.[15] The tone nevertheless changed quickly: Nóbrega reported that Sardinha forbade the Jesuits from practicing their "disciplines" (public flagellations) and that confessions could no longer be said in Tupi. Sardinha also instituted a sales tax on local products and apparently collected the monies for himself.[16] Much to the chagrin of the missionaries, he personified an aristocratic and bureaucratic Christianity that offended their missionary fervor.[17] After the bishop's death, Father Nóbrega wrote that Sardinha believed the Amerindians "incapable of all doctrine due to their brutishness and bestiality." The bishop was clear that the "savages" did not belong to his flock, "and not even Christ would be willing to have them as his flock either."[18]

After a long and intricate sequence of controversies with settlers and the colonial administration in the city of Salvador, Bishop Sardinha hit a stalemate in his episcopacy and was asked to return to Lisbon.[19] Thus began his via crucis to the stomach of the Caeté warrior. On the night of June 15, 1556, through wind and rain, Sardinha's ship hit a reef and sank. He and his companions managed to reach the beach without casualties. The area was, however, enemy territory. The Caetés, native to those lands, had a lasting commercial partnership with the French and an increasing rivalry with the Portuguese. Within a day of the shipwreck, all but three members of the Portuguese party had been captured and devoured by the Caetés in an anthropophagic ritual.

In many accounts of his life and death in the centuries to come, Bishop Sardinha's body became a sacrament of Christian zeal.[20] Father Vicente do Salvador witnesses the birth of a tradition that claimed that in the place where the bishop was killed, no grass grew, "as if his blood was clamoring for God from the land against those who shed that blood."[21] Father Carlos Augusto Peixoto de Alencar, writing in 1864, goes so far as to rebuke

Father Nóbrega, a well-established figure in the Brazilian pantheon of missionary saints, for his critiques of the bishop.[22] Historian Pedro Calmon, writing in the 1940s, adds an imaginary component to his description of Sardinha's death:

> Master of the Sorbonne, codisciple of Ignatius of Loyola, of Francis Xavier, confessor of the late thoughts of D. João de Castro; illustrious in France, remarkable in Évora, a principal in India, first in America—he allowed himself to be conducted to the immolation just like the martyrs of faith. All there was of seigniorial in his temper, the intransigency, the dogmatic word, the stubborn will, was transformed at last in humility before God's face. . . . And enveloped in an aura of decency, the most modest and the most resigned among all victims, knelt down facing the immense Indian that managed above his bald and slightly bended head the wooden *tacape*.[23]

With that single blow of hagiography, Calmon turns the devouring of Bishop Sardinha into a reenactment of the crucifixion.

The death of Bishop Sardinha echoes a common scene that captivated the imagination of colonial records and depictions of the New World. Dr. Diego Alvarez Chanca, who accompanied Christopher Columbus on his second voyage to the Caribbean in 1494, reported that they interfaced with "people who eat human flesh."[24] Not long after Columbus encountered Europe's first cannibals, a Tupinamba from Brazil was taken to the courts of the young French King Charles IX, where he met the philosopher Michel de Montaigne, author of the tract "Des Cannibales," which would definitively inscribe cannibalism as a topic for European philosophy—and horror.[25] The Flemish painter Jan van der Straet (1523–1604) added the anthropophagic ritual to his famous depiction of Amerigo Vespucci's arrival in the New World, probably painted in 1575, suggesting that at this time anthropophagy was already established in the European mindset as the symbol of the savage ethos of the Amerindians.

In the case of Brazil, the anthropophagic ritual also quickly stands out as the symbol par excellence of the savagery of the natives. A few weeks after his arrival in Salvador, Father Nóbrega, for instance, already had a fairly accurate description of the ritual. For him, this was "the greatest abomination that exists among this people."[26] Reports of anthropophagic rituals among the Tupi tribes of the Brazilian Atlantic coast are abundant. The most impressive ones come from the French Calvinist pastor Jean de Léry (1534–1611) and the German merchant Hans Staten, who was arrested and lived among the Tamoios in the southern tip of the Portuguese colony in Brazil for nearly a year in 1554 and witnessed several executions (he escaped after convincing his owner that he was not Portuguese).[27]

Anthropophagy, as practiced by numerous Tupi peoples of the Brazilian Atlantic coast, was a war ritual. It was a rite of vengeance designed, as Léry noted, not for "nourishment . . . , although all of them confess human flesh to be wonderfully good and delicate," but as a way of striking "fear and terror into the hearts of the living."[28] After the battle, the enemy was imprisoned and brought to the victorious village, where he was received with a series of insults, only to be later integrated into the tribe's routine. A woman was offered to him, normally a daughter or sister of his capturer, and he could walk freely in the village as long as he remained there. When the time of the execution arrived, a weeklong ritual began. The victim was then prepared for execution: he was shaved, painted, and covered with feathers and eggshells. In the morning, after a feast, he was brought to the village and, tied by his feet, heard from his capturer: "Aren't you a member of [such] tribe, our enemies? Haven't you killed and eaten, yourself, many of our relatives?" This is the prisoner's moment of glory: "Yes!," he responds. "I am very brave, I have killed and devoured many, and after I am dead, many of my friends will come and kill and eat you!" The executor then killed the victim with a single strike with a *tacape* (a long, heavy club). The body was then scalded to remove the outer skin, split, cooked (a way of cooking "unknown to us," says Léry), and finally shared among the villagers.[29] In the philosophical and ritualistic world of the Tupi, there is no better grave for a warrior than the enemy's belly. Through the killing and devouring of the other, the enemy's strengths become part of one's personhood—the enemy is *incorporated*.[30]

The Other, Swallowed

THIS FLESHLY MODE OF BECOMING one with the other is closely scrutinized in Sigmund Freud's study of "primitive societies" in *Totem and Taboo*, where he pins the very core of the human psyche and the development of human civilization to the devouring of the other. For Freud, human subjectivity is fundamentally structured by an anthropophagic logic. He opens his reflections by explaining that totems, usually an animal that names and represents a clan, are tied to two essential taboos: the prohibition of eating the totem animal and the rejection of sexual intercourse with members of the same clan.[31] For Freud, these taboos are encoded in the oedipal structure of the human psyche. Primitive totemism is the social embodiment of this psychic structure: "If this equation is anything more than a misleading trick of chance, it must enable us . . . to make it probable that the totemic system . . . was a product of the conditions involved in the Oedipus complex."[32]

In this context, the cannibal jumps into Freud's text. After establishing the connection between totemism and the Oedipus complex, Freud paints the following scene: in primitive groups, a single man ruled the clan by rule of force. At a certain point, however, a group of "brothers" who had been excluded from the clan banded together to kill the alpha male. Their fear of the leader was matched only by the solidarity of their coalition, which culminated in the first coup in human history. But killing the band leader was not enough: "*Cannibal* savages as they were, it goes without saying that they devoured their victim as well as killing him."[33] Freud gives no further details on this drive to devour the victim, but the figure of the cannibal is the segue Freud needs to outline his elegant conclusion: "The violent primal father had doubtless been the feared and envied model of each of the company of brothers: and in the act of devouring him they accomplished their identification with him. . . . The totem meal . . . would thus be a repetition and a commemoration of this memorable and criminal deed, which was the beginning of so many things—of social organization, of moral restrictions and of religion."[34] And so we arrive at subjective identification through incorporation. Freud will stress that subjectification and civilizing processes require incorporation. In *Totem and Taboo*, he describes it as the desire to become like the father "by incorporating parts of their father's surrogate in the totem meal."[35] Freud stresses the "emotional ambivalence" of the act as the brothers both admire and resent the band's leader. Their violent assassination of the father is matched by their desire to incorporate his memory, his legacy, his strength. In this view, the devouring of the father figure is fundamental to the formation of the self but is also a world-shaping event. Through it, societies, moral codes, and religious systems are built.

In part owing to Freud's studies and the generalized interest in primitivism in European academic and artistic circles, the Brazilian modernist movement of the mid-1920s adopted cannibalism as a sign of a general "ancestral syndrome" of human culture.[36] In their hands, however, the cannibal scene gained a different taste. The logic of filiation that grounds Freud's analysis is filtered through the lenses of the Brazilian colonial legacy, where the one being devoured is not a father figure—or the envied leader of the band—but the Christian invader. The ambivalence at play is not so much the psychological interplay between admiration and resentment but generated by power differentials established by colonialism, between "savages" and "civilized."

In the colonial setting, cannibalism is a tactic of resistance through incorporation—it is the killing of the colonizers but not their annihilation. Brazilian philosophers, poets, and artists have approached the story of the swallowing of Bishop Sardinha as a mythical point of departure for what Brazil would come to be. Brazil becomes, they argue, by this eucharistic swallowing of the Portuguese settler.

Poet and philosopher Oswald de Andrade identified anthropophagy as the source for a new poetics and a new politics. For him, after some centuries of indigestion, Bishop Sardinha remains at the bottom of the Brazilian stomach. Written in 1928, Andrade's "Cannibalist Manifesto" is a poem-manifesto that defends something akin to a cannibal aesthetics. At the conclusion of the poem, Andrade winks at the story of Bishop Sardinha by dating the poem thus: "In Piratininga, in the 374th Year of the Swallowing of Bishop Sardinha."[37] Savoring the intensity of the story, Andrade assumes anthropophagy as the leitmotif of his philosophical and aesthetic program.

The famous opening words of the manifesto read:

Cannibalism alone unites us. Socially. Economically. Philosophically.
    The world's single law. Disguised expression of all individualism, of all collectivisms. Of all religions. Of all peace treaties.
    Tupi or not tupi, that is the question.[38]

From its first aphorism, the manifesto introduces anthropophagy as fleshly bricolage, uniting all things into one body. In the stomach of the cannibal, the Shakespearean quest for identity—to be or not to be—is transubstantiated into the quest for the incorporation of the other. Andrade performs his literary cannibalism by bringing *Hamlet*'s signature quest for being into the stomach of the Tupi warrior. The homonyms *to be* and *Tupi* establish the manifesto's relation to the canon of western aesthetics along with its political and colonial legacy, while showing that this tradition is accepted and incorporated into the Tupi anthropophagic context.

Andrade's Shakespearean allusion signals the anthropophagic dilemma of marking a difference while also dissolving any possible separation between self and others. In cannibalism, all is brought together. But the mode of this uniting is not a mere melting. The individual is not so much contrasted to the collective (cannibalism is the disguised expression of "all individualism" and of "all collectivisms") as conjoined with it. This collective body denies the possibility of a separation between the self and the collective while remaining aware of their irrevocable difference. Testifying to the blurring of the lines between the individual and the collective, the manifesto gestures toward a mythical retrieval of an Indigenous past combined with manifesto-like calls for resistance: "We want the Carib Revolution. Greater than the French Revolution. The unification of all productive revolts for the progress of humanity. Without us, Europe wouldn't even have its meager declaration of the rights of man."[39] One notices in this passage Andrade's perceptive claim that the formation of some of the noblest political ideals in Europe cannot be separated from its colonial underside. Like in Freud's analysis of totemism and the formation of the self, one cannot do without the shadowy presence of the flesh eater—be it our own sense of self, be it the Declaration of the Rights of Man. Andrade nevertheless constantly seasons his rejection of the colonial legacy with winks that indicate a playful acceptance of a certain European inheritance. Later in the poem, for example, Andrade recognizes that "those who came here weren't crusaders" but rather "fugitives" of a civilization that charged its own outcasts with the task of colonizing other lands. Naturally, the manifesto expresses the desire to eat this civilization brought by its fugitives.[40]

The Brazilian philosopher Benedito Nunes posits that by casting Sardinha's death as the starting point of a timeline that culminates with his manifesto, Andrade disidentifies with and troubles foundational myths of Brazilian origins.[41] Brazil, in this scheme, has no "ontological" existence, in the words of literary critic Haroldo de Campos. Rather, the cannibal affords a "modal, differential nationalism" that assumes the nation as a "dialogical movement" of differentiations and disidentifications, of "rupture instead of the linear course."[42] Anthropophagy disarms what Campos appropriately calls *ontological nationalism* by exposing the nonbeings secreted by the logocentric logic of the colonial nation-state and offering in its stead the playful possibility of a differential nation. Andrade's cannibal aesthetic troubles not only Brazil's opaque origins but also the idea of a Brazilian essential nature, instead affirming that identification gains shape only through incorporation of the other. The nation is what it consumes and, yes, also what it secretes.

With the antifoundationalist view of Brazilian culture, Andrade probes the aporia of thinking of Brazil before its colonial origins. "Before the Portuguese discovered Brazil, Brazil had discovered happiness."[43] The impossibility of a precolonial "Brazil" is not so much neglected by the manifesto as in fact accepted as the condition of possibility of a happy Brazil. Primitivism is the fiction deployed by Andrade to depict an alternative cultural trajectory for a country steeped in coloniality. Andrade writes playfully, with another gesture toward Freud:

> Cannibalism. Absorption of the sacred enemy. To transform him into a totem. The human adventure. The earthly goal. Even so, only the pure elites managed to realize carnal cannibalism, which carries within itself the highest meaning of life and avoids all the ills identified by Freud— catechist ills. What results is not sublimation of the sexual instinct. It is the thermometrical scale of the cannibal instinct. Carnal at first, this instinct becomes elective, and creates friendship. When it is affective, it creates love.[44]

For the manifesto, cannibalism is the utter expression of an infinite desire for the flesh of others. While accepting Freud's provocation about the entanglement between totemism and cannibalism, Andrade rejects the Freudian thesis that the taboo is the internalization of the primordial totem and, as such, a step beyond barbarism and into civilization. As noticed by Nunes, what marks the passage to civilization in Freud's narrative is the internationalization of the paternal rule. Andrade, in contrast, rejects the patriarchal logic of filiation by embracing the totem.[45] "Cannibalism. The permanent transformation of the [taboo] into a totem."[46] The forbidden incorporation, for Andrade, ought to be made incarnate—not vaporized into moral and religious codes. The desire for the flesh of others need not be sublimated into taboos; in fact, it has to be incarnated in the work of art.[47] For the manifesto, the desire to become one flesh with the other is the condition of possibility of friendship and love.

Take and Eat, This Is My Body

WE MAY NOW RETURN to the barbecue by the beach that brought Bishop Sardinha into the stomach of the Caeté warrior. We recall this gravest of scenes: the bishop, appointed to deploy his office in the aid of the colonial project, sinks with his boat, only to become flesh for the hunger of a Caeté warrior. For the hagiographic record that followed him, Sardinha died as a martyr. For Andrade's cannibal aesthetics, Sardinha was hosted in the stomach of the warrior to give flesh to a new thing. Cannibal subjectivity refuses to be an isolated self—it directs itself toward the incorporation of others into its body. The "law of the cannibal," Andrade states, concerns itself with the other: "I am only concerned with what is not mine."[48] And inside the cannibal stomach is the world: "From the equation 'Self, part of the Cosmos' to the axiom 'Cosmos, part of the Self.'"[49] The visceral problem for the cannibal is precisely this disposition toward the other—the infinite desire of becoming one flesh with the other.

The literary critic Maggie Kilgour theorizes that this is the real promise of cannibalism as a literary and cultural gesture. She argues that the idea of cannibalism contains an intriguing connection to the concept of communion as that which both produces and dissolves the apparently fixed boundaries between outside and inside, here and there. Drawing from Mikhail Bakhtin's work, Kilgour points out that the very mundane act of eating exposes the ambivalence between these antitheses: eating "is the most material need yet is invested with a great deal of significance, an act that involves both desire and aggression, as it creates a total identity between eater and eaten while insisting on total control—the literal consumption—of the latter by the former."[50] One may actually think that the cannibal act is not one of unification, as Kilgour suggests, but a mode of incorporation that maintains *something* of the eaten alive in such a way as to transform the eater. The idea of "incorporation . . . depends upon and enforces an absolute division between inside and outside; but in the act itself that opposition disappears, dissolving the structure it appears to produce."[51] If the maxim that "we are what we eat" is true, anthropophagy leads us into a more mysterious—in fact, even sacramental—understanding of human subjectivity. By swallowing the other, the cannibal in-fleshes otherness.

In the colonial context, the act of devouring the Christian settler marks the irreducible difference between colonizer and colonized while also digesting that opposition. As literary critic Peter Hulme points out, anthropophagy is central to coloniality insofar as it is "inseparable from considerations of difference and distinction," particularly as European colonizers sought mechanisms to represent the barbarism of Indigenous peoples.[52] In the colonial world, cannibalism was the mark of the colonial difference separating civilization from savagery. In the hands of coloniality, the cannibal is the embodiment of a savagery ready to be conquered by the civilizing mission. In Andrade's cannibal aesthetic, in contrast, cannibalism is the mechanism that unhinges the colonial logic of demarcation between them and us. Anthropophagy ingrains the other into the materiality of the body to unhinge colonial demarcations of land, body, and food.

As Campos suggests, the poetic and political force of Andrade's anthropophagy and its possibilities for a new form of world art is shaped by a "Marxilary dialectics," a political manifesto that chews and dissects the colonial legacy to form a new aesthetics.[53] This anthropophagic mixture of Marxism and the maxillary resists colonial forces by introducing them to the "new barbarians who . . . have been devouring them and making them flesh of their flesh and bone of their bone, who have been resynthesizing them chemically by means of an impetuous and unrestrainable metabolism of difference."[54] Campos focuses our attention on the jaws of the cannibal:

> For some time, these new barbarians' devouring jaws have been gnawing at the "ruining" of a cultural heritage that is ever more global. . . . In contrast, the combinatory and ludibrious poly-culturalism, that parodic transmutation of meaning and values, the open, multi-lingual hybridization, are the devices responsible for the constant feeding and re-feeding of this Baroque soul moment, the carnivalized transencyclopedia of the new barbarians, where everything can coexist with everything. They are mechanisms which crush the material of tradition with the teeth of a tropical sugar-mill, changing stalks and protective coverings into husks and cane syrup.[55]

These cannibal jaws squash coloniality not out of an appetite for destruction but as a "regenerative cannibalism" that seeks to deconstruct coloniality.[56] Andrade's cannibal aesthetics might then engender a decolonial sensibility: "[his] originality," critic Sérgio Luiz Prado Bellei points out, "lies precisely in the attempt to use . . . backwardness, with its mixture of primitivism and absurdity . . . as a possible Brazilian contribution for a society less unjust and bourgeois."[57] The dismantling of coloniality—and its complicity in the formation of the bourgeoisie—comes through the swallowing of the colonial legacy, bringing it inside the body of conquered peoples. Their stomach fluids are the deconstructive lever that can digest a postcolonial world into existence.

Might these same fluids reopen the Christian appetite for flesh? Kilgour teases out the uncanny anthropophagic sensibility one finds in Christian writings about the mystery of the incarnation. She highlights, for example, that Augustine's conversion is punctuated by food metaphors: from the lack of nourishment in Manichaean doctrine to an encounter with a God that fully consumes Augustine. He states in his *Confessions*, "And I found myself far from you . . . and heard as it were your voice from on high: 'I am the food of the fully grown; grow and you will feed on me. *And you will not change me into you like the food your flesh eats, but you will be changed into me.*'"[58] Cannibal indeed. The food Augustine finds in God is not consumed as one eats it but instead consumes the hungry subject. As Kilgour suggests, while this may seem just another affirmation of God's ultimate separation from the "earthly nutrients," Augustine's *Confessions* belie an acute passion for the flesh.

Equally haunted by the mystery of the flesh of others, Andrade's manifesto is also concerned with incarnation. In the cannibal aesthetic, however, the Christian event of incarnation is transplanted to the tropics: "We were never catechized. We live by a somnambulistic law. We made Christ to be born in Bahia. Or in Belém do Pará."[59] Andrade's transference of the place of Christ's birth from Bethlehem to Bahia or Belém do Pará—in Portuguese, Belém means Bethlehem—radicalizes the theological affirmation of the incarnation by multiplying its sites and its fleshes. It showcases the possibility of an alter-carnation of the divine assuming flesh in the colonies. "We were never catechized," the manifesto insists again, only to reiterate: "What we really made was Carnaval [*sic*]. The Indian dressed as a Senator of the Empire."[60] The impossibility of catechesis in the aphorism does not indicate the refusal of the Christian message but a magical appropriation and transference of the motif of the incarnation into a new cultural territory. Christian instruction is not so much denied as unnecessary in a culture that has already incorporated the Christ. The feast of the flesh, carnival, becomes the "totemic meal" marking this new variety of the Christian trope of the Eucharist.

By transposing and multiplying the sites of incarnation, Andrade's cannibal reverses the logic of the eucharistic host brought by Christ's vicar, Bishop Sardinha. The host, lifted up by the bishop and transubstantiated into the body of Christ, is now hosted in the stomach of the Caeté warrior. The two are now one flesh. As theologian Mayra Rivera reminds us, incarnation is not the coming to flesh of a preexisting entity, as if the Eucharist celebrated by the bishop introduced to the tropics the coming of the incarnate Christ. Rather, incarnation is fundamentally about the "patterns by which social-material flesh is distributed, transformed as it is given, and transforms those who participate in these processes." Each incarnation is an "interpretation shaped by the unique textures and rhythms of each body."[61] As Sardinha is received into the Tupi communion, this incarnation constitutes a new social-material-subjective reality.

Could the body of Christ have resisted such a tasty banquet? The uncanny presence of the cannibal in Andrade's thought is a lasting reminder of the fleshly Eucharist that we are. The manifesto brilliantly states, "The spirit refuses to conceive a spirit without a body. Anthropomorphism. Need for the cannibalistic vaccine."[62] This anthropophagic vaccine is this shot of flesh into the spirit. It is the eucharistic vision of the self as the incarnation of other fleshes. For Rivera, this is the promise of the "carnal strand" of Christian theology, namely, its insight that all that I can claim as "my" flesh comes from the other: "Unless I can embrace my own flesh, and its beginnings in the flesh of another, I cannot love other fleshly beings—nor can I understand the incarnation."[63] What anthropophagy offers is thus not simply a way to consider the dynamic of establishing and dissolving difference but rather a way to cement radical otherness in the event of incorporation. The bodily formation of the subject, its material constitution through incorporation, is an act of alter-carnation. It is the mystery of the host that we take as the body of God, through which we become like gods.

In the cannibal aesthetic, Andrade resurrects the memory of the swallowing of Bishop Sardinha to disentangle our clan's origins from the colonial invasion and hence imagine new incarnations. Sardinha, the embodiment of our enmity against colonial Christianity and its hosts, continues to be digested. Sardinha is the figure we, on occasion, incorporate through carnivalesque meals. *Sardinha*, the Portuguese word for "sardine," our totemic delight.

Notes

1 See Hulme and Whitehead, *Wild Majesty*, 354–55; Walton, *Our Cannibals, Ourselves*, 2–3; and Petrinovich, *Cannibal Within*, 4–5.

2 For the original Portuguese version of the manifesto, see Andrade, "Manifesto antropófago."

3 King John III's chronicler, Francisco de Andrada, recognized this in the early seventeenth century: "After Pedro Álvares Cabral discovered the land of the Holy Cross, now known as Brazil, and possessed it for the crown of these kingdoms . . . [As] the King's primary occupation and his council's are devoted to the matters of India for they are of the highest importance, Brazil's matters were seconded." Andrada, *Crônica de D. João III*, 975. All translations of non-English sources are by the author.

4 King John III's particular concern in colonizing Brazil was part of a broad and complex cluster of political issues, the turbulent Portuguese relations with France being chief among these. It is reported that French merchants had developed commerce on the Brazilian coast quite early, in clear breach of the Treaty of Tordesillas; in 1552, for instance, a French ship was intercepted in the Mediterranean, and Portuguese officials found enormous amounts of brazilwood and animals from Brazil. The event was decisive in King John III's decision to create the hereditary captaincies. For more information, see Bueno, *Capitães do Brasil*, 7–9.

5 Bueno, *A coroa, a cruz e a espada*, 25.

6 In fact, one of the reasons for Coutinho's downfall was his relationship with the amusing Mr. Caramuru, a Portuguese sailor by the name of Diogo Álvares, who shipwrecked on those seas between 1509 and 1510 and survived to marry a cacique's daughter, and lived amid the Tupinamba of Bahia after that. Caramuru was in charge of a complex system of wood trafficking with French merchants, a commerce so extensive in the first three decades of the sixteenth century that French cartography from the period identifies this region as "Pointe du Carammorou." See Bueno, *A coroa, a cruz e a espada*, 25–29.

7 Bueno, *A coroa, a cruz e a espada*, 56.

8 Andrada, *Crônica de D. João III*, 975.

9 Nóbrega, *Cartas do Brasil*, 19.

10 Bueno, *A coroa, a cruz e a espada*, 132.

11 In a letter dated August 10, 1549, Father Nóbrega relates that a hundred people had recently been baptized and that another "six hundred or seven hundred" catechumens were to be baptized soon, "who are all learning very well and walk after us asking when shall we baptize them, with great desire and promising to live according to our ordinances." Nóbrega, *Cartas do Brasil*, 51.

12 Nóbrega, *Cartas do Brasil*, 36.

13 Calmon, *História da fundação da Bahia*, 184n2. Some doubt remains whether Álvaro Gomes was in fact Sardinha's brother or just a close friend. The latter opinion is presented in Van Der Vat, *Princípios da igreja no Brasil*, 267.

14 The historical record on Bishop Sardinha's life before his assignment to Brazil is minimal. Unlike other missionaries in the sixteenth century, Bishop Sardinha was not a prolific writer, and there are no records of his writing in this period. See Schurhammer, *Orientalia*, 151; and Van Der Vat, *Princípios da igreja no Brasil*, 367. For a more recent account of Bishop Sardinha's life in Brazil, see Bueno, *Capitães do Brasil*; Bueno, *A coroa, a cruz e a espada*; Bagetti, *História brasileira da infâmia*; and Lemos, *Dom Pedro Fernandes Sardinha*.

15 Letter to King John III, dated July 1552, in Nóbrega, *Cartas do Brasil*, 113, 117.

16 Bueno, *A coroa, a cruz e a espada*, 138. Accusations of greed were common during Bishop Sardinha's time in Brazil. In 1553, he is reported to have trav-

eled to the wealthier and better-structured captaincy of Pernambuco to "convert ecclesiastical penalties into pecuniary ones." Bueno, *A coroa, a cruz e a espada*, 209. As most historians recognize, by the time he left Salvador, Sardinha had accumulated a good amount of riches.

17 "Do not forget," the bishop once wrote to the king, "to send here some organs for these Gentiles are fond of novelties." Bueno, *A coroa, a cruz e a espada*, 138.

18 Nóbrega to Tomé de Sousa, July 5, 1559, in Nóbrega, *Cartas do Brasil*, 319.

19 The controversy was between Bishop Sardinha and Brazil's second governor-general, the nobleman Duarte da Costa, and his son, D. Álvaro da Costa, whom the bishop publicly accused of having inappropriate relations with married women. By October 1554, the conflict had become public and divided the city of Salvador into two camps. While the bishop appears to have had the trust of the king, in May 1555, a Tupinamba insurrection assaulted the colonial outpost in Salvador; this was followed by a successful counterattack, led by Álvaro da Costa. The military victory robbed Sardinha of his leverage with the crown, and not long after that, the king demanded his return to Portugal. For more on these events, see Johnson, Mauro, and Silva, *Império luso-brasileiro*, 150, 373–76; Bueno, *A coroa, a cruz e a espada*, 208–15; Van Der Vat, *Princípios da igreja no Brasil*, 359–60; and Nóbrega, *Cartas do Brasil*, 377–79.

20 Our first account of Sardinha's death comes from the Jesuit Antonio Blasques, who lamented his passing, saying that the city of Salvador suffered greatly from his loss. Letter to Fr. Ignácio [Ignatius of Loyola], June 10, 1557, in Cabral and Peixoto, *Cartas avulsas*, 177.

21 Salvador, *Historia do Brasil*, 166.

22 Alencar, *Roteiro dos bispados do Brasil*, 4.

23 Calmon, *História da fundação da Bahia*, 216.

24 "The Report of Dr. Chanca" (1494), in Hulme and Whitehead, *Wild Majesty*, 32.

25 Montaigne, *Essays*.

26 See letter to Dr. Martin de Azpicuelta Navarro, August 10, 1549, in Nóbrega, *Cartas do Brasil*, 48–49.

27 Léry, *History of a Voyage*, ch. 15; and Staden, *Hans Staden's True History*. For additional reports of anthropophagy in colonial Brazil, see Sousa and Varnhagen, *Tratado descritivo do Brasil*. For a good summary of documents and reports about the anthropophagic ritual in Brazil, see Maestri, *Os senhores do litoral*, 65–76. For good illustrations and a brief summary of the same ritual, see Bueno, *Brasil*, 20–21.

28 Léry, *History of a Voyage*, 127.

29 Léry, *History of a Voyage*, 126.

30 See Maestri, *Os senhores do litoral*, 74.

31 Freud, *Totem and Taboo*, 5–9.

32 Freud, *Totem and Taboo*, 164.

33 Freud, *Totem and Taboo*, 176 (emphasis mine).

34 Freud, *Totem and Taboo*, 176.

35 Freud, *Totem and Taboo*, 184.

36 Nunes, "Antropofagia e vanguarda," 319.

37 Andrade, "Cannibalist Manifesto," 44. The word *Piratininga* is the Indigenous name of the region where the city of São Paulo is presently located.

38 Andrade, "Cannibalist Manifesto," 38.

39 Andrade, "Cannibalist Manifesto," 39.

40 Andrade, "Cannibalist Manifesto," 41.

41 Nunes, "Anthropophagisme et surréalisme," 166.

42 Campos, "Rule of Anthropophagy," 323.

43 Andrade, "Cannibalist Manifesto," 42.

44 Andrade, "Cannibalist Manifesto," 43.

45 Nunes, "Anthropophagisme et surréalisme," 169–70.

46 Andrade, "Cannibalist Manifesto," 40.

47 See Bellei, "Brazilian Anthropophagy Revisited."

48 Andrade, "Cannibalist Manifesto," 38.

49 Andrade, "Cannibalist Manifesto," 40.

50 Kilgour, *From Communion to Cannibalism*, 7.

51 Kilgour, *From Communion to Cannibalism*, 4.

52 Hulme, "Introduction," 2.

53 Campos, "Rule of Anthropophagy," 334. In some of Andrade's writings, Marxiar was used as a pseudonym.

54 Campos, "Rule of Anthropophagy," 334.

55 Campos, "Rule of Anthropophagy," 334.

56 Hulme, "Introduction," 27–28.

57 Bellei, "Brazilian Anthropophagy Revisited," 105.

58 Augustine, *Confessions*, 123–24 (emphasis mine).

59 Andrade, "Cannibalist Manifesto," 39.

60 Andrade, "Cannibalist Manifesto," 40.

61 Rivera, *Poetics of the Flesh*, 145.

62 Andrade, "Cannibalist Manifesto," 39.

63 Rivera, *Poetics of the Flesh*, 154.

Bibliography

Alencar, Carlos Augusto Peixoto de. *Roteiro dos bispados do Brasil e dos seos respectivos bispos: Desde os primeiros tempos coloniaes até o presente.* Typ. Cearense, 1864.

Andrada, Francisco de. *Crônica de D. João III*. Edited by M. Lopes de Almeida. Porto: Lello & Irmão, 1976.

Andrade, Oswald de. "Cannibalist Manifesto." Translated by Leslie Bary. *Latin American Literary Review* 19, no. 38 (1991): 38–47.

Andrade, Oswald de. "Manifesto antropófago." *Revista de Antropofagia*, May 1928. http://www.ufrgs.br/cdrom/oandrade/oandrade.pdf.

Augustine. *Confessions*. Translated by Henry Chadwick. Oxford: Oxford University Press, 2008.

Bagetti, Werner Salles, dir. *História brasileira da infâmia*. São Paulo: Log On Editora Multimidia, 2005. DVD.

Bellei, Sérgio Luiz Prado. "Brazilian Anthropophagy Revisited." In *Cannibalism and the Colonial World*, edited by Francis Barker, Peter Hulme, and Margaret Iversen, 87–109. Cambridge: Cambridge University Press, 1998.

Bueno, Eduardo. *Brasil: Uma história; A incrível saga de um país*. São Paulo: Ática, 2006.

Bueno, Eduardo. *Capitães do Brasil: A saga dos primeiros colonizadores*. Rio de Janeiro: Objetiva, 2006.

Bueno, Eduardo. *A coroa, a cruz e a espada: Lei, ordem e corrupção no Brasil colônia, 1548–1558*. Rio de Janeiro: Objetiva, 2006.

Cabral, Alfredo do Valle, and Afrânio Peixoto, eds. *Cartas avulsas*. Rio de Janeiro: Officina Industrial Graphica, 1931.

Calmon, Pedro. *História da fundação da Bahia*. Salvador: Instituto Histórico Geográfico Brasileiro, 1949.

Campos, Haroldo de. "The Rule of Anthropophagy: Europe under the Sign of Devoration." In *Baroque New Worlds: Representation, Transculturation, Counterconquest*, edited by Lois Parkinson Zamora and Monika Kaup, translated by Maria Tai Wolff, 319–41. Durham, NC: Duke University Press, 2010.

Freud, Sigmund. *Totem and Taboo: Some Points of Agreement between the Mental Lives of Savages and Neurotics*. New York: Norton, 1989.

Hulme, Peter. "Introduction: The Cannibal Scene." In *Cannibalism and the Colonial World*, edited by Francis Barker, Peter Hulme, and Margaret Iversen, 1–38. Cambridge: Cambridge University Press, 1998.

Hulme, Peter, and Neil L. Whitehead, eds. *Wild Majesty: Encounters with Caribs from Columbus to the Present Day: An Anthology*. Oxford: Oxford University Press, 1992.

Johnson, Harold Benjamin, Frédéric Mauro, and Maria Beatriz Nizza da Silva. *O império luso-brasileiro, 1500–1620*. Lisbon: Estampa, 1992.

Kilgour, Maggie. *From Communion to Cannibalism: An Anatomy of Metaphors of Incorporation*. Princeton, NJ: Princeton University Press, 1990.

Lemos, João R. *Dom Pedro Fernandes Sardinha: Um bispo, mártir, em Coruripe*. Coruripe: Prefeitura Municipal de Coruripe, 2004.

Léry, Jean de. *History of a Voyage to the Land of Brazil, Otherwise Called America*. Translated by Janet Whatley. Berkeley: University of California Press, 1990.

Maestri, Mário. *Os senhores do litoral: Conquista portuguesa e agonia tupinambá no litoral brasileiro*. Porto Alegre: Universidade Federal do Rio Grande do Sul, 1994.

Montaigne, Michel de. *The Essays: A Selection*. Translated by M. A. Screech. London: Penguin Books, 1993.

Nóbrega, Manuel da. *Cartas do Brasil e mais escritos (opera omnia)*. Edited by Serafim Leite. Coimbra: Universidade de Coimbra, 1955.

Nunes, Benedito. "Anthropophagisme et surréalisme." In *Surréalisme périphérique: Actes du colloque "Portugal, Québec, Amérique Latine: Un Surréalisme Périphérique?,"* edited by Luis de Moura Sobral, 159–79. Montreal: Université de Montréal, 1984.

Nunes, Benedito. "Antropofagia e vanguarda: Acerca do canibalismo literário." *Literatura e Sociedade* 9, no. 7 (2004): 316–27.

Petrinovich, Lewis F. *The Cannibal Within*. New York: Aldine de Gruyter, 2000.

Rivera, Mayra. *Poetics of the Flesh*. Durham, NC: Duke University Press, 2015.

Salvador, Frei Vicente do. *Historia do Brasil*. Edited by Capistrano de Abreu, Rodolfo Garcia, and Venâncio Willeke. São Paulo: Melhoramentos, 1965.

Schurhammer, Georg. *Orientalia*. Lisbon: Centro de Estudos Historicos Ultramarinos, 1963.

Sousa, Gabriel Soares de, and Francisco Adolfo de Varnhagen, Visconde de Porto Seguro. *Tratado descritivo do Brasil em 1587*. Recife: Fundação Joaquim Nabuco and Massangana, 2000.

Staden, Hans. *Hans Staden's True History: An Account of Cannibal Captivity in Brazil*. Edited by Neil L. Whitehead and Michael Harbsmeier. Durham, NC: Duke University Press, 2008.

Van Der Vat, Odulfo, OFM. *Princípios da igreja no Brasil*. Petrópolis: Vozes, 1952.

Walton, Priscilla L. *Our Cannibals, Ourselves*. Urbana: University of Illinois Press, 2004.

Joseph R. Winters

9 The Sacred Gone Astray

Eliade, Fanon, Wynter, and
the Terror of Colonial Settlement

RACE, RELIGION, AND COLONIALITY make up a violent constellation, the
implications of which religious studies is still only beginning to confront. Scholars have demonstrated how modern conceptions of religion
emerge alongside the collisions between Europe and the darker denizens
of modernity. As David Chidester points out in his analysis of colonial
encounters in southern Africa and elsewhere, early modern European
missionaries and settlers assumed that Blacks and Indians lacked religion,
an assumption that "called into question the humanity" of Europe's external others.[1] To not have religion, or more specifically to exist outside of
the European Christian fold, signified an absence of those qualities that
distinguish humans from other species—law, order, and political structure. This imaginary justified conquest and settler projects in the name
of giving the law to anarchic populations.[2] In response to this predicament, Nelson Maldonado-Torres claims that "the concept of religion is
intimately linked with the modern concept of race, and that both play a
key role in the formation of modernity/coloniality."[3] To put it succinctly,
race and religion are coconstitutive in determining who counts as human.

One significant aspect of religious life is the fabrication of sacred value
and the endeavor to protect sacred objects from violation, from being profaned. The sacred is typically set apart by taboos and prohibitions as a

special domain that generates value, order, and cohesion. Consequently, the sacred needs to be buffered from entities that threaten to introduce disorder and contamination.[4] Since Black bodies and people of color have been marked by modern arrangements as signifiers of disorder and death, the logic of the sacred/profane is intimately bound up with coloniality, race, and anti-Blackness. In what follows, I extend the work on religion, race, and colonization by sharpening attention to a particular understanding of the sacred that underwrites and legitimates the colonial imaginary. To accomplish this, I return to the work of Mircea Eliade. Although Eliade has been dismissed by commentators for being ahistorical and uncritical, his distinction between the sacred and profane, which maps onto the distinction between being and nonbeing, or legible world and chaotic space, continues to illumine the complicity between sacrality and colonial terror.[5] To flesh out the dangers of Eliade's framework, dangers that he glosses over, I turn to the work of Frantz Fanon and Sylvia Wynter. While these authors are not as widely read in religious studies, I contend that their reflections on colonization and anti-Blackness rely on an implicit critique of the grammar of the sacred found in Eliade's account of religion. I conclude the essay by showing that Fanon's writing, particularly the style of *Black Skin, White Masks*, gestures toward an alternative sense of the sacred, a volatile sacred that departs from the logics of settlement and possession.

Eliade and the World-Establishing Sacred

ELIADE'S UNDERSTANDING of religion relies on a strong distinction between sacred and profane space, and religious and secular Man. While the contrast does not always hold, it does provide insights into the kinds of imaginaries that propel coloniality, or colonization and its afterlife. Borrowing from Rudolf Otto, Eliade contends that sacred space is made possible by an interruption of the wholly other into the natural world.[6] This manifestation of the sacred, made possible by the world-creating work of the gods, introduces a break into what would otherwise be homogeneous space. Sacred space is made possible by a rupture, a qualitative division within the space continuum, enabling religious people to experience that space as separate and unique. As Eliade writes, "There is, then, a sacred space, and hence a strong, significant space; there are other spaces that are not sacred and so are without structure or consistency, amorphous. . . . For religious man, this spatial nonhomogeneity finds expression in the experience of an opposition between space that is sacred—the only real and really existing space—and other space, the formless expanse surrounding it."[7] In Mary Douglas's language, we might read Eliade as saying that a hierophany enables the opposition between space that is coherent and meaningful and space that symbolizes dirt and matter out of place.[8] More strongly, the appearance of the sacred "ontologically founds the world" and "reveals an absolute fixed point, a center" that orients religious people.[9] As the center of the world and an expression of the real, the sacred is "power, efficacity, the source of life and fecundity."[10] For Eliade, sacred experience provides the conditions for participating in being, for escaping illusion and the threat of irrelevance.

Eliade consistently contrasts the qualities of the sacred (structure, foundation, reality) with the characteristics of the profane (chaos, formlessness, lack). There seems to be an ontological distinction between the two kinds of spaces and consequently between religious and nonreligious experience. Yet Eliade also suggests that there is some continuity between sacred and profane experience when he mentions nonreligious people who treat certain places—their birthplace, the first foreign city they visit—as extraordinary or set apart from the mundane. He also interprets various secular philosophies, such as Marxism, as unconsciously invested in religious themes like redemption (a classless society) and the collective messiah (the proletariat). In addition, he acknowledges that for humans to access the sacred, to have a religious experience, hierophanies must occur through profane objects and spaces. Consequently, Eliade identifies various thresholds, like a door to a temple, the top of a mountain, or a ritual that indicate a passage from the profane to the sacred domain. As he puts it, "The threshold is the limit, the boundary, the frontier that distinguishes and opposes two worlds—and at the same time the paradoxical place where those worlds communicate, where passage from the profane to the sacred world becomes possible."[11] While this notion of the threshold suggests a more fluid relationship between the sacred and the profane, this fluidity is superseded by a designation of the sacred as that which establishes order over and against figures of profanity.

One way that humans communicate with the gods is by participating in the creative work of the gods, an activity that involves the consecration of space and the construction of worlds. According to Eliade, "the ritual by which [man] constructs a sacred space is efficacious in the measure in which it reproduces the work of the gods."[12] One such ritual or liturgy that he mentions is the occupation of foreign land by a world or community that has already been ordered and organized by the sacred. If the sacred "fixes the limits and establishes the order of the world," it does so by opposing and engulfing territories and populations that embody chaos.[13] Eliade writes, "An unknown, foreign, and unoccupied territory (which often means unoccupied by our people) still shares in the fluid and larval modality of chaos. By occupying it, and above all, by settling in it, man symbolically transforms it into a cosmos through a ritual repetition of the cosmogony."[14] Eliade offers the example of Spanish and Portuguese conquistadores taking possession of Native American territory in the name of the cross. By planting the cross and the flag on foreign territory, this consecrating liturgy converts chaos into form, fluidity into solidity, uncultivated space into inhabitable land, and death into life.[15] This transforming practice creates a world that can be possessed, occupied, and settled. And the violence involved in this kind of colonial project is disavowed by the colonizer in the name of creating and giving new life. Within Eliade's grammar of the sacred and the profane, "settling in a [new] territory is equivalent to founding a world" and reenacting the original creation of god/s.[16] Settlement is a terrifying ritual that purportedly transforms profane land into a sacred world; in the process, the human (settler) becomes something like a divine power.

One might dismiss the cosmos/chaos binary that underwrites Eliade's idea of the sacred and the related grammar of settlement as emblematic of premodern myths, especially myths that narrated the beginning of time with gods slaying monsters and dragons in order to establish the world. On this reading, the colonial conquest is modeled after creation stories that secular reason has abandoned. But Eliade anticipates this move. He reminds the reader that the monsters that need to be slayed in ancient myths, especially the sea monster, are embodiments of "darkness, death, and night." The monster represents "everything that has not acquired a form."[17] Consequently, secular thought continues to be committed to something like the sacred/profane distinction insofar as it identifies certain bodies as signifiers of "ruin, disintegration, and death," as threats to the civilized world; insofar as prevailing practices and arrangements mark certain kinds of populations and territories as harbingers of disorder, as embodiments of the monstrous. Eliade has his finger on something here but does not develop a devastating insight: sacredness, which is reproduced by projects of settlement, is anti-Black. Here the term *Black*, following Fred Moten, refers not just to Black people but more generally to "disordering, deformational forces [that are] indispensable to normative order, normative form."[18] (Therefore, as Moten's work indicates, these qualities of Blackness resemble and overlap with those qualities associated with the feminine and the figure of the queer.) In line with the work of historian of religion Charles H. Long, whose work is in direct response to Eliade, we might say that the world-founding sacred is opposed to (but relies on) opacity.[19] Opacity for Long alludes to Red and Black peoples, Indigenous Americans and kidnapped Africans, populations that make up the traumatic kernel of American religious history. At the same time, the language of the opaque signifies that which frustrates and escapes the will to transparency or the yearning for stable distinctions, borders, and meanings. The opaque represents a kind of muddiness that threatens to unravel rigid boundaries and normative forms.[20] The opaque is what the project of settlement attempts to contain, transform (or impose form on), and eliminate.

While Eliade briefly describes how the sacred/profane framework accompanies and justifies colonial missions, he does not linger or tarry with the implications. In other words, he does not reflect on the constitutive relationship between the enactment of the sacred, or the procedures of settling erstwhile uninhabitable territory, and what Paul Gilroy alludes to as the "terror of modernity."[21] Consequently, he does not underscore how his understanding of the sacred is tethered to imaginaries and practices that rank peoples and lands, that position Europe and America as the sanctified sources of power, life, fecundity, and being. To put it differently, Eliade's reflections gesture toward a predicament in which whiteness is considered sacred and Blackness is associated with the dangers of profanity and the potential pollution of communities and spaces set apart as more valuable and more in touch with life. Perhaps because Eliade is so focused on reviving religiosity and a sense of transcendence in a secular age, he cannot sit with the underside of the sacred and its operations. And while Eliade acknowledges how a commitment to the redemptive sacred, or that which gives life to signifiers of death, is evident in religious and secular Man, we might say that there is more continuity than Eliade notices between these two personae—especially as it relates to the darker denizens of modernity. When Eliade claims that "religious man . . . expresses a desire to live in a pure and holy cosmos, as it was in the beginning, when it came fresh from the Creator's hands," we should acknowledge that this will to purity gets rearticulated in secular thought and practice, colonial regimes, and racial logics.[22] When it comes to the world-establishing sacred, religious and secular Man are often two sides of the same colonial, anti-Black coin. To flesh out an insight that Eliade refuses to expand on, I turn to the work of Wynter and Fanon.

Wynter, Fanon, and the Terror of Man

WYNTER AND FANON IMPLICITLY RESPOND to the kind of religious imaginary articulated by Eliade, one in which the production of sacred space is closely tied to settling territory, occupying foreign land, and containing the opaque. By thinking with these authors, we see how Eliade's sacred/profane distinction underwrites European colonial frameworks and maps onto what W. E. B. Du Bois calls the "color line," the hierarchical division between whites and Blacks, and Europeans and non-Europeans.[23] While Wynter offers a genealogical account of these sacred divisions, Fanon provides a more existential account of the enticements of the sacred for Black subjects who yearn to be inducted into the sphere of the human.

For Wynter, the long-lasting hierarchies and divisions within modernity are largely the result of a particular conception of the human, European Man, becoming the totalizing image of humanity. From the late fifteenth century to the present, European conceptions of what and who is human have dominated and excluded other ways of imagining the human. As Katherine McKittrick points out, Wynter endeavors "to re-present the fullness of human ontologies, which have been curtailed by what she describes as an over-representation of Man (western bourgeois Man) as if it/he were the only available mode of complete humanness."[24] In the effort to reinvent the human, Wynter unsettles the ground that equates the human with Man, a conflation that has implications for race, class, and gender arrangements. Or, to put it differently, Wynter exposes how certain visions and expressions of the human have become *settled* in opposition to bodies and territories that have come to signify a danger to settlement but that constitute the necessary occasions for colonial and settler projects. In the process, Wynter shows how this opposition or division relies on religious and theological patterns of thought even as discourses shift toward the secular.

In her well-known essay "Unsettling the Coloniality of Being/Power/Truth/Freedom," Wynter traces different stages of western Man, showing how each stage is a rearticulation of religious and theological paradigms. For Wynter, the Christian distinction between spirit and fallen flesh, and the related distinction between the redeemed and unredeemed, gets extended into the early modern era or the age of European discovery. She writes:

> The series of symbolically coded Spirit/Flesh representations mapped upon the "space of Otherness" of the physical cosmos had not only functioned to absolutize the theocentric descriptive statement of the human, its master code of symbolic life (the Spirit) and death (the Flesh). . . . It had also served to absolutize a "general order of existence," together with its "postulate of significant ill," whose mode of affliction then logically calls the particular "plan of salvation" or redemptive cure able to cure the specific ill that threatened all subjects of the order, in order to redeem them from its threat of nihilation/negation that is common to all religions.[25]

As this passage suggests, the contrast between spirit and flesh has something to do with a stable separation between life and death, cure and sickness. The flesh is associated with severability, scattering, and excess. As Mayra Rivera puts it, "Flesh is an ambivalent term that names a rather slippery materiality. . . . Flesh is conceived as formless and impermanent, crossing the boundaries between the individual body and the world."[26] While *spirit* can mean many things, when it is opposed to flesh, it typically represents unity and coherence; it marks a sort of elevation above, and a disciplining of, the dissipating qualities and desires associated with fleshliness. Thus, Wynter contends that the spirit/flesh demarcation operates to construct a "general order of existence." Within western Christianity, especially during the age of discovery, this schema includes distinctions between the heavens and "vile and base" matter, clergy and laity, the redeemed and the unredeemed, and inhabitable and uninhabitable territory. Some populations, including Africans and Native Americans, get associated with fallen flesh that requires redemption, while the respective territories, such as Africa and the Americas, were considered unlivable apart from the settling activities of missionaries and colonizers. Regions and populations associated with too much heat, excessive water, or wasted natural resources become figures of death (or nonbeing) and occasions for redemption via occupation.

What is crucial for Wynter is that the separation between spirit and flesh, and redeemed Christian and unredeemed other, gets reexpressed through racial language within the framework of colonial modernity. She writes, "In the wake of the West's reinvention of its True Christian Self in the transumed terms of the Rational Self of Man, however, it was to be the peoples of the militarily expropriated New World territories (i.e., Indians), as well as the enslaved peoples of Black Africa (i.e., Negroes), that were made to reoccupy the matrix slot of Otherness—to be made into the physical referent of the idea of the irrational/subrational Human Other."[27] Here the language of transumed and reoccupation suggests that the general schema of division and separation underwent a transformation and reinvention, with rational Man taking the space of the true Christian and the irrational Native American and subhuman Black assuming the position of the infidel. "The evangelizing mission of the Church" transformed into, and existed alongside, "the imperializing mission of the state based on its territorial expansion and conquest."[28] This transformation was enabled by an analogy between the obedient Christian, subject to ecclesial authority, and the rational European self, subordinate to the laws of the state.[29] European Man, an offspring of the true Christian self, emerges as the site of order and reason while non-Europeans signify wildness, disorder, and the undefinable space between animal and human. Consequently, the latter must be contained, disciplined, and civilized by the former. The idea of European civilization sublates, and retains, the Christian logic of salvation.

It might seem as if Wynter's story is too linear and abstract. Similarly, it could be argued that her story does not allow for differences between the church and the state, theology and politics. While these concerns are valid, they do not take away from her general claim that a particular way of carving up the earth, of imagining nonhomogeneity, propels and justifies violence against those on the stigmatized side of the division. This grammar of nonhomogeneity, according to Wynter, sneaks into religious and secular paradigms; it is part of Christianity and the secular religion of Man. And as Maldonado-Torres points out, this division, especially within the modern context, is ontological—western Man participates completely in being, while Blacks and other nonconforming peoples exist at the edges of being and nonbeing.[30] Man is positioned in the privileged space of capacity, power, life, and endurance, while Black flesh is the site of lack and excess, death, and instability. Here we should recall Eliade's claims about the intersection of religion and ontology. He writes, "The religious need [of living in a sacred world] expresses an unquenchable ontological thirst. Religious man thirsts for being. His terror of the chaos that surrounds his inhabited world corresponds to his terror of nothingness."[31] To thirst for being is to yearn for a secure position in the world in opposition to looming figures and signifiers of terror and nothingness. This desire involves fabricating rigid distinctions and borders, exemplified in the economy of the sacred or in the color line, as an effort to prevent embodiments of terror from infiltrating zones of being and life, an endeavor that re-creates these zones in order to self-identify as life. Consequently, the strong distinction between being and chaos justifies projects of terror by the agents of being, projects that go under the name of gift, mission, civilization, defense, or the spreading of democracy. The religion of Man, in its thirst for being, is terrifying.

Wynter anticipates the kind of argument that would accuse her of focusing on a particular phase of Man from the early modern period—the fifteenth to eighteenth centuries.[32] This phase includes an image of western bourgeois Man that resembles René Descartes's cogito, which is defined by its ability to represent the world in conformity with reason, or the Kantian subject, which is characterized as the self-legislating source of reason, morality, and value. Some might argue that these philosophical moments are indebted to an old, pre-Darwin metaphysics attached to permanence and stability as conditions for truth.[33] Charles Darwin's ideas, on this reading, introduce the primacy of contingency, variation, and uncertainty in human experience, qualities that would refuse the image of Man and its dualisms. Yet as Wynter points out, Darwin's thought repeats the dividing strategy as it makes a strong distinction between the selected and dysselected within the process of human evolution. According to Wynter, "This principle, that of bio-evolutionary Natural Selection was now to function at the level of the new bourgeois social order as a de facto new Argument-from-Design—one in which one's selected or dysselected status could not be known in advance, it would come to be verified by one's (or one's group's) success or failure in life."[34] Perhaps what is so insidious about Darwin's idea of natural selection is that over time, the term *natural* conceals that this is a reinvention of the human, a new way of carving up populations in terms of the livable and unlivable. This division between the selected and dysselected "would be embodied in . . . the Color line" and used to justify the "instituted relation of socioeconomic dominance/subordination between . . . the lighter and the darker peoples of the earth."[35] This demarcation is another way in which non-Europeans get subordinated to Man and a further way of reinstituting the sacred.

By supplementing Eliade's religious thought with Wynter's diagnosis of colonial modernity, I have shown that Man is a product of various binaries and divisions that resemble the separation between the sacred and the profane—livable/unlivable, inhabitable/uninhabitable, spirit/flesh, and being/nonbeing. Man, according to this framework, consecrates the world through territorial expansion, through "African enslavement, Latin American conquest, and Asian subjugation."[36] While we can consider the settlement of territory a quasi-religious liturgy for the colonizer, Fanon suggests that the colonized also participate in rituals that involve an imaginary passage from the profane to the sacred. In his influential text *Black Skin, White Masks*, Fanon provides a powerful account of the lived experience of Blackness under the regime of Western Man. While it is well known that Fanon uses clinical and psychoanalytic categories to diagnose the effects of the colonial encounter, particularly between France and its Caribbean and African colonies, he uses religious grammar as well.[37] Think, for instance, of an early remark in the introduction: "There is a zone of nonbeing, an extraordinarily sterile and arid region, an incline stripped bare of every essential from which a genuine new departure can emerge. In most cases, the black man cannot take advantage of this descent into a *veritable hell*."[38] The image of descending into hell involves a prior position above death, nonbeing, and the abyss. This assumes that hell is a possibility rather than an ontological condition—or the lot of those whose exclusion from the realm of being is a precondition of ontology. For Fanon, the colonial framework places Blacks in a situation of perpetual violence, suffering, and wretchedness. It produces a hell that Blacks do not have the privilege of descending to—like the dialectical thinker or avant-garde artist—in order to create and produce something new.

Fanon continues to read the condition of the Black through religious tropes in his discussion of language and coloniality. In this discussion, these tropes help to explain the enticements of Man, the attractions of being recognized as fully human, and the transformations that supposedly accompany this recognition. For Fanon, "we must attach a fundamental importance to the phenomenon of language" in part because "the more the black Antillean assimilates the French language, the whiter he gets— i.e., the closer he comes to becoming a true human being."[39] By "possessing language," the colonized subject begins to possess or secure a position in French civilization, the metropolitan culture, the realm of being. But of course this process of becoming human requires the Black to reject and abandon those aspects of their culture—such as dialect and vernacular— that cannot be assimilated into the civilizing movement. "The more the colonized has assimilated the cultural values of the metropolis, the more he will have escaped the bush. The more he rejects his blackness and the bush, the whiter he will become."⁴⁰ Here, Fanon gestures toward Du Bois's understanding of *double consciousness*, a term the latter uses to describe the condition of Blacks in the United States. Among other things, double consciousness names "a peculiar sensation . . . this sense of always looking at one's self through the eyes of others, of measuring one's soul by the tape of a world that looks on in amused contempt and pity."⁴¹ What Fanon and Du Bois are getting at is a certain cut in Georg Wilhelm Friedrich Hegel's notion of mutual recognition; within the framework of anti-Black racism, Black bodies are compelled to imitate values and modes of being that are central to maintaining that anti-Black framework. To learn proper French, to become a subject worthy of recognition, requires one to suppress those aspects of Blackness that are looked on with "contempt and pity." Induction into the human sphere demands a kind of self-alienation, an im/possible separation from one's Black flesh.

In Fanon's context, this duplicity is experienced especially by those who travel from the Caribbean to Europe. The aforementioned distinction between metropolis and bush, developed metropole and backward colony, is an extension of Eliade's contrast between a legible world at the center of the earth and an opaque territory located in the hinterland. By crossing the divide, by passing from the Antilles to France, the Black takes on a new character, a new relationship to being and life. Fanon writes, "The black man who has been to the metropole is a demigod. . . . After a fairly long stay in the metropole, many Antilleans return home to be deified. . . . The black man who has lived in France for a certain time returns home radically transformed."⁴² By becoming a demigod, still below the sanctified status of Man, the elevated Black "creates an aura of magic around himself," an aura that creates both disdain and awe in other Blacks.⁴³ This transformation attests to the fact that the colonizing country is treated as the "holy of holies," while the culture of the colonized people "has been committed to the grave."⁴⁴ As I take it, Fanon is identifying the rites of initiation that promise a conversion from the wretched to the human, from a figure of death to a subject of new life. These rites include language acquisition and a pilgrimage from uncivilized territories to the centers of the colonial world. In Eliade's language, these rites enable a passage from the profane to the sacred. But this enticing religious passage would always be incomplete because, as David Marriot points out in his reading of Fanon, "blackness is the [settled] world's aberration."⁴⁵ The task now is to develop a notion of the sacred and religiosity that is faithful to this aberration.

The Other Sacred and Fanonian Poetics

IN THE SAME WAY that Western Man does not exhaust our understanding of the human, the world-establishing sacred that underwrites coloniality and anti-Black racism does not completely determine how we imagine and perform the sacred. As Jeremy Biles points out, an ambivalence is intrinsic to the notion of the sacred. With a nod to Émile Durkheim and Georges Bataille, Biles distinguishes between the "right-hand" sacred that involves form and purity and the "left-hand" sacred, which is opaque, formless, and ecstatic.[46] The left-hand sacred prompts an engagement with qualities like unsettlement, anguish, and volatility—the necessary flip side of projects of territorial possession and expansion. Perhaps Eliade provides resources for thinking about this alternative religiosity.[47] Recall that Eliade draws from Otto's notion of the holy as a mysterious, awe-inspiring, and terrifying power that exceeds the laws of reason. For Eliade, the manifestation of the sacred is an interruption into the ordinary, an interruption that makes "man sense his profound nothingness."[48] By encountering the holy, Man experiences an identification with "ashes and dust." Hence, the sacred, before becoming the vehicle of settlement and order, is a site of ambivalence (both awe and anguish, attraction and repulsion); it is similarly in excess of form and coherence. In addition to this Otto-inspired description of the holy, Eliade's notion of the threshold can be interpreted against the tendency to bifurcate the sacred and the profane, or settled world and formless territory. He admits, for instance, that the sacred necessarily manifests itself through the profane and that the passage from one to the other, the threshold, is a paradoxical space of opposition and intimacy. Instead of the threshold being an occasion for form to be imposed on the opaque, perhaps the edge is that moment when reliable distinctions break down, when stable forms unravel, and when continuity interrupts the compulsion to be set apart and to set things apart. In other words, what if we associated the sacred with passage, movement, the jagged edge, intimacy, and deformation? And how is this version of the left-hand sacred related to Blackness, decolonizing practices, and alternative forms of sociality?

To read Eliade in this direction would bring him closer to an author like Georges Bataille, whom Biles associates with the left-hand sacred. In Bataille's religious thought, the profane world is defined by instrumental reasoning, meaning making, and the pursuit of projects. The profane world is the order of *things* in which humans separate themselves from other species and other humans through objectification. As beings invested in duration and self-preservation, humans treat the world as a toolbox, as an occasion to advance and further projects. In other words, human survival and endurance rely on treating others as objects and things that are subordinate to various ends and goals.[49] Treating another as an object entails both horizontal and vertical distance; it results from seeing other beings as discontinuous with ourselves. The sacred domain, in contrast, is associated with intimacy and anguish, with encounters and experiences that interrupt investments in being coherent, durable selves. Sacred experiences, such as mysticism, sexual activity, or a festival, momentarily restore the kind of continuity that humans long for but cannot completely attain because of the very qualities that distinguish humans from animals—particularly self-consciousness or the commitment to being a discrete self. Bataille writes, "Man is afraid of the intimate order that is not reconcilable with the order of things. . . . Because man is not squarely within [the intimate order] but only partakes of it through a thing that is threatened in its nature (in the projects that constitute it), intimacy, in the trembling of the individual, is holy, sacred, and suffused with anguish."[50] Religious experience cuts against the fantasy of a coherent self or community, and intimacy feels excessive and anguish filled because humans always have one foot in the order of things, the profane world, the realm that sets the self or collective apart and above others in the attempt to pursue projects. Therefore, Bataille underscores the "constant problem posed by the impossibility of being human without being a thing and of escaping the limits of things without returning to animal slumber."[51]

Unlike Wynter, Bataille does not think enough about the relationship between Man and Europe, or how the self that he takes for granted is the product of dominant western epistemes. At the same time, Bataille reminds us that any reinvention of the human, including Wynter's endeavor, must take seriously the violence internal to projects and the general will to preservation. In other words, any project invested in futurity, goals, and the fulfillment of meaning will, to some extent, restrain those beings, entities, or desires that threaten the success of that project. Consequently, Bataille does not contend that humans can live completely outside of the order of things. Rather, he promotes the kinds of projects and practices that wound our very investment in duration and coherence. If the sacred is that which opens up the self to excess and anguish, or to a "level where clarity . . . is no longer given," then we can still access the sacred only through the everyday realms of language, grammar, aesthetics, and the like.[52] In addition to fiction, music, and film, one genre that expresses this immanent excess is poetry. According to Bataille, "If poetry introduces the strange, it does so by means of the familiar. The poetic is the familiar dissolving into the strange, and ourselves with it."[53] Here, I take it that Bataille is making a connection between poetry and poetics, the latter being the more general study of the ways in which language and grammar operate in literature and on selves. Insofar as Bataille links the dissolution of the familiar within poetry to the dissolution of the self, he clearly sees poetics as more than a literary strategy. Poetics for him is an ethical site, a scene of interactions, tensions, and affective experiences that depart from the disavowed violence of settlement and stabilizing projects. Or, to put it differently, poetics names a mode of relating to the other, to the heterogeneous, that aims for communication through wounds and cuts.[54]

Fanon's *Black Skin, White Masks*, particularly in its style and form, offers a powerful example of poetics being an expression of the sacred that interrupts and overwhelms. As Marriott points out, Fanon's thought enacts a "poetics of dissolution" that cannot be rendered intelligible by the frameworks of meaning that underwrite the "current state of things."[55] Recall that Fanon ascribes much importance to language as a vehicle of colonial power; the acquisition of the French language by the colonized is a rite of initiation into the hallowed space of Western Man. Within this process, language, like civilization, is something to be possessed and taken as property. Yet Fanon also quotes the poet and essayist Paul Valéry's claim that language is "the god gone *astray* in the *flesh*."[56] To go astray is to go off target, to deviate from the normal course. To approach the flesh, as Wynter suggests in her analysis of the spirit/flesh distinction, is to plunge into dark matter that lacks coherence and clear form. Fleshliness is both an indication of permeability and a slippery excess that cannot be fully contained by language or grammar but that a certain way of using and arranging words can expose us to.[57] As I demonstrate, Fanon's writing exemplifies the sacred gone astray, a sense of the sacred that remains faithful to the opacity and surplus of the flesh. He also shows how the language of the colonizer can be used against colonial strategies, to express the dispossession and anguish that accompany projects of possession and capture.

Consider the style and format of "By Way of Conclusion," the final chapter in Fanon's classic text. In this concluding section, Fanon combines essay, aphorism, stream of consciousness, and even prayer. He invites the reader into a succession of exclamations, declarations, self-realizations, and questions, a sequence that does not always cohere. He begins the section by anticipating, "I can already see the faces of those who will ask me to clarify such and such a point or condemn such and such a behavior."[58] Here, Fanon is envisioning those who desire a conclusion that will resolve certain tensions or iron out the kinks in his diagnosis of anti-Blackness and colonial trauma. These might be readers who "believe that the appeals for reason or respect for human dignity can change reality" or appeals that reassure us that racial antagonisms can be overcome without struggle, force, and interruptions to the order of things (interruptions that involve exposing the violence that goes unnamed in the affirmation of reason and humanity).[59] For Fanon, this everyday violence against Blacks is the result of an "ossified" society, a social world that is defined by congealed borders. Fanon attempts to work poetically within this ossified space to gesture toward something different, a gesture that involves taking the reader through a series of tensions, torsions, and cuts. The cut is both a wound and an opening.

These tensions revolve around the relationship between past and future, self and other, and being and nonbeing. Regarding the modalities of time, Fanon seems to argue throughout the conclusion that the past does not determine the future. At times, his rhetoric mimics American optimism as he claims that "the density of History determines none of my acts" or that he has no interest in dwelling on the racial violence of the past.[60] At the same time, he acknowledges that Black selves are locked, to some extent, in a despised body, that "tons of chains, squalls of lashes, and rivers of spit stream over [their] shoulders."[61] Here the words *squall* and *river* connote turbulence and movement; the image of spit streaming alludes to the Black body as the target of ejected excess and flow (and perhaps the violent intimacy between whites and Blacks). By combining a history of cuts and wounds accumulated on Black bodies with signifiers of mobility, flow, and turbulence, Fanon beckons the reader to think beyond a stark contrast between moving forward and looking backward. In fact, when he claims that "still today they are organizing dehumanization rationally" after alluding to Black enslavement and white inhumanity, Fanon acknowledges that the past carries an afterlife that haunts the present and future.[62] Keep in mind that Fanon frequently sounds averse to gazing backward because the precolonial past can be treated as a privileged source of authenticity, meaning, and Eliade-like purity. In response to this tendency to search for an unscathed origin or ground for Blackness, Fanon writes, "But I have not the right to put down roots. I have not the right to admit the slightest patch of being into my existence. I have not the right to become mired by the determinations of the past."[63]

Here, Fanon associates being with roots, with having a secure place in the world, with being mired or held by what the past has established. But the Black past cannot give him a stable ground or foundation; similarly, the idea of a Black civilization cannot provide the assurance of possession, of overcoming the "have-not." Both attempt to cover over or cover up the abyss that Black bodies have been positioned to represent and to protect the non-Black world from.

The tensions and frictions that mark Fanon's relationship to time can also be felt in the way Fanon discusses the self, the "I" that becomes the privileged pronoun repeated throughout the conclusion. The repetitive self-references to an "I" culminate in a statement that riffs on the transcendental subject: "I am my own foundation."[64] While this sounds as though Fanon is elevating the self as the ground of its own existence, we must remember that white existence has relegated Blackness to the edges of being, to a zone of nonbeing. And since Fanon claims that he has been thrown into a world where "things are hurtful" and his words are "fringed with silence," the foundation that Fanon refers to must be wounded, torn, and something like an abyss.[65] Yet this wounded I is not necessarily stuck or incapacitated. Rather, Fanon claims that a kind of leap (through the abyss) involves "introducing invention into life" and imagining a world where creation outstrips confinement and ossification.[66] As mentioned earlier, western Man, the colonizing subject, is also motivated by the desire to create and discover new things; therefore, invention is historically intertwined with expansion, possession, and the erasure of beings and entities considered defunct, or obstacles to discovery and creation. This may explain why Fanon broaches the language of touching—"why not simply try to touch the other, feel the other, discover each other?"[67] The act of touching, and being touched, underscores receptivity and vulnerability in a manner that the logic of appropriation disavows.[68] Even if the touch can always become a violent attempt to clutch or hold the other, Fanon reminds the reader that these violent modes of relating to others are still expressions of touch, a gesture that exposes the self to the other in the moment of contact. Consequently, Fanon's inventing I is always already tied to, and undone by, intimate relationships with others.

The use of the interrogative in the passage just quoted is significant. Throughout the concluding section, Fanon interweaves questions into his declarations and claims. The interrogative, as Martin Heidegger suggests in *Being and Time*, enacts a certain way of relating to the world, of comporting oneself toward subject matter.[69] Rather than making an assertion or a judgment, which often entails a hasty endeavor to project the self onto the world, or the familiar onto the unfamiliar, the question can be a slow seeking after and opening up to something. The proverbial rhetorical question within a text like *Black Skin, White Masks* enables the reader to work through tensions, queries, and paths of thought without aiming for a resolution. In fact, a series of questions interrupts the reader and asks them to pause, stand still, and reflect. At the same time, these questions elicit a response; they prompt the reader to think, ponder, and imagine without the assurance of a definitive answer. Along these lines, Fanon ends the book by performing a prayer: "O my body, always make me a man who questions!"[70] In this final prayer, Fanon implores to be made a man, a dubious request since he has already told the reader that "a black is not a man."[71] Anticipating Wynter, Fanon's work shows how western Man both relies on and rejects Blackness. He gives us a poignant account of what it means to live the antagonistic relationship between Blackness and the human, as constructed by Euro-American modernity. At the same time, he also uses the term *man* throughout the final section and this final prayer to indicate a possibility that is not yet. This new humanity, this alternative sense of *man*, is defined by the question and perhaps comes into existence by questioning, for instance, the racial and gendered dimensions of man, the human, and so forth.[72] Finally, Fanon offers this prayer to his questioning *body*, a body he has already associated with chains, lashes, and spit, with the tornness and permeability of flesh. By calling this cry a "final prayer," Fanon suggests we read *Black Skin, White Masks* as a series of prayers, petitions, and cries toward the reader/listener.[73] And by linking prayer with the Black body, Fanon gestures toward an alternative sense of the sacred, a notion of the sacred that has gone astray in the flesh rather than becoming a placeholder for settlement and possession of the earth.

To be sure, Fanon's poetics only hint at this alternative framing of the sacred. Yet the implications of his thought for religious studies come into focus by juxtaposing his ideas with recent attempts to rethink sacrality and the human. Here, I am especially thinking of Carol Wayne White's brilliant text *Black Lives and Sacred Humanity*, a study that examines the works of Du Bois, Anna Julia Cooper, and James Baldwin in an effort to construct an African American religious naturalism. While I cannot get into the intricacies of White's book, she makes several pertinent moves. For instance, even though she appreciates Eliade's attempt to trace the sacred across different religious traditions, she rejects Eliade's "sense that the sacred is necessarily grounded in a supernatural reality or transcendent order."[74] For White, the sacred is immanent, part of the natural world, and experienced in the profane realm. Sacredness, she contends, is located in relationality and interconnectedness, in human beings' various entanglements with other humans, nonhuman animals, and the processes and vicissitudes of nature. As White puts it, "Sacrality is a specific affirmation and appreciation of that which is fundamentally important in life, or that which is ultimately valued: relational nature."[75] And this affirmation of interdependence resists the kinds of dualisms and oppositions that Wynter associated with nonhomogeneity, dualisms such as "soul/body, spirit/matter, male/female, human/animal, white/black, rich/poor, straight/gay—in which the second half of the pair is seen as alien and subject to the first."[76] Fanon's emphasis on the flesh, the touch, and questioning as a mode of engaging the other certainly has affinities with White's insistence on the relational. Yet Fanon's poetic cries expose White's tendency to link the sacred too closely with purpose, meaning, life, and wholeness, a tendency that diminishes how these well-intentioned ends and aspirations have been implicated in the decimation of the very earth that her project wants to honor. In other words, an ethics of interconnectedness would involve a puncturing/hole more than a will to wholeness, an openness to non-sense and existence at the edges of meaning, and a willingness to engage desires, entities, and beings that refuse teleological ordering. And while I applaud White's attempt to imagine humanity in terms of process and dependence, we must also keep in mind the specter of Man, how new ways of configuring the human are haunted by the coloniality of being, the terror that continues to accompany the human and its projects. An alternative, decolonial conception of the sacred would have to cut against the world-establishing sacred, including those practices and imaginaries that place too much emphasis on purpose and meaning, at the expense of opacity and things that go astray.

Conclusion

MALDONADO-TORRES CORRECTLY alludes to a gap between religious studies scholars and those who study race and politics. The former usually do not consider race and coloniality as central components of modern constructions of religion, while the latter assume that religion is already known and figured out.[77] Following Maldonado-Torres, I have attempted to bridge this gap by juxtaposing Eliade, Wynter, and Fanon. I have argued that a particular notion of the sacred as a signifier for settled territory and the imposition of form onto chaos, a notion of the sacred exemplified in Eliade's thought, provides the underpinning and legitimation for colonial projects. While Eliade briefly acknowledges the connection between the world-establishing sacred and aversion to the opaque and the flesh, Wynter and Fanon show how this antagonism between the sacred/Man and Blackness organizes and structures the modern world. Because a commitment to the sacred is prevalent in religious and secular projects (but often subtler in self-described secular projects), we cannot simply assume that abandoning religion and theological grammars will save us from anti-Black racism or the afterlife of colonization. Instead, I have argued for an alternative sense of the sacred, defined by excess, self-dissolution, and anguish. This volatile sacred, expressed in Fanon's writings and poetics, draws out the disavowed terror of Western Man and its redemptive endeavors. It also becomes a site where an author like Fanon can play with language and grammar in attempting to outline the invention of new forms of intimacy and sociality—through wounds and cuts. In a contemporary situation where Black football players are punished for "desecrating" the flag; where migrant workers from the U.S. South are captured and detained because they threaten to obscure the borders between life and death, us and them, purity and contamination; or where religious terror is primarily associated with radical Islam rather than imperial state projects of war and expansion, a reexamination of the relationship among race, coloniality, and the sacred may provide glimmers of hope within the current order of things.

Notes

1 Chidester, *Savage Systems*, 11.
2 Jonathan Z. Smith argues that the category "religion" will always bear the trace of being imposed from the outside onto Native populations. See Smith, "Religion, Religions, Religious."
3 Maldonado-Torres, "Race, Religion, and Ethics," 693.
4 See Douglas, *Purity and Danger*, 196–220.
5 For a critique of Eliade, see, for instance, McCutcheon, *Manufacturing Religion*. For a more sympathetic reading of Eliade and a critique of McCutcheon, see Biles, "Sacrifice of Domestication," 21–32.
6 Eliade is indebted to Otto's understanding of the divine as a *mysterium tremendum*, a site of awe, mystery, and terror. See Otto, *Idea of the Holy*.
7 Eliade, *Sacred and the Profane*, 20.

8 See Douglas, *Purity and Danger*, 196–220.

9 Eliade, *Sacred and the Profane*, 21.

10 Eliade, *Sacred and the Profane*, 28.

11 Eliade, *Sacred and the Profane*, 25.

12 Eliade, *Sacred and the Profane*, 29.

13 Eliade, *Sacred and the Profane*, 30.

14 Eliade, *Sacred and the Profane*, 31.

15 On a powerful articulation of the relationship between Christian theology, race, and modern spatial imaginaries, see Jennings, "Building Landscapes."

16 Eliade, *Sacred and the Profane*, 47.

17 Eliade, *Sacred and the Profane*, 48.

18 Moten, "Case of Blackness," 180.

19 See Long, *Significations*, 209–11.

20 While Long introduces the language of opacity in *Significations*, he does not develop the implications of the opaque for thinking about sociality, relationality, deterritorialization, excessive practice, and so on. For a more sustained account of opacity, see Glissant, *Poetics of Relation*. For an account of the relationship between opacity and Black aesthetic practice (the slave songs), see Hartman, *Scenes of Subjection*, 35–36.

21 Gilroy, *Black Atlantic*, 36.

22 Eliade, *Sacred and the Profane*, 65. On the relationship between modern racial reasoning and the will to purity (or the tendency toward self-enclosure), see Carter, *Race*. Also see Vesley-Flad, *Racial Purity and Dangerous Bodies*.

23 Du Bois, "Souls of Black Folk," 209.

24 McKittrick, *Demonic Grounds*, 123.

25 Wynter, "Unsettling the Coloniality," 279.

26 See Rivera, *Poetics of the Flesh*, 2. For a distinction between body and flesh, see Spillers, "Mama's Baby, Papa's Maybe," 206.

27 Wynter, "Unsettling the Coloniality," 266.

28 Wynter, "Unsettling the Coloniality," 286.

29 Wynter, "Unsettling the Coloniality," 277.

30 See Maldonado-Torres, "Race, Religion, and Ethics," 700.

31 Eliade, *Sacred and the Profane*, 64.

32 I do not focus on Wynter's distinction between Man 1 and Man 2. For a helpful discussion of the transition from one phase of Man to the other, see McKittrick, *Demonic Grounds*, 124–27. For my purposes, Wynter's story is too linear at this point—the transition from Man 1 to Man 2 maps onto a shift from religious to secular political domination.

33 See, for instance, Dewey, "Influence of Darwin on Philosophy."

34 Wynter, "Unsettling the Coloniality," 310.

35 Wynter, "Unsettling the Coloniality," 311.

36 Wynter, "Unsettling the Coloniality," 263.

37 David Marriott begins to connect the clinical to the spiritual/religious ideas in Fanon's thought in *Whither Fanon?* On this connection, also see J. Kameron Carter's lecture "The Disorders of Love."

38 Fanon, *Black Skin, White Masks*, xii.

39 Fanon, *Black Skin, White Masks*, 1, 2.

40 Fanon, *Black Skin, White Masks*, 2.

41 Du Bois, "Souls of Black Folk," 215.

42 Fanon, *Black Skin, White Masks*, 3.

43 Fanon, *Black Skin, White Masks*, 7.

44 Fanon, *Black Skin, White Masks*, 2.

45 Marriott, *Whither Fanon?*, 316.

46 See Biles, *Ecce Monstrum*, 3–4.

47 On this possibility, see Biles, "Sacrifice of Domestication."

48 Eliade, *Sacred and the Profane*, 10.

49 See Bataille, *Theory of Religion*, 17–42.

50 Bataille, *Theory of Religion*, 52.

51 Bataille, *Theory of Religion*, 53.

52 Bataille, *Theory of Religion*, 57.

53 Bataille, *Inner Experience*, 5.

54 See Bataille, *Inner Experience*, 37, 94.

55 See Marriott, *Whither Fanon?*, 36–37. Marriott makes several brief connections between Bataille and Fanon in this text. For a more sustained attempt to think about the affinities between Bataille and Fanon, see Marasco, *Highway of Despair*.

56 Quoted in Fanon, *Black Skin, White Masks*, 2.

57 For an account of the relationships among language, embodiment, and flesh, see Gordon, *What Fanon Said*, 25.

58 Fanon, *Black Skin, White Masks*, 198.

59 Fanon, *Black Skin, White Masks*, 199.

60 Fanon, *Black Skin, White Masks*, 205.

61 Fanon, *Black Skin, White Masks*, 204.

62 Fanon, *Black Skin, White Masks*, 205.

63 Fanon, *Black Skin, White Masks*, 204–5.

64 Fanon, *Black Skin, White Masks*, 205.

65 Fanon, *Black Skin, White Masks*, 203. For a treatment of the notion of the abyss in the context of decolonial thought, see An, *Decolonial Abyss*.

66 Fanon, *Black Skin, White Masks*, 204.

67 Fanon, *Black Skin, White Masks*, 206.

68 See Merleau-Ponty, *Visible and the Invisible*. Also see Irigaray, *Ethics of Sexual Difference*, 151–84.

69 See Heidegger, *Being and Time*, 24–28

70 Fanon, *Black Skin, White Masks*, 206.
71 Fanon, *Black Skin, White Masks*, xii.
72 For an essay on Fanon's new humanism that focuses on both its significance in Fanon's thought and his intentional reticence on this possibility, see Bernasconi, "Casting the Slough."
73 I am indebted to J. Kameron Carter for our conversations on this issue and insight.
74 White, *Black Lives and Sacred Humanity*, 33.
75 White, *Black Lives and Sacred Humanity*, 33.
76 White, *Black Lives and Sacred Humanity*, 35.
77 See Maldonado-Torres, "Race, Religion, and Ethics," 691–92.

Bibliography

An Yountae. *The Decolonial Abyss: Mysticism and Cosmopolitics from the Ruins.* New York: Fordham University Press, 2016.

Bataille, Georges. *Inner Experience.* Translated by Leslie Ann Boldt. Albany: State University of New York Press, 1988.

Bataille, Georges. *Theory of Religion.* Translated by Robert Hurley. New York: Zone Books, 1989.

Bernasconi, Robert. "Casting the Slough: Fanon's New Humanism for a New Humanity." In *Fanon: A Critical Reader*, edited by Lewis Gordon, T. Denean Sharpley-Whiting, and Renee White, 113–21. Cambridge, MA: Blackwell, 1996.

Biles, Jeremy. *Ecce Monstrum: Georges Bataille and the Sacrifice of Form.* New York: Fordham University Press, 2011.

Biles, Jeremy. "The Sacrifice of Domestication: Theorizing Religion." In *From Influence and Confluence to Difference and Indifference: Studies on History of Religions*, edited by Mihaela Gligor, 15–68. Cluj-Napoca, Romania: Presa Universitara Clujeana, 2015.

Carter, J. Kameron. "The Disorders of Love: A Meditation on the Theological Fanon." Sorensen Lecture, Yale University, April 5, 2011. https://www.youtube.com/watch?v=kr5RPoMlG_w.

Carter, J. Kameron. *Race: A Theological Account.* New York: Oxford University Press, 2008.

Chidester, David. *Savage Systems: Colonialism and Comparative Religion in Southern Africa.* Charlottesville: University of Virginia Press, 1996.

Dewey, John. "The Influence of Darwin on Philosophy." In *The Influence of Darwin on Philosophy and Other Essays*, 1–19. New York: Holt, 1910.

Douglas, Mary. *Purity and Danger: An Analysis of Concepts of Pollution and Taboo.* New York: Routledge, 2002.

Du Bois, W. E. B. "The Souls of Black Folk." In *Three Negro Classics*, 207–391. New York: Avon, 1965.

Eliade, Mircea. *The Sacred and the Profane: The Nature of Religion*. Translated by Willard Trask. New York: Harcourt Brace, 1987.

Fanon, Frantz. *Black Skin, White Masks*. Translated by Richard Philcox. New York: Grove, 2008.

Gilroy, Paul. *The Black Atlantic: Modernity and Double Consciousness*. Cambridge, MA: Harvard University Press, 1993.

Glissant, Édouard. *Poetics of Relation*. Translated by Betsy King. Ann Arbor: University of Michigan Press, 1997.

Gordon, Lewis. *What Fanon Said: A Philosophical Introduction to His Life and Thought*. New York: Fordham University Press, 2015.

Hartman, Saidiya. *Scenes of Subjection: Terror, Slavery, and Self-Making in Nineteenth-Century America*. New York: Oxford University Press, 1997.

Heidegger, Martin. *Being and Time*. Translated by John Macquarrie and Edward Robinson. Cambridge, MA: Blackwell, 1962.

Irigaray, Luce. *An Ethics of Sexual Difference*. Translated by Carolyn Burke and Gillian Gill. Ithaca, NY: Cornell University Press, 1993.

Jennings, Willie. "Building Landscapes: Secularism, Race, and the Spatial Modern." In *Race and Secularism in America*, edited by Jonathon Kahn and Vincent Lloyd, 207–38. New York: Columbia University Press, 2016.

Long, Charles H. *Significations: Signs, Symbols, and Images in the Interpretation of Religion*. Aurora, CO: Davies, 1999.

Maldonado-Torres, Nelson. "Race, Religion, and Ethics in the Modern/Colonial World." *Journal of Religious Ethics* 42, no. 4 (2014): 691–711.

Marasco, Robyn. *The Highway of Despair: Critical Theory after Hegel*. New York: Columbia University Press, 2015.

Marriott, David. *Whither Fanon? Studies in the Blackness of Being*. Stanford, CA: Stanford University Press, 2018.

McCutcheon, Russell. *Manufacturing Religion: The Discourse on Sui Generis Religion and the Politics of Nostalgia*. New York: Oxford University, 1997.

McKittrick, Katherine. *Demonic Grounds: Black Women and the Cartographies of Struggle*. Minneapolis: University of Minnesota Press, 2006.

Merleau-Ponty, Maurice. *The Visible and the Invisible*. Translated by Alphonso Lingis. Evanston, IL: Northwestern University Press, 1968.

Moten, Fred. "The Case of Blackness." *Criticism* 50, no. 2 (2008): 177–218.

Otto, Rudolf. *The Idea of the Holy*. Translated by John Harvey. New York: Oxford University Press, 1958.

Rivera, Mayra. *Poetics of the Flesh*. Durham, NC: Duke University Press, 2015.

Smith, Jonathan Z. "Religion, Religions, Religious." In *Critical Terms for Religious Studies*, edited by Mark Taylor, 269–82. Chicago: University of Chicago Press, 1998.

Spillers, Hortense. "Mama's Baby, Papa's Maybe: An American Grammar Book."
In *Black, White, and In Color: Essays on American Literature and Culture*,
203–29. Chicago: University of Chicago Press, 2003.

Vesley-Flad, Rima. *Racial Purity and Dangerous Bodies: Moral Pollution, Black
Lives, and the Struggle for Justice*. Minneapolis: Fortress, 2017.

White, Carol Wayne. *Black Lives and Sacred Humanity: Toward an African
American Religious Naturalism*. New York: Fordham University Press,
2016.

Wynter, Sylvia. "Unsettling the Coloniality of Being/Power/Truth/Freedom:
Towards the Human, after Man, Its Overrepresentation—an Argument."
CR: New Centennial Review 3, no. 3 (2003): 257–337.

Amy Hollywood

10 Response—
On Impassioned Claims

The Possibility of Doing Philosophy
of Religion Otherwise

> Your troubles
> aren't my troubles
> but that doesn't mean
> they aren't
> trouble.
>
> The arc breaks
> hangs precipitously,
> its jagged end
> promises nothing.
>
> We try to see in the dark,
> to see dark
> when only white is visible
> marking the other.
>
> There.

MAYBE IT HAS BEEN DIFFICULT for philosophy and philosophy of religion, as fields internal to the academy in the United States, Canada, Australia, New Zealand, and western Europe, to take up, to see the impossibility of *not* taking up, the issues of coloniality and race because that would entail acknowledging what Frantz Fanon named so concisely almost sixty years ago; "challenging the colonial world," Fanon argued, "is not a rational confrontation of viewpoints . . . but the impassioned claim by the colonized that *their world is fundamentally different*."[1] Too often, that difference is displaced onto the very definition of what constitutes philosophy and religion. The colonializing subject is said to do philosophy and to have religion—or its properly calibrated secular displacement—whereas the colonized, in their fundamental difference, are defined as not doing philosophy, not having religion, or not having the right *sort* of religion, one that can argue rationally, putatively dispassionately, for its positions and practices. Philosophy, in particular, insists it is the realm of rational argument rather than impassioned claims; only those who play by its rules, use its forms, engage with its terms, are welcome to the discussion. This belies the passion engendering philosophy within the west itself, of course, and more pertinently the passionate attachment to its forms through which it renders other modes of engagement impossible.

The essays collected here demonstrate the ways in which the very conception of philosophy in the modern west is coconstitutive with the colonial project. The stakes could not be higher. If philosophy and philosophy of religion are going to continue, they must be fundamentally dismantled, their terms subjected to detailed critical engagement, and claims to other modes of thought and practice placed not on the peripheries or in the margins of inquiry but at its very heart. To proceed otherwise is at best to consign one's intellectual labor to immediate obsolescence, at worst—and the worst is always in play—to actively maintain a colonialist imaginary and to participate in its ongoing, at times seemingly unkillable project. That project is itself murderous, not only to colonized subjects, as we see across this book, but to the earth itself. There is no way we can survive within its terms, *whoever* we may be, although some of us are able to live for the time being cushioned from that stark reality by the labor and suffering of others. Yet to live within that bubble, to imagine that long-term survival is possible without almost unimaginable changes in how those within the bubble—or those aspiring to it—think and act, is itself a form of irrationality, a madness and an insanity, that is the unhinged product of the western colonialist capitalist project itself. (Within the colonialist and capitalist logic of the modern west, there will always be *more*—more territory to conquer, more labor to exploit, more resources to deplete, more knowledge to gain, more problems to conquer. Hence the techno-cratic fantasy that the climate crisis can be *managed*, that new forms of technology will save us while at the same time allowing us to continue to grow, expand, take up as much room as humanly possible.)

A transformed philosophy and philosophy of religion demand atten-tion to particularity and with it to history. How to think the relationship between the particular claims of history and the putatively universal—I prefer the language of generalizable—claims of philosophy is of vital con-cern to the work in this volume and to the larger project of which it is a part.[2] Eleanor Craig argues, following Michel Foucault, that history is always a history of the present and yet also demonstrates that it is not only that. The assertion that modern philosophy is coconstitutive with colonialism is, among other things, a historical claim; as many contribu-tors show, it matters when and how this happened. As An Yountae argues, moreover, the idea that secularism is a putatively neutral "outside" to the specifically Christian project of early modern colonialism does not with-stand scrutiny. "The problem of colonialism exceeds the modern binary framework of religion and the secular," An rightly argues. "Colonialism is coconstitutive not only with religion but also with the secular" (chap-ter 7 in this volume).

And yet philosophy still matters. There are at least two reasons for this. First, as Joseph R. Winters and others insist, following Fanon, Sylvia Wynter, and, more recently, Nelson Maldonado-Torres, the constitution of Western Man (as Wynter names him) as distinct from all of his others is ontological; "Western Man participates completely in being, while Blacks and other nonconforming peoples exist at the edges of being and nonbeing" (Winters, chapter 9 in this volume).[3] Here, the discourses of colonialism and coloniality are supplemented by those of race and of other unspecified forms of nonconformity.[4] The question of how and when this occurs is also both a philosophical and a historical one.[5] What is clear is that within the logic of the western philosophical imaginary, the colo-nized, as they are variously configured racially, but most often and most starkly in terms of Blackness, become the paradoxically and murderously literal figure for both lack and excess, embodiment and death. Modern western ontology depends on this opposition, and as such the challenge must be an ontological one. To accept the opposition between the ontological fullness of Man and the contingency of all his lacking, dispersed, particular others would be to capitulate to the very philosophical logic that renders them invisible (and all too starkly visible as matter out of place and in need of erasure).

This leads to my second argument for why philosophy matters. The goal is not to replace the false universality of Western Man with another universal, itself inevitably destined to erase those who do not fit within it. The goal, instead, is to uncover the unquestioned generalizations with which we think and that shape our actions, our affective lives, and our very beings. Race and coloniality, as well as gender, sex, sexuality, ability, and class, are among the generalizable terms with which we think and in terms of which we live—not always everywhere and not inevitably but now in this time and here in this place. Other times and places may well work with different conceptual frames—and some of these other modes of generalizability might help contemporary philosophy in the west imagine itself differently. Some conception of god or the gods—perhaps better the sacred—and ideas about good and evil, about nature, and about the interplay of praxis and theory also shape the ways in which human lives and communities are constituted. For this reason, philosophy of religion in its particularity, but critically shorn of its overwhelmingly Christian grounding, remains vital to thinking decolonially, postcolonially, anticolonially.

Like many contributors to this volume, I do not think that philosophy is the only site in which valuable conceptual work happens—philosophers are not found only in departments of philosophy. Mayra Rivera, for example, in exploring Wynter's work on religion, points to literature as a crucial resource for thinking otherwise. At the same time, she asks whether literature can truly replace the counterhegemonic force Wynter at times finds within religion. While Rivera, like Wynter and like J. Kameron Carter and Filipe Maia in this volume, finds literature an important resource for thinking against the constraints of Western Man, she wonders whether more fully embodied rituals might be necessary to "cultivate affective orientations and intentionally re-create ourselves." "Are the humanities," Rivera asks, "equipped to guide us toward this sense of embodied counterpoetics as both imaginative discourse and transformative practice—to counter the colonial and capitalist forces that shape our being? Do we need to invent new rituals, a counteraesthetic and a counterethics?" (chapter 2 in this volume).

Rivera's questions serve as a reminder that for centuries within the west, philosophy was itself understood as a form of embodied practice, as of course is Christianity.[6] That these particular forms of practice were and are often debilitating ones grounded in claims to self-mastery over putatively recalcitrant passions, bodies, or flesh renders them no less apt as sites for reflection on the work we want philosophy and religion (and the arts) to play for us now. Of course, as Carter rightly notes, Christianity is not as hegemonic and singular as Wynter's "Western Man" might suggest (chapter 6 in this volume).

Philosophical or conceptual approaches to the issues of race and coloniality also serve as reminders that the problems are not solely historical. There is a real danger in certain forms of historicism that would seek some site of pure origins, a realm untouched by the colonializing and imperialist projects of western Europe. Such projects often result in forms of ascetic purification that are profoundly debilitating to the very communities they hope to serve. Moreover, as so many of the essays collected here show, coloniality is historically enacted not only on the bodies but also on the *imaginations* of its subjects, both the colonized and the colonizing. For the colonizer, or those who live in the space of colonizing privilege, giving up the material advantages that come with that position necessarily involves some form of mourning. Yet not only material privilege needs to be renounced and mourned. The *imaginary of coloniality*, as it affects both the colonized and the colonizer, is also an object of loss. To refuse to acknowledge that loss and think about its effects, is, I think, to run the danger of continually repeating the trauma of the colonial project itself. How this is experienced differentially by the colonizer and the colonized, moreover, is vital to present and future shared philosophical, political, ethical, and religious engagements. On the one hand, on some deep level, the losses that face the colonizer and those already undergone by the colonized might render it too soon even to talk about shared projects—and as the Bataillean aspects of a number of the essays collected here suggest, *project* may be the wrong word entirely. Yet, on the other hand, the very distinction between colonized and colonizer is often too sharp, too dualistic, too uncomplicated even to name our differences and what it would mean to work together in the face of them. (Where does gender fit here? Class, sexuality, ableism? The differences of colorism? There are no easy answers to these questions.)

What is clear to me is that the legacies of coloniality, capitalism, and racism are inextricably bound and are all linked in fundamental ways to religion, to loss, and so to mourning and melancholia. Sigmund Freud helps us to see this, even as his own work participates in that colonizing enterprise. His first substantive engagement with religion, the much-lambasted and long-ignored *Totem and Taboo* (1913), brings together issues vital to the essays collected here in ways that demand both acknowledgment and critical analysis. *Totem and Taboo* is about, among other things, the violence of the colonial project, the ambivalent jubilation and mourning to which that violence gives rise among the colonizers, the ways in which the murdered other is cannibalistically incorporated into its killer, and the haunting figure of the devoured other that continues to mark colonizing discourse. The enlightened modern western subject, Freud unwittingly shows, depends on the incorporation of the "savage" other for its authority. Following suggestions made here by Carter and Maia, I want to ask what happens if this act of cannibalism is acknowledged? How might— how can—it be redressed? And what if one is that other who has been devoured? What continuing life in death remains for the colonized? Even to ask these questions requires first that we understand what Freud, in *Totem and Taboo*, shows about the place of cannibalism within the constitution of the western psyche.

Critics have detailed *Totem and Taboo*'s racism, sexism, and reliance on an equally suspect—both ideologically and scientifically, if we can pretend to separate the two—anthropology.[7] Even the existence of the subject matter of the four essays—totemism, animism, and taboo—has been challenged (many would argue that totemism is undone by Claude Lévi-Strauss). In good psychoanalytic fashion, moreover, the book has been read as an enactment of the "scientific myth" it describes. Just as the father of the primal horde must fight off—and finally fails to fight off—the murderous rage of his sons, so Freud here fights off Carl Jung's challenge to Freud's supremacy within that "science" he purports to have discovered. Freud uses a story about the origins of civilization among the savages to stave off a threat to his preferred story about the origins of psychoanalysis.

I do not contest any of these arguments, all of which I think are right. I want to add to and nuance them, showing that by the end of *Totem and Taboo*—as also in Freud's later works on religion, morality, and civilization—the very antithesis between the savage and the civilized is profoundly troubled by their cannibalistic intertwining. On the one hand, Freud seems to argue, the most civilized are, finally, the most savage, at least toward themselves (in the texts written during and after World War I, clearly also toward each other). Some left-wing Freudians later try to argue that this makes the savage the most civilized, but Freud's wartime and postwar pessimism make it difficult to discern such a position in his work. For Freud, in the end, we are all savages. Yet even as I find something right and compelling about this set of claims, it is vital to see that Freud is also actively covering over the scene of his own crime—not toward Jung or other followers, although there might be crimes there as well, but toward the colonized, the so-called savages on whom his argument at least in part rests. By taking as given the stories of savage rituals and practices for which he admits there is no evidence, Freud covers over the crime of coloniality and the colonial "science" of anthropology itself.

But how do we get from savagery to civilization and then, as I want to argue, back again? What is exposed by Freud in this movement, and what is covered over? As I have mentioned, *Totem and Taboo* is above all else a story of origins. In it, Freud purports to show how the faint beginnings of civilization can be found among so-called primitive people and, more important, how these first prohibitions come about. He identifies the origin of human civilization with two founding prohibitions, prohibitions that he argues are essential to what anthropologists describe as totemism: the law against killing the totem animal and that against engaging in sexual acts with those attached to one's totem group. The theories of totemism with which Freud works argue that in primitive societies, groups identify with a specific animal—the totem—and often believe themselves to have descended from that animal. The animal cannot be killed, except at times in highly ritualized settings. In some societies, one cannot even say the name of the totem. And, according to these accounts, one can never marry inside one's totem group. Freud has to do a lot of maneuvering with the anthropological sources to get to the claim that there are *two* defining characteristics of totemism, for many more prohibitions are associated with totemism in the late nineteenth- and early twentieth-century anthropological literature. Freud himself admits that many anthropologists question whether there is a close connection between the two prohibitions he wants so keenly to link together, yet he insistently deploys their writings to argue that these two prohibitions are the key to totemism. Psychoanalysis, he claims, is not necessary to reach this conclusion.

Anthropologists, according to Freud, have not been able to explain where these prohibitions come from and whence their force. Here, Freud argues (although he will soon take back the claim), psychoanalysis is required. More modestly, he writes, psychoanalysis "casts a single beam of light."[8] The key, for Freud, lies in the close link between totemism's two prohibitions and those associated with the origins of the individual psyche as constituted through the Oedipus complex, Freud's understanding of the human psyche as constituted through and by the prohibition against killing the father and committing incest with the mother. Freud starts (over a hundred pages into the book) with the presumption that the totem animal is the father. "The first result of our substitution," Freud writes, "is very curious."

> If the totem animal is the father, then the two chief commandments of totemism, the two taboo prescriptions which form its nucleus, not to kill the totem and not to have sexual intercourse with any woman belonging to the totem, coincide in their content with the two crimes of Oedipus, who killed his father and took his mother as his wife, and with the two primal desires of the child, insufficient repression or reawakening of which perhaps forms the core of all psychoneuroses. If this equation is more than a misleading trick of chance, it should allow us to cast a light on the distant origins of totemism. In other words, we should succeed in making it appear likely that the totemistic system arose out of the conditions of the Oedipus complex. (132)

Yet does Freud make a case for understanding "this equation" as more than chance? And if it does have some purchase, what does it tell us about the origins of civilization, the origins of the individual psyche, and the relationship between the two? Even more pointedly, what does it tell us that we cannot learn elsewhere? (And why does this question—or does this question—matter to Freud?)

The last issue is crucial, for in order to make this equation between the totem and the father and to authorize the subsequent account of the way in which prohibitions are constituted and handed down in relationship to the totem or father, Freud places himself—and the authority of psychoanalysis—between two secular giants: Charles Darwin and W. Robertson Smith. (The latter is by far the less well known but, as I will show, the one for whom Freud reserves his highest accolades.) It is not quite right, then, to say that Freud starts with the presumption of the identity between the father and the totem (although one might say the psychoanalytic argument proper begins there), for Freud wishes also to locate this father within *history*. To do so, he turns to Darwin and certain anthropologists who elaborate on a hypothesis put forward by Darwin about "the primal social state of man." The question, remember, is whence the dread of incest stems.

> Darwin concluded from the habits of the higher primates that mankind, too, first lived in small hordes within which the jealousy of the oldest and strongest male prevented sexual promiscuity. . . . "Therefore, if we look far enough back in the stream of time . . . the most probable

view is that primaeval man aboriginally lived in small communities, each with as many wives as he could support and obtain, whom he would have jealously guarded against all other men. Or he may have lived with several wives by himself, like the gorilla; for all the natives 'agree that but one adult male is seen in a band; when the youngest male grows up, a contest takes place for mastery, and the strongest, by killing and driving out the others, establishes himself as the head of the community.' (Dr Savage, in *Boston Journal of Natural History*, vol. V, 1845–47, p. 423). The younger males, being thus expelled and wandering about, would, when at last successful in finding a partner, prevent too close interbreeding within the limits of the same family." [Freud is here citing Darwin's *Descent of Man*; Darwin cites Savage.] (126–27)

From the uncanny appearance of a "Dr. Savage" erupting within Freud's text to the relentless circularity of Freud's argument, there is much more to say about this passage than I have space for here. Freud juxtaposes this account of men and gorillas with a psychoanalytic case history, one in which a little boy's fear of his father takes the form of an animal phobia. He then moves to the conclusion just cited. Yet if he has Sandòr Ferenczi's "Little Árpàd," why does he need Darwin? (Why will he need Smith?) Freud wants both to claim a specific set of insights for psychoanalysis *and* to ground his account of the origins of civilization—and that of the origins of the psyche—not solely on psychoanalytic evidence but on history, or what he calls "the deed."

So also, then, Freud's turn to Smith, "the physicist, philologist, biblical exegete and classical researcher who died in 1894, a man as many-sided as he was clear-eyed and free-thinking" (133). From Darwin, Freud gets the primal horde of brothers, jealous of the father's wives, who then kill the father and bed the mother(s). The prohibitions against these two acts, Freud argues, are grounded in their commission. The question Freud never quite poses but that I think is crucial for *Totem and Taboo*, and specifically for Freud's turn to Smith, is how guilt over the murder of the father and incestuous relations with the mother is passed from generation to generation. Why do the sons' descendants share in their fathers' guilt and honor the prohibitions that guilt puts in place? How are the prohibitions that lead to totemism *handed down*? Once again, the key is not found within psychoanalysis itself but within the study of religion.

Smith is most famous for *The Religion of the Semites* (1889), in which he argues for the sacrificial nature of ancient religion. He shows, Freud writes, that sacrifice—the sacred act par excellence (sacrificium, ieronrgia)—originally had a meaning other than the one it acquired in later times: an offering to the deity in order to propitiate him or gain his favor. (It was from the subsidiary meaning of self-denial that the secular use of the word emerged.) At the first, the sacrifice was demonstrably nothing other than "an act of social fellowship between the deity and his worshippers," a communion of the faithful with their god. (133)[9]

Freud subordinates the later, secular meaning of the term *sacrifice*—self-denial or renunciation—to its putatively original meaning of fellowship with God. Yet he goes on to argue that (1) sacrifice binds the community together around its god; (2) the bonds depend on "repetition in order to be reinforced and made to endure" (135); and (3) the bonds are formed in and through the mourning and guilt occasioned by "the sacramental killing and communal consumption" of the father or of the totem associated with the father. The repetition of the primal murder—for that, finally, is what sacrifice is for Freud—also "refreshed and ensured" the community members' "likeness with the god" (138). The repetition is both an indulgence *and* a renunciation, for the killing of the father is both desired and mourned.

Mourning and guilt are at the center of sacrifice for Smith (according to Freud), and they are also key to Smith's hypothesis concerning what he calls "the totem meal." To get from the altar sacrifice of the Semites back to totemism (a move Smith finds necessary to make his claim about the sacrificial nature of all ancient religion), Smith has to hypothesize something like a sacrificial rite at the center of primitive society, hence the totem meal, in which the totem is ritually killed and eaten by the community. Freud himself acknowledges that there is no "direct observation" of the totem meal among primitive peoples (although he follows Smith in trying to suggest some possible examples.) Everything rests, for Smith as for Freud, on one story. "St. Nilus," Freud writes, a source putatively from the fifth century,

> gives an account of the sacrificial custom of the Bedouins in the Sinai Desert around the end of the fourth century AD. The sacrifice, a camel, was bound and laid upon a crude altar of stones; the leader of the tribe made the participants pass singing three times around the altar, inflicted the first wound upon the beast and greedily drank the blood that poured out; then the whole community fell upon the victim, hacked out pieces of its quivering flesh with their swords and devoured it raw in such haste that in the brief interval between the rising of the

morning star for which this sacrifice was made, and the fading of the stars before the sun's rays, the whole of the sacrificial animal, its body, bones, skins, flesh and innards had been devoured. This barbaric and clearly very ancient rite was, all indications suggest, not an isolated custom, but the universal and original form of the totemic sacrifice which would later be watered down in various ways. (138–39)

This sacrificial meal, then, comes together with Freud's Darwinian account of the primal horde to create what he will later call a "scientific myth" about the origin and continuity of civilization.

In this account, which appears in six dense pages of *Totem and Taboo*, Freud locates mourning and lamentation, guilt and remorse, as well as identification and desire, at the heart of human civilization. Freud poses the problem as one of bringing together the Darwinian primal horde and totemism, two (utterly speculative) historical "facts" that seem to have nothing to do with each other. The former depends on hierarchy; the latter is constituted by "bands of men consisting of members who enjoy equal rights and are subject to the restrictions of the totemistic system and inheritance along the matriarchal line" (141). How can the one emerge from the other? The totem meal brings the two together.

So Freud writes:

One day the expelled brothers joined forces, killed and devoured their father and thus put an end to the father's horde. United, they risked and accomplished something that the individual could not have achieved. (It might be that a cultural advance, perhaps the use of a new weapon, had given them a feeling of superiority.) It was thought natural among such cannibalistic savages to eat their victim. The violent primal father had certainly been the feared and envied model for each of the brothers. Now, by eating him, they accomplished their identification with him, and each of them appropriated a piece of his strength. The totem meal, perhaps humanity's first feast, could be seen as the repetition and commemoration of this curious, criminal deed that saw the beginning of so many institutions—social organization, moral restrictions and religion. (141–42)

Freud assumes here that one moves from the primal horde to cannibalism, thence to the ritual repetition of that act (the totem meal), and thence to totemism itself. In other words, the sacrifice precedes the totem. Yet what has most decisively occurred in this passage is the beginning of an account of how idealization, identification, and internalization (the putatively intrapsychic) are constituted and *handed down* (the interpsychic).

The sons identify with the father. They envy and idealize him, and when they kill him—when he is lost to them—they literally take him inside of themselves. Yet with this act of cannibalism, the sons not only come to be the father but also internalize the father's prohibitions. "The dead man," Freud writes, "now becomes stronger than the living man had been" (142). He becomes so strong, in fact, that he demands constant commemoration—and a constant re-creation of the crime against him—around which the community is formed and re-formed. The father haunts the sons, even as—perhaps even more powerfully because—he has been eaten by them. (Yet, of course, Freud is caught in a temporal a priori here, for the brothers must already have formed a community in order for the initial murder to have occurred.) We are born, then, into communities of mourning, melancholia, and haunting, communities founded on the murder of the father and the constantly repeated, recriminative internalization of his law.

Yet if the Oedipus complex itself explains the foundation of the ego and the superego—that critical agency in which the prohibitions of the father are internalized and we become self-critical, moral, scientific—in a word, secular—then why the insistence on the primal horde and the totem meal? Why the continual recursive and circular explanations of the one in terms of the other? Why turn to Darwin and Smith? Why take the intensively speculative risks of an invented history? At the end of the day, there is no historical evidence for the totem meal, that mechanism by which Freud claims that prohibition and guilt are handed down. Freud himself *shows* us this. So why does he continue to insist, against his own evidence, that there is or was *a deed*?

One answer lies in Freud's anxiety about the status of psychoanalytic argument itself. Freud, in *Totem and Taboo,* appears to fear the independence of psychoanalytic explanations, an independence for which he himself fought. Psychoanalysis, as Freud will worry in *The Future of an Illusion,* is itself in danger of looking too much like religion, like an illusion driven by the desire of its practitioners. So even as Freud insists on the desire and affect driving the primal horde and instituting totemism, he also insists on the *historicity* of *the deed* and, more pointedly, of the totem meal, the sacrifice at the heart of all culture. There must be a deed if psychoanalysis itself is to be rational, clear-eyed, real—secular.

There must be a deed if Freud's scientific myth is to be understood as something other than an illusion generated by his desire. If the deed is fantasy, then so too might be psychoanalysis and the society on which it is built. Yet it is Freud's desire that civilization restrain desire and that psychoanalytic knowledge might be untainted by desire that drives *Totem and Taboo*. He wants, finally, to transmute religious sacrifice into secular renunciation. Freud purports to renounce desire in the name of critique, even as he enacts the irrationality at the core of critical reason—the desire to renounce desire itself. Hence, the fantasy of the primal horde and the totem meal is the fantasy of a civilization grounded in renunciation and of a science that does not rest on fantasy.

That is one reading of Freud's bizarre speculations in *Totem and Taboo*, and I think it is right as far as it goes. But there is another, more pressing and more pertinent reading that speaks directly to the issues raised by the essays gathered here. For Freud's insistence on *the deed* covers over the founding crime on which his speculation rests, that of colonialism itself. The anthropological literature on which Freud depends is a vital part of the colonial enterprise. That project requires anthropology, in which European savagery is displaced, continuously, onto those whose land and resources and bodies it exploits. At the heart of these displacements and disfigurations is the figure of the cannibal, as Carter and Maia pointedly show. The question, always, is who is eating whom.[10] In the fever dream that is coloniality, the savage, the native, the other, eats the European or continually threatens to do so.[11] But as Carter shows in his reading of Aimé Césaire, Césaire knew that the true cannibal was the European himself, re-creating his Christian rituals through the incorporation of those others whose very existence he simultaneously refuses to acknowledge. Within such a system, the other can only be read as shit, detritus, that which literally cannot be absorbed into the colonializing digestive system (see Carter, chapter 6 in this volume).

So while I think Maia is right that some kind of cannibalism is always at work in our relationship to others and that we are always, in some way, haunted by those we incorporate—and hence there can never be a pure origin free of the intermixing logic of a sociality grounded in identification and incorporation—I also think the logic of coloniality submerged, buried, and negated in Freud's account of melancholic incorporation complicates the Freudian story in new ways (see Maia, chapter 8 in this volume). *Totem and Taboo* and "Mourning and Melancholia" are crucial texts in Freud's corpus, for they lead to his claim in *The Ego and the Id* (1923) that every psyche is structured melancholically. We are all cannibals, psychically, for we all incorporate those others we lose or fear to lose.

The superego is the incorporated, cannibalized father, the one whose pro-hibitions become, Freud insists, our own.

Yet what does it mean for Freud's account of the psyche if a key feature of its landscape comes to him not only through his work with Europeans on the couch but through his deployment of anthropological literature grounded in the colonial enterprise? This analysis of Freud leads me—a person of European descent, deeply implicated in the logics of Christian-ity, western philosophy, and psychoanalysis—to ask, Who am I, and to what extent does my very sense of self and community depend on the ex-ploited, colonized, devalued others whom I eat in order to sustain my-self? How can I recognize the other within without furthering the project of exploitation or simply shitting out that which is unassimilable to my delicate digestion? How does western European and American philoso-phy, which demands the questions psychoanalysis asks, decolonize itself? What Freud enables me to see clearly is that the liberal and neoliberal logic of inclusion will not do. Inclusion *is* cannibalism, yet another itera-tion of that murderous project.

The essays collected here lead me to that observation, but they them-selves often do a different kind of work. For my analysis of Freud, like many of the essays collected here, asks the crucial question, What of the colonized? What of those who are eaten, cannibalized by western colo-nialism and the philosophy, theology, and psychoanalysis that ground and are grounded by it? What does it mean to *be* the specter who haunts the western European and American imaginary? Is there, as Nicolas Abra-ham argues, some way in which a phantom always remains outside, un-incorporated and unincorporable, no matter how hard those riven with melancholia try to assimilate it fully through their ritual totem meals and feasts of psychic incorporation?[12] How might that phantom—always out-side even as it is also within—be configured as occupying a space in and out of which the other always and under duress continues to live? Not as shit, or not only as shit, but as human. (Of course, shit is brown or black, rendering the racialization of these issues inescapable.)[13] This is not to deny that the colonized also mourn.[14] On the contrary, mourning may be taken as constitutive of colonized life; the colonized mourn the losses they undergo as the subjects of colonialism—even as colonial ideology denies that these losses occur, that they are truly losses, or that they are losses in any way that matters, hence redoubling the trauma of mourning itself—but also, and even more complexly, the loss of the colonial imagi-nary as itself an ambivalently held attachment. (Fanon again is vital to telling this story.) But how that mourning is lived, experienced, configured, and reconfigured will differ radically for different groups, precisely because of the continuing violence wrought by colonialism.

All of us, everywhere, need different rituals, different imaginaries, different forms through which to mourn and through which to live. I do not know what they will look like. I do not know who has already invented them or who will bring them into the future. I suspect that they will involve what Georges Bataille called the left and the right sacred—abjection and ecstasy, rupture and rapture, fighting against the void and living together within it—even as these aspects of the sacred will be experienced in radically different ways by those with power and those without. And I know that the past will be hard to evade, the other within—the colonized in the colonizer; the disavowed, seemingly unmournable because never really human colonized in the colonized; *and* the colonizer in the colonized—will be difficult, perhaps impossible, ever fully to expel.[15] Attention to ghosts, to that which refuses assimilation into melancholic processes of incorporation and erasure, will be crucial. As I understand philosophy, if, as I hope, philosophy can be decolonized and decolonializing, if, as I know, philosophy always exists outside of the frame of its western appropriation, this is precisely the work philosophy requires, the work it is required to do—the therapeutic task of analysis, critique, and self-exposure through which "the impassioned claim by the colonized that their world is fundamentally different" can continue to be made and can be heard. This is a world in which the phantom speaks and mourns and lives.

Notes

1   Fanon, *Wretched of the Earth*, 6, quoted in An Yountae's chapter in this volume. The emphasis is An's. Fanon's book first appeared in French in 1961.
2   The work of Jacques Derrida is crucial to my thinking here, particularly early work in which generalizability is a key conceptual tool. See, for example, Derrida, "Signature Event Context."
3   For a powerful critique and deployment of Wynter's work, see Rivera, chapter 2 in this volume.
4   As An Yountae and Eleanor Craig show in the introduction to this volume, colonialism, postcolonialism, and coloniality are analytically distinct. The relationship of colonialism and imperialism, however, is largely unaddressed within the volume. It is also vital to remember that Western Europe is not

the only source of colonial and imperialist projects, although modern western forms of coloniality are the focus of this volume.

5 My thanks to Adrián Emmanuel Hernández for reminding me of this point. As Hernández rightly notes, Fanon himself moves from a focus on race in *Black Skin, White Masks* to one on coloniality in *The Wretched of the Earth*, yet Hernández insists that it would be wrong to read this as a progression or maturation in Fanon's work, as some have. Debates between Afropessimism and theories of decoloniality, Hernández shows, can be seen as emerging in part out of which aspect of Fanon is given primacy. Adrián Emmanuel Hernández, email to the author, November, 9, 2019. As Afropessimist thinkers show, anti-Blackness is crucial to the colonial enterprise, which is itself inextricably linked to capitalism. Given the conceptual and historical complexities of the issues involved and my own competencies, for the purposes of this response I will speak primarily in terms of colonialism and coloniality—even as Blackness haunts the essay, as it does much of my work in ways with which I still need to contend.

6 A crucial reference here is Hadot, *Philosophy as a Way of Life*.

7 Anthropologists were critical of the book very early on. The literature is large, but for a powerful account with a full bibliography, see Brickman, *Aboriginal Populations*. See also DiCenso, *Other Freud*.

8 Freud, *Totem and Taboo*, 127. Hereafter cited parenthetically in the text.

9 There are translation issues here that require further analysis.

10 There is also the question of the status of cannibal stories. For a skeptical account of claims to cannibalism among the Pacific Islanders, see Obeyesekere, *Cannibal Talk*. On thinking anthropology as philosophy, see Viveiros de Castro, *Cannibal Metaphysics*.

11 With "fever dream" I am echoing words recently said to me by Noreen Khawaji responding to a different piece of my writing. The event was at Yale University on November 1, 2019.

12 See Abraham, "Notes on the Phantom." Again, my thanks to Adrián Hernández for this crucial point.

13 There is an irony in the exception. Nothing suggests that a human organism is unhealthy more than white or pale shit.

14 There is a large and rich literature on mourning in Black life, for example. For one crucial recent discussion, see Sharpe, *In the Wake*.

15 Judith Butler's work on queer lives and the inability to recognize queer death as death echoes throughout my argument here, pointing to the key role that sexuality—and I would add gender—plays in this argument. The colonial other is not the only other whose death is unrecognizable. In addition, arguments close to that suggested here are made in trans studies. See, in particular, Awkward-Rich, "Trans, Feminism." My thanks to Siobhan Kelly for bringing this essay to my attention.

Bibliography

Abraham, Nicolas. "Notes on the Phantom: A Complement to Freud's Meta-psychology." Translated by Nicholas Rand. *Critical Inquiry* 13 (1987): 287–92.

Awkward-Rich, Cameron. "Trans, Feminism: Or Reading like a Depressed Transfeminist." *Signs* 42 (2017): 819–41.

Brickman, Celia. *Aboriginal Populations in the Mind: Race and Primitivity in Psychoanalysis*. New York: Columbia University Press, 2003.

Derrida, Jacques. "Signature Event Context." In *Margins of Philosophy*, by Jacques Derrida, translated by Alan Bass, 307–30. Chicago: University of Chicago Press, 1985.

DiCenso, James. *The Other Freud: Religion, Culture and Psychoanalysis*. New York: Routledge, 1998.

Fanon, Frantz. *Black Skin, White Masks*. 1952. Translated by Richard Philcox. New York: Grove, 2008.

Fanon, Frantz. *The Wretched of the Earth*. 1961. Translated by Constance Farrington. New York: Grove, 1963.

Freud, Sigmund, *The Ego and the Id*. 1923. Translated by James Strachey. New York: Norton, 1990.

Freud, Sigmund, *The Future of an Illusion*. 1927. Translated by James Strachey. New York: Norton, 1989.

Freud, Sigmund. "Mourning and Melancholia." 1917. In *On Murder, Mourning and Melancholia*, by Sigmund Freud, translated by Shaun Whiteside, 201–18. London: Penguin, 2005.

Freud, Sigmund. *Totem and Taboo*. 1913. In *On Murder, Mourning and Melancholia*, by Sigmund Freud, translated by Shaun Whiteside, 1–166. London: Penguin, 2005.

Hadot, Pierre. *Philosophy as a Way of Life: Spiritual Exercises from Socrates to Foucault*. Edited by Arnold Davidson. Hoboken, NJ: Wiley-Blackwell, 1995.

Obeyesekere, Gananath. *Cannibal Talk: The Man-Eating Myth and Human Sacrifice in the South Seas*. Berkeley: University of California Press, 2005.

Sharpe, Christina. *In the Wake: On Blackness and Being*. Durham, NC: Duke University Press, 2016.

Smith, William Robertson. *The Religion of the Semites*. 1894. New York: Routledge, 2017.

Viveiros de Castro, Eduardo. *Cannibal Metaphysics*. Edited and translated by Peter Skafish. Minneapolis: University of Minnesota Press, 2017.

CONTRIBUTORS

AN YOUNTAE is Assistant Professor of Religious Studies at California State University, Northridge. He specializes in religions of the Americas with a particular focus in Latin American intellectual history, Africana philosophy, and decolonial thought. He is the author of *The Decolonial Abyss: Mysticism and Cosmopolitics from the Ruins* (2016). He is currently completing his second monograph, tentatively titled "The Coloniality of the Secular: Theorizing Race and Religion in the Americas."

ELLEN ARMOUR is Associate Dean for Academic Affairs and the E. Rhodes and Leona Carpenter Chair in Feminist Theology at Vanderbilt Divinity School. Her research interests are in feminist theology; theories of sex, race, gender, disability and embodiment, and visual culture; and contemporary continental philosophy. She is the author of *Deconstruction, Feminist Theology, and the Problem of Difference: Subverting the Race/Gender Divide* (1999) and *Signs and Wonders: Theology after Modernity* (2016) and coeditor of *Bodily Citations: Judith Butler and Religion* (2006).

J. KAMERON CARTER is Professor of Religious Studies and Co-Director of the Center for Religion and the Human at Indiana University Bloomington. He works in Black studies, drawing on the tools and resources of religious studies, philosophical and political theology, and aesthetics in doing so. He is the author of *Race: A Theological Account* (2008) and *The Religion of Whiteness: An Apocalyptic Lyric* (forthcoming). Additionally, his book manuscript "Black Rapture: A Poetics of the Sacred" is in the final stages of preparation.

ELEANOR CRAIG is Program Director and Lecturer of the Standing Committee on Ethnicity, Migration, Rights at Harvard University's Faculty of Arts and Sciences. Craig's work explores the intersecting histories of race and religion in the Americas, using philosophical and literary approaches. A current book project, tentatively titled "Fated Falls: Racial Religious Imaginaries in the Study of

Trauma," analyzes the theological narratives that undergird trauma studies. Craig has published in *English Language Notes* and *Representations* and is a member of the founding cohort of Emerging Scholars in Political Theology.

AMY HOLLYWOOD is Elizabeth H. Monrad Professor of Christian Studies at Harvard University. Her publications include *Sensible Ecstasy: Mysticism, Sexual Difference, and the Demands of History* (2002) and *Acute Melancholia and Other Essays* (2016). Her most recent book project, *Devotion: Three Inquiries in Religion, Literature, and Political Imagination*, coauthored with Constance M. Furey and Sarah Hammerschalg, is forthcoming.

VINCENT LLOYD is Associate Professor in the Department of Theology and Religious Studies and the Director of Africana Studies at Villanova University. He coedits the journal *Political Theology* and directs the Villanova Political Theology Project, an interdisciplinary research hub. His recent publications include *Law and Transcendence* (2009), *The Problem with Grace: Reconfiguring Political Theology* (2011), *Black Natural Law* (2016) and the coedited *Race and Secularism in America* (2016). His most recent book, coauthored with Joshua Dubler, is *Break Every Yoke: Religion, Justice, and the Abolition of Prisons* (2019).

FILIPE MAIA is Assistant Professor of Theology at Boston University School of Theology. His teaching and research focus on liberation theologies and philosophies, theology and economics, and the Christian eschatological imagination. His current book project offers an analysis of the debate in critical theory addressing the financialization of capitalism to show how future talk is ubiquitous in financial discourse and how contemporary finance engenders a particular mode of temporality.

MAYRA RIVERA is Andrew W. Mellon Professor of Religion and Latinx Studies at Harvard University. Rivera works at the intersections among philosophy of religion, literature, and theories of coloniality, race, and gender—with particular attention to Caribbean thought. Her most recent book, *Poetics of the Flesh* (2015), analyzes theological, philosophical, and political descriptions of "flesh" as metaphors for understanding how social discourses materialize in human bodies. She is also the author of *The Touch of Transcendence* (2007), *Planetary Loves: Spivak, Postcoloniality, and Theology* (2010), and *Postcolonial Theologies: Divinity and Empire* (2004). Rivera is currently working on a project that explores narratives of catastrophe in Caribbean thought.

DEVIN SINGH is Associate Professor of Religion at Dartmouth College, where he teaches courses on modern religious thought in the west, social ethics, and the philosophy of religion. He is also a faculty associate in Dartmouth's Consortium of Studies in Race, Migration, and Sexuality. Singh is the author of *Divine Currency: The Theological Power of Money in the West* (2018) as well as articles in journals such as *Political Theology*, *Journal of Religious Ethics*, *Telos*, and *Harvard Theological Review*.

JOSEPH R. WINTERS is Associate Professor in Religious Studies and African and African American Studies at Duke University. He holds secondary appointments in English and Gender, Sexuality, and Feminist Studies. His interests lie at the intersection of African American religious thought, Black literature, and critical theory. He is the author of *Hope Draped in Black: Race, Melancholy, and the Agony of Progress* (2016) and is currently working on a manuscript tentatively titled "Disturbing Profanity: Hip Hop, Black Aesthetics, and the Volatile Sacred."

Charles IX (king), 230

Chidester, David, 245

Chinese philosophy, 11

Christianity: biopower and, 129; in Caribbean, 70–72; Césaire on, 153–54; coloniality and, 15; colonial theodicy, 207–10; conquest and, 61–66; hegemony of, 7–8; James's deconversion from, 108–9, 118–24, 125n16; medieval Christian order, 60–61; philosophy and, 272–73; photography and, 130–31, 134–35, 141–42, 148n56; race and, 18–19; visual theo-logics of, 133–35; Wynter on effects of, 57–58

Churchill, Winston, 113

church property, 41

Cipriani, Arthur, 112

citizenship, 137–42

The Civil Contract of Photography (Azoulay), 137–42

civil gaze, 20, 137–42

Civil Imagination: A Political Ontology of Photography (Azoulay), 137–42, 147n37

class structure, 113–24

C. L. R. James Reader, 116

collective activity, 19–20

colonialism and coloniality: anti-Blackness and, 15; cannibalism and, 22, 226–39; defined, 3–4; Eliade on, 248–50; Eucharist ritual and, 156–60, 162–71; excremental poetics and, 179–92; hemispheric thought and, 17–18; imaginary of, 273–83; Laws of Burgos and, 86–103; modernity and, 3–7, 33–34; moral philosophical justification of, 19; philosophy of religion and, 3, 6–7, 271–83; photographic truth and, 130–31; primitive accumulation and secularization and, 40–46; race and, 3–7, 14–15; as sacrament of race, 158–60; sovereign subjectivity and, 20–21; theodicy and, 204–5, 207–10; in western

philosophical imaginary, 271–83; Wynter on religion and, 58–59

Columbus, Christopher, 226–27, 230

community, 131–32

"Concerning Violence" (Fanon), 206, 211–16

Cone, James, 204

conquest, 61–66

conversion, 98–100

Cooper, Anna Julia, 261–62

Copeland, Shawn, 15

corpus mysticum, 168

Corregidora (Jones), 187–88

cosmos/chaos binary, 248–50

Costa, Álvaro da, 241n19

Costa, Duarte da, 241n19

Coste-Floret, Paul, 162–63

Cotubanamá cacique, 93–94

Council of Trent, 229

counter-natural generations, 176–77, 196n61

Coutinho, Francisco Pereira (the Rustic), 228, 240n6

Craig, Eleanor, 7, 19, 86–103, 207, 270

cultural practices, 32–34

Dakota Access Pipeline protests, 128

Damas, Léon-Gontran, 151

The Darker Nations (Prashad), 46

Darkwater: Voices from within the Veil (Du Bois), 153

Darwin, Charles, 64–65, 253–55, 276

Davis, Gregson, 189

decoloniality: Afro-pessimism and, 284n5; cannibalism and, 237–39; Césaire on intervention of, 158–60; countercolonial violence and, 212–16, 219; evolution of, 4–7, 15–26; Fanonian violence and, 210; hemispheric genealogy and, 17–18; photography and new media and, 127–43; redemptive theology and, 216–18; refiguration of, 46–50; secularism and, 32–50; typology of, 37–40; Wynter's legacy in, 58–59

Deitch, Selma, 116

Deleuze, Gilles, 185–86

Derrida, Jacques, 13, 38, 146n30, 214

Descartes, René, 253–55

Desjardins, 166

difference, 35–36

Discourse on Colonialism (Césaire), 153–54, 157–58, 160, 163, 171–72, 176–77, 186–88

divine suffering, 204–6

divine violence, 22, 212–16

domination, 110

double consciousness, 255

Douglas, Mary, 247

Du Bois, W. E. B., 153, 250, 255, 261–62

Dunayevskaya, Raya, 112

Durkheim, Émile, 163, 256

Dussel, Enrique, 4–5, 33–34, 37, 51n2, 89

Dyson, Rick, 90

economics, 42–46

The Ego and the Id (Freud), 281–82

Eliade, Mircea, 22–23, 246–62

Emanuel African Methodist Episcopal Church, 132

The Embodied Eye: Religious Visual Culture and the Social Life of Feeling (Morgan), 142–43

empire, 71–72

encomienda obligations, 99–100

English coloniality, 45–46

English Protestantism, 44

Enlightenment philosophies, 11, 19, 92, 207–10

enthusiasm, 43

Esposito, Roberto, 169

Eucharist ritual: cannibalism and coloniality and, 238–39; coloniality and, 156–60; excremental poetics of, 179–92; medieval transformation of, 172–77; violence of, 160–71

eudaimonia, 140–42

Eurocentrism: decoloniality and, 38–39; in Laws of Burgos, 99–100; moral justification of colonialism

and, 19; philosophy of religion and, 1–3, 8, 16–26; political thought and, 24–26; religion and race and, 7–15, 245; sacred/profane distinction in colonialism and, 250–55

European feminist philosophy, 14–15

European identity, 33–34

European Man, 3

European philosophy, 1–3, 8, 230

evangelism, 94, 252–55

excremental poetics, 171–92

Fabian, Johannes, 158–59

Facebook, 131–32

Facing Reality (James), 113–16, 122–23

Fanon, Frantz, 141, 147n55; anticolonialism of, 156; on Christianity and race, 65–66; on colonial theodicy, 204–10; colonization and anti-Blackness and, 246; on culture, 76; decoloniality and, 269; on decolonization and violence, 37–38, 217–18; Eliade and, 246; on gender and masculinity, 7; Marriott on, 152; on otherness, 14–15; phenomenology of, 14; on race and colonization, 5–6; sacred and poetics of, 256–62; vampire discourse of, 194n27; on violence and colonialism, 2, 21–22, 210–16, 218–21; on western Man, 219–21, 250–55, 271; Winters's discussion of, 22–23

fecopoetics, 21

Federici, Silvia, 173–77

Ferdinand II (emperor), 86

Ferenczi, Sandòr, 277

Ferreira da Silva, Denise, 155–56, 193n8

Feuerbach, Ludwig, 77, 109

flesh and spirit, 251–55, 258–62

Fonlup-Espéraber, Jacques, 165–66

Foucault, Michel, 38, 59–60, 128–29, 270

1492 worldview, 8–9

Foxe, John, 118

Fraser, Nancy, 45

Frederick II (emperor), 91

and role of, 157–60; Eurocentric concepts of, 250–55; Foucault's biodisciplinary power and, 129; gendered status of, 7; Hegel's concept of, 12–13; hegemonic representation of, 4–7; James's concept of, 109–10; liturgy of, 167–70; "problem of man" scholarship and, 193n8; sacred and role of, 23; terror of, 250–55; western Man concept, 219–21, 271–72; whiteness and being of, 219–21; Wynter on emergence of, 28n46, 59–66

Manicheanism, 2, 6, 21–22, 206–10

Maroon settlements, 68–69, 73–76

Marriott, David, 152, 183, 192, 255, 258, 265n55

Martin, Trayvon, 132, 145n23

Martínez, María Elena, 94, 102

Martinique, 161

Marx, Karl, 5, 40–41, 52n33, 77

Marxilary dialectics, 237

Marxism, 37–38, 109–11, 112, 115–24

master-slave dialectic (Hegel), 12–13

Masuzawa, Tomoko, 8, 10

Mbembe, Achille, 6, 14, 22, 53n34, 194n22, 216

McKittrick, Katherine, 250

McWhorter, LaDelle, 129

media, 20, 127–43, 145n22, 146n30

"Mediation or Mediatisation" (Morgan), 148nn59

medieval Christian theology, 60–61, 158–60, 168–77

Mehta, Uday Singh, 101

Melville, Herman, 113

Mendieta, Eduardo, 14

Merleau-Ponty, Maurice, 5–6

Metropolitan Community Church, 131–32

Meyer, Birgit, 141–42, 148nn58–59

middle-class thought, 20, 120–24

Middle Passage, 154, 176, 181–82, 192, 197n73

Mignolo, Walter, 4, 16, 26, 37–39, 46

military, 134–35

Mills, Charles, 14

Mitchell, W. J. T., 130–31

modernity: Brazilian modernist movement, 232; Césaire on, 160–71; coloniality and, 3–7; cultural reading of, 32–34; decoloniality and, 37–40; Gilroy on terror of, 249; hierarchies and divisions in, 250; photography and, 128–31; politics of, 152; racial ontological hierarchy and, 9; secularism and, 18; as totalitarian myth, 5

Moltmann, Jürgen, 204

Montaigne, Michel de, 230

Montesinos, Antonio de, 89, 100–101

moral religious philosophy, 87–88

Morant Bay rebellion, 70–71, 73

Morgan, David, 134, 142–43

Morris, Errol, 20

Moten, Fred, 159–60, 178, 186, 219, 248–50

Moutet, Marius, 162–63

Mulvey, Laura, 141, 147n55

Muñoz, José, 187

Muslims, 173

Musser, Amber Jamilla, 184–86

Mutu, Wangechi, 160

mythical law, 212–13

Nasser, Gamal Abdel, 38

national identity, 37–40

Natives of My Person (Lamming), 125n19

natural selection, 64–66

necropolitics, 216–18

"Necropolitics" (Mbembe), 6

Negri, Antonio, 206, 209–10, 222n14

négritude, 21, 67, 152, 171–77; Caribbean context of, 188–91; Christian sacraments and, 168–69; colonialism and, 159–60; excremental poetics and, 171–79

Neuromancer, 146n30

New York Times, 127–28

Nóbrega, Father Manoel da, 228–31, 240n11

www.ingramcontent.com/pod-product-compliance
Lightning Source LLC
Chambersburg PA
CBHW071732270326
41928CB00013B/2647